MiFID II AND PRIVATE LAW

In the wake of the global financial crisis, investors have suffered significant losses as a result of breaches of conduct of business rules in the distribution of financial instruments. MiFID II introduced new disclosure, distribution and product governance rules to strengthen the protection of investors but, like MiFID I, did not harmonise the civil law consequences for their violation.

This book asks whether, in spite of the silence of the EU legislators, the MiFID II conduct of business rules may produce civil law effects, enabling investors to enforce them against investment firms before national courts and alternative dispute resolution (ADR) mechanisms.

Building on the case law of the CJEU, the book shows the conditions under which the breach of MiFID II conduct of business rules should give rise to a private law remedy, and what remedies would be compatible with EU law.

MiFID II and Private Law is an essential contribution to academic research in EU and financial law and will be a key text for policy-makers and legal practitioners working in the field of investor protection regulation and mis-selling litigation.

Hart Studies in Commercial and Financial Law: Volume 2

Hart Studies in Commercial and Financial Law
Series Editor: John Linarelli

This series offers a venue for publishing works on commercial law as well as on the regulation of banking and finance and the law on insolvency and bankruptcy. It publishes works on the law on secured credit, the regulatory and transactional aspects of banking and finance, the transactional and regulatory institutions for financial markets, legal and policy aspects associated with access to commercial and consumer credit, new generation subjects having to do with the institutional architecture associated with innovation and the digital economy including works on blockchain technology, work on the relationship of law to economic growth, the harmonisation or unification of commercial law, transnational commercial law, and the global financial order. The series promotes interdisciplinary work. It publishes research on the law using the methods of empirical legal studies, behavioural economics, political economy, normative welfare economics, law and society inquiry, socio-legal studies, political theory, and historical methods. Its coverage includes international and comparative investigations of areas of law within its remit.

Volume 1: The Financialisation of the Citizen: Social and Financial Inclusion through European Private Law
Guido Comparato

MiFID II and Private Law

Enforcing EU Conduct of Business Rules

Federico Della Negra

•HART•

OXFORD • LONDON • NEW YORK • NEW DELHI • SYDNEY

HART PUBLISHING

Bloomsbury Publishing Plc

Kemp House, Chawley Park, Cumnor Hill, Oxford, OX2 9PH, UK

HART PUBLISHING, the Hart/Stag logo, BLOOMSBURY and the Diana logo are trademarks of Bloomsbury Publishing Plc

First published in Great Britain 2019

A catalogue record for this book is available from the British Library.

Library of Congress Cataloging-in-Publication data

Names: Della Negra, Federico, author.

Title: MiFID II and private law : enforcing EU conduct of business rules / Federico Della Negra.

Description: Oxford, UK ; Chicago, Illinois : Hart Publishing, 2019. | Series: Hart studies in commercial and financial law | Includes bibliographical references and index.

Identifiers: LCCN 2019001687 (print) | LCCN 2019005381 (ebook) | ISBN 9781509925315 (EPub) | ISBN 9781509925292 (hardback)

Subjects: LCSH: European Parliament. Directive 2014/65/EU of the European Parliament and of the Council of 15 May 2014 on markets in financial instruments. | Financial institutions—Law and legislation—European Union countries. | Actions and defenses—European Union countries. | BISAC: LAW / Banking.

Classification: LCC KJE2245.A432015 (ebook) | LCC KJE2245.A432015 D45 2019 (print) | DDC 346.24/08—dc23

LC record available at https://lccn.loc.gov/2019001687

ISBN: HB: 978-1-50992-529-2
ePDF: 978-1-50992-530-8
ePub: 978-1-50992-531-5

Typeset by Compuscript Ltd, Shannon

Ai miei genitori

FOREWORD

I.

EU law has increasingly regulated financial transactions but it has done so without harmonising the national private law which is applicable to these transactions.

MiFID I, adopted in 2004, harmonised regulation of investment services and replaced the Investment Services Directive (ISD) of 1993 which introduced, for the first time in the EU, rules on conduct of business between investment firms and their customers. In 2014 MiFID II replaced MiFID I, expanding and developing its conduct of business rules. MiFID II, like its predecessor, is a form of public interest regulation in the area of financial services. Klaus Hopt has called the directives and their transposition into national law the 'constitution' or '*Grundgesetz*' of capital market law in Europe and Stefan Grundmann has developed this approach and its consequences for private law at a general level.[1]

Within a wider framework of market regulation, the focus of the conduct of business rules is on the protection of investors. MiFID I and II provide for enforcement of the conduct of business rules by supervisory authorities and harmonise the powers of these authorities but these directives do not expressly or directly harmonise private law duties and remedies. Are the conduct of business rules part of administrative law without any consequences for private law or without any private law remedies? It is clear that conduct of business rules are supervised by financial market regulators, but less clear how far the duties of the regulators go. This cannot exclude any impact of conduct of business rules on private law or the availability of remedies in private law.

EU law does not rely on domestic distinctions between public and private law. Such a dichotomy may be unconvincing on a general conceptual level. As early as 1962, Jürgen Habermas in his work on the public sphere challenged the distinction between public and private law, *Habilitation*, on the *Strukturwandel der Öffentlichkeit*. Domestic lawyers disagree on where to draw the line and the consequences of doing so. And the line and consequences are not seen in the same way in the different national jurisdictions. So to apply this dichotomy would be practically very difficult in EU law. It would not render the conduct of business rules effective in the way that EU law requires.

[1] S Grundmann, 'Privatrecht un Regulierug', in Auyer et al *Privarechtsdogmatik im 21. Jahrhundert. Festschrift für Claus-Wilhelm Canaris* (Berlin, De Gruyter, 2017) 907.

There is increasing scholarship on the horizontal direct effect of EU law, and the way in which this limits the autonomy of national procedural and private law. Principles such as that of the effectiveness of EU law assist national courts in giving effect to EU law. The conduct of business rules that are the subject of this book originate in national private law. Those principles at the national level interact with the merging principles at the EU level. The relationship can be seen as a complex one, although when the common origin and aims of the principles are explored, it turns out to be much easier to make use of them in the clarification and development of the law. This is for the ECJ and national courts, and also to some extent for the domestic legislators where EU legislation leaves gaps.

Also, legal disciplines interact in complex ways. Legal disciplines often lay claim to autonomy. We know it from the ways in which EU law claims autonomy, and national law from EU law and other law from outside the national jurisdiction. The same applies within national jurisdictions, for instance private law from public law, or commercial law from private law or the other way around. National private law may base its claims of autonomy on most of these grounds. That creates a challenge for scholars on topics as that of Federico Della Negra's book. The challenge is to move freely over the boundaries, which seem to divide these fields of law and bring out the underlying unities. They are to be found in the principles which these fields of law are based on.

Dr Della Negra's book is about the private law impact of conduct of business rules. The relationship between public interest regulation and private law lies at the heart of his book. The conceptual framework builds on the extensive literature that has investigated the regulatory effects of general private law, including Hugh Collins' seminal work,[2] my own work with Guido Alpa[3] and Hans-W Micklitz's contributions.[4] Della Negra has written his book within a research project directed by Hans-W Micklitz on European regulatory private law.[5] This book provides one of the most important contributions to this project, 'testing' by means of an impressive number of judgments, decisions of ADR bodies and acts of supervisory authorities the impact of regulation on private law. One could effectively say, after reading this book, that EU conduct of business rules, designed as a 'self-sufficient' public law regime may, by virtue of general principles of EU law, influence the interpretation of general private law thus giving rise to a europeanisation of national private law.

[2] H Collins, *Regulating Contracts* (Oxford, OUP, 1999).

[3] G Alpa, M Andenas, *Fondamenti del diritto privato europeo*, in *Trattato di Diritto Privato*, a cura di G. Iudica e P. Zatti, (Milano, Giuffré, 2005).

[4] See, in particular, see H-W Micklitz, 'The Visible Hand of European Regulatory Private Law – The Transformation of European Private Law from Autonomy to Functionalism in Competition and Regulation' (2009) 28 *Yearbook of European Law* 1.

[5] The Visible Hand of European Regulatory Private Law (ERPL). The Transformation from Autonomy to Functionalism in Competition and Regulation (https://blogs.eui.eu/erc-erpl/project-description/).

Della Negra has an exceptional grasp of the literature and demonstrates a deep knowledge of, insight in, and attention to practical issues. He knows the academic literature and manages to make use of it for his analysis. This also applies to his command of the case law and other materials from a number of national legal systems. The fragmented literature is difficult to deal with within a book on this topic. Della Negra has placed his book in the context of the literature on financial market regulation, including my own work, in particular in *The Foundations and Future of Financial Regulation*[6] (with Iris Chiu) and the contributions by Olha Cherednychenko,[7] and Danny Busch.[8] This further includes the papers by Stefan Grundmann,[9] Christos Hadjiemmanuil[10] and Fabian Möslein[11] focusing on the impact of the European Banking Union and Single Rulebook on the relationship between private parties. Della Negra's book focuses on the civil law effects of conduct regulation but provides insights to understand the potential civil law effects stemming from the Single Rulebook (ie CRR, CRD and BRRD), and its implementation by national legislators may effectively shape the private law relationships between market participants.

II.

Harmonisation in EU law does often not provide for remedies and procedures. However, when EU law confers rights on individuals, national law must ensure that individuals have effective and equivalent remedies to enforce these rights. The scope and content of the right needs to be assessed having regard to the protective purpose of the rule at stake. The book shows under what conditions MiFID II's disclosure, distribution and product governance obligations confer rights on individual investors and therefore require national courts to interpret general private law in light with the principles of equivalence and effectiveness. The EU requirement that domestic law gives effect to EU law, is countered by claims to the autonomy of domestic law, and with particular strength in procedural law and private law. This accounts for some of the challenges. It also explains why Della Negra has had to explore EU and domestic law sources in such detail.

[6] M Andenas and I Chiu *The Foundations and Future of Financial Regulation* (2014).

[7] See, in particular, OO (Olha) Cherednychenko, 'Contract Governance in the EU: Conceptualising the Relationship between Investor Protection Regulation and Private Law' (2015) 21(4) *European Law Journal* 500–520.

[8] See, in particular, D Busch and C van Dam (eds), *A Bank's Duty of Care* (Oxford, Hart Publishing, 2017).

[9] See S Grundmann, 'The Banking Union Translated into (Private Law) Duties: Infrastructure and Rulebook', (2015) *European Business Organisation Law Review* 16:345–367.

[10] See C Hadjiemmanuil, "The Banking Union and Its Implications for Private Law: A Comment", (2015) *European Business Organisation Law Review* 16:383–400.

[11] See F Möslein, "Third Parties in the European Banking Union: Regulatory and Supervisory Effects on Private Law Relationships Between Banks and their Clients or Creditors", (2015) *European Business Organisation Law Review* 16:547–574.

Private law and private enforcement in the post-crisis EU retail financial regulation is undergoing a transformation. The process and outcome, also on the normative level, remains understudied, uncertain and is highly controversial. In an inchoate form this is reflected in a scholarship which remains fragmented along different lines. EU retail regulation, as Niamh Moloney showed, has become more paternalistic, transforming the retail client, from an investor to a consumer.[12] But this new approach has not included a harmonisation of the civil law effects of breaches of its conduct of business rules. Private law and private enforcement remain in the shadow of the administrative law aspects of EU conduct of business regulation and subject to national legislative choices.

The design of private law remedies for breaches of conduct of business rules remains crucially dependent on the interpretative approach of national courts. It is striking to see, as Della Negra's analysis shows, that while in continental Europe, courts tend to converge on the need to ensure civil law effects to conduct of business rules, in the UK courts are much more careful about 'importing' regulatory concepts into private law adjudication, especially in non-advised transactions.

Indeed, lack of express and direct private law harmonisation is problematic for investors, in particular for retail or private investors. It may appear unclear whether breach of conduct of business rules give rise to a private law remedy. It may be even more unclear if a private law remedy granted will be different across member states. So far, the Court of Justice of the European Union (CJEU) has provided limited guidance to solve these issues. The *Genil v Bankinter* judgment addressed the issue of the civil law effects of MiFID I, but left unanswered the crucial question of what type of remedies would be in line with the principle of equivalence and effectiveness and what are the criteria to assess compliance with these principles.

III.

The book answers these key questions showing that, notwithstanding the absence of any express or direct EU or national law provisions, MiFID II's conduct of business rules should be enforced by private law remedies, in parallel with the public or administrative law sanctions. Della Negra bases his argument on the doctrine of horizontal effects of EU law, the principles of equivalence, effectiveness and effective judicial protection. He argues convincingly how EU law should guide the national courts' interpretation in shaping the civil law effects of conduct of business rules. The broad scope of the analysis, which comprises four jurisdictions (UK, French, Italian and Spanish law) offers a comprehensive view on the different judicial approaches in dealing with the civil law effects of conduct of business rules.

[12] N Moloney, The Investor Model Underlying the EU's Investor Protection Regime: Consumers or Investors?' (2012) 13 *European Business Organization Law Review* 169.

This applies to the extra-judicial enforcement of conduct of business rules too. After the global financial crisis, Member states experienced a 'de-judicialisation' of retail client disputes that has inevitably reduced the role of courts in this type of dispute. The book devotes the necessary attention to the institutional and substantive law aspects of ADR adjudication in the four examined countries, showing that this type of dispute resolution may provide a positive outcome not only in terms of compensation but also deterrence in retail financial markets.

The civil law effects of conduct of business rules may arise also from acts adopted by EU and national supervisory authorities. The reason is that this type of act, even if not legally binding (like in the case of ESMA's acts) may nevertheless influence the interpretation of binding law applicable to financial transactions. The book innovatively shows the link between the new powers granted by EU law to the European Supervisory Authorities and the civil law effects stemming from these powers in relation to MiFID II's conduct of business rules.

In the current EU financial regulatory context, where soft-law and forms of administrative rule-making have gained increasing importance in shaping the content of EU regulatory requirements, technical expertise of ESMA and national supervisory authorities could facilitate the private (judicial and extra-judicial) enforcement of conduct of business rules. A challenge for these authorities will be to balance investor protection and financial stability's objectives. Building on the case law of the CJEU, Della Negra argues that the latter only under very specific circumstances can restrict the former.

The creation, via courts and ADR mechanisms, of what the book calls 'hybrid private law duties and remedies', will increase the protection of investors and strengthen the deterrent effect of conduct of business rules. It also ensures that the investors' confidence in financial markets is adequately protected, avoiding situations in which losses caused by mis-selling are not compensated. Going forward, legislative harmonisation of civil law effects of conduct of business rules would be beneficial to level the playing field but would probably not increase substantially the level of protection of investors, given that national courts have already imposed on investment firms obligations that are stricter than the ones laid down in MiFID I and have enforced conduct of business rules via private law remedies.

IV.

Della Negra contributes to an emerging scholarship where different traditions struggle for the upper hand. While offering alternative perspectives, there are few scholars that manage to combine a deeper understanding of private law and the technicalities of EU financial regulation. Applying these two perspectives to an analysis of private law and enforcement in the post-crisis EU retail financial markets is particularly challenging. Della Negra's strongest contribution is his analysis of how general principles of EU law developed by the CJEU can bridge traditional categories of private law and sectoral regulatory duties. Private law should be interpreted in light of EU law but its broad concepts, like good faith, duty of care and reasonableness, grant to national courts a necessary margin of manoeuvre to shape the private law remedy in light of the specific circumstances of the case.

EU law is undergoing a process of transformation, in terms of substantive law and enforcement. This applies no less to national private law, including the new forms of dispute settlement. The sources are rich, but their relationship and legal weight are not settled. Working at the interface between these dimensions is demanding.

To conclude, with this book Della Negra has made an outstanding contribution to legal scholarship. The book will be a core text for scholars of EU law, private law and financial market law and also essential for supervisory authorities and practitioners dealing with MiFID II's conduct of business rules.

Professor Mads Andenas

ACKNOWLEDGEMENTS

This book is a revised version of my PhD thesis which I wrote and defended at the European University Institute (EUI) of Florence in 2017.[1]

During the PhD's journey I had the opportunity to develop my passion for legal thinking and explore the interlinks between private law and EU financial regulation. I started to study this topic in my undergraduate studies in Pisa, at the Sant'Anna School of Advanced Studies and at the University of Pisa. I owe a lot to Professor Umberto Breccia, who has driven me in the study of private law and Professor Giovanni Comandè who opened up my mind towards comparative private law and EU law.

Since my first days in the EUI, I have had the privilege to be part of the research project European Regulatory Private Law (ERPL), led by Professor Hans-W Micklitz, my PhD supervisor.

I am particularly grateful to Professor Hans-W Micklitz for welcoming me in the ERPL project, teaching me with patience 'what is', 'why to do' and 'how to do' legal research and for his continuous support and strong engagement with my PhD's research topic.

Special thanks also to Professor Yane Svetiev and to Dr Guido Comparato for their precious support, especially on methodological aspects of the research, and Barend, Ronan, Marta, Lucila, Betül and Elena for their feedback and to Dr Thomas Roete for his inspiring thoughts on my research.

Being part of the ERPL project, I was involved in an intense research activity and I exchanged my ideas with outstanding academics from all over Europe. Among them, I am particularly indebted to Professor Mads Andenas for being an extraordinary support and source of inspiration for my PhD since the beginning of my studies in Florence, always encouraging to explore new horizons of the research.

Moreover, I owe a particular debit of gratitude to Professor Giuseppe Vettori for his interest in my research and for his precious support over the PhD's journey.

Without being possible to mention here all the people that have contributed to shape my research, I want to thank in particular Professor Stefan Grundmann, Professor Olha Cherednychenko, Professor Fernando Gómez Pomar, Professor Jan Dalhuisen, Professor Niamh Moloney, Professor Eva Lomnika, Professor Alexander Turk, Professor Rob van Gestel, Professor André Prüm, Professor Norbert Reich and Professor Valentina Calderai.

[1] The views expressed in this book are purely personal and they are in no way intended to represent those of the European Central Bank (ECB). All errors and omissions remain my own.

I thank also Raffaele D'Ambrosio for his feedback on the book's aspects related to EU financial supervision which helped me to develop this topic more comprehensively. Moreover, following with Professor René Smits the evolving case law of Union courts on the EU banking union, and the opportunity to discuss with him these complex judicial developments, allowed me to deepen the focus of the book on the interactions between prudential rules and private law rights of financial market participants.

I am also grateful for the very constructive comments that Professor Giorgio Monti and Professor Takis Tridimas, together with Professor Hans-W Micklitz and Professor Mads Andenas, made in the Phd examination and I which I tried to fully take into account when turning the PhD thesis into this book.

My research and this book have greatly benefitted from two important professional experiences, at the European Commission and at the European Central Bank (ECB).

My traineeship at the Legal Service of the European Commission helped me to ground the earlier stages of my research into solid EU law foundations and to develop the EU law dimension of the PhD's thesis. This was possible also thanks to the exchanges of views on my research that I had with Adrian Tokar, George Zavvos, Julio Baquero Cruz, Joan Rius, Elisabetta Montaguti and Enrico Traversa.

Working at the ECB as legal counsel in the Directorate General Secretariat to the Supervisory Board, and before as banking supervisor in the Directorate General Micro Prudential Supervision III, gives me every day the unique opportunity to look at the developments of EU banking regulation 'in action' and helped me to contextualise the book's topic into the bigger picture of the EU banking regulation. I am very grateful to Petra Senkovic and to Georg Gruber for all their support. I wish to thank also the team of the ECB Library for its precious assistance.

I am grateful to the anonymous reviewers and the work of the Hart publishing's team, in particular, Roberta Bassi, Tom Adams, Richard Cox, Paula Divine and Rose Wood, who made this book a reality.

My last words of gratitude are for the persons who are closest, my sister Anna and my parents, Gilberto and Daniela, to whom I dedicate this book. My gratitude for them is much bigger than what words can express. I would not be who and where I am now without their constant encouragement, support, patience and confidence.

CONTENTS

ABBREVIATIONS

AMF	Autorité des marchés financiers
BoA	Board of Appeal of the European Supervisory Authorities
CNMV	Comisión Nacional del Mercado de Valores
CONSOB	Commissione Nazionale per le Società e la Borsa
CESR	Committee of European Securities Regulators
CJEU	Court of Justice of the European Union
EBA	European Banking Authority
ECB	European Central Bank
ECHR	European Convention of Human Rights
ECtHR	European Court of Human Rights
EIOPA	European Insurance and Occupational Pensions Authority
ESMA	European Securities and Markets Authority
ESAs	European Supervisory Authorities
ESFS	European System of Financial Supervision
ESRB	European Systemic Risk Board
EU	European Union
FCA	Financial Conduct Authority
NCAs	National Competent Authorities
SRM	Single Resolution Mechanism
SSM	Single Supervisory Mechanism
TEU	Treaty on European Union
TFEU	Treaty on the Functioning of the European Union

TABLE OF CASES

Court of Justice of the European Union

UK courts

French courts

Italian courts

Spanish courts

German courts

European Court of Human Rights

TABLE OF LEGISLATION

European Union

United Kingdom (UK)

France

Italy

Spain

Germany

TABLE OF ACTS OF INTERNATIONAL, EUROPEAN AND NATIONAL COMPETENT AUTHORITIES

International Organization of Securities Commissions (IOSCO)

European Commission

Committee of European Securities Regulators (CESR)

European Supervisory Authorities (ESAs)

European Securities and Markets Authority (ESMA)

European Systemic Risk Board (ESRB)

Bank of England

Financial Services Authority (FSA) and Financial Conduct Authority (FCA)

Introduction

Directive 2014/65/EU on markets in financial instruments (MiFID II)[1] was adopted on 14 April 2014 and entered into force on 3 January 2018, repealing its predecessor, Directive 2004/39/EC on markets in financial instruments (MiFID I).[2] MiFID II is the cornerstone of investment services regulation in the European Union (EU) and is a fundamental regulatory tool to protect investors in financial transactions.

Although MiFID II is not a 'crisis-driven' measure, the significant losses suffered by retail clients due to mis-selling of complex financial instruments in the wake of the global financial crisis have shaped the regulatory design of its conduct of business rules.[3] MiFID II has tightened MiFID I's disclosure and distribution rules and introduced new product governance obligations. These new requirements aim to reduce the detrimental effects of mis-selling for individual investors, the society and financial markets as a whole.[4]

To achieve this objective, effective and credible enforcement is as important as regulation.

MiFID II strengthened the public enforcement and supervisory powers of national competent authorities (NCAs). MiFIR,[5] which also entered into force on 3 January 2018, conferred on the NCAs the European Securities and Markets Authority (ESMA) and the European Banking Authority (EBA) the incisive power to restrict the distribution of financial products. While public enforcement has been enhanced and further harmonised, private enforcement, despite its

[1] Directive 2014/65/EU of the European Parliament and of the Council of 15 May 2014 on markets in financial instruments and amending Directive 2002/92/EC and Directive 2011/61/EU ('MiFID II') [2014] OJ L 173/349.

[2] Directive 2004/39/EC of the European Parliament and of the Council of 21 April 2004 on markets in financial instruments amending Council Directives 85/611/EEC and 93/6/EEC and Directive 2000/12/EC of the European Parliament and of the Council and repealing Council Directive 93/22/EEC ('MiFID I') [2004] OJ L 145/1.

[3] The global financial crisis (hereinafter 'the financial crisis' or 'the crisis') was triggered by the insolvency of Lehman Brothers Holdings Inc (LBHI), which entered into administration on 15 September 2008 at 6.56 am London time.

[4] See especially recital No 5 of MiFID II. See also European Systemic Risk Board (ESRB) 'Report on Misconduct Risk in the Banking Sector', June 2015 and the International Organization of Securities Commissions (IOSCO) 'Credible Deterrence in the Enforcement of Securities Regulation', June 2015.

[5] Regulation (EU) No 600/2014 of the European Parliament and of the Council of 15 May 2014 on markets in financial instruments and amending Regulation (EU) No 648/2012 (MiFIR) [2014] OJ L 173/84.

important role in ensuring compensation to investors in the wake of the crisis,[6] remained in the 'shadow' of MiFID II. This directive reinforces the extra-judicial private enforcement of conduct of business rules but, like its predecessor, does not harmonise the civil law effects of regulatory duties, nor does it grant a private law remedy for breaches of conduct of business rules. Therefore, investors must continue to rely on their national private laws when seeking compensation for losses suffered as a result of breaches of MiFID II conduct of business rules.

The key problem that arises is whether and to what extent the bulk of increasingly detailed and prescriptive conduct of business rules introduced by MiFID II may have an effect on national contract law or tort law duties and remedies, notwithstanding of the absence of an express EU law provision in that sense. MiFID II's new conduct of business rules could create new possibilities for private enforcement. In addition, Level 2 of this directive, which contains more detailed conduct of business rules has been adopted in the form of a regulation,[7] which is a directly applicable act and may, in principle, produce horizontal direct effects. Another reason to consider the interplay between conduct of business rules and private law is that the Court of Justice of the European Union (CJEU) has so far provided little guidance on what the civil law effects of MiFID I should be.

The CJEU addressed for the first time the issue of the civil law effects of MiFID I in the *Genil v Bankinter* judgment handed down in 2013.[8] In this judgment, which arose from a swap mis-selling dispute, the CJEU held that it is for Member States to establish the contract law consequences of breaches of MiFID I appropriateness and suitability rules, subject to the principle of equivalence and effectiveness. Two years later, in *Banif Plus Bank Zrt v Márton Lantos*,[9] the CJEU reiterated that the contract law consequences of breaches of these rules fall within national procedural autonomy. These judgments, however, have left open key questions on what remedies would be in line with the principle of equivalence and effectiveness and how compliance with these principles should be assessed by national courts and ADR bodies.

The book builds upon a growing body of literature that, especially after the global financial crisis, has explored the theme of the civil law effects of pre-MiFID and MiFID I conduct of business rules across several jurisdictions, arguing that

[6] ESMA Securities and Markets Stakeholder Group, Investor Protection Aspects of the Consultation Paper on MiFID II and MiFIR, 8 August 2014 ESMA/2014/SMSG/035, 4.

[7] Commission Delegated Directive (EU) 2017/593 of 7 April 2016 supplementing Directive 2014/65/EU of the European Parliament and of the Council with regard to safeguarding of financial instruments and funds belonging to clients, product governance obligations and the rules applicable to the provision or reception of fees, commissions or any monetary or non-monetary benefits (Commission MiFID II Directive) [2017] OJ L 87/500 and Commission Delegated Regulation (EU) 2017/565 of 25 April 2016 supplementing Directive 2014/65/EU of the European Parliament and of the Council as regards organisational requirements and operating conditions for investment firms and defined terms for the purposes of that Directive (Commission MiFID II Regulation') [2017] OJ L 87/1.

[8] Case C-604/11, *Genil v Bankinter*, ECLI:EU:C:2013:344, para 57.

[9] Case C-312/14, *Banif Plus Bank Zrt v Márton Lantos*, ECLI:EU:C:2015:794.

conduct of business rules are relevant to determine the scope of private law duties and remedies.[10] However, this book goes beyond that scholarship in two main respects. On the one hand, while the discourse has been almost exclusively focused on the civil law effects of conduct of business rules before national courts, this research also considers the potential civil law effects of these rules before alternative dispute resolution (ADR) mechanisms, which played an increasingly important role in resolving retail clients disputes after the crisis. On the other hand, while academic attention so far has been devoted on the civil law effects stemming from regulation,[11] the centrality acquired by ESMA in regulatory and supervisory convergence after the crisis calls for an analysis of the impact of its acts on private law relations and their potential effects on national private law.

Against this backdrop, this book aims to examine the civil law effects of MiFID II conduct of business rules from a comparative and institutional perspective. More specifically, the book aims to determine whether regulatory duties may produce an effect on the firm's private law duties vis-à-vis their clients and whether and, if so, under what conditions, clients may have a private law remedy (ie compensation, avoidance of contracts) for breaches of these rules, despite the absence of any EU or national provision in that sense.

The book advances two main claims.

First, it argues, building on the analysis of the case law of national courts and the decisions of ADR bodies in the UK, France, Italy and Spain, that national courts and adjudicators have granted different civil law effects to pre-MiFID and MiFID I conduct of business rules, translating them into private law duties, and have granted to clients a remedy, based on general private law, to obtain compensation for losses suffered as a result of breaches of conduct of business rules. The importance of this claim is twofold. First, it shows that lack of EU harmonisation of private law remedies does not mean that conduct of business rules

[10] See before the financial crisis: PO Mülbert, 'The Eclipse of Contract Law in the Investment Firm-Client Relationship: The Impact of the MiFID on the Law of Contract from a German Perspective' in G Ferrarini and E Wymeersch (eds), *Investor Protection in Europe: Corporate Law Making, The MiFID and Beyond* (Oxford, Oxford University Press, 2006), 317. After the crisis, see in particular: M Tison (2010) 'The Civil Law Effects of MiFID in a Comparative Law Perspective' *Financial Law Institute Working Paper Series*; OO Cherednychenko, 'The Regulation of Retail Investment Services in the EU: Towards the Improvement of Investor Rights?' (2010) 33 *Journal of Consumer Policy* 403; F Della Negra, 'The Private Enforcement of the MiFID Conduct of Business Rules. An Overview of the Italian and Spanish Experiences' (2014) 10 *European Review of Contract Law* 571; P Reynolds, Selling Financial Products: The Interface between Regulatory and Common Law Standards' (2014) 29 *Journal of International Banking Law and Regulation* 269; D Busch, 'The Private Law Effect of MiFID I and MiFID II' in D Busch and G Ferrarini (eds), *Regulation of the EU Financial Markets. MiFID II & MiFIR* (Oxford, Oxford University Press, 2017), 176; M Andenas and F Della Negra, Between Contract Law and Financial Regulation: Towards the Europeanisation of General Contract Law' (2017) 4 *European Business Law Review* 499; D Busch and C van Dam (eds), *A Bank's Duty of Care* (Oxford, Hart Publishing, 2017).

[11] See, on this aspect, F Della Negra, 'The Effects of the ESMA's Powers on Domestic Contract Law' in M Andenas and G Deipenbrock (eds), *Regulating and Supervising European Financial Markets* (Leiden, Springer, 2016) 139.

cannot be enforced via general private law. Second, it shows that that the same conduct of business rule may produce different civil law effects not only across jurisdictions but also within the same jurisdiction but across different institutions (eg courts and ADR bodies). Conceptually, this type of judicially crafted private law duties and remedies have a hybrid nature: they are based on national private law but they are, in practice, 'designed' to achieve the investor protection objective of EU conduct of business rules.

The second claim of the book is that conduct of business rules should be enforced via private law. This normative claim builds on the critical analysis of the protective purpose of MiFID II conduct of business rules and the general principles of EU law, as interpreted by the CJEU. The book offers guidance on how the doctrine of horizontal effects of EU law, the principles of equivalence and effectiveness as well as the EU fundamental rights could (and should) lead to the imposition of hybrid private law duties on investment firms and confer private law remedies on investors, notwithstanding the absence of an EU or national law provision in that sense. This analysis shows that the creation of hybrid private law duties and remedies is legally justified on the basis of EU law and it is necessary to ensure the effective application of MiFID II conduct of business rules and an effective protection of investors.

The book will also discuss the implications of hybrid private law from a private enforcement perspective. The term 'private enforcement' will be used to describe the actions of private individuals or undertakings aimed to enforce (ie obtain compensation for breaches of) regulatory duties via courts or out-of-court dispute resolution mechanisms. The private enforceability of conduct of business rules not only ensures an effective compensation for clients' losses, but it also strengthens the deterrent effect of conduct of business rules, supplementing the public enforcement and supervisory actions of NCAs. At the same time, the book argues that an optimal system for the private enforcement of conduct of business rules would require specific regulatory mechanisms to ensure that adequate incentives are given to the most vulnerable clients to bring a civil law action and to ensure that better coordination exists between private and public enforcement mechanisms.

The book innovatively looks at the theme of civil law effects of conduct of business rules from a broader institutional perspective. By bringing ADR bodies as well as supervisory authorities into the scope of the analysis, the research will take a holistic view of the interplay between sectoral financial regulation and general private law, investigating linkages and relationships between regulation, soft law and contracts. This institutional approach will also show that the protection of investors in the EU is not only dependent on the 'law on the books', more and more determined by EU regulatory choices, but by the 'law in action', which derives from the application of EU rules by national authorities.

The institutional approach will be complemented by a comparative analysis of four jurisdictions (ie the United Kingdom (UK), France, Italy and Spain). These countries will be used as case studies to explore the civil law effects of conduct of business rules in their multifaceted institutional dimensions. In fact, these jurisdictions have experienced widespread mis-selling which resulted in an abundant case law for breaches of pre-MiFID I and MiFID I conduct of business rules.[12] In addition, in these jurisdictions large volumes of complex products have been distributed to retail clients, exposing them to a high risk of unforeseen losses, thus making the analysis of these legal systems particularly relevant.[13] The inclusion of the UK and thus common law in the scope of the study is meaningful because the UK, unlike the continental jurisdictions examined, provides for a statutory right of action for breaches of conduct of business rules, and English courts play a key role in adjudicating complex financial derivatives disputes.[14] These two factors offer a basis for a comparison with France, Italy and Spain where investors have to rely on general private law to obtain compensation (ie there is no statutory right of action) and litigation mostly concerns retail client disputes. The Brexit referendum (hereinafter 'Brexit')[15] may reduce the role and impact of EU law in the UK in the next years. However, the issues related to the interplay between national conduct of business rules and general common law will remain of interest for investors and investment firms operating in the UK.

The themes of the book are developed in seven chapters.

Chapter 1 provides a conceptual framework to examine the civil law effects of conduct of business rules. After illustrating the milestones of the EU investor protection regulation (ISD, MiFID I and MiFID II), it provides an account of the principles of EU law that may facilitate the private enforcement of conduct of business rules before national courts and ADR bodies. It then elaborates on the concept of the Europeanisation of national private law and the normative models to identify the interactions between general private law and sectoral EU regulatory duties (eg separation, substitution and hybridisation).

Chapter 2 undertakes an in-depth analysis of MiFID II conduct of business rules (disclosure, distribution and product governance rules), examining their content and purpose. The aim of this analysis is to show which conduct of business rules may grant a legally enforceable right to clients and could therefore be

[12] In Italy, the mis-selling of bonds issued by the Republic of Argentina ('Argentina bonds'), the Cirio Group ('Cirio bonds') and the Parmalat Group ('Parmalat bonds'). In Spain the large scale mis-selling of *participationes preferents* and other hybrid financial instruments. In the UK the mis-selling of payment protection insurances and complex derivatives.

[13] In 2017, Italy and France accounted for the highest sale volumes of structured retail products in the EU. See ESMA, 'Report on Trends, Risks and Vulnerabilities, No 2' (2018) at 57. In Q3/2017, Italy and France, together with Germany, accounted for the Euro area countries with highest holdings of banks' debt securities (EBA and ESMA, 'Statement of the EBA and ESMA on the Treatment of Retail Holdings of Debt Financial Instruments Subject to the Bank Recovery and Resolution Directive', EBA/Op/2018/03 30/05/2018, 6). In Spain, retail investors held 83% of bail-inable instruments before 2012 see (Bank of Spain, 'Report on the Financial and Banking Crisis in Spain, 2008–2014', Madrid, 2017, 172).

[14] UK law is used as a synonym of common law as referred to in the legal system of England and Wales.

[15] On 29 March 2017, the UK notified the European Council of its intention to withdraw from the European Union, in accordance with Article 50(2) of the Treaty on the European Union (TEU), as a result of the referendum of 23 June 2016.

enforced via a private law remedy. The chapter concludes with an account of the conduct of business rules in the UK, France, Italy and Spain.

Chapter 3 examines ESMA's 'conduct of business handbook' to understand whether and to what extent it can produce horizontal effects in firm–client relations. After illustrating the institutional set up of ESMA, it shows how this has strengthened disclosure, distribution and product governance requirements and provides an overview of the measures adopted by the NCA in the examined jurisdictions to strengthen investor protection in these areas. Finally, it highlights the horizontal or civil law effects of ESMA's acts, building on the relevant case law of the CJEU.

Having examined the 'law on the books', in Chapter 4 the analysis moves to the 'law in action', investigating the civil law effects of conduct of business rules before ADR bodies. After illustrating the main innovations of the ADR Directive and MiFID II on extra-judicial enforcement, the chapter examines how national ADR bodies have enforced the fair treatment, suitability and appropriateness duties. The chapter provides a comparative assessment of the role played by regulatory and private law standards in adjudication, as well as what remedies have been granted to clients. It is argued that, even if ADR bodies are not required to decide the disputes based on legal rules, national private law and regulation have been increasingly taken into account in dispute resolution.

Chapter 5 complements the analysis of the 'law in action' examining the civil law effects of conduct of business rules before national courts. To this purpose, it shows for each examined jurisdiction the impact of EU conduct of business rules on general private law duties (ie duty of care and good faith) and remedies and conducts a comparative assessment of the different civil law effects as well as remedies granted by courts for breaches of conduct of business rules.

Chapter 6 provides a normative analysis of hybrid private law. Building on the critical analysis of the relevant case law of the CJEU, it examines the extent to which the emergence of hybrid private law could be justified by EU law. The chapter shows that the doctrine of horizontal effects of EU legal acts and the principles of equivalence and effectiveness should ensure that civil law effects are granted to conduct of business rules and under certain conditions, should grant investors a private law remedy to enforce breaches of conduct of business rules in a civil proceeding, notwithstanding an express EU or national law provision in that sense.

Finally, moving from the substantive to the enforcement level of contract governance, the last chapter examines how hybrid private law fits into the debate on the private and public enforcement of securities regulation. It is argued that, given the high costs of legal proceedings and the fact that clients are not best positioned to detect wrongdoings, regulatory mechanisms are needed to incentivise clients to bring compensation claims and to strengthen coordination between public and private enforcement, ensuring that, in certain circumstances, the assessments of supervisory authorities are taken into account by national courts and ADR bodies in resolving disputes.

1

The Rise of EU Investor Protection Regulation and the Role of Private Law

I. Harmonisation in EU Securities Markets: From Liberalisation to Regulation

The harmonisation of national laws is one of the most important tools to establish the internal market.

It is generally accepted that harmonisation has both market integration goals, aimed at removing barriers to cross-border trade, and regulatory goals, aimed at protecting consumers and strengthening their confidence in the internal market.[1] In EU securities law, harmonisation has gradually moved from liberalisation to regulation.[2] The traditional goals of securities regulation (protecting investors, ensuring the safety of individual firms and the stability of the financial system)[3] have been re-orientated towards the ultimate goal of strengthening the internal market. The shift from liberalisation to regulation is well documented in the development of the EU conduct of business regime. The Investment Service Directive (ISD), adopted in 1993, introduced the single passport for investment firms and minimum conduct of business principles that had to be implemented by Member States. The MiFID I, adopted in 2004, while aimed at achieving market integration, introduced numerous conduct of business rules for investment firms to protect investors. In the same vein, the MiFID II, adopted ten years later, has tightened conduct of business rules, reaffirming the need to ensure an effective protection of investors.

MiFID II also harmonised supervisory and enforcement powers to sanction breaches of these rules of competent authorities and required Member States to strengthen extra-judicial mechanisms to compensate investors' losses. However,

[1] See L Azoulai, 'The Complex Waive of Harmonization' in A Arnull and D Chalmers (eds), *The Oxford Handbook of European Union Law* (Oxford, Oxford University Press, 2015) 599. See also for a critical view H Unberath and A Johnston, 'The Double-Headed Approach of the ECJ concerning Consumer Protection' (2007) 44 *Common Market Law Review* 1237, 1255.

[2] See especially N Moloney, *EU Securities and Financial Markets Regulation*, 3rd edn (Oxford, Oxford University Press, 2014) 19 and M Andenas, 'Harmonising and regulating financial markets' in M Andenas and C Baasch Andersen (eds), Theory and Practice of Harmonisation (Cheltenham, Edward Elgar, 2012) 1–29.

[3] See, in particular, C Goodhart, P Hartman, DT Llewellyn, L Rojas-Suarez and S Weisbrod, *Financial Regulation: Why, How and Where Now?* (London and New York, Routledge, 1998) 2.

like its predecessor, it did not harmonise rules on formation, performance, validity of that contract, nor the rules for remedies for its breach and avoidance.[4] Therefore, these private law rules remain based on national law and are subject to the procedural autonomy of Member States.

As a consequence, conduct of business rules have grown as a comprehensive sectoral regulatory regime without formally replacing or interfering with general private laws enshrined in civil codes and common law. While investment firms should comply with both set of duties, the civil law effects of non-compliance with regulatory duties are not clarified by these directives. In particular, it is not clear if breaches of regulatory duties may give rise to general private law remedies, whether regulatory duties may produce horizontal effects and what the impact of EU law should be in shaping these civil law effects. In fact, the EU does not have its own body of general private law to supplement its sectoral requirements. However, the CJEU in preliminary ruling proceedings has developed several important principles to facilitate the private enforcement of EU derived rights and secure the effectiveness of EU law (ie that EU rules achieve their practical purpose).[5]

It is argued that the application of these judge-made principles (ie duty to conform interpretation, principle of equivalence and effectiveness) may have far-reaching consequences on national private law duties and remedies, namely by giving horizontal (direct and indirect) effects to regulatory duties and requiring national courts to provide effective remedies to ensure that these regulatory duties are effective.

This chapter aims to provide a conceptual framework to examine the potential civil law effects of conduct of business rules. It begins by illustrating the milestones of the EU investor protection regulation (ISD, MiFID I and MiFID II). It will then provide an account of the principles of EU law that may facilitate the private enforcement of conduct of business rules before national courts. Finally, it discusses the Europeanisation of national private law and identifies the normative models that may serve to identify the interactions between general private law and sectoral EU regulatory duties.

II. The Development of EU Investor Protection Regulation

A. ISD

In 1966, the Group of Experts appointed by the Commission and headed by Claudio Segrè delivered a report ('Segrè Report') which recommended that

[4] See, in particular, J Köndgen, 'Rules of Conduct: Further Harmonisation?' in G Ferrarini (ed), *European Securities Markets: The Investment Services Directive and Beyond* (London-The Hague-Boston, Kluwer Law International, 1998), 117.

[5] For more detail on the concept of effectiveness in EU law, see P Pescatore, 'The Doctrine of "Direct Effect": An Infant Disease of Community Law': reprinted in (2015) 2 *European Law Review* 135.

EU institutions harmonise capital raising and disclosure rules to strengthen the integration between national financial markets.[6] The Segrè Report paved the way for the adoption, at the beginning of the 1970s, of several directives that liberalised capital movements and introduced prudential requirements for credit institutions and minimum listing and disclosure requirements for companies to facilitate the raising of capital across the EU.[7] Prudential and disclosure requirements ensured a minimum level of protection for the depositor and the prudent saver by ensuring that credit institutions were sufficiently capitalised.[8]

The first EU initiative specifically aimed at protecting investors in secondary market transactions is the European Code of Conduct Relating to Transactions in Transferable Securities adopted by the Commission in 1977. The code set out recommendations for financial intermediaries, including disclosure, conflict of interest and best execution rules, in order to promote the effective functioning of securities markets and to safeguard investors' confidence in the fairness of the market.[9]

In the 1985 White Paper on the completion of the internal market, the Commission underlined the importance of facilitating the exchange of financial products across the European Community to achieve a greater integration in EU financial markets.[10] To achieve this objective, firms who obtained authorisation in their home state, were allowed to provide services across the EU under the supervision of the home state's authorities ('single passport'). The single passport was first granted to collective investment schemes,[11] then to credit institutions[12] and eventually to investment firms, by the ISD.[13]

This directive was adopted, after long negotiations,[14] with the main aim of fostering integration in investment services markets. In addition to the single passport and minimum authorisation requirements, the ISD laid down the first 'EU generation' of conduct of business rules. The final version of the ISD required Member States to draw up rules of conduct which investment firms would observe

[6] C Segre, 'The Development of a European Capital Market.' Report of a Group of Experts appointed by the EEC Commission, November 1966.

[7] See in more detail Moloney, *EU Securities and Financial Markets Regulation* 22.

[8] See A Marcacci, *Regulating Investor Protection under EU Law. The Unbridgeable Gaps with the US and the Way Forward* (Palgrave, 2018) 38–39.

[9] Commission, Recommendation on European Code of Conduct Relating to Transactions in Transferable Securities [1977] OJ L 212/37.

[10] Commission, White Paper on Completing the Internal Market (COM(85) 310), paras 102–103.

[11] Council Directive 85/611 on the Coordination of Laws, Regulations and Administrative Provisions Relating to Undertakings for CollectiveInvestment in Transferable Securities [1985] OJ L 375/3.

[12] Council Directive 89/646 on the Coordination of Laws, Regulations and Administrative Provisions Relating to the Taking Up and Pursuit of the Business of Credit Institutions [1989] OJ L 386/1.

[13] Council Directive 93/22/EEC of 10 May 1993 on investment services in the securities field (ISD) [1993] OJ L 141/27.

[14] Negotiations featured numerous divergences between the so-called 'Club Med' (France, Italy, Spain, Portugal, Greece and Belgium) and the 'North Sea Alliance' (the United Kingdom, Germany, Ireland, Luxembourg, the Netherlands and Denmark). See, in particular, MG Warren, 'The European Union's Investment Services Directive' (1994) 15 *University of Pennsylvania Journal of International Business Law* 193.

at all times and which implemented at least seven 'conduct of business principles', taking into account the professional nature of the person for whom the service was provided.[15] Conduct of business principles remained under the supervision of the host country with the effect that cross-border transactions remained subject to 12 different conduct of business regimes.[16] For this reason, and given that at the time of ISD's adoption Member States had already put in place much more detailed conduct of business rules, the impact of the ISD on the harmonisation of national conduct of business rules was minimal.[17]

The content of the ISD's conduct of business principles reflected that of the principles adopted by IOSCO in 1990.[18] The general phrasing of the ISD's principles aimed to avoid regulatory arbitrage and the risk of interfering with national private laws.[19] Although the conduct of business principles apply to all investment firms irrespective of their business model, the broker-dealer business model, prevalent in continental Europe,[20] was eventually reflected in the directive. In fact, investment advice was not included among the financial services, contrary to the view of the the UK and the Commission,[21] but among the 'non-core services', which were not passportable.

B. MiFID I

In 1999, the Commission presented a Financial Services Action Plan which proposed the adoption of more than 40 action points to accelerate the integration between financial markets in the EU.[22] The FSAP, together with the Lamfallussy Report adopted in 2001 – which laid down the four-layer regulatory approach for financial regulation[23] – is commonly regarded as a milestone towards the

[15] Conduct of business rules were not included in the two Commission proposals, due to the divergences emerged among Member States.

[16] See M Andenas, 'Rules of Conduct and the Principle of Subsidiarity' (1994) 15 *Company Lawyer* 60. See, on the harmonisation scope of ISD, Case C-356/00, *Testa, Lazzeri and Commissione Nazionale per le Società e la Borsa (Consob)*, ECLI:EU:C:2002:703, para 36.

[17] C Cruickshank, 'Is there a Need to Harmonise Conduct of Business Rules?' in G Ferrarini (ed), *European Securities Markets. The Investment Services Directive and Beyond* 132.

[18] International Conduct of Business Principles, 9 July 1990.

[19] See E Wymeersch, 'The Implementation of the ISD and CAD in National Legal Systems' in G Ferrarini (ed), *European Securities Markets. The Investment Services Directive and Beyond* 40.

[20] See Warren, *The European Union's Investment Services Directive*, 194.

[21] Investment advice was, however, included in the passportable services by the Commission Proposal (COM/88/778).

[22] Commission, Financial Services: Implementing the Framework for Financial Markets: Action Plan (FSAP) (COM(99) 232), 3. See, previously, Financial Services: Building a Framework for Action (COM(1998) 625).

[23] Final Report of the Committee of Wise Men on the Regulation of European Securities Markets 2001 (Lamfalussy Report). Level 1: Framework principles adopted by Directives or Regulations under the ordinary legislative procedures of Art 294 TFEU; Level 2: Implementing measures taken by the Commission by means of delegated delegated or implementing acts under Arts 290 and 291 of the TFEU, with the support of ESMA's technical advice and delegated and implementing acts endorsing

federalisation of EU financial regulation for its ambition and efforts towards a greater harmonisation.

The FSAP underlined the urgent need to upgrade the ISD, 'if it is to serve as the cornerstone of an integrated securities market' and to reconsider the host country principle for conduct of business rules.[24] The Commission indicated in the 'judicious ex ante harmonisation of conduct of business protection for retail investors, arrangements to facilitate the negotiation, conclusion and arbitration of cross-border contractual relationships' the priorities for the revision of the ISD.[25] The revision of the ISD was also needed to harmonise the divergences arisen across Member States in the implementation of the ISD's conduct of business principles.[26]

MiFID I was adopted in 2004, two years after the Commission's proposal,[27] in order to 'create an integrated financial market, in which investors are effectively protected and the efficiency and integrity of the overall market are safeguarded'.[28] MiFID I introduced the notion of retail client and set out specific conduct of business rules, further detailed by the 2006 Commission MiFID I Directive,[29] to protect this type of client against misconduct, thus promoting a shift from the prudent saver who 'invests' into riskless bank deposits, to the retail client, who is willing to invest into more risky products.[30]

To foster access to financial markets for investors, MiFID I removed the host state power to implement and supervise conduct of business rules and introduced an, in principle, maximum harmonisation standard for these rules.[31] Building on the work of CESR,[32] MiFID I introduced disclosure, distribution and general product governance rules. In particular, it extended the boundaries of the ISD's

draft regulatory or implementing technical standards according to Arts 10 and 15 of the ESMA Regulation; Level 3: Measures (eg recommendations, guidelines and compares regulatory practice by way of peer review) adopted by ESMA, previously CESR, to ensure consistent implementation and application of the rules adopted; Level 4: Commission checks Member States' compliance with EU legislation and may take legal action against non-compliant Member States.

[24] COM(99) 232, 3.

[25] Commission, *Upgrading the Investment Services Directive* (93/22/EEC) (COM (2000) 729) 3.

[26] Commission, The application of conduct of business rules under Art 11 of the investment services Directive (93/22/EEC) (COM(2000) 722), 11. The Commission identified one area of divergence in 'the typology of contract terms; and documentation as well as 'fragmented state of contractual and extra-contractual frameworks and enforcement systems'.

[27] COM (2002), 625.

[28] Recital No 71 of MiFID I.

[29] Commission Directive 2006/73/EC of 10 August 2006 implementing Directive 2004/39/EC of the European Parliament and of the Council as regards organisational requirements and operating conditions for investment firms and defined terms for the purposes of that Directive ('Commission MiFID I Directive') [2006] OJ L 241/26.

[30] N Moloney, *How to Protect Investors. Lessons from the EC and the UK* (Cambridge, Cambridge University Press, 2010) 39.

[31] See Chapter 2 for more detail on the level of MiFID I harmonisation.

[32] CESR, *A European Regime of Investor Protection. The Harmonization of Conduct of Business Rules.* April, 2002 (CESR/01-014d), 17.

services (by including investment advice) and instruments (by including financial derivatives), introduced differentiated categories of clients (retail, professional and eligible counterparties) and new conduct of business rules (in particular, the suitability and appropriateness rules) calibrated on the type of client, service (advised and non-advised) and financial instrument offered (complex and non-complex).

MiFID I also harmonised the supervisory powers of competent authorities, required Member States to lay down effective, proportionate and dissuasive administrative measures or sanctions or administrative sanctions for breaches of the Directive and encouraged Member States to set up extra-judicial mechanisms for out-of-court resolution of consumer disputes.[33] MiFID I did not introduce rules to harmonise the civil law consequences of breaches of conduct of business rules or other requirements.

C. MiFID II

After the global financial crisis, the EU has re-shaped the regulatory and supervisory architecture of EU financial markets.[34] The reformative effort was driven by two interrelated goals. The first goal was to strengthen the safety and soundness of credit institutions and the stability of the financial system, minimising systemic risks arising from key financial market actors (ie credit institutions, hedge funds, credit rating agencies). This led to the adoption of legislative measures, such as the AIFMD or the short-selling regulation, driven by the international agenda and, later on, when the Euro-zone crisis unfolded, to the creation of the Single Supervisory Mechanism (SSM) and Single Resolution Mechanism (SRM), which together with the single-rulebook (CRR/CRDIV), form the European Banking Union.

The second goal was to further develop the harmonisation within the EU financial market. The underlying rationale, highlighted by the Report of the De Larosière Group, was that the increasing integration across national markets required a deepening of regulatory integration to restore the (lost) confidence of European citizens in financial markets and facilitate intermediation between those with financial resources and those with investment needs.[35]

MiFID II and MiFIR, adopted on 15 May 2014 and entered into force on 3 January 2018,[36] are the key measures to achieve this goal. Although MiFID II

[33] Art s 50, 51 and 53 of MiFID I.

[34] For a detailed overview of the post-crisis EU financial regulation, see House of Lords, 'The Post-crisis EU Financial Regulatory Framework: Do the Pieces Fit?' European Union Committee 5th Report of Session 2014–15, 2 February 2015.

[35] The High-Level Group on Financial Supervision in the EU, Brussels, 25 February 2009, para 40.

[36] The MiFID II Commission Proposal was submitted in 2011, the directive was adopted in 2014 and the entry into force of the MiFID II, originally planned for 3 January 2017, has been deferred, due to technical difficulties in its implementation faced by ESMA and NCAs, to 3 January 2018.

is not a crisis-driven measure,[37] it was 'coloured'[38] by the large detriment suffered by retail clients due to mis-selling in the wake of the financial crisis. In fact, its recitals reflect the need to enhance the protection of investors, particularly retail investors, against the poor conduct of firms, taking into account the limited ability of these investors to estimate risks and take informed investment decisions.[39]

These regulatory concerns account for the tightening of conduct of business rules, the introduction of new product governance obligations and product intervention powers for competent authorities.[40] MiFID II's conduct of business rules are broadly based on those of MiFID I, but several changes have been introduced to reinforce the protection of investors, both in advisory and non-advisory services. MiFID II strengthens supervisory powers and administrative enforcement (by detailing the list of breaches that shall be regarded as an infrigement of the directive) and requires Member States to establish mechanisms to compensate clients for losses suffered as a result of breaches of the directive and to set up extra-judicial mechanisms for the out-of-court resolution of consumer disputes.[41] However, MiFID II does not introduce rules to harmonise the civil law consequences of the breach of conduct of business rules, although some attempts were made by the Commission and the European Parliament.

In the course of MiFID I's review, the Commission, due to the regular number of complaints received especially from retail investors on the firms' breach of conduct of business rules, considered that 'a principle of civil liability of investment services providers would be essential for ensuring an equal level of investor protection in the EU'.[42] However, this principle was not included in the MiFID II Commission proposal. The European Parliament proposed to harmonise rules for the civil and criminal liability of members of the management board but this proposal was not included in the final text of the directive.[43]

III. Protecting Investors without Private Law: The Reasons for (The Lack of) Private Law Harmonisation

The ISD, MiFID I and MiFID II have not harmonised the civil law consequences for breaches of conduct of business rules. MiFID I and MiFID II ensured

[37] MiFID I review started in 2008 by way of the review clause of Art 65 of MiFID I.

[38] See Moloney, *EU Securities and Financial Markets Regulation*, 35 and 339.

[39] Recitals No 5 and 104 of MiFID II.

[40] See Chapter 2.

[41] Arts 69, 70(3), 75(1) of MiFID II.

[42] Commission, Review of the MiFID, Consultation 8 December 2010, 18.

[43] European Parliament, Report on the proposal for a directive of the European Parliament and of the Council on markets in financial instruments repealing Directive 2004/39/EC of the European Parliament and of the Council (COM(2011)0656 – C7-0382/2011 – 2011/0298(COD)) A7-0306/2012 5 October 2012 (Art 9(8a)).

compliance of these rules via administrative enforcement and supervision. At the same time, however, MiFID I and, more significantly, MiFID II have strengthened the out-of-court dispute resolution mechanisms for client disputes,[44] thus showing the legislators' intention to strengthen private enforcement of conduct of business rules.

Although in the wake of the crisis, investors have triggered a high number of mis-selling disputes and national courts and ADR bodies have granted different type of remedies, determining different degrees of legal protection across the EU, MiFID II has refrained from harmonising civil law consequences of breaches of these rules. In our view, leaving aside for the moment the question of whether private laws harmonisation would be appropriate, this regulatory choice can be explained by competence-based, policy-based and institutional-based reasons.

A first reason might be related to the lack of an express EU law competence to harmonise national private laws.[45] However, especially after the global financial crisis, new harmonisation regimes have been introduced on the basis of Article 114 of TFEU (Prospectus Directive,[46] Transparency Directive,[47] AIFM Directive,[48] EMIR Regulation,[49] CRA Regulation,[50] PRIIPs Regulation,[51] UCITS V Directive[52]).

The purposive and cross-sectoral nature of Article 114 of TFEU[53] and the flexible approach of the CJEU in assessing its limitations,[54] have indeed

[44] See Chapter 4.

[45] The EU has only an express competence only to harmonise rules on civil procedure, access to justice, international private law having cross-border implications (Art 81(2)(f) of TFEU).

[46] Art 6 of Directive 2003/71/EC of the European Parliament and of the Council of 4 November 2003 on the prospectus to be published when securities are offered to the public or admitted to trading and amending Directive 2001/34/EC ('Prospectus Directive') [2003] OJ L 345/64.

[47] Art 7 of Directive 2004/109/EC of the European Parliament and of the Council of 15 December 2004 on the harmonisation of transparency requirements in relation to information about issuers whose securities are admitted to trading on a regulated market and amending Directive 2001/34/EC ('Transparency Directive') [2004] OJ L 390/38.

[48] Art 21 of Directive 2011/61/EU of the European Parliament and of the Council of 8 June 2011 on Alternative Investment Fund Managers and amending Directives 2003/41/EC and 2009/65/EC and Regulations (EC) No 1060/2009 and (EU) No 1095/2010 ('AIFM Directive') [2011] OJ L 174/1.

[49] Art 12(3) of Regulation (EU) No 648/2012 of the European Parliament and of the Council of 4 July 2012 on OTC derivatives, central counterparties and trade repositories (EMIR) [2012] OJ L 201/1.

[50] Art 1(22) of Regulation (EU) No 462/2013 of the European Parliament and of the Council of 21 May 2013 amending Regulation (EC) No 1060/2009 on credit rating agencies (CRA Regulation) [2013] OJ L 146/1 which introduced Art 35a into Regulation (EC) No 1060/2009.

[51] Art 11 of Regulation (EU) No 1286/2014 of the European Parliament and of the Council of 26 November 2014 on key information documents for packaged retail and insurance-based investment products (PRIIPs Regulation) [2014] OJ L 352/1.

[52] Art 24 of Directive 2014/91/EU of the European Parliament and of the Council of 23 July 2014 amending Directive 2009/65/EC on the coordination of laws, regulations and administrative provisions relating to undertakings for collective investment in transferable securities (UCITS) as regards depositary functions, remuneration policies and sanctions (UCITS V Directive) [2014] OJ L 257/186.

[53] See G Davies, 'Democracy and Legitimacy in the Shadow of Purposive Competence' (2015) 21 *European Law Journal* 2.

[54] Case C-376/98, *Germany v Parliament and Council*, ECLI:EU:C:2000:544. For a critical appraisal of this case law, see S Weatherill, The Limits of Legislative Harmonization Ten Years after Tobacco

facilitated private law harmonisation also in other sectors of the internal market (ie consumer law), strengthening the private enforcement of EU law.[55]

Since MiFID I and MiFID II have been based on the freedom of establishment,[56] the powerful tool of Article 114 of TFEU was not available to co-legislators to harmonise the civil liability of investment service providers. However, from a legal perspective, the harmonisation of private law rules may also be justified for regulatory measures that ultimately aim to foster freedom of establishment. The main rationale would be to facilitate the investors' confidence in the EU financial markets, ensuring a greater degree of uniformity of private law and civil liability standards.[57] These standards would contribute to ensure, together with regulatory duties, 'the competence and trustworthiness of the financial intermediaries on whom investors are particularly reliant'.[58]

Second, more than the strictly legal concerns, policy-related considerations may have played an important role in the co-legislator's choice not to harmonise the civil law consequences for breaches of conduct of business rules.[59] These type of concerns did not become 'explicit' but, as in the case of MiFID II, they might have led to a rejection of both the Commission and European Parliament's proposals to introduce rules on firm's liability in the directive.[60] One reason for this rejection is the fear that harmonisation would provoke politically sensitive inroads into national private laws.[61] This has driven the public-enforcement and functional approach to securities regulation which, since the ISD, has sought to level the playing field in conduct regulation without interfering with the different philosophical conceptions of private law and cultural approaches to private litigation existing across the EU.[62]

Another reason for the absence of private law's harmonisation is that harmonisation would tighten the standards of civil liability for financial market participants and would give rise to excessive levels of litigation that could endanger

Advertising: How the Court's Case Law has become a "Drafting Guide" (2011) 12 *German Law Journal* 843.

[55] See, in particular, F Wilman, *Private Enforcement of EU Law Before National Courts. The EU Legislative Framework* (Cheltenham, Edward Elgar, 2015) 399 and H-W Micklitz, 'The EU as a Federal Order of Competences and the Private Law' in L Azoulai, *The Question of Competence in the European Union* (Oxford, Oxford University Press, 2014) 125, 133.

[56] MiFID I was based on Art 47(1) of Treaty establishing the European Community (TEC) [2002] OJ C 325/33 and MiFID II is based on Art 53(1) of Treaty Consolidated Version of the Treaty on the Functioning of the European Union (TFEU) [2012] OJ C 326/47.

[57] Notably, MiFID II, like MiFID I, already harmonises contract law aspects of the firm-client relationship, such as that of concluding a written client agreement.

[58] Case C-384/93, *Alpine Investments BV v Minister van Financiën*, ECLI:EU:C:1995:126, para 42.

[59] See, in general, Wilman, *Private Enforcement of EU Law Before National Courts* 411.

[60] See Chapter 2.

[61] T Tridimas, 'EU Financial Regulation: Federalization, Crisis Management and Law Reform' in P Craig and G De Burca (eds), *The Evolution of EU Law*, 2nd edn (Oxford, Oxford University Press, 2011) 794.

[62] See CESR, *Draft Technical Advice on Possible Implementing Measures of the Directive 2004/39/EC on Markets in Financial Instruments*, Second set of Mandates October 2004. CESR/04-562, 13.

the efficiency and stability of financial markets.[63] Some of the post-crisis regulatory measures reflect the concerns for vexatious litigation and its potential negative systemic spillovers. The EMIR expressly provides that the infringement clearing, reporting and risk mitigation obligations by the parties to an OTC derivative contract shall neither affect the validity of that contract nor the possibility for the parties to enforce the provisions of an OTC derivative contract and shall not give rise to any right to compensation from a party to an OTC derivative contract.[64] The AIFM Directive requires alternative investment funds to have additional own funds to cover potential liability risks arising from professional negligence.[65] However, in retail markets, this type of risk is much less pronounced, since retail clients have generally weak incentives to bring a civil law action given the high cost of legal proceedings and the relatively low value of their claims.[66]

IV. Bridging EU Conduct of Business Rules and National Private Law via EU General Principles

A. The EU Judge-Made Law on Remedies

There is also a broader institutional reason that underpinned MiFID's 'public-enforcement approach' to conduct of business regulation. As Reich put it, 'the liberal deregulation and privatisation movement as undertaken by the EU has been quite successful in reducing state functions and in opening public services, traditionally provided by state institutions, to private competition [but] it has […] not been able to transfer with similar success the obligations flowing out of these services to private actors'.[67] As a result, 'whereas rights originate in themselves as far as their "vertical" state orientation is concerned; obligations need a much different and longer track before becoming effective'.[68] MiFID II (like MiFID I)

[63] See I MacNeil, 'Enforcement and Sanctioning' in E Ferran, N Moloney, N Payne (eds), *Oxford Handbook on Financial Regulation* (Oxford, Oxford University Press, 2015) 293; N Moloney, 'Liability of Asset Managers: A Comment' (2012) 4 *CMLJ* 421. See in relation to the concerns raised by the UK's Financial Markets Law Committee (FMLC) on the risk of vexatious litigation due to Art 28(1) of the Transparency Directive, the Letter sent to Lord Woolf, FMLC on 3 May 2006, by Alexander Schaub, on behalf of the European Commission. Available at: http://fmlc.org/wp-content/uploads/2018/02/Issue-76-Letter-from-Alexander-Schaub-re-Transparency-Directive.pdf.

[64] Art 12(3) of EMIR.

[65] Art 9(7) of AIFMD.

[66] See Chapter 7.

[67] N Reich, 'The Interrelation between Rights and Duties in EU Law: Reflections on the State of Liability Law in the Multilevel Governance System of the Union: Is There a Need for a More Coherent Approach in European Private Law?' (2010) 29 *Yearbook of European Law* 121.

[68] Ibid at 122.

reflects the imbalance between rights and obligations. Its conduct of business rules are able to confer rights on individual investors but these rules are not 'backed' by an EU law remedy, but only by administrative enforcement and supervision. Individuals need to rely on national (private) law to enforce these rights 'horizontally' via a civil proceeding.

However, to ensure that rights derived from EU law do not remain 'naked' and individuals have an effective way to enforce them via their national courts and national laws,[69] the CJEU has developed a 'genuine European system of rights, remedies and procedures'[70] which comprises the doctrine of direct effect of EU law and the principle of equivalence and effectiveness.

B. Horizontal Effects of Conduct of Business Rules

Under certain conditions, EU law provisions that are intended to bind only Member States and their public authorities ('vertical effects') may also produce effects against private parties ('horizontal effects').

The type of horizontal effects depends on the nature of the EU legal act. Regulations and other directly applicable acts, if clear, precise and unconditional, may be invoked against the state and private parties in a civil proceeding ('horizontal direct effect').[71] The doctrine of horizontal direct effect is particularly relevant for the conduct of business rules enacted in the Commission MiFID II Regulation. These conduct of business rules may, in principle, be invoked by an investor in a civil proceeding against the firm to label a private act as null and void or unlawful[72] or to trigger civil liability for breaches of EU law.[73]

[69] See, in particular, Wilman, *Private Enforcement of EU Law Before National Courts* 431.

[70] H-W Micklitz, 'The ECJ Between the Individual Citizen and the Member States – A Plea for a Judge-Made European Law on Remedies' in H-W Micklitz and B De Witte (eds), *The European Court of Justice and the Autonomy of the Member States* (Cambridge, Antwerp, Intersentia, 2012) 350.

[71] Case C-149/77, *Defrenne v Société anonyme belge de navigation aérienne Sabena* ECLI:EU:C:1978:130 (with regard to Art 157 TFEU, formerly Art 141 TEC); Case C-9/70, *Franz Grad v Finanzamt Traunstein*, ECLI:EU:C:1970:78, para 10 (with regard to Decisions); see Case C-144/04, *Mangold v Rüdiger Helm* ECLI:EU:C:2005:709, para 78 and Case C-555/07, *Kücükdeveci v Swedex GmbH & Co KG*, ECLI:EU:C:2010:21, para 55 (with regard to the general prinicple of non-discrimination on grounds of age), Case C-253/00, *Muñoz y Cia SA and Superior Fruiticola SA v Frumar Ltd and Redbridge Produce Marketing Ltd*, ECLI:EU:C:2002:497 (with regard to Regulations).

[72] See C Timmermans 'Horizontal Direct/Indirect Effect or Direct/Indirect Horizontal Effect: What's in a Name?' (2016) *European Review of Private Law* 677.

[73] Case C-453/99, *Courage Ltd and Bernard Crehan*, ECLI:EU:C:2001:465, para 24. For the opinion that the principle of horizontal liability cannot be generalised to other cases see D Leczykiewicz, 'Private Party Liability in EU Law: In Search of the General Regime' (2009–2010) 12 *Cambridge Yearbook of European Legal Studies* 257 and K Havu 'Horizontal Liability for Damages in EU Law – the Changing Relationship of EU and National Law' (2012) 18 *European Law Journal* 425. For a more open approach, see T Tridimas, *The General Principles of EU Law* (Oxford, Oxford University Press, 2006) 544 and Wilman, *Private Enforcement of EU Law Before National Courts* 478.

Directives, which are not directly applicable, cannot produce horizontal direct effects.[74] Therefore, they may be invoked only against the state but not against another individual.[75] Nevertheless, to ensure the full effectiveness of directives in cases where transposition is lacking or inadequate, the CJEU has held that directives, under certain conditions, may produce two types of horizontal indirect effects.

First, a party may rely upon a directive's provision, which was not correctly tranposed into national law, to set aside the national provisions that are incompatible with the directive in a civil proceeding ('exclusionary effect').[76] This type of horizontal indirect effect cannot lead to impose on a private party duties set out in the directive but it may deprive the defendant from a defence that he would have had under national law[77] or may disable the plaintiff from enforcing national law in contrast with the directive.[78]

Second, national courts have the duty to interpret national law as far as possible in line with the wording and purpose of the directive ('duty to consistent or conform interpretation').[79] It requires national courts to interpret national law taking into account not only the national transposition law[80] but also the whole body of domestic law pre-dating the directive[81] and the settled domestic case law.[82] This duty, which may lead to the disapplication of national law or the introduction of new private law remedies into national law,[83] applies only if (i) the national law provision is not in itself clear and unambiguous; (ii) the conform interpretation does not lead to an interpretation of national law *contra legem*,[84] does not

[74] For a critical overview of this case law see P Craig, 'The Legal Effect of Directives: Policy, Rules and Exceptions' (2009) 34 *European Law Review* 352.

[75] Case C-91/92, *Paola Faccini Dori v Recreb Srl.*, ECLI:EU:C:1994:292, paras 22–24 and Case C-201/02, *R (on the application of Wells) v Secretary of State for Transport, Local Government and the Regions*, ECLI:EU:C:2004:12, para 56.

[76] T Tridimas, 'Black, White, and Shades of Grey: Horizontality of Directives Revisited' (2001) 21 *Yearbook of European law* 330.

[77] Case C-194/94, *CIA Security International SA v Signalson SA and Securitel SPRL*, ECLI:EU:C:1996:172; Case C-443/98, *Unilever Italia SpA v Central Food SpA*, ECLI:EU:C:2000:496, para 51 and Case C-381/98, *Ingmar GB Ltd v Eaton Leonard Technologies Inc.*, ECLI:EU:C:2000:605, para 33.

[78] Case C-77/97, *Österreichische Unilever GmbH and Smithkline Beecham Markenartikel GmbH*, ECLI:EU:C:1999:30.

[79] See Joined Cases C-397/01–C-403/01, *Bernhard Pfeiffer* et al., ECLI:EU:C:2004:584, para 114.

[80] Case C-306/12, *Spedition Welter GmbH v Avanssur SA*, ECLI:EU:C:2013:650 (the duty of conform interpretation applies also to directive provisions that have been transposed word-for-word into national law).

[81] Case C-106/89, *Marleasing SA gegen La Comercial Internacional de Alimentacion SA.*, ECLI:EU:C:1990:395, para 8; case C-282/10, *Dominguez v Centre informatique du Centre Ouest Atlantique and Préfet de la région Centre*, ECLI:EU:C:2012:33, para 24.

[82] Case C-456/98, *Centrosteel Srl v Adipol GmbH*, ECLI:EU:C:2000:402, para 17.

[83] Case C-456/98, *Centrosteel Srl v Adipol GmbH*, ECLI:EU:C:2000:402, para 17.

[84] See, inter alia, case C-268/06 *Impact v Minister for Agriculture and Food and Others* ECLI:EU:C:2008:223, para 100.

aggraviate the criminal liability of the individual[85] and respects the general principles of law, in particular the principles of legal certainty and non-retroactivity.[86]

C. The Procedural Autonomy of Member States: A Private Law Remedy Based on EU Law?

The doctrine of horizontal effects was primarily developed to avoid the risk that the full effect of regulations and directives were exclusively dependent on national transposition legislation. However, whilst the 'invocability' of an EU law provision in civil proceedings – the main corollary of the horizontal effects – ensures an effective defence against the application of national law in contrast with EU law, it does not grant to the plaintiff a private law remedy to obtain compensation for losses caused by the other party's non-compliance with EU law.[87] Where EU law is silent on the remedial consequences of breaches of regulatory duties, the remedy should be based on national law.

Nevertheless, since the landmark *Rewe* judgment, the CJEU held that:

> in the absence of Union rules on the subject, the rights conferred by EU law must be exercised before the national courts in accordance with the conditions laid down by national law (ie procedural autonomy[88]), provided that the procedural conditions governing the action are not be less favourable than those relating to similar actions of a domestic nature (ie the principle of equivalence) and do not make it impossible in practice or excessively difficult to exercise the rights which are based upon or derived from EU law (ie the principle of effectiveness).[89]

Therefore, national (private) law plays an instrumental or 'ancillary' role in ensuring the effective application of substantive EU law.[90] The pre-condition is that the EU law provision at stake confers a right on the individual. Rights can be conferred directly (ie by way of a provision which entitles the individual to a certain benefit) or indirectly (ie by way of provisions imposing requirements on

[85] See Case C-168/95, *Criminal Proceedings against Luciano Arcaro,* ECLI:EU:C:1996:363, para 42. For the opinion that Arcaro should be interpreted restrictively, as referred only to the criminal liability (and not civil liability) see the Opinion of Advocate General Jacobs in *Centrosteel* (case C-456/98, EU:C:2000:137, para 34).

[86] See in particular Case C-268/06 *Impact,* para 100.

[87] See T Eilmansenberger 'The Relationship Between Rights and Remedies in EC Law: In Search of the Missing Link' (2004) 41 *Common Market Law Review* 1217.

[88] On the principle of procedural autonomy see, in particular: CN Kakouris 'Do the Member States possess Judicial Procedural "Autonomy"?' (1997) 34 *Common Market Law Review* 1389; S Prechal, 'Community Law in National Courts: The Lessons from Van Schijndel' (1998) 35 *Common Market Law Review* 681; Wilman, *Private Enforcement of EU Law Before National Courts* 405.

[89] Case 33/76, *Rewe v Landwirtschaftskammer für das Saarland.,* ECLI:EU:C:1976:188 and Case 45/76, *Comet BV v Produktschap voor Siergewassen,* ECLI:EU:C:1976:191.

[90] Kakouris, 'Do the Member States Possess Judicial Procedural "Autonomy"?' 1390.

another party).[91] While in some judgments, mainly concerning directly applicable provisions, the CJEU considered it sufficient for a provision to be sufficiently clear and precise to be right-conferring,[92] in others the CJEU required something more, namely that the provision 'by its content and purport affords protection to the interests which he is invoking in law' ('protective purpose').[93] The fact that a directive intends to protect investors is not enough to conclude that its provisions confer a legally enforceable right on these investors.[94] It is necessary that its provisions by their content,[95] the need for protection of the addressee of the rule,[96] their level of detail[97] and their legal nature[98] grant a legally enforceable right to the investor.

Finally, the scope of procedural autonomy depends on the scope of EU law harmonisation. When EU law harmonises only the constitutive conditions of the remedy,[99] (ie whether a private law remedy must be granted (ie the Prospectus Directive)), the principles of equivalence and effectiveness apply only to the detailed rules (or executive conditions) of the remedy (ie causation, measure of damages), whilst the stricter principle of primacy of EU law applies to the constitutive remedial conditions. This principle entails that if national law is in contrast with a directly applicable EU law provision and no interpretation in conformity is available the national law provision must be disapplied.[100]

When EU law harmonises only the regulatory duties to be imposed on market participants (ie MiFID I and MiFID II), and these provisions confer individual rights, both the constitutive and executive remedial conditions are subject to the principles of equivalence and effectiveness. This means that, in principle, a greater leeway should be given to national courts to determine the civil law consequences of breaches of conduct of business rules. When EU law provisions do not harmonise remedies and do not confer rights on individuals, Member States remain free

[91] Eilsemberger, 'The Relationship between Rights and Remedies in EC Law' 1207.

[92] See Case C-253/00, *Munoz*, para 27 and joined cases C-6/90 and C-9/90, *Francovich and Bonifaci v Italy*, ECLI:EU:C:1991:42, para 39.

[93] Opinion of AG Geelhoed in case C-253/00, *Muñoz*, ECLI:EU:C:2001:697, para 47.

[94] Case C-222/02, *Peter Paul and Others v Bundesrepublik Deutschland*, ECLI:EU:C:2004:606, para 41. See also case C-219/15, *Schmitt v TÜV*, ECLI:EU:C:2017:128, para 55 and case C-571/16, *Nikolay Kantarev v Balgarska Narodna Banka*, ECLI:EU:C:2018:807, para 90.

[95] See M Ruffert, 'Rights and Remedies in European Community Law: A Comparative View' (1997) 34 *Common Market Law Review* 307.

[96] See N Reich, 'Horizontal Liability in EC Law – Hybridisation of Remedies for Compensation in Case of Beach of EC Rights' (2007) 44 *Common Market Law Review* 704 at 718.

[97] Case C-101/08, *Audiolux SA e.a v Groupe Bruxelles Lambert SA (GBL) and Others*, ECLI:EU:C:2009:626, para 62. See also case C-131/88, *Commission v Federal Republic of Germany* ECLI:EU:C:1991:87, para 7S.

[98] Opinion of AG Geelhoed in case C-253/00, *Muñoz*, para 47 (if it is a directly applicable act the right conferring test should be less strict).

[99] For the notion of constitutive and executive remedial conditions, see W Van Gerven, 'Of Rights, Remedies and Procedures (2001) 37 *Common Market Law Review* 525.

[100] Wilman, *Private Enforcement of EU Law Before National Courts* 409.

to decide the civil law consequences for violation of these provisions. The only limit, in this case, is represented by the EU fundamental rights.

D. EU Fundamental Rights: The Right to an Effective Judicial Protection

Member States shall respect the EU fundamental rights not only where national law is transposing EU law but also in situations where they are acting within the scope of application of EU law.[101] Of particular importance, in the context of retail financial disputes, is the fundamental right of effective judicial protection, which is a general principle of EU law stemming from the constitutional traditions common to the Member States[102] and is enshrined in Articles 6 (right to a fair trial) and 13 (right to an effective remedy) of the ECHR, Article 47 of the Charter of Fundamental Rights[103] and reaffirmed in Article 19 of the TEU. This fundamental right must be respected 'at, all levels of EU law adjudication, irrespective of the degree of autonomy left to the Member States'.[104]

Even if there is certain degree of interference between the principle of effectiveness, developed by the CJEU since *Rewe* and the fundamental right of effective judicial protection,[105] there are two main differences between these principles.

First, whilst the principle of effectiveness, aims to ensure the Member States' compliance with the obligations imposed by EU law,[106] the fundamental right of effective judicial protection aims to ensure that the individuals' rights are protected against Member States, Union institutions and private parties. This entails that the fundamental right should ensure not only the minimum level of protection that is necessary to implement EU law but the level of protection that, given the specific circumstances of the case, is adequate to protect the individual.[107]

[101] Case C-617/10, *Åklagaren v Hans Åkerberg Fransson*, ECLI:EU:C:2013:280, para 19.

[102] Case 222/84, *Johnston v Chief Constable of the Royal Ulster Constabulary*, ECLI:EU:C:1986:206, paras 18 and 19.

[103] Charter of Fundamental Rights of the European Union (the Charter) [2012] OJ C 326/391.

[104] M Safjan and D Dusterhaus, 'A Union of Effective Judicial Protection: Addressing a Multi-level Challenge through the Lens of Art 47 CFREU' (2014) *Yearbook of European Law* 24.

[105] In some judgments the CJEU held that the principle of effectiveness incorporates the principle of effective judicial protection (Case C-432/05 *Unibet*, ECLI:EU:C:2007:163, para 37; Case C-268/06, *Impact*, ECLI:EU:C:2008:223, para 47; Case C-169/14, *Sánchez Morcillo and others v Banco Bilbao Vizcaya Argentaria SA*, ECLI:EU:C:2014:2099, para 35; Case C-483/16, *Zsolt Sziber v ERSTE Bank Hungary Zrt.*, ECLI:EU:C:2018:367, para 49); in others the CJEU treated effectiveness and fundamental right of effective judicial protection as different principles, thus conducting two different assessments (Joined cases C-317/08, C-318/08, C-319/08 and C-320/08 *Rosalba Alassini and others*, EU:C:2010:146, para 61).

[106] See P Nebbia, 'The Double Life of Effectiveness' (2007–2008) 10 *Cambridge Yearbook of European Legal Studies* 288.

[107] See N Reich, *General Principles of EU Civil Law* (Cambridge, Intersentia, 2013) 97.

Second, whilst the principle of effectiveness can be limited in light of the principles of the domestic legal system (ie principle of legal certainty, adversarial principle), the principle of effective judicial protection may be limited only if limitations correspond 'to objectives of general interest pursued by the measure in question and that they do not involve, with regard to the objectives pursued, a disproportionate and intolerable interference which infringes upon the very substance of the rights guaranteed'.[108] In private law relations, where both parties could legitimately claim that their fundamental rights are at stake, the fundamental rights of each party need to be assessed in light of the proportionality principle, taking into account the fact that the legitimate aim that may justify an interference with the fundamental rights of one party may coincide with the fundamental rights of the other party.[109] This means that to restrict the right of effective judicial protection a justification based on the 'autonomy' of domestic law is not sufficient but it is necessary to explain why the national law at stake it is necessary to achieve, in a proportionate manner, an objective of general interest.

V. The Interplay between EU Sectoral Regulation and National General Private Law: Towards Hybridisation of National Private Law?

The case law of the CJEU may offer to national courts and ADR bodies powerful tools to ensure the civil law effects of conduct of business rules. Conceptually, this means that, on the one hand, lack of private law harmonisation does not mean that EU law is indifferent to the private enforcement of its rules, and on the other, that the EU law general principles examined above require the adjustment or instrumentalisation of national private law to the extent that it is necessary to give full effects to conduct of business rules.[110]

In practice, instrumentalisation may be difficult to achieve given the different goals pursued by regulatory and private law duties.[111] Conduct of business rules

[108] See R Widdershoven and S Prechal, 'Redefining the Relationship between "Rewe-effectiveness" and Effective Judicial Protection' (2011) 2 *Review of European Administrative Law* 44.

[109] See H Collins, 'On the (In)compatibility of Human Rights Discourse and Private Law' in H-W Micklitz (ed), *Constitutionalization of European Private Law* (Oxford, Oxford University Press, 2014) 50.

[110] See in more detail on Europeanisation M Claes, 'The European Union, its Member States and their Citizens' in D Leczykiewicz and Stephen Weatherill (eds), *The Involvement of EU Law in Private Law Relationships* (Hart Publishing, Oxford, 2013), 35 and P Giliker. *The Europeanisation of English Tort Law* (Oxford, Hart Publishing, 2014) 210. See especially OO Cherednychenko, 'Contract Governance in the EU: Conceptualising the Relationship between Investor Protection Regulation and Private Law' (2015) 21 *European Law Journal* 500 and, from a broader perspective, see H-W Micklitz, 'The Visible Hand of European Regulatory Private Law – The Transformation of European Private Law from Autonomy to Functionalism in Competition and Regulation' (2009) 28 *Yearbook of European Law* 1.

[111] See especially S Grundmann, 'The Banking Union Translated into (Private Law) Duties: Infrastructure and Rulebook' (2015) *European Business Organization Law Review* 1.

primarily aim at protecting clients, private law duties primarily aim to protect freedom of contract of market participants. Whereas general private law rules are based on the assumption of the equality of contracting parties, conduct of business rules are based on the assumption of the inequality of contracting parties as regards their information and bargaining power asymmetry. Could these different goals be reconciled? Or, to put it differently, may the divergence of goals between these rules prevent the full effect of conduct of business rules?

As this study will show,[112] conflicts between the client-protective purpose of conduct of business rules and the freedom of contract's purpose of general private law have arisen in the case law and, in certain instances, have reduced the effectiveness of conduct-of-business rules. These type of conflicts are, in our view, physiological in the EU legal order because private law is not harmonised; it therefore reflects national philosophical, economical and sociological conceptions of private relations within the society, which may be at odds with the internal-market-building objective pursued by the EU.

However, regulation and autonomy do not necessarily conflict. It has been argued that in the EU legal order, private autonomy should not only be understood in the negative meaning of lack of public interferences but also in a positive meaning of promotion of the freedoms granted to individuals by the Treaties.[113] In numerous sectors of the internal market, harmonisation of private laws, served to enhance, after market liberalisation, consumer protection and competition – two key goals of EU law enshrined in Article 3(3) of the Treaty on European Union (TEU)[114] – rather than 'the pursuit of autonomous interests of the parties'.[115] The essence of EU rules governing transactions in goods and services – also named the European Regulatory Private Law (ERPL)[116] – is therefore in a 'regulated autonomy' rather than a 'private autonomy'. As a result, in a legal order where autonomy and heteronomy, private and public become blurred and the rights granted by EU law to the individuals need to be protected (via EU or national authorities) the divergent public and private goals of EU and national law rules should not affect the degree of protection of the individual citizen.[117]

[112] See Chapter 6.

[113] See H-W Micklitz, G Comparato, Y Svetiev, 'The Regulatory Character of European Private Law' in C Twigg-Flesner (ed), *Research Handbook on EU Consumer and Contract Law* (Cheltenham, Edward Edgar, 2016) 46. See also S Cassese, 'Quattro paradossi sui rapporti tra poteri pubblici ed autonomie private' (2000) 2 *Rivista Trimestrale di Diritto Pubblico* (2000): 389.

[114] See especially Micklitz, 'The Visible Hand of European Regulatory Private Law' at 1; M. W. Hesselink, 'Contract Theory and EU Contract Law' in C. Twigg-Flesner (ed), *Research Handbook on EU Consumer and Contract Law* (Cheltenham, Edward Elgar, 2016) 50; A Zoppini, 'Diritto Privato vs Diritto Amministrativo (ovvero alla ricerca dei confini tra stato e mercato)' (2013) 3 *Rivista di diritto civile* 527.

[115] F Möslein and K Riesenhuber, 'Contract Governance – A Draft Research Agenda' (2009) 3 *European Review of Contract Law* 293.

[116] Micklitz, 'The Visible Hand of European Regulatory Private Law' at 3.

[117] C. Hadjiemmanuil, 'The Banking Union and Its Implications for Private Law' 16(3) *European Business Organization Law Review* 383–400 at 393.

What matters is whether the protective scope of the EU law rule at stake, irrespective of its nature, includes that person.

That said, when the EU sectoral regulation intersects national general private law, four types of interaction, as Hans-W Micklitz put it, can be observed depending on the sector of the internal market and the EU legislative technique: intrusion and substitution, conflict and resistance, hybridisation and convergence.[118] Similarly, but in the context of investment services regulation, Olha O Cherenychenko[119] identified four models of interaction: substitution, separation, complementarity and integration. This chapter focuses the attention on three conceptual models: separation, substitution and hybridisation.[120]

The model of separation envisages the co-existence, without interference, of traditional private law and financial regulation.[121] Under this model, which can be seen, for instance, in the UK, investors can benefit from a statutory right of action to enforce regulatory duties in civil proceedings. This model avoids the conflict of goals mentioned above because investors do not need to resort to general private law to enforce regulatory duties and can rely on 'in principle' a more favourable private law remedy. This also ensures a high degree of legal and commercial certainty because investment firms know in advance that unsophisticated retail clients may have 'alternative' routes to traditional private law to recover investment losses and this may produce positive effects in terms of deterrence.[122] However, the flipside is that this special private law regime may create unequal treatment in similar situations and may also bar investors from relying on general private law, where statutory rights of action do not provide for a satisfactory remedy.

At the other extreme of the separation model lies the model of substitution in which the sectoral financial regulatory duties and remedies replace and substitute the general ones, thus becoming the only private law governing the transaction. This model entails that the breach of regulatory duties can give rise only to a certain private law remedy. No discretion is left to national courts or adjudicators. This model ensures a high degree of uniformity across national jurisdictions and that private law rules are aligned with the expertise of regulators, but it restricts regulatory competition and can have a disruptive effect on national private law, bringing about a full or partial pre-emption of the more favourable national private laws.[123]

[118] See H-W Micklitz, Y Svetiev, G Comparato (eds), 'European Regulatory Private Law – The Paradigms Tested' LAW 2014/04 Department of Law European Regulatory Private Law Project (ERC-ERPL-07) European Research Council (ERC) Grant.

[119] See Cherednychenko, 'Contract Governance in the EU' at 508.

[120] In the proposed categorisation, the model of separation includes characteristics of the separation and complementarity models put forward by Cherednychenko, 'Contract Governance in the EU' at 511–513.

[121] See, for this view, A Hudson, *Law of Finance* (London, Sweet & Maxwell, 2013) 39 and I H-Y Chiu, 'Regulatory Duties for Directors in the Financial Services Sector and Directors' Duties in Company Law: Bifurcation and Interfaces' (2016) 6 *Journal of Business Law* 489.

[122] See Cherednychenko, 'Contract Governance in the EU' at 512.

[123] See, for an example of pre-emption, Art 12(3) of EMIR.

The hybridisation model is somehow in between the previous two models and represents the general normative model of interaction between general private law and special regimes in the EU legal order.[124] Although legal hybrids are vague concepts,[125] in EU law they indicate the ambivalent nature (ie neither exclusively national nor exclusively European) of private law remedies and procedures aimed at protecting EU-derived rights. [126] The model of hybridisation reflects the fact that EU private law and national private law, albeit driven by different rationales (ie regulation and private autonomy) are intertwined in the sense that the rights, obligations and remedies of contracting parties cannot be determined with certainty by referring exclusively to either national or EU law.[127] Hybridisation may also refer, more generally, to the synthesis between sectoral, regulatory duties and general private law duties,[128] which may take place also at the national level.

Our hypothesis is that this model seems to be implicitly endorsed by MiFID I and MIFID II, given that they leave Member States free to determine the civil law consequences of any violation of their conduct of business rules but, via the general principles of EU law, require, under certain conditions, national courts to grant civil law effects to these rules. The adaptability of general private law to the specific need of protection of the client is the main strength of hybridisation but, at the same time, it is its Achilles' heel because it could make private law adjudication excessively reliant upon courts or the decisions of ADR entities and this is a risk for legal and commercial certainty.[129] For this reason, it is necessary to examine in-depth the EU legal grounds for the creation of hybrid private law duties and remedies.

VI. Preliminary Conclusion

EU law has traditionally favoured a public enforcement of securities and financial regulation.

[124] H-W Micklitz, 'Monistic Ideology versus Pluralistic Reality – Towards a Normative Design for European Private Law' in L Niglia (ed), *Pluralism and European Private Law* (Oxford, Hart Publishing, 2013) 47.

[125] See, in particular, K Tuori, 'On Legal Hybrids and Perspectivism' in M Maduro, K Tuori, and S Sankari (eds), *Transnational Law: Rethinking European Law and Legal Thinking* (Cambridge, Cambridge University Press, 2014) 14 who argues that we use legal hybrids when 'our inherited conceptual framework is unable to capture and imprison in a determined conceptual box'.

[126] See Reich, 'Horizontal Liability in EC Law' at 709.

[127] See Hesselink, 'Contract Theory and EU Contract Law' at 523.

[128] See AS Hudson, 'The Synthesis of Public and Private in Finance Law' in K. Barker and D. Jensen (eds), *Private Law: Key Encounters with Public Law* (Cambridge, Cambridge University Press, 2013) 233.

[129] See JA Grundfest, 'Damages and Reliance Under Section 10(b) of the Exchange Act' *Stanford Law School and The Rock Center for Corporate Governance* 28 August 2013, 25 who argued that the creation of implied rights of action under s 10(b) of the 1933 US Securities Act is 'is entirely a creature of the judicial imagination, and it comes as no surprise that the courts have played a crucial role in the evolution of Section 10(b) jurisprudence'.

After the global financial crisis, the EU introduced new rules to harmonise the civil liability of key market participants (ie credit rating agencies, fund depositaries) but did not harmonise the civil law consequences for breaches of MiFID II's conduct of business rules. The reasons for lack of private law harmonisation in MiFID's transactions should be found in policy-related concerns for the fear of vexatious litigation and in the difficulties in harmonising divergent national private laws.

However, lack of private law harmonisation, does not mean that EU law remains indifferent to the private enforcement of MiFID II conduct of business rules.

A distinctive feature of the EU legal order is that individuals have to rely on their national courts and (generally) on national remedies and procedures to enforce rights derived from EU law. However, to ensure an adequate level of protection for EU-derived rights, Member States must ensure that remedies and procedures comply with the principles of equivalence and effectiveness and with the EU fundamental rights.

This chapter has shown that these judge-made principles, together with the doctrine of the horizontal effects of EU law, should bridge conduct of business rules with private law, requiring national courts to interpret general private law in light of detailed regulatory duties and, under certain conditions, to grant a civil law remedy for breaches of these rules. General private law should assist or facilitate conduct of business rules in achieving their policy goals. This instrumentalisation of private law gives a prominent role to national courts and ADR bodies, which should define, ex post, once a dispute has arisen, the private law duty and remedy required to ensure that clients have effective protection.

The extent to which general private law concepts (ie duty of care, causation) may be influenced by the judge-made principles developed by the CJEU will, depend on the scope, content and purpose of the specific rule at stake. Therefore, the next chapter will examine in more detail the MiFID II conduct of business rules to identify their content and purpose.

2

Regulatory Design of MiFID II's Conduct of Business Rules

I. Rationales of Conduct of Business Rules

Conduct of business rules govern the process through which securities are distributed to clients. They do not indicate a uniform set of rules but comprise disclosure, distribution and product governance rules which have the common rationale of ensuring that firms treat their customers fairly. The need to introduce specific rules to ensure the 'fair behaviour' of investment firms vis-à-vis clients depends on the peculiar nature of financial instruments and services. Unlike most consumer goods, financial instruments are 'credence goods' because their value can be ascertained only after purchase and this is often determined by the behaviour of the supplier after the purchase.[1] Financial services are 'skills' that the client seeks to buy to reduce the risks connected to the nature of financial instruments but, like financial instruments, they are credence goods that can be assessed only after their 'purchase'.[2] The peculiar nature of these goods and services increases the risk of information and bargaining power asymmetry as well as agency problems between intermediary firms and clients.

The central role played by financial services in the economy and society attaches an important 'supra-transactional' rationale to conduct of business rules, namely to protect the confidence of investors in the fair and efficient functioning of financial markets. In 1934 the US Securities Exchange Act recognised that 'transactions in securities [...] are effected with a national public interest which makes it necessary to provide for regulation and control of such transactions'.[3] In 1993 the CJEU in the landmark *Alpine Investments BV* judgment held that 'given the speculative nature and the complexity of commodities futures contracts, the smooth operation of financial markets is largely contingent on the confidence

[1] See especially D Llewellyn, *The Economic Rationale for Financial Regulation*. FSA Occasional Paper Series 1. April 1999, 11.

[2] See FH Easterbrook and DR Fischel, 'Optimal Damages in Securities Cases' (1985) 52 *The University of Chicago Law Review* 651.

[3] Securities Exchange Act of 1934, § 2 15 US Code § 78b.

they inspire in investors'.[4] After the global financial crisis, MiFID II acknowledges the link between the transactional and the supra-transactional dimension of these rules: 'incorrect conduct of firms providing services to clients may lead to investor detriment and loss of investor confidence'.[5] Yet, differently from the US, in the EU, conduct of business rules were not a crisis-driven measure nor were they aimed at correcting 'failures' of national private laws;[6] instead they were part of the EU regulatory strategy to achieve an internal market.[7]

MiFID II pursues this strategy by tightening MiFID I disclosure and distribution rules and introducing new product governance requirements. To understand whether these regulatory innovations strenghten the horizontal/civil law effects of conduct of business rules, it is necessary to examine their content and purpose. Understanding the primary purpose of these rules is crucial to drive national courts in the correct interpretation of national law transposing MiFID II and, more importantly, to determine the extent to which, under the principles of equivalence and effectiveness, a private law remedy should be granted for their violation.

This chapter is organised as follows. It first illustrates the content and purpose of the main MiFID II's conduct of business rules. It then considers the scope and intensity of private law harmonisation in this directive. Finally, it provides a brief account of the national conduct of business regimes in the UK, France, Italy and Spain.

II. The Scope of Conduct of Business Rules

MiFID conduct of business rules apply to investment firms and credit institutions when they are providing investment services to third parties or performing an investment activity. Unlike the US legislation where different conduct of business rules apply to brokers–dealers and advisors, MiFID does not differentiate conduct of business rules based on a firm's business model but on the type of service it offers to clients. Investment services and activities are in turn defined by reference to any of the financial instruments listed in the MiFID's annex.[8] Recent CJEU case law suggests the notion of investment service should be interpreted

[4] Case C-384/93, *Alpine Investments BV v Minister van Financiën*, para 42.

[5] Recital No 5 of MiFID II.

[6] See J Köndgen, 'Rules of Conduct: Further Harmonisation? in G. Ferrarini (ed), *European Securities Markets: The Investment Services Directive and Beyond* (London-The Hague-Boston, Kluwer Law International, 1998) 116.

[7] See, in particular, EE Avgouleas, 'The Harmonisation of Rules of Conduct in EU Financial Markets: Economic Analysis, Subsidiarity and Investor Protection' (2000) 6 *European Law Journal* 74.

[8] An exception concerns structured deposits which are not classified as financial instrument.

narrowly and cannot be used to extend MiFID's conduct of business rules to services and instruments which are not expressly included in the directive.[9]

MiFID II, like its predecessor, does not define the notion of 'financial instrument'[10] but sets out a list of financial instruments which include both transferable securities and financial contracts (ie derivatives).

MiFID II extended the list of financial instruments (eg by adding emission allowances) and brought structured deposits within the scope of application of its conduct of business.[11] The rationale is to ensure an adequate level of investor protection for products that can be used as substitutes for financial instruments.[12] As regards financial services, the main change of MiFID II is the inclusion of the 'conclusion of agreements to sell financial instruments issued by an investment firm or a credit institution at the moment of issuance (Article 4(1)(5))', previously regarded as an instance of 'dealing in own account', into the scope of the 'execution of orders on behalf of clients'.[13] This novelty aims to extend conduct of business rules to the practice of firms selling proprietary financial instruments to its own clients ('self-placement'),[14] which has proved to be detrimental for retail clients in the wake of the financial crisis.[15] This change may have important

[9] Case C-678/15, *Mohammad Zadeh Khorassani*, ECLI:EU:C:2017:451, para 42 (the investor protection objective cannot justify allowing a particularly broad meaning to be attached to the definition of 'investment service' to the point of encompassing brokering with a view to concluding a contract covering portfolio management services) and case C-312/14, *Banif Plus Bank Zrt v Márton Lantos*, ECLI:EU:C:2015:794, para 76 (an investment service or activity does not encompass certain foreign exchange transactions, effected by a credit institution under clauses of a foreign currency denominated loan agreement, consisting in fixing the amount of the loan on the basis of the purchase price of the currency applicable when the funds are advanced and in determining the amounts of the monthly instalments on the basis of the sale price of that currency applicable when each monthly instalment is calculated).

[10] Compare with Art 4(50) of the Regulation (EU) No 575/2013 of the European Parliament and of the Council of 26 June 2013 on prudential requirements for credit institutions and investment firms and amending Regulation (EU) No 648/2012 (CRR) [2013] OJ L 176/1 and Directive 2014/59/EU of the European Parliament and of the Council of 15 May 2014 establishing a framework for the recovery and resolution of credit institutions and investment firms and amending Council Directive 82/891/EEC, and Directives 2001/24/EC, 2002/47/EC, 2004/25/EC, 2005/56/EC, 2007/36/EC, 2011/35/EU, 2012/30/EU and 2013/36/EU, and Regulations (EU) No 1093/2010 and (EU) No 648/2012, of the European Parliament and of the Council ('BRRD') [2014] OJ L 173/190.

[11] See K Lieverse, 'The Scope of MiFID II' in D Busch and G Ferrarini, *Regulation of the EU Financial Markets. MiFID II and MiFIR* (Oxford, Oxford University Press, 2017) 37.

[12] Structured deposits means a deposit which is fully repayable at maturity on terms under which interest or a premium will be paid or is at risk, according to a formula containing factors such as an index, a financial instrument, a commodity a foreign exchange rate or a combination thereof (Art 4(1)(43) of MiFID II). Structured deposits are also subject to PRIIPs Regulation (Art 2(2)(c)). Deposits and deposits linked solely to interest rates remain outside the scope of MiFID II and PRIIPs Regulation.

[13] MiFID II has also included the operation of an organised trading facility (OTF) in the list of investment services

[14] ESAs, Placement of Financial Instruments with Depositors, Retail Investors and Policy Holders ('Self placement') (JC 2014 62).

[15] See P-H Conac, *Mis-selling of Financial Products: Subordinated Debt and Self-placement*, Study Requested by the ECON committee, IP/A/ECON/2016-17. June 2018, 11.

repercussions. For instance, it has been argued that where a firm acts as a contractual counterparty in a swap contract under MiFID II, it is executing an order on behalf of a client and should therefore be subject to the applicable conduct of business rules, including the best interest duty.[16]

III. The Clients' Categorisation Rules

A. Overview

MiFID II, like its predecessor, classifies clients into retail clients, professional clients and eligible counterparties. Rules on clients' categorisation are crucial to determine clients' degree of protection and the scope of the application of conduct of business rules.

Professional clients are those who possess the experience, knowledge and expertise to make their own investment decisions and properly assess the risks that this incurs. MiFID distinguishes between clients who should be automatically considered as professional clients and clients who would be automatically considered to be retail clients but who choose to be treated as professional clients.

Retail clients comprise clients who are not professional clients and professional clients who have asked to be treated as retail clients. It can be inferred that a retail client is a client who lacks the experience, knowledge and expertise to make its own investment decisions and properly assess the risks that it incurs. Differently from the EU law's notion of consumer (a natural person who concludes a transaction for purposes which are outside his trade, business or profession) MIFID does not attach relevance to the purpose of the transaction nor the legal incorporation. Retail clients can therefore be both natural and legal persons (ie small and medium enterprises, non-profit organisations and under MiFID II municipalities and local public authorities), acting either within or outside their profession.[17]

Eligible counterparties include highly sophisticated investors who are legal persons. Like MiFID I, MIFID II distinguishes between mandatorily eligible counterparties (eg undertakings that must be recognised as eligible counterparties (ie investment firms, credit institutions, insurance companies, national governments, central banks) and optionally eligible counterparties (ie undertakings that may be recognised as eligible counterparties by Member States if some requirements are met)).

[16] See D Busch and C van Dam, 'Conduct-of-Business Rules under MiFID I and II' in D Busch and C van Dam (eds), *A Bank's Duty of Care* (Oxford: Hart Publishing, 2017) 16. See, however, for a more dubitative view, L Enriques and M Gargantini, 'The Expanding Boundaries of MiFID's Duty to Act in the Client's Best Interest: The Italian Case' (2017) 3 *The Italian Law Journal* 496.

[17] Recital No 104 of MiFID II.

This regime aims to allow investment firms to conduct transactions 'between equals', without having to comply with the conduct of business rules.[18] For this reason, only typical wholesale securities markets transactions are subject to this regime (ie reception and transmission of orders, the execution of orders, and dealing on own account). However, MiFID II extended to these clients several conduct of business rules: the fair treatment clause, some disclosure duties, the duty to provide clients with adequate reports on the service offered.[19] Conflict of interest rules and product governance obligations also apply to these transactions.

B. The Retail Client: Consumer or Investor?

MiFID II, like MiFID I, has given the broadest possible scope to the category of retail client. This may include very different types of clients ranging from the 'prudent saver', to the gambler who is willing to take some risks to obtain a higher yield, to SMEs who enter into financial transactions to hedge against previous exposures.[20]

MiFID II does not take an express stance on whether the 'retail client' should be treated as a consumer or as an investor.[21] In theory, if the retail client is regarded as a consumer, regulation should introduce mechanisms that reduce ex ante the risks of clients incurring losses. If they are regarded as an investor, any regulation should aim to remedy only market failures, leaving the client free to pursue its investment objectives and take risks.[22]

The issue of the scope and significance of the retail clients' notion has arisen in *Banif Plus Bank* where the referring court asked the CJEU whether certain foreign exchange transactions fall within the notion of investment service. In answering this question, Advocate General Jaaskinen held that 'an investor in the sense of [MiFID I] is somebody who invests or intends to invest his own or borrowed capital in a financial instrument with a view to gaining revenue, or at least protecting the value of his capital'. Given that the client did not intend to invest any capital but to borrow from the bank the sum needed to finance the purchase of a car, the Advocate General concluded that 'investment protection under Directive 2004/39 is not intended to cover situations in which consumers are financing consumption,

[18] See especially M Kruithof and W Van Gerven, 'A Differentiated Approach to Client Protection: The Example of MiFID' *Financial Law Institute WP* 2010/07, 37.

[19] Art 30(2) of MiFID II.

[20] See N Moloney, *How to Protect Investors: Lessons from the EC and the UK* (Cambridge, Cambridge University Press, 2010) 31 and 39.

[21] See especially N Moloney, 'The Investor Model Underlying the EU's Investor Protection Regime: Consumers or Investors?' (2012) 13 *European Business Organization Law Review* 169, underlying a process of consumerisation of retail clients in post-crisis regulation.

[22] D Kingsford Smith and O Dixon, 'The Consumer Interest and the Financial Markets' in N Moloney, E Ferran, J Payne (eds), *The Oxford Handbook of Financial Regulation* (Oxford, Oxford University Press, 2015) 698.

in contradistinction to investments, which in economic terms are a form of saving'.[23] Although this Opinion is *plus dixit quam voluit* because MiFID I is not concerned with the individual purpose of a transaction, it supports the idea that this directive is based on an 'empowering investor' regulatory strategy, which relies upon the model of the retail client as a well informed and responsible investor.[24]

MiFID II/MiFIR made some corrections to this model, namely by reducing the scope for the client's decision making in execution-only services by introducing new product governance obligations which seek to prevent a potential mismatch between the product's design and the client's profile and by granting to the supervisory authorities the power to ban financial instruments if there is significant investor protection concern.[25] Nevertheless, EU law did not go so far as to introduce a pre-approval of financial instruments or a duty to mandatorily assess the suitability of retail clients (also for non-advised services) and does not require firms to assess the clients' behavioural biases (ie financial ignorance, overconfidence, present bias, susceptibility to persuasion),[26] although the 2018 ESMA's Guidelines on suitability take some steps in this direction.[27]

Client's vulnerabilities, therefore, may become legally relevant only via litigation and dispute resolution. The principle of effectiveness and the fundamental right of effective judicial protection require courts and ADR bodies to interpret general regulatory (ie fair treatment clause) or private law (ie duty of good faith) concepts on the basis of the concrete vulnerabilities (ie personal, economic and social) of retail clients, thus ensuring that the retail client is treated as a consumer, rather than an investor, where the concrete circumstances of the case indicates an imbalance between the parties.

Finally, MiFID I and MiFID II also make reference to the 'consumer' in relation to the Member State's obligation to ensure the setting-up of efficient and effective complaints and redress procedures ('Extra-judicial mechanism for consumers complaints') for the out-of-court settlement of 'consumer disputes'.[28] The term 'consumer' should not be interpreted in the technical meaning of 'natural person acting outside his business, trade or profession' because this would run counter to MiFID's objective to ensure a high level of investor protection but as 'consumers of financial services and instruments', which encompass all categories of investors.[29]

[23] Opinion of the Advocate General Jääskinen in case C-312/14, *Banif Plus Bank Zrt*, ECLI:EU:C:2015:621, para 37. The Advocate General concluded that the reference was inadmissible but, in substance, held that this financial product is not covered by MiFID.

[24] See N Moloney, 'Effective Policy Design for the Retail Investment Services Market: Challenges and Choices Post-FSAP' in G Ferrarini and E Wymeersch (eds), *Investor Protection in Europe. Corporate Law Making, the MiFID and Beyond* (Oxford, Oxford University Press, 2007) 391.

[25] See Moloney, 'The Investor Model Underlying the EU's Investor Protection Regime: Consumers or Investors?' 169.

[26] For more details on investors' cognitive limitations, see S Grundmann and P Hacker, 'Conflicts of Interest' in D Busch and G Ferrarini (eds), *Regulation of the EU Financial Markets* 176.

[27] See Chapter 3, below.

[28] Art 53(1) of MiFID I and Art 75(1) of MiFID II.

[29] In support of this argument see also Art 81(3)(f) of MiFID II (Art 58(3)(f) of MiFID I) which establishes that competent authorities may only use confidential information received from other

IV. Regulating Investment Firms' Conduct

A. Fair Treatment and Best Interest Duties

(i) Content

According to Article 24(1) of MiFID II, investment firms 'shall act honestly, fairly and professionally in accordance with the best interests of its clients and comply with the principles of Article 24 and 25'. In MiFID II, these principles now include product governance obligations.[30]

This provision comprises a 'fair treatment' and a 'best interest' duty. As regards the fair treatment duty, it is noteworthy that MiFID I and MiFID II translated the 'duty of skill and care', expressly mentioned by CESR in its 'Conduct of Business Handbook',[31] into the duty to 'act professionally' and removed the reference made by the ISD to the fact that the fair treatment duty should also be exercised for the sake of market integrity. In addition to MiFID II, this duty shall apply also to eligible counterparties.[32]

The 'best interest duty' is autonomous from the 'fair treatment duty' and requires investment firms to understand the features of the financial instruments offered or recommended and establish and review effective policies.[33] It reflects the fiduciary obligations which have traditionally characterised the regulatory regime for investment advisors, as opposed to broker-dealers in the US.[34] The novelty of MiFID I (followed by MiFID II) was that it also imposed this duty on non-advised services and/or in circumstances where more detailed conduct of business rules do not apply (ie execution-only transactions), except for those services offered to eligible counterparties, where only the fair treatment duty applies. In these circumstances, the application of this duty may be problematic given that firms have less information to assess the client's interest.[35] The most important application of the fair treatment and best interest duties is in execution-only transactions (ie execution or reception and for transmission of trading orders concerning non-complex financial instruments at the client's initiative). In this case, the firm shall respect these general duties towards retail and professional clients (if the client is an eligible counterparty only the fair treatment duty will be respected) even if no other conduct of business rule applies.

authorities in the course of their duties and, in particular, 'in the extra-judicial mechanism for investors' complaints provided for in Article 75'.

[30] Art 24(2) of MiFID II.

[31] CESR, A European Regime of Investor Protection. The Harmonization of Conduct of Business Rules. April, 2002. CESR/01-014d, 47.

[32] Art 30(1) of MiFID II. See Recital Nos 86 and 104 of MiFID II.

[33] Recital No 71 of MiFID II.

[34] See A Tuch, 'Conduct of Business Regulation' in N Moloney, E Ferran, and J Payne (eds), *The Oxford Handbook of Financial Regulation*, (Oxford, OUP, 2015) 547.

[35] See especially Enriques and Gargantini, 'The Expanding Boundaries of MiFID's Duty to Act in the Client's Best Interest' 496.

(ii) Purpose

The fair treatment and the best interest duties aim to protect investors against misconduct that is not captured by more detailed rules or against conduct that ensures only a formal compliance with the rules. Therefore, these general duties may be breached even if a more specific duty is not.[36] For example, the fair treatment duty would be breached notwithstanding the absence of other breaches where firms offer 'general recommendations' outside the suitability rule.[37] Legally, it is important to clarify that the general nature of these duties does not mean that they are unable to confer rights on the investors. The investor, in our view, has a legally enforceable right, which is clearly defined by the norm, to be treated fairly, honestly and professionally and that the firm acts in their best interest. The difference between more detailed conduct of business rules (disclosure, suitability) and these general conduct of business rules is only a matter of legislative drafting technique. To strengthen the 'anti-elusive' purpose of the fair treatment and best interest duties, legislators have designed them by reference to a standard (ie fairness, best interest), rather than to a specific conduct.

Standards 'delegate' the national court or adjudicator to determine, on the basis of the circumstances of the case, how a specific conduct should be legally qualified (ie compliant or non-compliant).[38] The soft-law acts of ESMA will play a crucial role in better determining the content of these standards; they also provide guidance to market participants, national courts and ADR bodies.

B. Disclosure Rules

(i) Content

MiFID II sets out a general disclosure duty that all information, including marketing communications addressed by the investment firm to clients or potential clients shall be fair, clear and not misleading.[39] The Commission MiFID II Regulation extends this obligation to professional clients and, following ESMA's advice, introduces further requirements to enhance clients' ability to process information. For example, firms should use 'a font size in the indication of relevant risks that is at least equal to the predominant font size used throughout the information provided, as well as a layout ensuring such indication is prominent'. All information and

[36] See also Kruithof and Van Gerven, 'A Differentiated Approach to Client Protection', 40.

[37] See P Giudici, 'Independent Financial Advice' in D Busch and G Ferrarini (eds), *Regulation of The EU Financial Markets*, 162. Unlike personal recommendations, general recommendations are not held out as being suited to, or based on a consideration of, the client's personal circumstances but are intended for distribution channels or for the public'. See CESR, 'Understanding the definition of advice under MiFID', 19 April 2010. CESR/10-293, 6.

[38] See Chapter 6.

[39] Recital No 15 of Commission MiFID II Regulation.

marketing materials should be presented in the same language unless the client has agreed to receive information in more than one language.[40]

In addition, Article 24(4) of MiFID II requires firms to provide appropriate information in good time to clients or potential clients with regard to the investment firm and its services, the financial instruments and proposed investment strategies, execution venues and all costs and related charges. Disclosure duties are further specified, in great detail, by Articles 44–51 of Commission MiFID II Regulation. Like Commisison MiFID I, this directive states that the information should be sufficient for, and presented in a way that is likely to be understood by, an average member of the group to whom it is directed or by whom it is likely to be received.[41]

In comparison to MiFID I, MIFID II introduces new disclosure requirements for independent and non-independent advice,[42] bundled packages of services and products,[43] cost and associated charges.[44] However, like MiFID I (Article 19(3)),[45] MiFID II (Article 24(5)) does not require firms to provide information about a specific financial instrument but only about a 'specific type' of financial instrument.

MiFID II places more emphasis than MiFID I on the need to provide information regarding the future performance of financial instruments: investment firms must ensure that the information is based on performance scenarios in different market conditions and reflects the nature and risks of the specific types of instruments included in the analysis.[46] The Commission MiFID II Regulation added that the description should also include 'the risks associated with insolvency of the issuer or related events, such as bail in' and 'information on impediments or restrictions for disinvestment'.[47]

MiFID II has also removed a firm's power to provide the above information in a standardised format, giving Member States the task of deciding whether information can be provided in this format.[48]

Finally, where sufficient information in relation to the costs and associated charges or to the risks in respect of the financial instrument itself is provided in accordance with other EU law (ie the UCITS Directives and PRIIPs Regulation)

[40] Art 44(2)(c) and (f) of Commission MiFID II Regulation.

[41] Ibid, Art 44(2)(d).

[42] Ibid, Arts 24(4) and 52. See D Busch, 'Conduct-of-Business Rules under MiFID I and II' in D Busch and C van Dam (eds), *A Bank's Duty of Care*, 27 arguing that MiFID II should have instead introduced basic requirements for all forms of advice.

[43] Art 24(11) of MiFID II.

[44] Art 50(1) of Commission MiFID II Regulation.

[45] See PO Mülbert, *The Eclipse of Contract Law in the Investment Firm-Client Relationship* (Oxford, Oxford University Press, 2006) 307.

[46] Art 44(6)(d) and Art 48(1) of Commission MiFID II Regulation.

[47] Ibid, Art 48(2).

[48] Art 24(5) of MiFID II.

that information should be regarded as appropriate for the purposes of providing information to clients under MiFID II.[49]

The analysis of the actual capacity of these new disclosure requirements to enhance the client's understanding of investments' risks goes beyond the purpose of this study and has long been debated in literature.[50] It could be said, however, that the new disclosure duties confirm that the average client continues to be seen as an informed and rationale investor, capable of taking autonomous investment choices, rather than a vulnerable consumer, who is unlikely to be able to assess this type of information. Unfortunately, MiFID II does not introduce mechanisms (ie UCITS' key investor document and PRIIPs' key information document) to simplify, standardise and enhance the comparability of disclosed information. There is, therefore, a risk that the new disclosure duties will not not overcome the problems that especially retail clients face when processing complex financial information.[51]

(ii) Purpose

The specific purpose of disclosure rules in MiFID II is to 'ensure that clients or potential clients are reasonably able to understand the nature and risks of the investment service and of the specific type of financial instrument that is being offered and, consequently, to take investment decisions on an informed basis'.[52] Although disclosure duties play an important 'supra-individual' function in securing the allocative efficiency of securities markets,[53] their main function is to secure the full understanding of risks by the individual client. The transactional dimension of these rules is confirmed by their level of detail and the fact that, like all the other MiFID II conduct of business rules, they are now contained into directly applicable acts (Commission MiFID II Regulation). This regulatory technique shows the legislators' intention to grant to individual clients (not just supervisory authorities) a right to enforce these duties in a civil proceeding.

C. Suitability Rule

(i) Content

The key innovation of MiFID I was the introduction of the suitability and appropriateness requirements.

[49] See Recital No 78 of MiFID II. See in more detail also V Colaert, 'MiFID II in Relation to Other Investor Protection Regulation. Picking Up the Crumbs of a Piecemeal Approach' in D Busch and G Ferrarini (eds) *Regulation of The EU Financial Markets*, 600.

[50] See, in particular, M Andenas and I H-Y Chiu, *The Foundations and Future of Financial Regulation* (London and New York, Routledge 2014) 242.

[51] See 'Consumer Decision-Making in Retail Investment Services: A Behavioural Economics Perspective' Final Report November 2010, p 19.

[52] Art 24(5) of MiFID II.

[53] See Avgouleas, 'The Harmonisation of Rules of Conduct in EU Financial Markets' 74.

The suitability rule requires firms which provide investment advice[54] or portfolio management[55] to 'obtain the necessary information regarding the client's or potential client's knowledge and experience in the investment field relevant to the specific type of product or service, financial situation and investment objectives, so as to enable the firm to recommend to the client or potential client the investment services and financial instruments that are suitable for him'.[56]

MiFID I has designed the suitability as a process-based requirement: emphasis is placed on the (procedural) duty to obtain certain information from the client (ie 'know your customer' principle) rather than on the duty to provide a suitable advice.[57] The suitability rule is modulated on the basis of the nature of the client: if the client is a professional, the firm can assume that this client has the necessary level of experience and knowledge and is able financially to bear any related investment risks consistent with his investment objectives.[58]

MiFID I established that if the firm does not obtain the information to conduct the suitability assesment, it shall not recommend investment services or financial instruments to the client or potential client.[59] It has been correctly argued that the duty to refuse the transaction should also apply when the firm determines that the transaction is unsuitable.[60] ,[61]

MiFID II reinforced the suitability rule with new distribution-related and organisational requirements.

First, the firm must assess, in addition to the client's knowledge and experience, their financial situation and objectives, risk tolerance and ability to bear losses.[62] The firm should therefore assess both the client's 'risk appetite' and 'risk capacity', two aspects that are often affected by behavioural biases, in particular over-confidence.[63]

[54] Investment advice means 'the provision of personal recommendations to a client, either upon its request or at the initiative of the investment firm, in respect of one or more transactions relating to financial instruments (Art 1(4)(4) of MiFID II). This does not include 'generic advice' (ie personal advice that refers to a type or types of financial instrument rather than a particular financial instrument). See, on the definition of investment advice: case C-604/11, *Genil 48 SL v Bankinter*, ECLI:EU:C:2013:344, para 55.

[55] For the exclusion of a brokering of a portfolio management agreement from the MiFID I investment service, see case C-678/15, *Mohammad Zadeh Khorassani v Kathrin Pflanz* ECLI:EU:C:2017:100.

[56] The predecessor of the suitability rule is the ISD's principle that firms shall 'seeks from its clients information regarding their financial situations, investment experience and objectives as regards the services requested' (Art11(1) fourth indent).

[57] This procedural approach deviates from the CESR's proposal to design the suitability rule, similarly to the US and UK experiences, as to require firms to have 'reasonable grounds to believe' that the advice is suitable. See CESR, A European Regime of Investor Protection, 28.

[58] Art 19(3)(4) of MiFID I.

[59] Art 35(5) of Commission MiFID I Directive.

[60] See especially Moloney, *EU Securities and Financial Markets Regulation*, 806.

[61] Art 35(5) of Commission MiFID I Directive.

[62] Art 25(2) of MiFID II. Reference to the need to assess 'risk tolerance' and 'ability to bear losses' was added by the European Parliament, in its position at first reading on 15 April 2014 (EP-PE_TC1-COD(2011)0298).

[63] Consumer Decision-Making in Retail Investment Services: A Behavioural Economics Perspective, p 19.

Second, MiFID II adds that when investment advice concerns a package of bundled services or products, the overall bundled package is suitable.

Third, the Comission MiFID II Regulation appropriately broadens the duty to refuse a transaction specifying that this not only applies where the firm does not obtain the information to assess the suitability,[64] but also where the firm concludes that a decision whether to trade, buy, hold or sell an investment is unsuitable.[65]

Fourth, when providing investment advice to a retail client, the firm must, provide the client with a statement on suitability in a durable medium specifying the advice given and how that meets their preferences, objectives and other characteristics before the transaction takes place.[66] This is important because it gives the client an opportunity to assess why and how its investment was deemed to be suitable and to provide evidence of how the suitability test was conducted in potential civil proceedings.

Finally, from an organisational perspective, MiFID II requires firms to have in place adequate policies and procedures to ensure that they understand the nature, features, including the cost and risks of investment services and financial instruments selected for their clients and that they assess, while taking into account cost and complexity, whether equivalent investment services or financial instruments can meet their client's profile.[67] While this requirement does not go so far as to require firms to recommend products that would be cheaper or less complex,[68] it nevertheless requires them to assess, also in the non-independent business model, the availability of products that, in light of their cost and complexity, would place the investor in a better position.

(ii) Purpose

The suitability rule was first introduced in the US as part of the regulatory measures culminated in the Securities Act 1933 and Securities Exchange Act of 1934 to restore investors' confidence in securities markets after the brokers' misconduct in the roaring Twenties.[69] It became apparent that the general private law

[64] Art 55(8) of Commission MiFID II Regulation.

[65] Art 25(2) of MiFID II and Art 54(10) of Commission MiFID II Regulation. See also Recital No 87.

[66] Art 25(6) of MiFID II.

[67] Art 54(9) of Commission MiFID II Regulation.

[68] The financial industry expressed concerns that a similar requirement would go beyond MiFID II and create legal uncertainty. See ESMA, *Technical Advice to the Commission on MiFID II and MiFIR* (Technical Advice) (ESMA/2014/1569) 150.

[69] The first suitability rule was included in Art 3, s 2 of the NASD Rules of Fair Practice adopted in 1939: 'in recommending to a customer the purchase, sale or exchange of any security, a member shall have reasonable grounds for believing that the recommendation is suitable for such customer upon the basis of the facts, if any, disclosed by such customer as to his other security holdings and as to his financial situation and needs'. See in more detail See SB Cohen, 'The Suitability Rule and Economic Theory' (1971) 80 *Yale Law Journal* 1604.

of agency and fiduciary duties could not adequately protect investors where the broker formally respected clients' orders but did not act in their best interests (eg by recommending an unsuitable security).

The main aim of the suitability rule is indeed to reduce the principal–agent problems between clients and intermediary firms.[70] Inter-mediation aims to reduce the risk that issuers of securities (agents) pursue their own interests instead of those of the investor (principals). However, financial intermediaries enjoy significant informational and positioning advantages vis-à-vis their clients that can be exploited to their detriment (ie recommending instruments issued by the firm itself or by firms that are financially linked).[71] The suitability rule ensures that the financial instrument distributed to the client matches its own investment interest and, consequently, prohibits the firm from carrying out a transaction with an unsuitable instrument.

The difference between general private law and the suitability rule is clear.

The private law requirements for the formation and performance of contractual obligations ensure that the parties' consent is free from abuse or unfair exploitation but, and except for the cases of lack or defect of consent (eg mistake, fraud, threat or unfair exploitation), do not allow a party to 'exit' from a contract solely because the good purchased is not economically convenient or it is too risky for the buyer. Likewise, the private law of agency or mandate ensures the correspondence between the principal's will and the agent's actions but puts on the principal the burden of taking an autonomous decision that the agent needs to implement. The suitability rule has 'revolutionary flavor' because it shifts the responsibility for making inappropriate investment decisions from the customer to the broker-dealer.[72]

The suitability rule is clearly different also from disclosure rules because it requires firms to take positive action that goes beyond informing the client and contains an express prohibition for a firm to distribute, via the suitability rule, an unsuitable financial instrument. Nevertheless, the current regulatory framework leaves on the client the (crucial) responsibility to choose the more protective (and generally more expensive) advisory services covered by the suitability rule or for the less protective (and less expensive) non-advisory services.[73] The problem is that since the quality of advice is hard to assess ex ante, clients may not be willing to spend the money, unless they are able to understand the risk of non-advised sales. The propensity to ask for advice is positively correlated with

[70] See Llewellyn, *The Economic Rationale for Financial Regulation* 11.

[71] See S Grundmann, W Kerber, 'Information Intermediaries and Party Autonomy' in S Grundmann, W Kerber, S Weatherill (eds), *Party Autonomy and the Role of Information in the Internal Market* (Berlin, Walter de Gruyter, 2001) 290 and K Judge, 'Intermediary Influence' (2015) 82 *University of Chicago Law Review* 573.

[72] RH Mundheim, 'Professional Responsibilities of Brokers-Dealers: the Suitability Doctrine' (1965) 3 *Duke Law Journal* 449.

[73] See Moloney, 'Effective Policy Design for the Retail Investment Services Market', 400.

financial education and 'financial advice acts as a complement rather than as a substitute of financial literacy'.[74]

From a legal perspective, the aim and formulation of the suitability rule are strong indicators in favour of its right-conferring nature. In *Genil v Bankinter*,[75] the CJEU has implicitly confirmed that the suitability rule enshrined in MiFID I conferred a right on clients.[76] The question may arise whether MiFID II grants the client only a 'procedural right' to be asked certain information or whether it grants also 'substantive right' to receive a suitable recommendation. Even if MiFID literally requires that firms only request certain information from clients, the firms must act honestly, fairly and professionally with clients and in their best interests. This means that firms have a duty to assess the information they receive and they cannot limit themselves to asking for certain information. The MiFID II requirement to provide a suitability statement confirms that the suitability rule entails an evaluative assessment of the client's needs and objectives. Finally, Article 54(10) of the Commission MiFID II Regulation implies that to determine that 'none of the services or instruments are suitable for the client', the firm must assess the suitability of that service or instrument.

D. Appropriateness Rule

(i) Content

When providing investment services other than investment advice or portfolio management (ie the reception, transmission and execution of orders), the firm shall ask the client or potential client to provide information regarding his knowledge and experience in the investment field relevant to the specific type of product or service offered or requested. Unlike the suitability rule, the firm does not need to obtain information about a client's financial situation, objectives, risk tolerance and their ability to bear losses. This is because the investment firm is supposed to merely execute or implement an investment decision taken by the client.

If the client is a professional client, firms can presume that they have the necessary experience and knowledge to understand the risks involved in the transaction.[77] Hence, de facto, the appropriateness rule does not apply for professional clients.

The difference between suitability and appropriateness is also clear with regard to the consequences of the negative assessment made by the firm. If the financial

[74] M Gentile, N Linciano, P Soccorso, 'Financial Advice Seeking, Financial Knowledge and Overconfidence. Evidence from the Italian Market', CONSOB Quaderni di Finanza, No 83, March 2016, 33.

[75] Case C-604/11, *Genil v Bankinter*, ECLI:EU:C:2013:344, para 57.

[76] The suitability's organisational requirements may not be able to grant a right to clients given that they do not directly affect the performance of a transaction.

[77] Art 56(1) of MiFID II.

instrument or service is not appropriate or the client decides not to provide information or provides insufficient information regarding his knowledge and experience, the firm can still provide the service but must warn the client (this can be provided in a standardised format).[78]

MiFID II adds that where a bundle of services or products is envisaged pursuant to Article 24(11), the assessment shall consider whether the overall bundled package is appropriate and requires firms to keep a record of the appropriateness assessment and the warnings given to clients. [79] However, unlike the suitability assessment, firms do not have a duty to deliver this record to clients; this may render it more difficult for these clients to demonstrate that the appropriateness test was not properly conducted.

It is important to mention that if the firm offers only execution and/or the reception and transmission of client orders, and some additional conditions are met (ie the service is offered at the client's initiative and the financial instrument is not complex),[80] the appropriateness rule does not apply. This regime reflected 'the popularity of the execution only service with investors and the policy assumption that investor choice at a low cost, low protection service should be supported'.[81] As I mentioned, in this case, only the fair treatment duty (and, if the client is not an eligible counterparty, the best interest duty) shall apply. However, MiFID II has reduced the scope of execution-only transactions. In particular, it expanded the scope of 'complex financial instruments', by extending the notion of complex financial instruments to shares in non-UCITS collective investment undertakings and shares that embed a derivative, money-market instruments,[82] bonds and structured deposits that 'incorporate a structure which makes it difficult for the client to understand the risk of return or the cost of exiting the product before term'[83] and it included in the notion of 'execution of orders on behalf of clients' the practice of self-placement.

(ii) Purpose

The appropriateness rule protects clients in investment services where the firm should have a marginal role in the client's investment-decision making. This does not mean, however, that mis-selling risks are also marginal. To the contrary, if the client is unsophisticated, these transactions carry higher mis-selling risk than advised transactions because firms may 'informally' recommed certain financial instruments outside the boundaries of the suitability rule.[84] For this reason,

[78] Art 19(5) of MiFID I.
[79] Art 56(2) of Commission MiFID II Regulation.
[80] Art 19(6) of MiFID I and Art 25(4) of MiFID II.
[81] Moloney, 'Effective Policy Design for the Retail Investment Services Market', 401.
[82] Money market instruments shall be regarded as complex if they embed a derivative.
[83] Art 25(4)(v) of MiFID II.
[84] See M Maggiolo, *Servizi ed attività di investimento, Prestatori e prestazione*, in *Tratt. Cicu-Messineo-Mengoni-Schlesinger* (Milano, Giuffré, 2012) 396.

especially in execution-only transactions, the respect of the fair treatment and best interest duties is crucial to protect investors. That said, the detailed formulation of the appropriateness rule and its clear transactional nature show that this rule confers rights on clients. Like the suitability rule, this right comprises not only a right to be asked certain information but a right that the financial instrument offered or demanded is appropriate to the clients' knowledge and experience.

E. Conflict of Interest Rules

(i) Content

In line with MiFID I, the MiFID II regime for conflicts of interest comprises both organisational and disclosure requirements. MiFID II does not define the notion of 'conflict of interest' but requires investment firms, to take all appropriate steps to identify and to prevent or manage conflicts of interest between themselves and their clients or between one client and another that arise in the course of providing any investment and ancillary services, or combinations thereof.[85] Therefore, conflict of interests are not prohibited. MiFID II increases the standard of care for firms (they must not only take reasonable steps, but all appropriate steps to prevent conflicts of interest) and requires them to consider also conflicts of interest caused by the receipt of inducements from third parties or by the investment firm's own remuneration and other incentive structures.[86] In particular, Article 24(10) of MiFID II prohibits firms from establishing remuneration arrangements (ie sales targets) that would incentivise staff to recommend a particular financial instrument to a retail client when it could offer one which would better meet that client's needs. An important change, introduced by Article 41(2) of Commission MiFID II Regulation is that where firms engage in self-placement they shall establish, implement and maintain clear and effective arrangements for the identification, prevention or management of the potential conflicts of interest that arise in relation to this type of activity. These include consideration of refraining from engaging in the activity, where conflicts of interest cannot be appropriately managed so as to prevent any adverse effects on clients.

Where these organisational or administrative arrangements are not sufficient to ensure, with reasonable confidence, that the risk of damage to client interests will be prevented, investment firms shall clearly disclose to the client the general nature and/or sources of conflicts of interest.[87] In addition to MiFID I, disclosure should concern the steps taken to mitigate those risks before undertaking business on its behalf, must be made in a durable medium and must include

[85] Art 16(3) of MiFID II.
[86] See, in more detail, Moloney, *EU Securities and Financial Markets Regulation*, 809.
[87] Art 23(2) of MiFID II.

sufficient detail, taking into account the nature of the client, to enable that client to take an informed decision with respect to the service in the context of which the conflict of interest arises.

(ii) Purpose

The organisational requirements around conflicts of interest aim to prevent a potential conflict of interest ex ante while leaving firms free to devise the best internal processes to achieve this objective. The general wording of the rules reflects the need to provide incentives for innovation without stifling the firm with rules that are too rigid.[88] However, this makes it difficult to capture the interest protected by this requirement in terms of a legally enforceable right. The same, in our view, holds true for the self-placement conflict of interest rule. While this rule makes a remarkable change in comparison to MiFID I it imposes an organisational duty and does not directly prohibit a firm from conducting this type of transaction.[89] Conflict of interest disclosure rules, as updated by MiFID II, seek to enhance investors' ability to make an informed decision and for this reason, similarly to the other disclosure rules, they may confer a legally enforceable right to clients. However, potential infringements of conflict of interest rules are not easily observable; clients may have difficulty proving in front of a judge that the organisational requirements were not sufficient to prevent the risk of damage to client interests. The effectiveness of the conflict of interest regime will, therefore, mostly depend on supervision and public enforcement rather than private enforcement actions.[90]

F. Inducements Rules

(i) Content

Article 24(9) of MiFID II introduces a general prohibition for firms to pay or receive a fee or commission in relation to the provision of investment services, unless the payment or benefit aims to enhance the quality of the service, does not impair the firm's compliance with the fair treatement and best interest duties and is clearly disclosed to the client.[91] These exceptions reflect the need to find a balanced approach in the regulation of distribution practices in Member States.

[88] See Grundmann and Hacker, 'Conflicts of Interest' 182.

[89] Compare Art 41(2) with Art 54(8) and (10) of Commission MIFID II Regulation. See instead Enriques and Gargantini, 'The Expanding Boundaries of MiFID's Duty to Act in the Client's Best Interest' 503.

[90] See Moloney, *EU Securities and Financial Markets Regulation*, 374.

[91] See in detail on the inducement ban, L Silverentand, J Sprecher and L Simons, 'Inducements' in D Busch and G Ferrarini (eds), *Regulation of The EU Financial Markets*, 205.

A radical ban on inducements would have prejudiced the industry in some countries (ie Germany, France and Italy) and would have favoured countries where advice on independent basis is more widespread and advisers are paid only by a client's fee (ie the UK and the Netherlands).[92]

Where inducements are given or received in relation to independent advice and portfolio management, the only exception to the ban concerns the minor non-monetary benefits.[93]

(ii) Purpose

The general prohibition of inducements implements the general fair treatment clause and aims to prevent the conflict of interest to which clients are exposed in the situations where the firm receive payments or benefits from third parties in connection with the provision of financial services.[94] The prohibition of inducements has a clear investor protection purpose and is sufficiently clear and detailed. However, like for breaches of conflict of interest requirements, it may be very difficult for the client to detect a breach (ie that the inducement was paid or received) and allege an infringement of these rules.[95] The investment firm would have a clear procedural advantage in demonstrating that the payment or benefit was designed to enhance the quality of the relevant service to the client and does not impair the firm's compliance with the investment firm's duty to act honestly, fairly and professionally in accordance with Article 25(9)(a) and (b) of MiFID II. Therefore, enforcement of inducement rules will mostly rely upon supervision and public enforcement.

G. Product Governance Rules

(i) Content

MiFID II introduced specific product governance obligations for firms that produce (manufacturers) and distribute financial instruments (distributors).[96]

[92] See A Perrone, Tanto rumore per nulla? Per un ripensamento della disciplina sugli inducements (2016) 2 *Banca Borsa Titoli di Credito* 129.

[93] Art 12 of Commission MiFID II Directive.

[94] See D Busch, 'Conduct-of-Business Rules under MiFID I and II' in D Busch and C van Dam (eds), *A Bank's Duty of Care*, 53.

[95] Once the allegation is made, it should be for the firm to prove that the inducement is covered by the exceptions of Art 24(7)(8)(9) of MiFID II. In this sense, see A. Perrone, 'Tanto rumore per nulla? Per un ripensamento della disciplina sugli inducements' 134.

[96] For the notion of creator and distributor, see Arts 9(1) and 10(1) of the MiFID II Delegated Directive. Although MiFID II refers these requirements only to investment firms, a teleological interpretation based on the client protection purpose of these rules suggests that credit institutions, UCITS and AIFM management companies should be subject to them when providing MiFID services and instruments to clients. See ESMA, 'Technical Advice' 52.

Product governance obligations can be distinguished, from a functional perspective, into corporate governance requirements, investor protection and organisational requirements.[97]

Corporate governance-related requirements are centred on the duty of the firm management body (for both manufacturers and distributors) to define, approve and oversee policies as to services, activities, products and operations.[98] MiFID II, in line with the recommendations of IOSCO,[99] does not require competent authorities to pre-approve financial products but relies on the firm to conduct internally such approval process.[100]

Investor protection requirements aim to minimise the risks that the product's design of distributed products does not match the client's profile.[101] To this end, manufacturers must ensure that products meet the needs of the identified target market, that the distribution strategy is consistent with the identified target market and that they take reasonable steps to ensure that the product is distributed to the identified target market. The target market shall be identified at 'a sufficiently granular level'.[102] In accordance with the proportionality principle, the target market should be identified with less detail for more common products than more complicated products, such as bail-inable instruments.[103]

For their part, distributors must understand the products they offer or recommend and assess whether they are compatible with the target market. Product governance requirements do not prejudice the application of the suitability/appriopriateness requirements.[104] If a financial instrument is compatible with the client's needs, in accordance with the target market, but is unsuitable (eg because it does not meet the client's ability to bear losses) the firm should not distribute it. Conversely, a firm must not distribute a product that is not targeted at the client, even if it would be suitable or appropriate.

Organisational requirements ensure that firms adopt adequate internal processes to comply with product governance rules. In particular, manufacturers must have in place procedures to approve financial products, to ensure that products comply with the requirements on proper management of conflicts of interest, to ensure that the staff possess the necessary expertise to understand the characteristics and risks of the financial instruments and to review the financial

[97] See D Busch, 'Product Governance and Product Intervention under MiFID II/MiFIR', in D Busch and G Ferrarini (eds), *Regulation of The EU Financial Markets*, 127.

[98] Art 9(3)(b) of MiFID II.

[99] IOSCO, Regulation of Retail Structured Products Final Report (FR14/13) 29.

[100] See, in this sense Art 44(8) and Recital No 91 of theMiFID II Regulation.

[101] For an overview of the product intervention measures adopted by national legislators and supervisory authorities, see ESMA Stakeholder Group 'Own Initiative Report on Product Intervention under MiFIR 2017' (ESMA22-106-264).

[102] Art 9(9) of Commission MiFID II Directive.

[103] Ibid, Recital No 18.

[104] Ibid, Recital No 15.

instruments they manufacture on a regular basis.[105] Distributors do not need to have a product approval process in place but must have in place procedures to ensure that the products and services they intend to offer or recommend are compatible with the identified target market; to review and update their product governance arrangements; to ensure that their staff possess the necessary expertise to understand the characteristics and risks of the products that they intend to offer or recommend; and that their compliance function oversees the development and periodic review of product governance arrangements to detect any risk of failure to comply with the product governance obligations.[106]

Finally, it is worth mentioning that if an investment firm breaches its product governance obligations, the competent authorities can suspend the marketing or sale of financial instruments or structured deposits.[107]

(ii) Purpose

The purpose of product governance requirements is manifold. Some requirements, including the key target market identification requirements, aim primarily to protect investors, thus reducing 'the need for recourse to alternative dispute resolution systems or the courts for compensation'.[108] Other requirements aim to ensure that adequate internal corporate processes arrangements are in place. Finally, a broader objective pursued by all product governance obligations is to ensure the orderly functioning and stability of financial markets to reduce the risk of creating a financial instrument that might create systemic risks because of its characterisitcs (ie complexity, illiquidity).

To understand the protective purpose of these requirements, it is therefore necessary to identify, for each specific rule, which of these purposes is prevalent. In general, while rules requiring firms to have internal processes or procedures in place are unsuitable to create legally enforceable rights for the end-clients, the requirement (for manufacturers) to identify a target market or the requirement (for distributors) to distribute products that are compatible with that market may confer a legally enforceable right. What is crucial, in this regard, is whether the obligation is intended to protect a specific class of persons and whether the end-client is part of this class. Although the duty to identify the target market does not apply to one individual client, it sufficiently defines the scope of its addresees ('the firm shall 'specify the type(s) of client for whose needs, characteristics and objectives the financial instrument is compatible' and 'any group(s) of

[105] Art 9 of Commission MiFID II Directive.

[106] Art 10 of Commission MiFID II Directive.

[107] Art 69(2)(t) of MiFID II.

[108] EBA, 'Guidelines on Product Oversight and Governance Arrangements for Retail Banking Product' (EBA/GL/2015/18) 40.

clients for whose needs, characteristics and objectives the financial instrument is not compatible'). In addition, if an event that would affect the potential risk or return expectations of the financial instrument, occurs, the firm must take appropriate action which may consist, inter alia, of changing the financial instrument to avoid unfair contract terms.[109] Therefore, the failure to correctly identify the target market may affect the contract concluded by the client. This provides another argument in support of the thesis that the the duty to identify the target market is transactional in nature and may give rise to a legally enforceable right.

For the same reasons, it appears clear that the investor protection-driven product governance obligations of distributors are imposed for the benefit of the client to whom the financial instrument is distributed. In that case, therefore, the end-client could invoke against the distributor a breach of these obligations, in addition to the potential breaches of conduct of business rules.

V. Private Law Duties and Remedies (in the Shadow of) MiFID II

A. Scope of Harmonisation

Like MiFID I, MiFID II does not generally harmonise private law duties applicable to the contractual or non-contractual relationship between investment firms and clients. The only contract-law aspect harmonised by MiFID I and MiFID II is the requirement to set out a written client agreement.

The MiFID I written agreement requirement[110] had a limited impact on national private laws since at the time it was adopted, most Member States required investment firms to conclude investment contracts in written form.[111] The Commission MiFID I Directive pointed out that apart from this requirement, no other obligation was imposed 'as to the form, content and performance of contracts for the provisions of investment or ancillary services'.[112]

Notably, MiFID II removed this 'non-prejudice clause', broadened the scope of the written agreement requirement (which now extends to any investment service and to both professional and existing clients[113]) and detailed precise requirements for its content. The agreement describes the services and, where relevant, the

[109] Art 9(15)(d) of Commission MiFID II Directive.

[110] Art 39 of Commission MiFID I Directive.

[111] See (COM(2000) 722) 9.

[112] Recital No 41 of Commission MiFID I Directive. See also CESR, 'Technical Advice on Possible Implementing Measures of MiFID I. First Set of Mandates' CESR/05-024c ('the advice is not intended to interfere with the way in which contracts are concluded, amended, renewed or terminated underthe applicable law of the Member States').

[113] Contrary to ESMA, 'Technical Advice' 164, the Commission deleted the reference to 'new client'.

nature and extent of the investment advice to be provided;[114] the types of financial instruments that may be purchased and sold; the types of transactions that may be undertaken on behalf of the client, as well as any instruments or transactions prohibited, in case of portfolio management; and a description of the main features of any ancillary services to be provided.[115] These changes reflect the legislators' intention to use the writen client agreement as a tool to complement disclosure and distribution rules to strengthen client protection.

Finally, differently from other experiences in Europe[116] and abroad[117] MiFID II, like its predecessor, did not grant investors a private law remedy for breaches of its conduct of business rules nor did it define the civil law consequences stemming for their violation. As a result, given that these aspects fall outside its scope for harmonisation, Member States remain free to govern them subject to the principle of equivalence and effectiveness.[118]

B. Intensity of Harmonisation

When harmonising national laws in a particular field of its competence, the EU may decide to grant Member States the right to impose stricter requirements where necessary to achieve a specific objective (minimum harmonisation) or to prohibit Member States from doing so, typically to ensure a level playing field (maximum harmonisation).

The 1999 Commission Financial Services Action Plan (FSAP) is traditionally seen as the watershed between minimum and maximum harmonisation in investment services regulation. Prior to the FSAP, harmonisation aimed to remove intra-state barriers to free movement of financial services and to set out minimum requirements for the provision of financial services across the Community; after the FSAP, harmonisation aimed to re-regulate the internal market through uniform rules. However, most of the directives adopted after the FSAP do not contain an express maximum harmonisation clause.

This is the case in MiFID I, which did not expressly prohibit Member States from introducing or maintaining stricter requirements.[119] However, the Commission

[114] The Commission appropriately broadens the requirement in comparison to the ESMA's advice which restricted it to the case where the firm provides a periodic assessment of the suitability of the financial instruments (ESMA, 'Technical Advice' 164).

[115] Also in this case the Commisison appropriately extends the ESMA's advice, which was restricted to custody services (ibid).

[116] See in the UK s 138D of the Financial Services and Markets Act (FSMA), in Ireland s 44 of the Central Bank (Supervision and Enforcement) Act 2013 (No 26/2013) and, in Portugal, Art 304a of Código dos Valores Mobiliários (Decreto-Lei n. 486/99) Diário da República nº 265/1999, Série I-A de 1999-11-13.

[117] See in Singapore: s 25 of the Financial Advisers Act (Chapter 110, 2007 (Revised Edition) 1B).

[118] Case C-604/11, *Genil 48 GL v Bankinter*, para 57.

[119] Lack of an express 'maximum harmonisation' clause, however, is not enough to conclude that the directive achieves only minimum harmonisation. See, in particular, M Dougan, 'Minimum

MiFID I Directive, adopted two years later, allowed Member States to introduce additional requirements to address specific risks to investor protection or to market integrity only in exceptional circumstances ('gold-plating prohibition').[120] Given the heterogeneous nature of EU retail markets, this prohibition was criticised for lowering the standards of investor protection in the EU.[121] It has therefore been argued that MiFID I introduced a de facto maximum harmonisation, given that Member States left some room to introduce stricter requirements (but only in exceptional circumstances).[122]

With MiFID II, the gold-plating prohibition of the Commission MiFID I Directive has been shifted to Level 1 legislation.[123] This indicates the co-legislators' intention to reaffirm the general principle of maximum harmonisation of the conduct of business rules, thus resolving the doubts relating to the potential illegality of the Commission MiFID I Directive's gold plating prohibition, introduced in the absence of an express Level 1 provision.[124]

VI. National Conduct of Business Rules

The UK, France, Italy and Spain introduced conduct of business rules at the end of the 1980s/ beginning of the 1990s, after a wave of de-regulation of stock exchanges and securities markets that started in the UK with the so-called 'Big Bang day' (27 October 1986).[125] The pressure to compete with London's standards pushed continental jurisdictions to adopt similar reforms (ie the removal of fixed commission rates, the opening up of stock exchange membership to outsiders) and to introduce rules to protect investors against abuse from broker-dealers and insider dealing.[126] Therefore, at the beginning of the Nineties, the regulation of

Harmonization and the Internal Market' (2000) 37 *Common Market Law Review* 853. See also the opinion of AG Kokott in Case C-45/08, *Spector v Commissie voor het Bank-, Financie-en Assurantiewezen*, ECLI:EU:C:2009:534, para 81 and Case C-154/00, *Commission v Hellenic Republic* ECLI:EU:C:2002:254, para 12.

[120] Art 4(1) of MiFID I. In favour of a minimum harmonisation approach, see CESR's 'Technical Advice on Possible Implementing Measures of the Directive 2004/39/EC on Markets in Financial Instruments First Set of Mandates'.

[121] See Moloney, *How to Protect Investors: Lessons from the EC and the UK*, 15.

[122] See, in favour of maximum harmonisation, PO Mülbert 'The Eclipse of Contract Law in the Investment Firm–Client Relationship', 299. *Contra* OO Cherednychenko, 'Full Harmonisation of Retail Financial Services Contract Law in Europe: A Success or a Failure?' in S Grundmann and YM Atamer (eds), *Financial Services, Financial Crisis and General European Contract Law*, (Alphenaan den Rijn, Kluwer, 2011) 243 and Moloney, *How to Protect Investors: Lessons from the EC and the UK*, 28.

[123] Art 24(12) of MiFID II.

[124] See G Walker and R Purves (eds), *Financial Services Law* (Oxford, Oxford University Press, 2014) 117.

[125] See, R Dale, *International Banking Deregulation* (Oxford, Blackwell, 1992) 107.

[126] See NS Poser, *International Securities Regulation: London's 'Big Bang' and the European Securities Markets* (New York, Little, Brown & Co, 1990) 376.

securities markets moved from 'radical de-regulation' to 'radical re-regulation'.[127] The following sections provide a synthetic account of the development of conduct of business rules in the four examined jurisdictions.

A. The UK

In 1958, the Prevention of Fraud (Investments) Act introduced licensing requirements for undertakings dealing with the business of securities transactions and required the Board of Trade to adopt conduct of business rules.[128] In 1983, the Board of Trade introduced a set of conduct of business rules, including the suitability rule, which required authorised brokers to recommend a financial instrument only if there was 'an adequate and reasonable basis for that recommendation'.[129]

However, the impact of the Prevention of Fraud Act was very limited because broker members of stock exchange (thus essentially, The Stock Exchange) and/or of a recognised association of dealers in securities were exempted from its requirements.[130] After the Big Bang reforms, the City was hit by some financial scandals[131] which undermined investors' confidence in financial markets. This called for a comprehensive reform of the self-regulatory regime and for stronger investor protection rules. The Financial Services Act 1986 (FSA 1986), following the recommendations of Professor Gower,[132] set up a new regulatory system based on 'self-regulation within a statutory framework'.

The Securities and Investments Board (SIB), a private company funded by the industry, was given rule-making and enforcement powers. It could recognise self-regulatory organisations (SROs) as its members if their rules afforded a level of investor protection at least equivalent to that affored by the SIB's rules.[133]

Section 62 of the FSA 1986 allowed a private person to claim compensation for the damages suffered as a result of the breach of the SIB and SROs rules. In 1987 the SIB enacted new Financial Services (Conduct of Business) Rules which introduced a system of client classification (based on nine type of clients) and a

[127] RD Kelemen, *Eurolegalism. The Transformation of Law and Regulation in the European Union* (Cambridge, MA, Harvard University Press, 2011) 95.

[128] Section 10(2) (a) of the Licensed Dealers (Conduct of Business) Rules 1983.

[129] Ibid.

[130] See LCB Gower, 'Big Bang' and City Regulation' (1988) 51 *Modern Law Review* 7.

[131] See GF Pimlott, *The Reform of Investor Protection in the UK – An Examination of the Proposals of the Gower Report and the UK Government's White Paper of January 1985* (1985) 7 *Journal of Comparative Business and Capital Market Law* 144.

[132] LCB Gower, 'Review of Investor Protection, Report: Part I (London, 1984) and Part II (London, 1985)'.

[133] See E Lomnika, 'Private Damages Claims for Breaches of Securities Regulation Law: The US and the UK Approaches' in R Plender (ed), *Legal History and Comparative Law. Essays in Honour of Albert Kiralfy* (London, Frank Cass, 1990) 129.

suitability rule that prohibited firms from carrying out unsuitable transactions unless authorised by the client and to abstain from transactions with unnecessary frequency or excessive size (churning).[134]

The Investment Services Regulations 1995 implemented the ISD 1993 in the UK, allowing EU investment firms to provide in the UK any listed service which it is authorised to provide in its home State.

The Financial Services and Markets Act 2000 (FSMA 2000) replaced the SIB and the SROs[135] with the Financial Service Authority (FSA) which adopted a conduct of business sourcebook (COB sourcebook) which is part of the FSA Handbook. The COB sourcebook established clients' classification rules (private customers, intermediate customers and market counterparties), a suitability rule applicable only when the firm makes a personal recommendation or effects a discretionary transaction with a private customer (COB 5.3.5), the duty to provide a suitability letter to the private customer, if the transaction was carried out, explaining why the transaction is suitable and its possible disadvantages (COB 5.3.14) and prohibition for firms to carry out certain transactions with private customers unless they understood the nature of the risks involved (COB 5.4.3).

MiFID I has been transposed by the COB sourcebook which entered into force on 1 November 2007.[136] The COB rules introduced the appropriateness test (now COB 10A.2.1) and the duty for the firm to refuse a transaction if the firm does not obtain the firm required (now COB 9A.2.13). In 2017, the content of MiFID II was loyaly transposed in the COB rules.[137]

On 14 November 2018, the draft withdrawal agreement, as agreed at negotiators' level by the EU and the UK after Brexit, was published. This draft agreement foresees a transition period which would apply from after the entry into force of the withdrawal agreement (in the current draft agreement that date is 30 March 2019) until no later than 31 December 2020.[138] Until that point, the UK would

[134] Rule § 5.01(1) of the Financial Services (Conduct Of Business) Rules 1987.

[135] The original members were the Association of Futures Brokers and Dealers (AFBD); the Financial Intermediaries, Managers and Brokers Regulatory Association (FIMBRA); the Investment Management Regulatory Organisation (IMRO); and the Securities Association (TSA). For more detail on the SIB and SROs, see E Lomnika. 'Private Damages Claims for Breaches of Securities Regulation Law' in R Plender (ed), *Legal History and Comparative Law. Essays in Honour of Albert Kiralfi*, 133.

[136] FSA, 'Policy Statement: Reforming Conduct of Business Regulation – Final feedback on CP06/19' (PS07/14), 87.

[137] FCA, 'Glossary (MiFID 2) Instrument 2017', FCA 2017/36. See for more details, FCA, 'Markets in Financial Instruments Directive II Implementation – Policy Statement II', PS17/14 July 2017. In March 2017, the FCA issued additional implementing rules (FEES (MiFID 2 Application Fees) Instrument 2017, FCA 2017/20), see FCA, 'Markets in Financial Instruments Directive II Implementation – Policy Statement I', PS17/5, 31 March 2017. A distinction is made between 'non-MiFID provisions' for firms falling outside the scope of the Directive and 'MiFID-provisions' for firms falling inside its scope.

[138] Commission, 'Draft Agreement on the withdrawal of the United Kingdom of Great Britain and Northern Ireland from the European Union and the European Atomic Energy Community' (Article 126) (TF50 (2018) 55 – Commission to EU27) 14 November 2018. Available at: https://ec.europa.eu/.

continue to be treated as part of the EU's single market in financial services, meaning that EU law would continue to apply to UK firms as it does now and firms will be able to operate on the same basis.[139]

B. France

In France the regulatory system was also initially based on the co-existence of regulation and self-regulation. However, in comparison to the UK's experience, French rules, until the transposition of MiFID I, were drafted in a language which reflected the general private law duties of care and good faith.

The first organic law to regulate securities market was adopted in 1988.[140] It granted to the *Commission des opérations de bourse* (COB), a government agency set up in 1967, the power to make and enforce investor protection regulations. COB was supported by self-regulatory organisations (ie the *Conseil des Bourses de Valeurs* (CBV) and the *Conseil du marché a terme* (CMT)) who were given regulatory powers to enact conduct of business rules.[141] The regulations of CBV and CMT required firms to conclude written contracts for the execution of orders,[142] to provide sufficient information on risks and to ask for information about their clients' needs, but did not expressly require a duty to provide a suitable advice (*devoir de conseil*).[143] Importantly, these regulations required firms to ask clients for enough collateral to cover risks in short-selling transactions to protect them against the risk of speculative transactions.[144] As I will show, the violation of this regulatory duty, now laid down Articles 516–4(2) and 516–5(1) of AMF general regulation (*règlement general AMF*),[145] has triggered numerous disputes before the French courts, fuelling the debate on the civil law consequences of breaches of financial regulatory duties.

Law No 96/597[146] transposed the ISD's conduct principles. These prinicples were then codified in the monetary and financial code (*code monétaire et financier*),[147]

[139] Bank of England, The Bank of England's Approach to Financial Services Legislation under the European Union (Withdrawal) Act. 27 June 2018. Available at: www.bankofengland.co.uk/.

[140] Loi n°88-70 du 22 janvier 1988 sur les bourses de valeurs (NOR: ECOX8700048L).

[141] Art s 2-6-1 to 2-6-9 of Règlement général du conseil des bourses de valeurs of 22 September 1988 (CBV Regulation) (JO du 25 september 1988) and Art s 4-1-1-1 to 4-1-1-7 of Règlement général du conseil du marché à terme of 12 January 1990 (CMT Regulation) (JORF n°70 du 23 mars 1990).

[142] Art 3-5-0-1 of CMT Regulation and Art 2-3-2 of CBV Regulation.

[143] Art fr4-1-1-3 of CMT Regulation and Art 2-6-3 of CBV Regulation.

[144] Art 3-4-0-1 of CMT Regulation and 4-6-1 of CBV Regulation.

[145] M Storck, 'La responsabilité encourue pour le défaut d'exigence de couverture sur le marché à terme' (2001) *Revue trimestrielle de droit commercial* 175.

[146] Loi n° 96-597 du 2 juillet 1996 de modernisation des activités financières (NOR: ECOX9500164L).

[147] Livre V of the Code monétaire et financier. Ordonnance n° 2000-1223 du 14 décembre 2000 relative à la partie législative du code monétaire et financier (JO décembre 2000).

which replaced the CBV and the CMT with the *Conseil des marchés financiers* (CMF). The CMF, which was mainly responsible for the supervision of conduct of business rules and the COB, which was mainly responsible for supervision of issuers' disclosure and investment funds, implemented the ISD's principles into more detailed conduct of business rules, including 'know your customer' rules for advised[148] and non-advised[149] services.

In 2003, the CMF and COB merged to become the AMF which was made responsible for adopting conduct of business rules for market participants.[150] This introduced specific rules for investment advice and disclosure for financial advisers (*conseillers en investissements financiers*).[151]

The AMF general regulation (*règlement general AMF*) transposed the MiFID I. Order No 2016-827 and the General Regulation of AMF transposed MiFID II.[152] One striking aspect of this is that after the transposition of MIFID II, the duty to refuse a transaction, previously laid down in Article L 533-13 of CMF, is no longer expressly established in French law.[153]

C. Italy

Until the introduction of Law No 1/1991,[154] the protection of the client vis-à-vis brokers (*agenti di cambio*) was ensured only by general contract law rules, authorisation requirements and the single capacity (duty to carry out only one transaction).[155] Law No 1/1991 marked an important regulatory change. It introduced the suitability rule: a duty for investment firms to obtain information from clients about their financial situation and required firms not to advise or carry out transactions with a frequency or for amounts that were excessive in comparison to the client's financial situation.[156] It also established that in civil proceedings,

[148] Règlement COB n 90-10 sur la commercialisation des valeurs, des contrats à terme et des produits financiers négociés sur un marché étranger (homologué par arrêt du 20 septembre 1991, JO 29 septembre 1991) (Art 2 introduced a suitability rule); Règlements COB n 96-02 sur les prestataires de service d'investissement effectuant une activité de gestion de portefeuille pour le compte de tiers (JORF n°303 du 29 décembre 1996 p 19418) and règlement COB n 96-03 relatif aux règles de bonne conduite applicables au service de gestion de portefeuille pour le compte de tiers (JORF n 18 du 22 janvier 1997) (Arts 19 and 20 set out a suitability rule.)

[149] Règlement général CMF (JORF n° 205 du 5 septembre 1998) which governed conduct of business rules in non-advised services. (Art 3-3-7 set out a suitability rule.)

[150] Loi n° 2003-706 du 1er août 2003 de sécurité financière (JORF n°177 du 2 août 2003 page 13220),

[151] Art 55 which introduced in the re IV du livre V du code monétaire et financier Art s 541-1–541-7.

[152] Ordonnance n° 2016-827 du 23 juin 2016 relative aux marchés d'instruments financiers (JORF n°0146 du 24 juin 2016, texte n° 17).

[153] See, in more detail, T Bonneau, 'France' in D Busch and C van Dam, *A Bank's Duty of Care* 115.

[154] Legge 2 gennaio 1991, n 1 Disciplina dell'attivita' di intermediazione mobiliare e disposizioni sull'organizzazione dei mercati mobiliari (GU Serie Generale n 3 del 04-01-1991).

[155] See Poser, *International Securities Regulation*, 417.

[156] These rules have been further implemented by CONSOB, Regolamenti nn. 5387/1991 and 8850/1994.

for the compensation of damages suffered for any breach of these rules, it is for the firm to prove that it acted with the required diligence.[157] In this initial regulatory phase, Italy, differently from the UK and France, detailed conduct of business rules in the 'primary legislative level', leaving little to secondary regulatory levels and SROs.

Legislative Decree No 415/1996 transposed the ISD, setting out general conduct of business principles.[158] CONSOB Regulation No 10943/1997, detailed the conduct of business rules, including the suitability rule which remained in place only at 'secondary regulatory level'.[159]

Legislative Decree No 58/1998 (*Testo Unico della Finanza*, TUF) codified existing legislative rules, and was supplemented by CONSOB Regulation No 1152/1998.[160] Its Article 29(3) detailed the 'pre-MiFID suitability rule' which applied to both advisory and non-advisory services in relation to transactions with retail clients[161] and formed the main legal basis for financial litigation until the entry into force of MIFID I. Firms were required not to conduct transactions that were unsuitable for type, frequency or size and were required to inform clients if a transaction was not suitable and why it was not advisable to proceed. The firm was allowed to execute the transaction only if the client gave a written order or for orders via the phone, a registered order.

Legislative Decree No 164/2007 and CONSOB Regulation No 16190/2007, which transposed MiFID I into Italian law,[162] introduced a full calibration of the conduct of business rules with the type of financial service/instrument and the distinction between suitability, appropriateness and the execution-only regime. MiFID II has been transposed by Legislative Decree No 129/2017[163] and CONSOB Regulation No 20307/2018.[164]

D. Spain

In Spain, as in Italy, the liberalisation of the stock exchanges did not lead to the adoption of a mixed statutory and self-regulatory model for conduct regulation but

[157] Art 13(10) of Law 1/1991.

[158] Decreto Legislativo 23 luglio 1996, n 415 Recepimento della direttiva 93/22/CEE del 10 maggio 1993 relativa ai servizi di investimento del settore dei valori mobiliari e della direttiva 93/6/CEE del 15 marzo 1993 relativa all'adeguatezza patrimoniale delle imprese di investimento e degli enti creditizi (GU n 186 del 9 agosto 1996 – SO n 133).

[159] Decreto Legislativo 24 febbraio 1998, n 58 Testo unico delle disposizioni in materia di intermediazione finanziaria, ai sensi degli articoli 8 e 21 della legge 6 febbraio 1996, n 52 (GU n 71 del 26 marzo 1998 – SO n 52) and CONSOB, Regolamento 1 Luglio 1998, n 1152 (GU 17 luglio 1998, n 165, S O n 125).'

[160] CONSOB, Regolamento 1 Luglio 1998, n 1152 (GU 17 luglio 1998, n 165 – SO n 125).

[161] Art 31 of CONSOB Regulation n 1152/1998 excluded the applicability of this rule in relation to qualified investors (operatori qualificati), unless the parties agreed to it.

[162] CONSOB, Regolamento 29 Ottobre 2007, n 16190 (GU n 255 of 2 novembre 2007, SO n 222).

[163] Decreto Legislativo 3 agosto 2017, n 129, di attuazione della Direttiva 2014/65/UE del Parlamento europeo e del Consiglio, del 15 maggio 2014, relativa ai mercati degli strumenti finanziari (GU n 198 del 25 agosto 2017).

[164] CONSOB, Regolamento 15 febbraio 2018 n 20307 (GU n 41 del 19 febbraio 2018, SO n 7).

to the re-regulation of securities markets via primary and secondary regulations. Article 79 of Law 24/1998 (*Ley del Mercado de Valores*, LMV)[165] introduced general conduct of business rules that were implemented by the Royal Decree No 629/1993.[166] The Order of the Ministry of Economy of 25 October 1995,[167] which transposed the ISD into more detailed rules, required firms to obtain information about the appropriate financial situation, experience and objectives for either advisory or non-advisory services.

Law No 47/2007, which transposed MiFID I, introduced the distinction between retail and non-retail clients, advisory and non-advisory services and complex and non-complex financial instruments.[168]

More detailed rules on the conduct of business obligations were contained in Royal Decree No 217/2008.[169] On 20 July 2012, Spain signed a Memorandum of Understanding (MoU) with the European Commission to obtain the financial support from the European Financial Stability Facility (EFSF) and, subsequently, the European Stability Mechanism (ESM) to recapitalise its banking sector.

Overseen by the European Commission, the ESM and the International Monetary Fund, Spain adopted important reforms to strengthen prudential and conduct regulation.[170] To restore the investors' confidence in securities markets, which had been hit by large-scale misconduct in the distribution of *participationes preferentes* and other hybrid financial instruments, Law No 9/2012[171] introduced limits for the issue and distribution of hybrid financial instruments[172] and tightened the suitability and appropriateness rules.[173] *De facto* anticipating MiFID II, Law No 9/2012 requires firms to provide clients in advised services with a document stating how the recommendation meets their requirements and objectives. For non-advised services, firms must provid an assessment document and are required to keep a register of assessed clients and financial instruments for which the appropriateness assessment is negative.[174]

[165] Ley 24/1988 del Mercado de Valores (BOE n 181, de 29 de julio de 1988, p 23405).

[166] Real Decreto 629/1993, de 3 de mayo, sobre normas de actuación en los mercados de valores y registros obligatorios (BOE n. 121, de 21 de mayo de 1993, p 15389).

[167] Orden de 25 de octubre de 1995, de desarrollo parcial del Real Decreto 629/1993, de 3 de mayo, sobre normas de actuación en los mercados de valores y registros obligatorios (BOE n 262, de 2 de noviembre de 1995, p 31850).

[168] Ley 47/2007, de 19 de diciembre, por la que se modifica la Ley 24/1988, de 28 de julio, del Mercado de Valores (BOE n 304, de 20 de diciembre de 2007, p 52335).

[169] Real Decreto 217/2008, de 15 de febrero, sobre el régimen jurídico de las empresas de servicios de inversión y de las demás entidades que prestan servicios de inversión y por el que se modifica parcialmente el Reglamento de la Ley 35/2003, de 4 de noviembre, de Instituciones de Inversión Colectiva, aprobado por el Real Decreto 1309/2005, de 4 de noviembre (BOE n 41, de 16 de febrero de 2008, p 8706).

[170] See, for the most important measures thereby established, CNMV, Annual report 2012, 291.

[171] Ley 9/2012, de 14 de noviembre, de reestructuración y resolución de entidades de crédito (BOE n. 275, de 15 de noviembre de 2012, p 79604).

[172] See the thirteenth additional provision of the Law 9/2012.

[173] See the new Art 79 bis (6 and 7) of the LMV.

[174] Arts 214 and 215 (former Art s 79bis(6) and (7)) of the LMV.

In 2015, the LMV was recast to bring together the MiFID I transposition laws and the post-financial crisis legislative acts.[175] Royal Decree Law No 21/2017[176] has transposed MiFID II provisions on trading venues and Royal Decree No 14/2018 has transposed MiFID II conduct of business rules.[177]

VII. Preliminary Conclusion

MiFID I was a watershed in the regulation of investment services in the EU.

After this directive, conduct regulation, which had previously been based on general principles, developed into a sophisticated regulatory regime composed of 'status-based', 'transaction-based' and 'product-based' rules. The intensity of regulatory requirements not only depend on the status of the party (as in EU consumer law) but also on the nature of the transaction and the type of financial instrument. These regulatory duties, which MiFID II has further reinforced, mark a clear difference with general private law duties (ie pre-contractual good faith and duty of care) which apply to all types of transactions and could be 'modulated' based on the circumstances of the case only *ex post* by judges.

This chapter has shown that general private law and sectoral financial regulation have remained generally unconnected in legislative terms. Continental jurisdictions, except for Italy, where the burden of proof was reversed in civil liability claims, considered conduct of business rules to be a separate regime from general private law. In fact, until the litigation triggered by the financial crisis or, in Italy by infamous bankruptcies between 2000 and 2003, in continental Europe 'private enforcement of securities regulation' was almost unheard of.[178] In the UK, the legislator introduced in 1986 a statutory right of action for breaches of conduct of business rules with the purpose of protecting investors, although, as I will show later on, the scope of this provision was subsequently narrowed down due to fears of vexatious litigation.

It has been argued that the EU law doctrine of direct effect and the theory of the conferral of rights could bridge EU conduct of business rules with national private law, thereby granting investors a remedy for any breach of these rules. The mere fact that MiFID II conduct of business rules aim to protect investors is

[175] Real Decreto Legislativo 4/2015, de 23 de octubre, por el que se aprueba el texto refundido de la Ley del Mercado de Valores (BOE n. 255, de 24 de octubre de 2015, p. 100356).

[176] Real Decreto-ley 21/2017, de 29 de diciembre, de medidas urgentes para la adaptación del derecho español a la normativa de la Unión Europea en materia del mercado de valores (BOE n 317, de 30 de diciembre de 2017, p 130580).

[177] Real Decreto-ley 14/2018, de 28 de septiembre, por el que se modifica el texto refundido de la Ley del Mercado de Valores, aprobado por el Real Decreto Legislativo 4/2015, de 23 de octubre (BOE n 236, de 29 de septiembre de 2018, p 93738). On 19 July 2018, the Commission referred Spain and Slovenia to the CJEU for failure to transpose MiFID II and the Commission MiFID II Regulation.

[178] RD Kelemen, *Eurolegalism*, 94.

not sufficient to confer on them a legally enforceable right that could be enforced in a civil proceeding. Yet, this chapter has shown that MiFID II's disclosure and distribution rules, given their rationale, the level of detail and their transactional nature are capable of conferring on investors a legally enforceable right. In addition, MiFID II's inclusion of these rules in a Level 2 directly applicable act will give horizontal direct effect to these rules, enabling investors to invoke them against firms in a civil proceeding. For organisational and product governance requirements, a case-by-case assessment is required to understand whether the rule at stake is sufficiently detailed and has a transactional nature that enables this rule to confer rights on investors.

The content and purpose of MiFID II conduct of business rules could be also affected by the quasi-regulatory acts adopted by ESMA. The role of ESMA will be crucial to assist national courts and ADR bodies in the enforcement of general conduct of business rules (ie fair treatment and best interest duties). Therefore, in the next chapter, the analysis moves to examine the civil law or horizontal effects of ESMA's acts on national private law.

3

Civil Law Effects of ESMA's 'Conduct of Business Handbook'

I. Conduct Supervision and Private Law: The Issues at Stake

The global financial crisis led to an overhaul of the institutional architecture for financial supervision in the EU.

Following the recommendations of the high-level group chaired by Jacques De Larosière, in 2010 the EU legislators created the European System of Financial Supervision (ESFS) which is composed of European Supervisory Authorities (ESAs) – the European Securities and Markets Authority (ESMA), the European Banking Authority (EBA), the European Insurance and Occupational Pensions Authority (EIOPA) – ESAs Joint Committee, national competent authorities (NCAs) and the European Systemic Risk Board (ESRB). The ESAs are responsible for micro-prudential tasks, whereas ESRB is responsible for macro-prudential tasks. NCAs continue to carry out day-to-day supervision over market participants and ESAs have a defined number of tasks and powers to ensure the stability and effectiveness of the EU financial system.

The conferral of significant tasks and powers to EU agencies without changing the Treaties has been mostly analysed from an administrative and constitutional law perspective.[1] The new powers of ESAs may also have implications for private law relations between financial market participants.[2] Supervisory acts not only have vertical effects against (or in favour of) the supervised entities but they also produce horizontal effects (ie they may affect the private law relations between

[1] See, in particular, T Tridimas, 'Financial Supervision and Agency Power: Reflections on ESMA' in N Shuibhne and LW Gormley (eds), *From Single Market to Economic Union* (Oxford, Oxford University Press, 2012) 56; I Iris H-Y Chiu, 'Power and Accountability in the EU Financial Regulatory Architecture: Examining Inter-Agency Relations, Agency Independence and Accountability' (2015) 8 *European Journal of Legal Studies* 68 and M Simoncini, *Administrative Regulation Beyond the Non-Delegation Doctrine. A Study on EU Agencies* (Oxford, Hart Publishing, 2018).

[2] See also F Della Negra, 'The Effects of the ESMA's Powers on Domestic Contract Law' in M Andenas and G Deipenbrock (eds), *Regulating and Supervising European Financial Markets: More Risks than Achievements* (Berlin/Heidelberg, Springer, 2016), 139.

the supervised entity and its clients).[3] For instance, supervisory acts may prohibit firms from distributing a financial instrument to clients or may introduce requirements and make recommendations as to how regulatory requirements should be interpreted. The ESAs, differently from NCAs, do not have regulatory powers. However, they may adopt non-binding acts of general application (ie guidelines) and, in limited circumstances, binding legal acts addressed to NCAs or individual market participants.

This chapter seeks to understand the horizontal effects of the acts adopted by ESMA to supplement MiFID II conduct of business rules. It is argued that the 'conduct of business handbook' built up by ESMA may have significant horizontal or civil law effects, affecting, under certain conditions, the interpretation of national private law duties and defining their scope and limitations in light of EU law.

To demonstrate this hypothesis, this chapter begins by illustrating ESMA's objectives, tasks and powers and examines the main aspects of its 'conduct of business handbook'. The chapter goes on to examine the most relevant national supervisory measures adopted to strengthen compliance with conduct of business rules. Finally, it discusses the horizontal direct and indirect effects of ESMA's acts based on the case law of the CJEU.

II. ESMA's Institutional Design

A. Objectives and Tasks

Although CESR and the other Lamfallussy Committees improved supervisory convergence, mainly through guidelines and Q&As,[4] they proved to be ill-suited to ensure adequate cooperation and information exchange between NCAs and to take effective action to ensure a consistent application of EU law.[5] To overcome these deficiencies, the co-legislators established the ESAs, on the basis of Article 114 of TFEU, 'in order to protect the public interest by contributing to the short, medium and long-term stability and effectiveness of the financial system, for the Union economy, its citizens and businesses'.[6]

[3] See F Möslein, 'Third Parties in the European Banking Union: Regulatory and Supervisory Effects on Private Law Relationships Between Banks and their Clients or Creditors' (2015) 16 *European Business Organization Law Review* 547; O O Cherednychenko, 'Public Supervision over Private Relationships: Towards European Supervision Private Law?' (2014) 1 *European Review of Private Law* 37.

[4] See P Schammo, *EU Prospectus Law. New Perspectives on Regulatory Competition in Securities Markets* (Cambridge, Cambridge University Press, 2011) 21.

[5] See J De Larosiere, Report, para 162. See also A Turner, 'The Turner Review. A Regulatory Response to the Global Banking Crisis'. March 2009, 36.

[6] Art 5(1) of Regulation (EU) No 1095/2010 of the European Parliament and of the Council of 24 November 2010 establishing a European Supervisory Authority (European Securities and Markets Authority), amending Decision No 716/2009/EC and repealing Commission Decision 2009/77/EC

The protection of investors takes up a central role in ESAs' architecture. ESMA shall contribute to enhance 'customer protection'[7] and has an express 'consumer protection' task which consists of promoting transparency, simplicity and fairness in the market for consumer financial products or services.[8] In our view, this enables ESMA to act with regard to clients who do not qualify as consumers *stricto sensu* (ie natural persons, who act outside their trade, business or profession) provided that it acts within the scope of the legislative acts mentioned by Article 1(2) of ESMA Regulation.[9] The consumer protection task shall include (but it is not limited to) reviewing and coordinating financial literacy and education initiatives by the NCAs and contributing to the development of common disclosure rules. As part of this task, ESMA gathers aggregate data on customer complaints made to the NCAs and, where applicable, ADR bodies relating to the provision of financial instruments and analyses trends and likely drivers for these trends.[10]

Strengthening the powers and role of ESMA is a priority for the Commission,[11] culminating in the proposal for a review of ESFS.[12] The Commission's 2017 proposal to revise the ESA Regulations confers new product intervention powers on ESMA, grants it the power to approve certain prospectus, introduces a more independent and effective governance system, ensuring the adequate representation of consumers' interest in the Board of Supervisors and gives ESAs a more adequate funding mechanism to fulfil their tasks.[13]

(ESMA Regulation) [2010] OJ L 331/84. For the notion of financial stability in EU law, see G Lo Schiavo, *The Role of Financial Stability in EU Law and Policy* (Alphen aan den Rijn: Wolters Kluwer, 2017) 52 and, for a theory of harmonisation of financial supervision in the EU, even before the outbreak of the crisis, see M Andenas, 'Who is Going to Supervise Europe's Financial Markets' in M Andenas and Y Avgerinos (eds) *Financial Markets in Europe: Towards a Single Regulator?* (London, The Hague, New York, Kluwer Law International, 2003) xv–xxvi.

[7] Art 5(a)(f) of ESMA Regulation. In the Commission proposal, investor protection ranked as the second objective of ESMA, before the stability of the financial system, after the functioning of the internal market (Art 1(4) of the Commission Proposal for a Regulation of the European Parliament and of the Council establishing a European Securities and Markets Authority Brussels (COM(2009) 503 final). The Parliament, in its first reading, placed financial stability and client protection on the same level and conferred on ESMA the task related to consumer protection and financial activities (EU Parliament. Position at first reading on 22 September 2010 with a view to the adoption of Regulation (EU) No …/2010 of the European Parliament and of the Council establishing a European Supervisory Authority (European Securities and Markets Authority) OJ C 50E/217.). Subsequently, the Council introduced a clearer hierarchy between financial stability, which became ESMA's overriding objective, and other objectives, to which ESMA shall contribute.

[8] Art 9(1) of ESMA Regulation.

[9] ESMA Regulation also makes reference to the task of 'fostering *investor* protection' (Art 8(1)(h)), whilst indicating, as mentioned, that it will contribute to enhancing '*customer* protection' (Art 1(5)(f)).

[10] ESMA, *Report on Trends, Risks and Vulnerabilities*, n 1/2017, 37.

[11] European Commission, 'Mid-Term Review of the Capital Markets Union Action Plan', Brussels, 8.6.2017 COM(2017) 292.

[12] See D Busch, 'A Stronger Role for the European Supervisry Authorities' in D Busch, E Avgouleas, G Ferrarini (eds), *Capital Markets Union in Europe* (Oxford, Oxford University Press, 2018) 28.

[13] European Commission, 'Proposal for a Regulation of the European Parliament and of the Council amending ESAs Regulations', Brussels (COM(2017) 536).

B. Powers

(i) Regulatory Convergence

In the current legal framework, ESMA may adopt non-legally binding acts of general application aimed to ensure regulatory and supervisory convergence. In some clearly defined circumstances, it may also adopt individual binding acts addressed to NCAs and market participants.

ESMA strengthens regulatory convergence by participating in the Level 2 rule-making and by adopting guidelines and recommendations.

ESMA may provide its technical advice to the Commission for adoption of delegated acts or may adopt, upon legislative delegation, draft regulatory and implementing technical standards which have to be endorsed and enacted by the Commission, in the form of delegated or implementing acts, under Articles 290 and 291 of TFEU, to acquire binding legal effects. To respect the limitations set out by the *Meroni* judgment,[14] substantially reaffirmed in the 'short-selling judgment',[15] ESMA Regulation specifies that these standards shall be technical and shall not imply strategic decisions or policy choices.[16] Nevertheless, doubts have been raised on whether constraints placed on the Commission if it decides not to endorse or to amend a draft technical standard fully respect its prerogatives under Articles 290 and 291 of TFEU.[17] Moreover, the distinction between acts that are merely technical and acts which imply strategic decisions or policy choices is not straightforward and may ultimately depend on how important a certain issue is for political authorities (ie a decision perceived to be uncontentious is accepted as being technical).[18]

In relation to MiFID II, ESMA gave its technical advice to the Commission for adoption of Level 2 legislation.[19] The technical advice covered large parts of the conduct of business rules, including product governance obligations and product intervention powers. In fact, the EU legislators favoured the instrument of delegated acts to implement conduct of business rules[20] and confined draft

[14] Case C-9/56 *Meroni v High Authority*, EU:C:1958:7.

[15] Case C-270/12, *UK v European Parliament and Council*, ECLI:EU:C:2014:18.

[16] Arts 10(1) and 15(1) of ESMA Regulation. For the difference between regulatory and technical standards see in more detail T Tridimas, 'Financial Supervision and Agency Power: Reflections on ESMA', 70. The Declaration (No 39) on Art 290 of the TFEU annexed to the Final Act of the Intergovernmental Conference which adopted the Treaty of Lisbon, recognised the role of technical expertise to adopt delegated legislation in the financial services area.

[17] See Commission, Proposal for a PRIIPS Regulation, 3 July 2012COM(2012) 352 final, 6. See also M Chamon, 'EU Agencies between Meroni and Romano or the Devil and the Deep Blue Sea' (2011) 48 *Common Market Law Review* 1055 and P Schammo, 'The European Securities and Markets Authority: Lifting the Veil on the Allocation of Powers' (2011) 48 *Common Market Law Review* 1879.

[18] See especially Moloney, *EU Securities and Financial Markets* Regulation, 925 and L Quaglia, 'Financial Sector Committee Governance in the European Union' (2008) 30 *European Integration* 572.

[19] ESMA, *Technical Advice.*

[20] The Declaration (No 39) on Art 290 of the Treaty on the Functioning of the European Union (TFEU), annexed to the Final Act of the Intergovernmental Conference which adopted the

regulatory technical standards to certain technical aspects of the best execution rule.[21] This suggests that the development of Level 2 conduct of business rules was perceived as a potentially controversial matter, involving policy choices.

Guidelines play a central role in ensuring the uniform and consistent application of EU financial regulation. ESMA may adopt guidelines on its own initiative or based on a legislative delegation. Differently from the CESR guidelines, NCAs and financial market participants 'shall make every effort to comply with those guidelines and recommendations' and NCAs 'shall confirm whether they intend to comply or not with that guideline or recommendation' (financial market participants have the duty to report compliance only if requested by the guideline/recommendation). These two obligations 'harden'[22] the soft-law nature which is traditionally attributed to these instruments[23] and place public pressure on the NCAs to implement guidelines, thus fostering the consistent application of EU law across Member States.[24]

(ii) Supervisory Convergence

Within the EFSF, the supervision of financial market participants remains in the hands of the NCAs. Only in exceptional circumstances may ESMA adopt individual binding legal acts addressed to financial market participants and/or NCAs. Leaving aside the cases where ESMA conducts ongoing supervision on CRAs and trade repositories,[25] in the cases defined by Articles 17, 18 and 19 of ESMA Regulation, ESMA may act as 'supervisor of supervisors'[26] and may take a legally binding decision where necessary to ensure the effective application of EU law or to address developments that could jeopardise the orderly functioning and integrity of financial markets or the stability of the whole or part of the financial system in the Union or to settle disagreements between competent authorities in cross-border situations. A financial market participant can be directly addressed by a decision only if the NCA fails to comply with the relevant ESMA decision or Commission opinion.

However, ESMA Regulation introduced several procedural restrictions for the use of these incisive powers. Moreover, private investors are not entitled to request

Treaty of Lisbon, recognised the role of technical expertise to adopt delegated legislation in the financial services area.

[21] Art 27(10) of MiFID II.

[22] M van Rijsbergen, 'On the Enforceability of EU Agencies' Soft Law at the National Level: The Case of the European Securities and Markets Authority' (2014) 10, www.utrechtlawreview.org 116.

[23] See Tridimas, Financial Supervision and Agency Power: Reflections on ESMA 71; Moloney. *EU Securities and Markets Regulation* 929.

[24] See Simoncini, *Administrative Regulation Beyond the Non-delegation Doctrine*, 72.

[25] Arts 14–17 and Arts 21–25 of CRA Regulation and Arts 55–59 and Arts 60–74 of EMIR.

[26] N Moloney, *EU Securities and Financial Markets Regulation* (Oxford, Oxford Univesity Press, 2014) 973 and P Schammo, 'EU Day-to-Day Supervision or Intervention-based Supervision: Which Way Forward for the European System of Financial Supervision?' (2012) 32 *Oxford Journal of Legal Studies* 790.

an investigation on the alleged breach of EU law[27] and the ESAs cannot use these powers 'to provide individual protection or redress in disputes between a natural or legal person and a competent authority at the national level'.[28]

In addition to these binding legal acts, ESMA may adopt a wide range of non-legally binding acts to enhance convergence in supervisory practices. In particular, peer review is a fundamental instrument to asses the effectiveness and the degree of convergence of enforcement of the provisions adopted in the implementation of Union law and can be taken into account to issue guidelines and recommendations and developing draft regulatory technical or implementing technical standards.[29]

Questions and answers (Q&As) provide practical guidance to NCAs and financial market participants in the application of MiFID's requirements. Even if Q&As are not legally binding, ESMA stressed that their application will be rigorously scrutinised given their practical significance to achieve a level-playing field.

Supervisory coordination powers are significantly enhanced by the Commission proposal amending ESMA Regulation. In particular, the ESAs will be required to set EU-wide priorities for supervision in the form of a 'Strategic Supervisory Plan' against which all competent authorities will be assessed.[30]

Finally, ESMA may adopt warnings to make clients aware about emerging risks.[31]

(iii) Product Intervention

Product intervention's powers deserve particular attention for their repercussions on private law relations. Article 9(5) of ESMA Regulation, empowers the Authority to temporarily prohibit or restrict certain financial activities that threaten the orderly functioning and integrity of financial markets or the stability of the whole or part of the financial system in the Union in the cases specified by the law or in an emergency situation, in accordance with Article 18 of ESMA Regulation.[32] On the basis of this general provision, MiFIR empowers ESMA, EBA

[27] Case C-577/15 P, *SV Capital OÜ v EBA*, ECLI:EU:C:2016:947, paras 39–41. See also Case T-660/14, *SV Capital v EBA*, EU:T:2015:608, para 47 and Case T-590/15, *Onix Asigurări SA v EIOPA*, ECLI:EU:T:2016:374, para 53. See the decisions of ESAs Board of Appeal in *SV Capital OÜ v European Banking Authority* (BoA 2013-008) at para 30 and *BoA, Investor Protection Europe Sprl v ESMA* (BoA 2014-05) at para 32.

[28] Case T-590/15, *Onix Asigurări SA v EIOPA*, ECLI:EU:T:2016:374, para 55.

[29] N Moloney, 'Institutional Governance and Capital Markets Union: Incrementalism or a "Big Bang"?' (2016) 2 *European Company and Financial Review* 418.

[30] Art 29a of amended ESA Regulations.

[31] ESMA, Trading in foreign exchange (forex), 5 December 2011; ESMA, Pitfalls on online investing, 10 September 2012; ESMA, Contracts for difference (CFDs), 28 February 2013; ESMA, Risks of investing in complex products, 7 February 2014. ESMA alerts firms involved in *Initial Coin Offerings* (ICOs) to the need to meet relevant regulatory requirements, 13 November 2017 (ESMA 50-157-828) and alerted investors ESMA, *Initial Coin Offerings* (ICOs), 13 November 2017 ESMA50-157-829. On 12 February 2018, ESAs issued a joint warning on the risks involved in virtual currencies.

[32] The Commission's proposal to convert this Article into a self-standing empowerment. (Commission. Report to the Parliament and the Council on the operation of the European Supervisory

and the NCAs to prohibit, also on a precautionary basis, the marketing, distribution or sale of certain financial instruments or a type of financial activity or practice.[33] This power may be used not only to address a threat to the orderly functioning and integrity of financial markets or to the stability of the financial system but also a significant investor protection concern. The Commission MiFIR Regulation, in line with ESMA's technical advice, clarifies that the 'threat' requires a greater concern than a 'significant concern' for ESMA to act.[34]

ESMA's product intervention powers may be used only on a temporary basis and are a last-resort measure: ESMA can adopt these measures only if the regulatory requirements under EU law that are applicable to the relevant financial instrument or activity do not address the threat and NCAs have not taken action (or adequate action) to address it.[35] However, ESMA's measures shall prevail over any previous action taken by a competent authority.[36]

ESMA must take into account the criteria set out by Commission MiFIR Regulation to assess whether there is a significant investor protection concern or a threat to market integrity or financial stability.[37] These factors relate to aspects of the financial instrument (eg pricing, leverage, degree of innovation and complexity), the client (eg his skills and abilities, level of education, economic situation) and the relationship between the firm and the client (eg selling practices). The existence of one the factors is sufficient to determine a significant investor protection concern, a threat to the orderly functioning and integrity of financial or commodity markets or to the stability of the whole or part of the financial system. Following ESMA's technical advice,[38] the Commission laid down an exhaustive list of criteria for ESMA and EBA and a non-exhaustive list of criteria for NCA to respect the limitations set out by the *Meroni* judgment.[39] However, ESMA will

Authorities (ESAs) and the European System of Financial Supervision (ESFS) has been abandoned in the draft regulation on the reform of the ESAs (COM(2017) 536.)

[33] ESMA has also product intervention powers on positions or exposures in derivatives under Art 45 MiFIR and under Art 28 of the short selling regulation. EIOPA has been granted such powers under Art 16 of Regulation No 1286/2014.

[34] Recital No 18 of Commission Delegated Regulation (EU) 2017/567 of 18 May 2016 supplementing Regulation (EU) No 600/2014 of the European Parliament and of the Council with regard to definitions, transparency, portfolio compression and supervisory measures on product intervention and positions ('Commission MiFIR Regulation') [2017] OJ L 87/90. See, for a critical view, R D'Ambrosio, 'The Temporary Intervention Powers of the European Banking Authority and the European Securities and Markets Authority: Content and Limits' (2018) *ERA Forum*.

[35] See, in more detail, D Busch, 'Product Governance and Product Intervention under MiFID II/MiFIR' in D Busch and G Ferrarini (eds), *Regulation of the EU Financial Markets* (Oxford, Oxford University Press, 2017) 137.

[36] Art 40(7) of MiFIR.

[37] Art 19(2) of the Commission Delegated Regulation (EU) 2017/567 of 18 May 2016 supplementing Regulation (EU) No 600/2014 of the European Parliament and of the Council with regard to definitions, transparency, portfolio compression and supervisory measures on product intervention and positions (Commission MiFIR Regulation) [2017] OJ L 87/90.

[38] See ESMA, *Technical Advice* 191 (specifying that the list should not be exhausting).

[39] Arts 19(2) and 21(2) of Commission MiFIR Regulation.

inevitably exercise some discretion when applying these criteria, especially those drafted in broad language.[40]

Before MiFIR came into force, several NCAs adopted measures to restrict distribution of certain complex financial instruments to retail clients.[41] On 22 May 2018, after a public consultation,[42] ESMA adopted two decisions to restrict the marketing, distribution or sale of contracts for differences (CFDs) to retail clients[43] and to prohibit the marketing, distribution or sale of binary options to these clients.[44] These measures, in effect since 2 July 2018 (for binary options) and 1 August 2018 (for CFDs), have been renewed for a further three-month period from 2 January 2019 (for binary options) and from 1 February 2019 (for CFDs), were taken on the ground that there is significant investor protection concern determined by the complexity and lack of transparency of CFDs and binary options.

III. ESMA's 'Conduct of Business Handbook'

ESMA has already adopted numerous acts to supplement MiFID II Level 1 and Level 2 legislation.

Its 'conduct of business handbook' comprises the guidelines on suitability requirements,[45] product governance[46] and complex debt instruments,[47] the opinions on good practices for product governance and MiFID practices for firms selling complex products[48] and the Q&A on MiFID II and MiFIR investor

[40] See, in particular, the criterion of Art 19(2)(u). In this sense also D'Ambrosio, The Temporary Intervention Powers of the European Banking Authority and the European Securities and Markets Authority'.

[41] See, in detail, ESMA Securities and Markets Stakeholder Group, 'Own Initiative Report on Product Intervention under MiFIR', 16 June 2017 (ESMA22-106-264).

[42] On 18 January 2018, ESMA published a call for evidence on proposed product intervention measures on the offer of CFDs and binary options to retail investors. This ran until 5 February 2018. ESMA received almost 18,500 responses.

[43] ESMA, Decision (EU) 2018/796 of 22 May 2018 to temporarily restrict contracts for differences in the Union in accordance with Art 40 of Regulation (EU) No 600/2014 of the European Parliament and of the Council (Decision on CFDs) [2018] OJ L 136/50).

[44] ESMA, Decision (EU) 2018/795 of 22 May 2018 to temporarily prohibit the marketing, distribution or sale of binary options to retail clients in the Union in accordance with Art 40 of Regulation (EU) No 600/2014 of the European Parliament and of the Council (Decision on binary options) [2018] OJ L 136/31.

[45] ESMA, Guidelines on certain aspects of the MiFID II suitability requirements, 28 May 2018 ESMA 35-43-869.

[46] ESMA, Guidelines on MiFID II product governance requirements, 2 June 2017 ESMA 35-43-620.

[47] ESMA, Guidelines on complex debt instruments and structured deposits, 4 February 2016, ESMA/2015/1787.

[48] ESMA, Opinion on structured Retail Products – Good practices for product governance arrangements, 27 March 2014, ESMA/2014/332 and opinion on MiFID practices for firms selling complex products, 7 February 2014 ESMA/2014/146.

protection and intermediaries topics.[49] This handbook not only conveys to the NCAs ESMA's expectations on how to apply regulatory requirements but it also affects the way general private law duties should be interpreted. The following sections provide an account of the most relevant ESMA's (soft law) rules applicable to the firm–client private law relations.

A. Fair Treatment Clause

ESMA gave a specific interpretation of the fair treatment clause in its opinion on MiFID practices for firms selling complex products. In particular, it clarified that the 'fair, clear and not misleading' principle entails, in particular, that firms should explain the potential benefits and returns in the simplest way possible, avoiding jargon and explaining technical terms in a straightforward manner (eg avoiding ambiguous terms such as 'absolute' or 'hedged').[50] Where offering leveraged products or products that embed a derivative, firms should make sure equal prominence is given to the risks as well as the benefits of such features (eg for leveraged products, firms should indicate the risk of multiplying losses and not only focus on the potential for increased returns).

B. Investment Advice and (Irrelevance of) Advisory Contracts

An important aspect underlined by ESMA and its predecessor (CESR) is that to determine whether advice was given, it is not necessary to prove that an advisory contract was concluded but that the personal recommendation, from the perspective of 'a reasonable observer' would be presented as suitable or would be based on a consideration of a clients circumstances.[51] This approach was motivated by the fact that, as CESR pointed out in its technical advice on MiFID I, 'some jurisdictions provide for concepts such as pre-contractual liability or implied agreement without consideration, while others do not. Since the principles of contract law are not harmonised throughout Europe, the conditions for formation of a contract and liability might vary according to the relevant jurisdiction.

[49] ESMA, Questions and Answers On MiFID II and MiFIR investor protection and intermediaries topics. 3 October 2017 (ESMA35-43-349).

[50] ESMA, Opinion on MiFID practices for firms selling complex products, 6.

[51] ESMA, Guidelines on suitability, 34 and CESR, *Understanding the Definition of Advice under MiFID*, 6. To be considered investment advice, CESR points out that five key tests should be met: the service constitutes a recommendation; the recommendation is given in relation to one or more transactions in financial instruments; the recommendation is presented as suitable or is based on a consideration of the personal circumstances; the recommendation is issued otherwise than exclusively through distribution channels or to the public; the recommendation is made to a person in his capacity as investor or potential investor or an agent for an investor or potential investor.

Though a regulatory approach may influence the interpretation by some courts, the regulatory approach should not depend on unharmonised principles of private law'.[52]

In the 2018 guidelines on suitability, ESMA reiterated that contractual dislaimers cannot limit the firms' responsibility under the suitability rule. In addition, in the Q&A on investor protection topics, with regard to Article 42 of MiFID II, which regulates the provision of services by third-country firms at the exclusive initiative of the client established in the EU, ESMA pointed out that 'the client's own exclusive initiative shall be assessed *in concreto* on a case-by-case basis for each investment service or activity provided, regardless of any contractual clause or disclaimer purporting to state, for example, that the third-country firm will be deemed to respond to the exclusive initiative of the client'.[53]

C. Suitability Rule

The governance of investment advice plays a central role in ESMA activity. Effective compliance with suitability requirements is key with specific regard to investors with lower level of financial literacy.[54] The 2018 guidelines on suitability, which replaced the previous guidelines issued in 2012, provide more clarity on the application of MiFID II requirements and promote greater convergence in the application of these requirements. An interesting aspect is that ESMA was mindful of avoiding potential ambiguities on the binding force of its guidelines. In fact, it specified that: 'guidelines do not reflect absolute obligations. For this reason, the word "should" is often used. However, the words "shall", "must" or "required to/" are used when describing a MiFID II requirement'.[55]

As regards their content, ESMA pointed out that 'firms should inform their clients clearly and simply about the suitability assessment and its purpose which is to enable the firm to act in the client's best interest' (General Guideline 1). ESMA supported this guideline specifying that 'firms should avoid stating, or giving the impression, that it is the client who decides on the suitability' and that 'any disclaimers (or other similar types of statements) aimed at limiting the firm's responsibility for the suitability assessment would not in any way impact the characterisation of the service provided in practice to clients nor the assessment of the firm's compliance to the corresponding requirements'.[56] This supporting

[52] CESR, *Draft Technical Advice on Possible Implementing Measures of MiFID I*, Second Set of Mandates 13.

[53] ESMA, Questions and answers on MiFID II and MiFIR 96.

[54] ESMA, *Financial Education and Investor Protection in Europe: The Role of ESMA*. Speech of Steven Maijoor at the IOSCO World Investor Week – FSMA Conference. 3 October 2017 (ESMA35-42-597) 4.

[55] ESMA, Guidelines suitability requirements para 34.

[56] Ibid at para 19.

guideline aims to reduce the risk that the MiFID's standard of protection is lowered by means of contract clauses negotiated by the client who is placed in a 'take it or leave it' situation due to the asymmetry of bargaining power vis-à-vis the firm. However, this guideline was criticised by some market participants for unduly interfering with national private law and limiting the private autonomy of market participants.[57]

Firms should also collect all 'necessary information' about the client's knowledge and experience, financial situation and investment objectives (General Guideline 3), taking into account of whether the financial instrument is complex, risky or illiquid and the vulnerability of the client due to his age or inexperience (Supporting Guideline 3). Reference to 'vulnerable clients' is consistent with the purpose of MiFID II to increase protection for 'investors most in need of protection'.[58]

Building on MiFID II organisation requirements for suitability, the guidelines recommend firms to ensure that the information collected from clients is reliable, 'without unduly relying on clients' self-assessments' (General Guideline 4). This is supported by the fact that 'any agreement signed by the client, or disclosure made by the firm that would aim at limiting the responsibility of the firm with regard to the sutiability assessment' would not be in line with MiFID II. Firms should adopt mechanisms to address the risk that clients may tend to overestimate their knowledge and experience, particularly where robo-advice is provided, since the risk of overestimation by clients may be higher when they provide information through an automated (or semi-automated) system (Supporting Guideline 4). Even if these guidelines go beyond the wording of Article 55(3) of MiFID II Delegated Regulation, this seems to be justified based on the purpose of that legislative provision to avoid that firms take advantage of their client's lack or inaccurate information.

Firms 'should also take reasonable steps to assess the client's understanding of investment risks as well as the relationship between risk and return' (Supporting Guideline 8) and that a thorough assessment of the possible investment alternatives is undertaken, taking into account the products' cost and complexity (General Guideline 9). These guidelines go beyond the letter of Articles 54(2)(c) and 54(9) of Commission MiFID II Regulation but they introduce a specification of existing requirements that is compatible with the need to ensure a high level of client protection.

Useful indications to interpret the suitability rule are also contained in ESMA's Q&A on investor protection. In particular, ESMA clarified that the firm must provide a suitability report irrespective of whether a transaction is concluded

[57] See response of European Banking Federation to the consultation paper, and the German Banking Industry Committee to the consultation paper (ESMA35-43-748). The responses to the consultation paper are available at: www.esma.europa.eu/press-news/consultations/consultation-guidelines-certain-aspects-mifid-ii-suitability-requirements#TODO.

[58] Recital No 104 of MiFID II.

or the specific recommendation given and that the suitability rule is breached where the purchase of a specific financial instrument cannot be recommended to a client because that instrument is unsuitable for him and the firm influences that client to proceed with the transaction at his/her own initiative for an unsuitable instrument or where the firm purposely changes the client's profile (without there being any real change in the client's situation that would justify such a modification of the profile) to make suitable a financial instrument that is unsuitable for him/her, so as to be able to recommend it.[59]

D. Appropriateness Rule

Although ESMA has not adopted specific guidelines on the appropriateness rule, it has strengthened this rule in the Level 2 legislative process. In its technical advice on MiFID II/MiFIR, ESMA recommended that the Commission further restricted the cases where a financial instrument can be considered as non-complex by adding two additional criteria to those of Article 38 of the Commission MiFID I Directive[60] and requiring firms to maintain records of the appropriateness test in several circumstances, including where an appropriateness assessment concluded that an investment service or product was not appropriate for a client.[61] In addition, in its opinion on MiFID practices for firms selling complex products, ESMA reminded NCAs that they should monitor firms who choose to have standardised processes in place to assess appropriateness so they do not simply use this process as a self-certifying exercise. ESMA also specified that a long and complicated risk warning, followed by a single 'tick box' that a client has understood the risks of a product, is unlikely to clearly indicate that the client has sufficient knowledge and experience.[62]

E. Governance of Structured and Complex Products

The risk posed to retail clients by structured retail products and complex financial instruments is a key concern for ESMA.

Low returns from more traditional forms of investments or ordinary deposits and volatility in the markets, have led investment firms to offer structured and complex financial products[63] which were previously available only to professional

[59] ESMA, Questions and Answers on MiFID II and MiFIR 32.
[60] See Art 57(d)(e) of Commission MiFID II Regulation.
[61] ESMA, *Technical Advice* 161 incorporated into Art 56(2) of Commission MiFID II Regulation.
[62] ESMA, Opinion on MiFID practices for firms selling complex products, 5.
[63] Structured products are investment products whose return is linked to the performance of one or more reference index, price or rate. According to ESMA, the vast majority of structured products are complex products (ie contracts for difference (CFDs); binary options; turbos; convertible bonds; and subordinated bonds). See ESMA, Opinion on MiFID practices for firms selling complex products, 3.

clients. Product complexity makes it difficult for retail clients to understand the risks, costs, expected returns and process-related pre-contractual information, thus increasing the risk of unforeseen losses. ESMA has taken several initiatives to address these risks.

Building on its 2013 report on 'Retailisation in the EU',[64] ESMA issued – before the adoption of MiFID II and MiFIR – two opinions detailing some practices to be followed when offering complex financial instruments. Further, the guidelines on product governance requirements aim to provide more clarity on the MiFID II's product governance obligations for manufacturers, distributors and both manufacturers and distributors. Therefore, ESMA looked at product complexity from an organisational and distribution perspective.

From an organisational perspective, ESMA's guidelines, building on the good practices for product governance arrangements developed in the 2014 opinion,[65] specifiy the MiFID II product governance requirements, reinforcing the duties of distributors. Whereas manufacturers, who do not have direct contact with clients, may identify the target market based on their theoretical knowledge and experience of the product, distributors should define the target market on a more concrete level and should take into account the type of clients to which they provide investment services, the nature of the investment products and the type of investment services they provide. Distributors' responsibility is further tightened because they should not deviate from the target market but, at the same time, cannot just rely on the manufacturer's target market without considering how that, as defined by the manufacturer, would fit their client base.

From a product distribution perspective, the 2014 opinion on selling practices recommends that firms ensure effective compliance with MiFID I distribution and disclosure rules. Remarkably, ESMA specifies that 'if, following firms' due diligence, it appears that a particular complex product will never meet the best interests of their clients, or there is a lack of sufficient information available to ascertain the main features and risks of a product, NCAs should monitor that firms do not offer advice on that envisaged product, or sell it at all'. Although this recommendation does not create a legally binding effect on firms, it may nevertheless influence the interpretation of applicable regulatory requirements, indicating a breach of product governance and/or 'know your customer' duties.

Another area of concern for ESMA is the mis-selling risk connected to financial instruments (ie debt securities and cocos) distributed by credit institutions to meet the regulatory requirements for own funds and the minimum requirement for eligible liability (MREL). There is a tension between ensuring that firms optimize their capital structure with affordable loss absorption instruments and

[64] ESMA found, analysing a sample of around 2,750 products, that understanding the risk and reward profile of structured products requires substantial financial expertise.

[65] ESMA, Opinion on Structured Retail Products – Good practices for product governance arrangements.

the need to protect retail clients against risks deriving from highly complex financial instruments.[66] In 2014, the ESAs reminded credit institutions and insurance undertakings about MiFID-applicable regulatory requirements when distributing to their own client base financial instruments that they themselves have issued ('self-placement'). ESAs have also stressed that the holders of these instruments are also exposed to the risk of bail in.[67] Mis-selling risk and bail-in risk are clearly different (retail clients can be exposed to bail-in irrespective of mis-selling practices) but they are intertwined (aggressive distribution practices of bail-in-able debt instruments might increase the risk that inexperienced clients access riskier products and are therefore subject to bail in). Following the approach already adopted in Italy by CONSOB, in 2016 ESMA recommended firms to strenghten disclosure and know your customer requirements recalling that 'the obligation for intermediaries to act in the best interest of their clients should not be compromised as a result of prudential pressures'.[68]

IV. National Supervisory Models

NCAs have a crucial role in the governance and effectiveness of ESMA. NCAs have voting rights on ESMA's Board of Supervisors and they conduct the day-to-day supervision of financial market participants thus 'implementing' ESMA's acts.[69] In its 2016 peer review on MiFID I, ESMA found that the majority of NCAs adopt a 'holistic' approach to supervision, meaning that they typically supervise compliance with respect to the suitability requirements as part of their general and overarching supervision of a firm's conduct, identifying issues as and when they arise on an incidental basis and that in the examined jurisdictions, NCAs conduct an effective supervision.[70]

Although an analysis of the horizontal effects of NCAs supervisory acts is beyond the scope of this book, it is relevant to know what type of acts have been adopted by the NCAs to strengthen distribution, product governance requirements and how these relate to ESMA's conduct of business handbook.

[66] ESMA, Statement on Potential Risks Associated with Investing in Contingent Convertible Instruments, 31 July 2014 (ESMA/2014/944).

[67] ESAs, Placement of Financial Instruments with Depositors, Retail Investors and Policy Holders, 31 July 2014 (JC 2014/62) para 14.

[68] ESMA, Statement MiFID practices for firms selling financial instruments subject to the BRRD resolution regime, 2 June 2016 (ESMA/2016/902), 2.

[69] See E Ferran, 'The Existential Search of the European Banking Authority' (2016) 17 *European Business Organization Law Review* 290.

[70] ESMA, MiFID suitability requirements. 'Peer Review Report', 7 April 2016 (ESMA/2016/584) para 39. ESMA made findings in ten NCAs, including the UK (for insufficient information on whether firms operating on a branch basis and on freedom to provide services were providing investment advice). In the 2018 follow-up 'Report to the Peer Review on MiFID Suitability Requirements' 24 July 2018 (ESMA 42-111-4653), ESMA assessed the progress made by the NCA in remediating these findings.

A. The UK

After the global financial crisis, the UK profoundly changed the architecture of financial supervision shifting from a sectoral tripartite system to a twin-peaks supervisory model.[71] The tripartite system was based on the Financial Service Authority (FSA), entrusted with the prudential and conduct supervision of banking, financial and insurance firms; the Bank of England, responsible for the overall stability of the financial system; and the Treasury, responsible for the institutional structure of the financial regulatory system.

In 2012, the Financial Conduct Authority (FCA) replaced the FSA and became responsible for conduct supervision, whereas the Prudential Regulatory Authority (PRA) which is now part of the Bank of England, was tasked with the micro-prudential supervision of banking, financial and insurance firms.[72] PRA has the power to give 'directions' to FCA, in particular when it is necessary to protect the stability of the UK financial system.[73] The Financial Policy Committee (FPC), created within the Bank of England, is responsible for the macro-prudential supervision and has the power to issue legally binding directions to both FCA and PRA.[74]

The strategic objective of FCA is to 'ensure that the relevant markets function well'. Its operational objectives are securing an appropriate degree of protection for consumers to protect and enhance the integrity of the UK financial system and to promote effective competition in the interests of consumers in the market.[75] The consumer protection objective should be pursued taking into account the general principle that consumers should take responsibility for their decisions.[76]

As part of its rule-making powers, FCA may adopt rules setting up consumer redress schemes by which firms can be required to compensate clients for breach of conduct of business rules[77] and adopt product intervention rules.[78]

[71] See A Hudson, *The Law of Financial Derivatives* (London, Sweet and Maxwell, 2013) 894 who noted that this change was mostly driven by the political willingness to replace the FSA which has been closely identified with the previous Labour government.

[72] The Financial Services Act 2010 conferred on the FSA the financial stability objective and new powers, including a ban on short selling. It required the establishment of a 'consumer financial education body'. On 1 March 2017, in accordance with the Bank of England and Financial Services Act 2016, the PRA Board was replaced by the Prudential Regulation Committee (PRC) and PRA became part of the single legal entity of the Bank of England.

[73] Section 3H of the Financial Services and Markets Act 2000.

[74] Sections 9B and 9H of the Bank of England Act 1998, as amended by the Financial Services Act 2012.

[75] Section 1B(2)(3) of FSMA 2000.

[76] Ibid, s 1C(d).

[77] See Chapter 4.

[78] Section 137D (1)(2) of FSMA. Product governance and product intervention rules have been included in the PROD Product Intervention and Product Governance Sourcebook. The product prohibition or restriction, which can also be permanent, can be adopted not only to achieve the consumer protection objective but also the efficiency and choice objective, but in this case only with the prior permission of the Treasury, the integrity objective (which includes the soundness, stability

The FCA also has private enforcement powers. It may require a firm to compensate losses suffered by clients as a result of breaches of regulatory requirements and may apply to civil courts for an injunction order.[79] It will take into account several criteria before exercising these powers, including whether the loss suffered is large, whether other means of redress are available (Financial Ombudsman Service (FOS) and consumer redress schemes) and whether the person can bring its own civil proceedings.[80] Therefore, FCA expects to exercise its formal restitution powers on rare occasions only.[81]

Turning now to the main initiatives taken by FCA to protect clients against mis-selling, in 2001 FSA started Treating Customers Fairly (TCF) which required firms to act with a view of achieving six consumer outcomes, which built on the principles for business set out in the FCA Handbook, and include compliance with fair treatment clause, suitability rule and obligation to identify a target market for financial instruments.[82] FSA noted that 'consumer responsibility is vital to the effectiveness of financial markets' but this does not mean that 'consumers must always bear such responsibility regardless of what was said or done to them' and 'to shift responsibility onto the consumer just on the basis that he or she has not read the written contract'.[83] TCF was criticised because it relied too much on the capacity of the regulatees to remedy their deficiencies.[84] However, the financial industry complained it risked creating a new regulatory layer, leaving aside the principle of caveat emptor embedded in UK law.[85]

TCF's initiative was complemented by the Retail Distribution Review (RDR) which was launched in 2007 to address the market failures (eg poor quality of advice and conflict of interest triggered by remuneration structures) connected to the provision of investment advice to retail clients.[86] RDR led to the introduction of new COBS rules on remuneration of investment advice offer to retail clients.[87]

and resilience, of the UK financial system) Section 2.8.1 PROD. Similarly to EU product intervention, in the UK the trigger for the FCA's intervention is lower for prohibition/restrictions based on the consumer protection objective (FCA must demonstrate that the measure is necessary to reduce or prevent consumer detriment) than the integrity or competition objective (FCA must demonstrate the existance of a threat) (PROD 2.5.1).

[79] Section 380 (injunction orders) and s 382 (restitutions orders) of FSMA 2000.

[80] FCA, Enforcement guide, para 11.3.

[81] Ibid, para 11.1.

[82] See FSA, 'Treating Customers Fairly after the Point of Sale'. FSA Discussion Paper 7 (2001).

[83] See FSA, 'Treating Customers Fairly – Towards Fair Outcomes for Consumers'. July 2006, 15–16.

[84] See A Georgosouli, 'The FSA's "Treating Customers Fairly" (TCF) Initiative: What is So Good About It and Why It May Not Work' (2011) 38 *Journal of Law and Society* 424 and J Black, 'The Rise, Fall and Fate of Principles-based Regulation', LSE Law, Society and Economy Working Papers 17/2010, 18.

[85] Financial Services Practitioners Panel, Annual Report for 2004/2005, 10.

[86] FSA, 'A Review of Retail Distribution', June 2007.

[87] See in detail M Andenas and I H-Y Chiu, *The Foundations and Future of Financial Regulation* (Abingdon: Taylor and Francis, 2013) 247–248.

In 2015, HM Treasury and FCA started the Financial Advice Market Review (FAMR) to improve the quality, accessibility and affordability of advice for retail clients. This led to the adoption of recommendations to the government, FCA and FOS.[88] One of the most important recommendations, which reflected the fact that advice is costly for firms but not always available for retail clients was to develop a clear framework that gives firms the confidence to provide streamlined advice on simple consumer needs in a proportionate way.[89] Following this recommendation, FCA issued guidance (a non-legally binding act) which detailed the conditions for firms offering 'streamlined advice'.[90] This allows firms to reduce the amount of information collected from the client in a proportionate manner, without lowering the suitability requirements.[91] In addition, following the firms' concerns that FOS' decisions increase legal uncertainty, the review recommended FOS to undertake regular 'Best Practice' roundtables with industry and trade bodies where both sides can discuss relevant issues such as the evidence used when considering historic sales and suitability requirements and improve the transparency of its decisions.[92] A 2017 FCA thematic review of the suitability of pension and investment advice showed that suitable advice was provided in 93.1 per cent of cases.[93]

After the global financial crisis, in addition to supervisory actions aimed at monitoring distribution rules, FSA and the Treasury both acknowledged the need to adopt 'a more proactive, interventionist approach […] so that actual or potential risk is acted upon before it crystallises in significant detriment'.[94] In the 2011 Discussion Paper on product intervention, FSA indicated its intention to shift its supervisory focus from transactions at the point-of-sale to the product manufacturing and design phase.[95] This new approach was complemented by post-sale thematic reviews on complex financial instruments[96] and by the

[88] HM Treasury and FCA, Financial Advice Market Review. March 2016.

[89] The FAMR recommended also to HMT should consult on amending the definition of regulated advice in the existing FSMA Regulated Activities Order (RAO) 2001 (Art 53). The RAO's notion of advice is broader than the MiFIDs because it include sales advice which is not based on a personal recommendation.

[90] FCA, 'Streamlined Advice and Related Consolidated Guidance. Finalised Guidance', September 2017, FG17/8.

Within streamlined advice, the FCA distinguishes between simplified advice, where the firm sets the boundaries of the service and focused advice, where the clients sets the boundaries.

[91] FCA, 'Annual Report and Accounts 2017/18' (for the year ended 31 March 2018), 66.

[92] HM Treasury and FCA, 'Financial Advice Market Review' 52.

[93] FCA, 'Annual Report and Accounts 2017/18', 64.

[94] HM Treasury, 'A New Approach to Financial Regulation: The Blueprint for Reform' (2011) 70.

[95] FCA, 'Product Intervention', DP 11/1. January 2011, 16.

[96] FSA, 'Retail Product Development and Governance – Structured Product Review', March 2012 and the review on contract for difference (CFD) products which resulted in the request to firms to consider whether their client take-on processes for CFD business comply with legal requirements (FCA, 'Dear CEO Letter, "Client take-on review in firms offering contract for difference (CFD) products"', 2 February 2016. Available at: www.fca.org.uk/publication/correspondence/dear-ceo-letter-cfd.pdf 'CFD Firms Fail to Meet our Expectations on Appropriateness Assessments', 29 June 2017. Available at: www.fca.org.uk/publications/multi-firm-reviews/cfd-firms-fail-expectations-appropriateness-assessments) and the Review on Interest Rate Hedging Products (IRHPs)).

adoption of several product intervention rules, based on the new powers conferred by FSA 2012, to restrict the distribution of Cocos,[97] common equity tier 1 (CET1) share instruments issued by mutual societies[98] and unregulated collective investment schemes to retail clients.[99]

B. France

The *Autorité des marchés financiers* (AMF), established in 2003, is responsible for the protection of investors and efficient functioning of financial markets. Since 2010, the *Autorité de contrôle prudentiel*, now *Autorité de contrôle prudentiel et de résolution* (ACPR), is responsible for the micro-prudential supervision and the protection of clients of credit and insurance firms. AMF has regulatory, supervisory and enforcement powers. Besides a wide range of intervention powers regarding securities trading and issuances, the AMF may, at the request of one or more financial service providers or a trade association and after hearing from the Banque de France, certify contracts on financial instruments. To this end, the AMF will assess the conformity of contract terms with the provisions of the AMF General Regulation.

AMF has taken several initiatives to ensure adequate disclosure for complex financial instruments.

In 2010, AMF recommended that firms, through a *position*, should submit the marketing documentation for complex financial instruments for approval before their distribution via advised and non-advised services – except for portfolio management – and to include a specific warning on the complexity of the financial instrument for retail clients.[100] While this measure is not legally binding, failure to comply with it could entail sanctions for non-compliance with other rules (eg those applying to the public solicitation and the requirement to provide investors with an information which is fair, clear and non-misleading). As reported by ESMA's Stakeholder Group, since its publication in 2010, AMF's *position* has contributed to an improvement in product intelligibility.[101]

[97] FCA product intervention rules are laid down in COBS 22.

[98] FCA, 'Restrictions on the Retail Distribution of Regulatory Capital Instruments', October 2014, CP 14/23 and FCA, 'Product Intervention (Contingent Convertible Instruments and Mutual Society Shares) Instrument 2015', 4 June 2015, 2015/29, The new rules entered into force on 1 July 2015 for mutual society shares and on 1 October 2015 for CoCos (COBS 22.2. (mutual society shares) and COBS 22.3 (CoCos)).

[99] FCA, 'Restrictions on the Retail Distribution of Unregulated Collective Investment Schemes and Close Substitutes. Feedback to CP12/19 Including Final Rules, PS13/3'. June 2013. The rules take effect from 1 January 2014.

[100] AMF, '*Position* – La commercialisation des instruments financiers complexes' (DOC-2010-05).

[101] See IMF, 'France: Country Report No 13/182. June 2013' 124–130; ESMA, 'Peer Review 2016', para 115 and ESMA, 'Securities and Markets Stakeholder Group, Own Initiative Report on Product Intervention under MiFIR', 17.

In 2013, in line with Article L533–12 of CMF, AMF issued another *position* recommending some practices for the compilation of contractual documentation related to structured debt instruments.[102] AMF has also anticipated the position expressed by ESAs some years later in connection to self-placement practices.[103]

In line with this supervisory measure, Law No 1691/2016 (*Loi Sapin* 2)[104] prohibited financial firms from sending marketing information to potential retail clients on financial instruments identified by AMF as having one of the following characteristics: the maximum risk is not known when the contract is concluded; the loss can be higher than the initial capital subscribed; and the risk of loss, in comparison to the possible returns, is not 'reasonably comprehensible' taking into account the specific nature of the contract.[105] Based on this provision, on 27 February 2017, AMF prohibited the sending of electronic marketing related to highly speculative and risky financial contracts to retail clients.[106] This ban was originally meant to target binary bets, CFDs and foreign exchange products but, due to resistance expressed by the industry for a 'name-and-shame' effect for such products,[107] was eventually addressed to complex financial instruments with certain characteristics.

C. Italy

The *Commissione Nazionale per le Società e la Borsa* (CONSOB), set up in 1974, is responsible for 'transparency and fairness of conducts' of financial

[102] AMF, '*Position* – Recommandation AMF n° 2013-13 – Guide pour la rédaction des documents commerciaux dans le cadre de la commercialisation des titres de créance structurés'. In 2011, the AMF recommended practices for the marketing of UCITS '*Position* – Recommandation AMF. Guide pour la rédaction des documents commerciaux et la commercialisation des OPC' (DOC-2011-24).

[103] AMF, '*Position* – Placement et commercialisation d'instruments financiers' (DOC-2012-08). Available at: www.amf-france.org/Reglementation/Doctrine/Doctrine-list/Doctrine?docId=workspace %3A%2F%2Financial firmacesStore%2Ff8f0fcf0-0fc4-43f3-8030-984291031bd9&category=III+-+ Prestataires.

[104] Loi n° 2016-1691 du 9 décembre 2016 relative à la transparence, à la lutte contre la corruption et à la modernisation de la vie économique (JORF n°0287 du 10 décembre 2016). The law introduced into the consumer code a general and outright prohibition to sed, either directly or indirectly, electronic advertising to retail clients who are not professional clients (Art 222-16-1 of the Code de la consommation).

[105] Art 533-12-7 of CMF.

[106] AMF, Order of 27 February 2017, Official Journal of 7 March 2017 amending Règlement général de l'AMF Art 314-31-1. The AMF has also conducted a review of the online foreign exchange (forex or FX) market which shown that around 89% of clients had, over a four-year investment period, lost money in CFDs, binary options and other complex financial products (see AMF 'Study of investment performance of individuals trading in CFDs and forex in France' 13 October 2014).

[107] AMF, 'Bilan de la consultation publique de l'AMF clôturée le 30 septembre 2016 relative à l'interdiction de la publicité portant sur certains contrats financiers hautement spéculatifs et risqués' 10 Janvier 2017. Available at: www.amf-france.org/Actualites/Communiques-de-presse/AMF/annee-2017.html?docId=workspace%3A%2F%2FinancialfirmacesStore%2Ff12bcdf3-0a29-4cde-912f-616b0f8f45c8.

services providers, whereas Banca d'Italia is primarily responsible for the micro- and macro-prudential supervision of credit institutions and investment firms and for the conduct supervision of banking services providers.[108]

CONSOB has regulatory, supervisory and enforcement powers. In particular, it may restrict the business, operations or any service where the breach could prejudice general interests and where there is an urgent need to protect investors[109] and may determine the content for financial instruments.[110] CONSOB will adopt the MiFIR's product intervention measures only if there is a significant investor protection concern or a threat to market integrity, whereas Banca d'Italia will be competent if there is a threat to the stability of whole or part of the financial system.[111] In addition to MiFIR product-intervention powers, CONSOB and Banca d'Italia have been vested with the power to suspend for a period of time not exceeding 60 days the marketing and sale of financial instruments and structured deposits if the conditions of Articles 40, 41 and 42 of MiFIR are met.[112] Even if the two authorities must hear each other before taking any product intervention measure,[113] the allocation of product intervention powers along supervisory objectives could be problematic for the effective and consistent application of MiFIR because the two authorities may have different views regarding the interpretation of the criteria and factors to determine the existence of a threat to market integrity, financial stability or the significant investor protection concern.

A distinctive feature of the Italian securities markets is that retail investors hold a large share of bail-inable debt[114] and rely, more than in other EU jurisdictions, on sovereign and corporate bonds.[115] CONSOB has also stressed that investors have a low level of financial education, which is reflected in the low propensity to ask for investment advice, and has taken numerous initiatives in 2017 (ie conferences in schools and universities) to strengthen financial education.[116]

[108] See Art 5(3) of the TUF and Art 127(01) of the Legislative Decree No 385/1993 (Testo Unico Bancario, TUB).

[109] Art 51 of TUF.

[110] Ibid, Art 95(4). On the CONSOB's powers to intervene on financial contracts see, in detail, R D'Ambrosio, 'La borsa e la finanza' in E Galanti, R D'Ambrosio, AV Guccione (eds), *Storia della legislazione bancaria finanziaria e assicurativa Dall'Unità d'Italia al 2011* (Venezia, Marsilio Editori, 2012), 308, 370, 477.

[111] Art 2(6) of Legislative Decree No 129/2017.

[112] Art 7bis(5) of TUF.

[113] Ibid, Art 7bis(6).

[114] EBA, Statement, 6.

[115] For instance, whilst in Italy bonds represent 9% of household financial wealth, they account for 3% in Germany, 2% in France and 1% in Spain. By contrast, shares of listed companies account for 2% of household financial wealth in Italy, 5% in France and Germany and 6% in Spain (see CONSOB, Annual Report 2017, 192).

[116] CONSOB, Annual Report 2017, 31 March 2018 38. M Gentile, N Linciano, P Soccorso, *Financial Advice Seeking, Financial Knowledge and Overconfidence.* Evidence from the Italian market. CONSOB Quaderni di Finanza, No 83, March 2016, 30 and See also N Linciano and P Soccorso, 'Challenges in Ensuring Financial Competencies – Essays on How to Measure Financial Knowledge, Target Beneficiaries *and Deliver Educational Programmes' Quaderni di Finanza,* n 84. October 2017.

CONSOB has complemented its focus on financial education with supervisory acts aimed at ensuring compliance with suitability rule in the distribution of complex financial instruments and bail-inable debt. Before the crisis, in 2007, CONSOB recommended investment firms to establish mechanisms (not only organisational but also contractual) to ensure effective compliance with firms' employees with MiFID suitability requirement given that activities like self-placement may in practice result into investment advice.[117]

In 2009 CONSOB recommendeded that firms (a) provide adequate information about potential risks in disinvestment of illiquid financial instruments (eg bonds issued by credit institutions, insurance policies and OTC derivatives), (b) identify the target market and give specific information about the cost components (eg fair value and price) of financial instruments and (c) carry out the suitability test when distributing OTC derivatives to clients.[118]

Even if after the crisis CONSOB has not taken binding measures to restrict or prohibit the distribution of financial instruments, in 2014 it recommended that firms do not distribute certain complex financial instruments (eg instruments derived from securitisation, instruments which foresee a conversion into equity or write down, instruments that are credit linked, and OTC derivatives with speculative purposes).[119] If a firm does not comply with this recommendation, CONSOB recommends that its management must inform the client that CONSOB does not consider these instruments to be appropriate for retail clients. Non-compliance can trigger supervisory action.

In 2015, in anticipation of ESMA's 2016 statement on MiFID practice for firms selling instruments subject to the BRRD, CONSOB recommended that firms provided appropriate information about the fact that capital instruments may be subject to write down or conversion and revised their internal processes for the assessment of suitability and appropriateness in light of these regulatory innovations.[120] In 2016, CONSOB launched a public consultation on a recommendation that clients should be provided with a standardised document setting out information about the financial instrument.[121] According to CONSOB, these

[117] CONSOB, Prime linee di indirizzo in tema di consulenza in materia di investimenti – Esito delle consultazioni. 30 ottobre 2007, 4.

[118] CONSOB, Comunicazione n. 9019104 del 2 Marzo 2009 sul dovere di correttezza e trasparenza dell'intermediario in sede di distribuzione di prodotti finanziari illiquidi. Available at: www.consob.it/documents/46180/46181/c9019104.pdf/64f86e70-2bb0-460a-8f60-3dd079b6341d.

[119] CONSOB, Comunicazione n. 0097996 del 22 dicembre 2014 sulla distribuzione di prodotti finanziari complessi ai clienti *retail*. Available at: www.consob.it/main/documenti/bollettino2014/c0097996.htm.

[120] CONSOB, Comunicazione n. 0090430 del 24 November 2015. Decreti legislativi nn. 180 e 181 del 16 novembre 2015 di recepimento della direttiva 2014/59/UE. Prestazione dei servizi e delle attività di investimento, nonché dei servizi accessori. Available at: www.consob.it/documents/46180/46181/c0090430.pdf/09b990c7-1e84-486c-bc24-9875e68e63cd.

[121] CONSOB, *Documento di consultazione. Principi guida sulle informazioni chiave da fornire ai clienti al dettaglio nella distribuzione di prodotti finanziari*. The consultation was open from 9 May to 6 June 2016. Available at: www.consob.it/documents/46180/46181/cons_20160509_inf_chiave.pdf/71c2a00a-4303-474e-bda8-f870a7eed943.

measures contributed to an increase in the proportion of debt retail holdings being distributed on an advice basis as well as to a significant overall decrease in domestic retail holdings of bank debt instruments.[122] It was noted, however, that the monitoring and supervision of these soft-law acts adopted in the aftermath of the crisis was not always adequate and *de facto* has not prevented the distribution of large amounts of subordinated debt to retail unsophisticated clients.[123]

D. Spain

The *Comisión Nacional del Mercado de Valores* (CNMV) was established in 1988 to ensure the transparency of financial markets, the correct formation of prices and the protection of investors. *Banco de España* is responsible for the micro and macro-prudential supervision of financial market participants and conduct supervision of banking service providers. The CNMV has regulatory, supervisory and enforcement powers. After the financial crisis, its investor protection mandate was driven by the need to reduce detriment connected with the distribution of hybrid financial products, especially *participaciones preferentes* to retail clients. *Participaciones preferentes* are perpetual and variable income financial instruments with no voting rights or shareholding, which rank below subordinate debt in the case of the issuer's insolvency. Over the last ten years these hybrid financial instruments represented the most important capital-raising vehicle for saving banks (*cajas*).[124] Between 1998 and 2012, €115 billion (1.2% of Spanish GDP) was issued and subscribed by 3.1 million retail clients. However, at the end of 2008, financial firms could no longer repurchase/redeem *participaciones preferentes* and institutional investors stopped purchasing them. As a result, firms engaged in aggressive distribution practices, selling these instruments to unsophisticated retail investors without any suitability or appropriateness tests and without providing adequate information on their risks.

The large detriment caused by mis-selling led national authorities to adopt, albeit some years later, incisive measures to limit the issuance of complex financial products,[125] to strengthen out-of-court resolution for these disputes[126]

[122] EBA and ESMA, 'Statement on the Treatment of Retail Holdings of Debt Financial Instruments' 23. In particular, these decreased from €415.6 billion (38.1% of total retail stock of financial instruments) in December 2011 to €122 billion (12.7% of total retail stock of financial instruments) in September 2017.

[123] See F Capriglione, La nuova finanza: operatività, supervisione, tutela giurisdizionale. Il caso «Italia». Considerazioni introduttive (la finanza post-crisi: forme operative e meccanismi di controllo) (2017) *Contratto e Impresa* 75.

[124] See especially P-H Conac, *Mis-selling of Financial Products: Subordinated Debt and Self-placement*, European Think Tank, 12 June 2018, 18.

[125] Thirteenth additional provision of Law No 9/2012. See Chapter 2.

[126] See Chapter 3, below.

and to enhance investors' awarness about these products. In 2013, the CNMV Circular 3/2013[127] required firms to provide a suitability statement to clients, explaining how the recommendation met their needs. The circular also mandates firms to include a specific warning in the event that the assessment cannot be carried out or that it has found the product to be inappropriate. In addition, if investment firms wish to include a generic clause in the contractual documentation indicating that the client recognises that it has not received advice, the client must provide a handwritten note confirming that advice has not been provided when purchasing a complex product. The aim of this measure is to make clients aware whether or not advice has been given. Although ESMA criticised this measure because a handwritten note 'could be used by firms to protect themselves in any supervisory case or litigation that sought to establish whether advice had been provided to the client',[128] CNMV held that it discourages firms from including those types of generic clause in the documents.[129]

In 2015, the Spanish Ministry of Economy and Competitiveness issued an order, in line with a CNMV proposal[130] requiring financial firms to classify financial instruments on the basis of a risk indicator reflected in a six-colour scale.[131] The level of risk of the financial instrument and warnings regarding the risk of liquidity and complexity was to be made public when the instrument was marketed to clients.

CNMV did not adopt any measures to restrict the distribution of financial instruments but, in 2017, it required firms distributing CFDs or forex products with leverage of over 10 times or binary options to expressly inform clients that these productys were not suitable for retail clients.[132]

V. A Comparative Assessment

NCAs have introduced several measures to supplement distribution and product governance requirements. Supervisory measures and approaches vary across

[127] Circular 3/2013, de 12 de junio, de la Comisión Nacional del Mercado de Valores, sobre el desarrollo de determinadas obligaciones de información a los clientes a los que se les prestan servicios de inversión, en relación con la evaluación de la conveniencia e idoneidad de los instrumentos financieros (BOE n 146, miércoles 19 de junio de 2013, p 46150).

[128] ESMA, 'MiFID suitability requirements. Peer Review' para 122.

[129] Ibid, para 136.

[130] CNMV, *Proyecto de circular sobre advertencias relativas a instrumentos financieros*, Enero 2015.

[131] Ministerio de Economía y Competitividad, Orden ECC/2316/2015, de 4 de noviembre, relativa a las obligaciones de información y clasificación de productos financieros (BOE n 265, 5 de noviembre de 2015, p 104567).

[132] CNMV, *Medidas en relación con la comercialización de CFD y otros productos especulativos entre clientes minoristas.* 21 de marzo 2017. Previously, the CNMV had conducted a thematic review on contracts for difference (CFD) and found that 75% of people investing in CFDs between 1 January 2012 and 31 October 2013 had lost money). See, in more detail, CNMV. Annual report 2014, 172.

jurisdictions. The AMF targeted complex financial instruments,[133] trying to avoid detriment, *ex ante*, through approval processes on marketing material. Other NCAs, like CONSOB and CNMV focused on the distribution process ensuring clients received effective information about complex financial instruments.[134] The FCA has taken several intiatives to improve the quality of advice and has adopted binding measures to restrict the distribution of complex financial products to retail clients. National financial market specificities play a crucial role in determining the supervisory approach. For instance, CONSOB's focus on illiquid securities and bail-inable debt is driven by the fact that Italy is the Eurozone country with the highest volume of retail bank debt holdings. AMF's focus on complex financial instruments is driven by the fact that France registered the highest volume of structured retail products sales in 2017.[135] FCA's focus on investment advice reflects the fact that UK retail clients rely on advice and independent advice much more than continental clients.

The overview of national supervisory measures has also shown that the influence between ESMA and the NCAs is bi-univocal. In certain instances, NCA's measures have driven ESMA's supervisory approach. For instance, ESMA's ban on CFDs and binary options[136] or its measures to foster disclosure on bail-inable instruments have been *de facto* anticipated by similar measures taken by the NCAs some years before.[137] In other instances and, particularly with regard to the supervision of the suitability rule, ESMA has played a driving role in promoting and ensuring the full compliance of market participants, via peer review and guidelines.

Legally, an interesting aspect which has emerged across these jurisdictions is that, even if all the NCAs have broad investor protection mandates and the formal power to ban financial instruments, they have preferred to resort to non-legally binding measures to convey their supervisory expectations. Only the FCA, introduced before MiFIR came into force, restrictions to the sale of certain financial instruments. Other NCAs, which are outside the scope of this book (eg German BaFin and the Belgian FSMA) adopted a mixed-approach, seeking voluntary commitments with the industry to limit the sale of complex finanical products and adopting binding product intervention measures for certain specific products.[138]

Recourse to non-legally binding acts could be explained by the need to limit potential (legal) risks arising from the enhanced supervisory attention concerning

[133] AMF, *Position* n 2010-05.

[134] See CONSOB, Comunicazione n 9019104 and CNMV, Circular 3/2013.

[135] ESMA, Report on risks, trends, 57.

[136] See Recital No 35 of ESMA Decision on CFDs.

[137] See CONSOB's measures mentioned above.

[138] See in detail ESMA Securities and Markets Stakeholder Group, 'Own Initiative Report on Product Intervention under MiFIR', 10.

the substance of the contractual relationship between firms and clients.[139] Even if soft-law acts do not, per se, reduce the effectiveness of the supervisory action, given that NCAs have the power to follow-up on potential non-compliance in their ongoing supervision, they may reveal their preference for soft rather than hard product intervention measures.[140] It is therefore likely that EU product intervention measures will only be taken when other investor protection and previous NCA measures fail to produce the desired effect,[141] and ESMA will convey its supervisory expectations on complex financial products via soft-law instruments. However, these add a 'quasi-regulatory' layer of 'contract governance'; this begs the question on what civil law effects retail clients and firm should expect from this type of supervisory acts.

VI. Shaping Private Law Through Supervisory Standards

A. Horizontal Direct Effects: Product Intervention

In our view, horizontal or civil law effects may derive from both binding and non-binding legal acts. However, the intensity of the horizontal effect depends on the nature of the act. To begin with, only legally binding acts, if directly applicable and sufficiently detailed, may affect the contractual rights of financial market participants (horizontal direct effects), for instance, by suspending or terminating them. In practice, these type of effects may be triggered by MiFIR's product intervention measures which have a direct bearing on the substance of the contractual rights and duties of the parties.[142] Since these measures encroach on the freedom to conduct a business of financial market participants, which is protected by Article 16 of the Charter, their legality, from a judicial review perspective, needs to be assessed in light of Article 52 of the Charter.

The CJEU has consistently held that freedom to conduct a business is not absolute, but must be viewed in relation to its social function. This freedom may be subject to a broad range of interventions on the part of public authorities, which may limit the exercise of economic activity in the public interest.[143]

[139] See Y Svetiev, A Ottow. 'Financial Supervision in the Interstices Between Private and Public Law' 10(4) *European Review of Contract Law* 496–544 at 542–543.

[140] See also ESMA, MiFID suitability requirements 'Peer Review', para 50 (with regard to some NCAs (BE, FR, IT, PT) ESMA defined as 'more conservative' the supervisory approach to operate voluntary agreements from firms not to sell complex products to retail investors or by issuing warning notices that some complex products may not be, à priori, suitable for retail investors.

[141] See, in this regard, ESMA Securities and Markets Stakeholder Group, 'Own Initiative Report on Product Intervention under MiFIR', 8.

[142] For the direct applicability of decisions, see Case C-9/70, *Franz Grad v Finanzamt Traunstein*, ECLI:EU:C:1970:78, para 5.

[143] Case C-283/11, *Sky Österreich GmbH v Österreichischer Rundfunk*, ECLI:EU:C:2013:28, para 46.

The need to reduce mis-selling risks and restore retail clients' confidence in financial markets – which ESMA considered as the main rationales for banning CFDs and binary options[144] – are objectives of general interest recognised by EU law. The temporary nature of the measure would also ensure that the essence of the freedom is not undermined.[145]

MiFIR literally limits product restrictions and prohibitions to the 'marketing, sale and distribution of financial instruments' (thus for the future) and does not expressly empower ESAs and NCAs to suspend or terminate contractual obligations.[146] For this reason, it seems that product intervention measures should not produce retroactive effects, namely they should not affect the contracts concluded before their entry into force and whose obligations have not yet completely discharged by the parties. In this vein, ESMA clarified, after its decisions restricting the distribution of CFDs and binary options, that firms are not required to apply the product intervention measures to CFDs sold to retail clients prior to this date. Firms exercising their discretion to close the existing CFD and binary option positions of retail clients, other than in accordance with existing terms and conditions and prior to the measures coming into effect, without their clients' express consent, would be in breach of Article 24 of MiFID II.[147] This means that clients must comply with the contractual obligations they entered into before the measures came into force.[148]

However, MiFIR allows competent authorities to restrict or prohibit 'a type of financial activity or practice' (ie cross-selling). This leaves open the question of whether ESMA or NCAs could, in fact, restrict activities that have started but have not yet been concluded. In our view, this is legally possible.

EU courts have accepted the legitimacy of EU law acts which adversely affect the rights of the addressee in the future but have an impact on past events which have not yet been concluded (so-called apparent retroactivity),[149] provided that

[144] ESMA, Decision on Binary Options, paras 93–94 and Decision on CFDs, para 142.

[145] See D'Ambrosio, 'The Temporary Intervention Powers of the European Banking Authority and the European Securities and Markets Authority', 1.

[146] See in contrast Arts 49(2) and 69 of the Bank Recovery and Resolution Directive (2014/59/EU) (BRRD).

[147] ESMA, Questions and Answers on ESMA's Temporary Product Intervention Measures on the Marketing, Distribution or Sale of CFDs and Binary Options to Retail Clients, 20 July 2018 (ESMA35-36-1262).

[148] However, ESMA clarified that the measure only restricts offering of these instruments, not their trading. Retail clients can transfer their contractual position to a third party. See for more detail on the civil law effects of this transfer, JH Dalhuisen, *Dalhuisen on Transnational Comparative, Commercial, Financial and Trade Law. Financial Products, Financial Services and Financial Regulation*, vol. 3 (Oxford, Hart Publishing, 2016) 264.

[149] Only in exceptional circumstances, have Union courts accepted the legitimacy of measures affecting situations that have already been concluded (actual retroactivity). For more details, see Herwig CH Hofmann, Gerard C Rowe, and Alexander H Türk, *Administrative Law and Policy of the European Union* (Oxford, Oxford University Press, 2011) 181.

the public interest underlying the measure overrides the private interest in maintaining the existing legal situation[150] and that the change was foreseeable for a prudent and well-informed addressee.[151]

Finally, MiFIR does not detail the civil law consequences for breaching a product intervention measure.[152] However, it is argued that, given the direct applicability of the act and the need to ensure its practical purpose, if after the entry into force of the measure, the parties conclude a contract in breach of these measures, the contractual obligations will not be binding on the parties. The specific civil law consequence (ie nullity, annullability, unenforceability) will be determined in accordance with the principles of effectiveness and equivalence, taking into account the nature and importance of the public interest (ie protecting investors or ensuring the financial stability of the Union) underlying the measure.[153] However, in order not to make the enforcement of their rights excessively difficult, it should be sufficient for the client to prove that the contract was subject to a product intervention rule and that they entered into it after the relevant product intervention rule came into effect.[154]

B. Horizontal Indirect Effects

(i) Guidelines

ESMA's non-binding legal acts of general application may offer valuable aid to national courts in the interpretation of MiFID II regulatory duties and general concepts of national private law (horizontal indirect effects). This applies, in particular, to ESMA's guidelines which may be defined as 'rules of conduct that are laid down in instruments which have not been attributed legally binding force as such, but nevertheless may have certain (indirect) legal effects, and that are aimed

[150] Case C-84/78, *Tomadini Snc v Amministrazione delle finanze dello Stato*, ECLI:EU:C:1979:129, para 20.

[151] Case C-350/88, *Société française des Biscuits Delacre and others v Commission*, ECLI:EU:C:1990:71, para 37.

[152] Section 137D(7) of the FSMA (FCA may decide that an agreement concluded in breach of these rules is unenforceable or that any money or other property paid or transferred under a relevant agreement or obligation by any person shall be recovered or that compensation shall be paid for any loss resulting from paying or transferring any money or other property under that agreement).

[153] Product intervention measures may qualify as an event which occurs out of some failure connected with one of the parties, beyond their control and that makes it unlawful to comply with the contractual obligations (eg payment). See also the definition of termination event due to illegality under s 5(b)(i) of the ISDA Master Agreement 2002, as supplemented by ISDA, Illegality/Force Majeure Protocol published on 11 July 2012. The Master Agreement sets out also specific provisions for the deferral of the payment due in case of a termination event due to illegality (s 5(d) ISDA MA 2002).

[154] Section PROD 2.3.1. By contrast, clients holding contracts made before the introduction of product intervention rules would either need to demonstrate that the advice they received was unsuitable or that they had bought the product after receiving a misleading financial promotion.

at and may produce practical effects'.[155] In the same vein, the CJEU has repeatedly held that soft-law instruments are not 'rules of law' but 'rules of practice' that produce two types of effect. First, in an individual case, the EU institution or body cannot depart from the guideline without giving reasons that are compatible with the principles of equal treatment and protection of legitimate expectations.[156] Second, national courts must take soft law into account in their interpretation of EU law.[157] This second effect, which is a variety of horizontal indirect effects, should be examined more in detail.

In *Grimaldi*, the CJEU held that national courts are 'bound to take recommendations into consideration in order to decide disputes submitted to them, in particular where they cast light on the interpretation of national measures adopted in order to implement them or where they are designed to supplement binding Community provisions'.[158] In this judgment, the CJEU tranformed a recommendation from a 'voluntary interpretation aid', into a 'mandatory interpretation aid' for national courts:[159] courts do not have the duty to ensure full application of soft-law rules but must take them into account when interpreting EU law.

This principle has been further developed in the recent *Koninklijke KPN NV v ACM*[160] where the referring court asked the CJEU what importance should be attached to the fact that a decision adopted by the Dutch competent authority for the telecommunications sector, setting price caps for fixed and mobile call termination services, was based on the cost methodology described in a Commission Recommendation.[161]

The CJEU reiterated that 'courts have the duty to take recommendations into account where the recommendations cast light on the interpretation of national

[155] See L Senden, *Soft Law in European Community Law* (Oxford, Hart Publishing, 2004) 112. See also F Terpan, 'Soft Law in the European Union – The Changing Nature of EU Law' (2015) 21 *European Law Journal* 71.

[156] See, in particular, case C-526/14, *Kotnik and Others v Državni zbor Republike Slovenije*, ECLI:EU:C:2016:570, para 40.

[157] Joined cases C-189/02 P, C-202/02 P, C-205/02 P to C-208/02 P and C-213/02 P, *Dansk Rørindustri and Others v Commission*, ECLI:EU:C:2005:408, para 211 (with regard to Commission guidelines); opinion of AG in case C-628/13, *Jean-Bernard Lafonta* ECLI:EU:C:2015:162, para 41 (with regard to CESR, 'Market Abuse Directive Level 3 – Second set of CESR Guidance and Information on the Common Operation of the Directive to the Market'. July 2007 (CESR/06-562b)); Case T-712/15, *Crédit Mutuel Arkéa v ECB*, ECLI:EU:T:2017:900, para 78 (with regard to CEBS guidelines); ESAs Board of Appeal, *SV Capital OU v EBA* 24 June 2013. BoA 2014–C1–02, para 56 (with regard to EBA, 'Guidelines on the Assessment of the Suitability of Members of the Management Body and Key Function Holders', 22 November 2012 (EBA/GL/2012/06)).

[158] Case C-322/88, *Grimaldi v Fonds des maladies professionnelles*, ECLI:EU:C:1989:646, para 18. See also case C-188/91, *Deutsche Shell AG v Hauptzollamt Hamburg-Harburg*, ECLI:EU:C:1993:24, para 18

[159] See Senden, *Soft Law in European Community Law*, 391.

[160] Case C-28/15, *Koninklijke KPN NV v ACM*, ECLI:EU:C:2016:692, para 52.

[161] Commission Recommendation 2009/396/EC of 7 May 2009 on the Regulatory Treatment of Fixed and Mobile Termination Rates in the EU [2009] OJ L 124/67). Competent authorities are required to take the utmost account of those recommendations in carrying out their tasks and where a national regulatory authority chooses not to follow a recommendation, it must inform the Commission, giving the reasons for its position.

measures adopted in order to implement them or where they are designed to supplement binding EU provisions'. Importantly, it added that a national court 'may depart from Recommendation 2009/396 only where it considers that this is required on grounds related to the facts of the individual case, in particular the specific characteristics of the market of the Member State in question'.[162] In practice, this introduces a duty for national courts to give reasons for deviations from soft-law instruments,[163] thus extending to national courts the duty of the national regulatory authorities to take the Commission's Recommendation (set out by Directive 2002/21/EC) into account.[164]

The case law confirms that soft-law rules should guide judicial interpretation not only where they clarify or specify existing requirements but also where they introduce new requirements that supplement (ie complete[165]) existing legislative requirements. In that case, even if national law does not give rise to interpretative doubts, national courts should make an effort (without being obliged) to interpret EU law in light of the soft-law rule. Clearly, the standardisation effects of soft law may be facilitated (or may simply be unavoidable) where regulatory requirements are broadly phrased.[166] To understand where ESMA's soft-law instruments introduce requirements that go beyond regulatory requirements it is necessary to assess the purpose of the rule at stake. For example, it is consistent with the purposes of Articles 54(1) and 55(3) of Commission MiFID II Regulation that firms should not contract out their liability for breach of the suitability rule. If a firm, which unilaterally drafts standard contract terms, were to be allowed to contract out its liability for any breaches of conduct of business rules, the purpose of these rules would be completely undermined.

Finally, even if soft-law rules cannot trigger a duty to conform interpretation, the duty of sincere cooperation between national and EU institutions, requires courts to motivate potential deviation from the recommendation expressed in a guideline.

(ii) Other Quasi-regulatory Acts

The duty to take into account guidelines for interpretation of EU and national law should apply to draft technical standards as well as Q&A and other soft-law

[162] Case C-28/15, *Koninklijke KPN NV* v ACM, paras 41–42. See, case C-526/14, *Kotnik and Others*, para 44 where the CJEU held that the Banking Communication 'is not capable of imposing independent obligations on the Member States'. This conclusion, however, cannot be read as overturning *Grimaldi* because it did not concern the effects of soft law towards national courts.

[163] This duty was spelt out more clearly by AG Kokott in Case 226/11, *Expedia Inc*, ECLI:EU:C:2012:544, para 39 but the CJEU did not follow the AG's view in that case.

[164] Art 19(2) of Directive 2002/21/EC of the European Parliament and of the Council of 7 March 2002 on a common regulatory framework for electronic communications networks and services (Framework Directive) (OJ 2002 L 108, p 33).

[165] The term 'supplement' has been translated into completare (Italian), compléter (French), completar (Spanish).

[166] See Simoncini, *Administrative Regulation Beyond the Non-delegation Doctrine*, 84.

instruments adopted by ESMA. The potential horizontal effects of draft technical standards was considered by Advocate General Jaskiinen, in his opinion in *UK v European Parliament and Council*, where the UK sought the annulment of certain provisions of the CRD IV on remuneration contesting, inter alia, the fact that Article 94(2) of this directive empowers EBA to develop a draft regulatory technical standard implying the 'taking of strategic decisions or policy choices'. However, the Advocate General dismissed this argument concluding that 'draft measures have no legal effects going beyond the internal decision-making process of the Commission [...] and thus "are in themselves incapable of harmonizing any national provisions or affecting the rights and obligations of individuals"'.[167] This conclusion denies horizontal direct effects of draft technical standards, but it does not prevent the possibility that these are used by national courts when it is necessary to resolve a problem in the interpretation or to supplement existing legislative provisions.

VII. Preliminary Conclusion

This chapter has shown that ESMA's acts will have a significant effect on the private law relationship between firms and their clients.

ESMA's binding legal acts addressed to market participants, like product intervention measures, create horizontal direct effects. This, therefore, enables an investor to invoke in a civil proceeding any act where the investment firm eihter concludes a contract or imposes a contract term that is in contrast with these measures.

Due to procedural constraints on the adoption of binding legal acts and the preference expressed by the examined NCAs for soft-law forms of 'product-related' measures, it could be supposed that ESMA will use soft-law instruments (eg guidelines, statements, Q&As) much more frequently than product intervention powers to convey its supervisory expectations to NCAs and market participants. Although this type of act neither creates rights nor imposes obligations on third parties, it can nevertheless produce horizontal effects which greatly increase the protection of clients vis-à-vis firms in contractual relations. As the CJEU held in recent judgments, national courts have a duty to take into account soft law, when interpreting national law.

This form of horizontal indirect effect is not as strong as the horizontal indirect effect of legislation (courts are not obliged to give full effect to soft-law rules, only to take them into account) but it will increase the uniform application of general regulatory duties, providing guidance on how they should be interpreted

[167] Opinion of the AG Jääskinen, in case C-507/13, *UK v European Parliament and Council of the European Union*, ECLI:EU:C:2014:2394, para 64. Subsequently, on 9 December 2014, the UK withdrew its application and the case has been removed from the court registry.

in specific circumstances.[168] The horizontal indirect effects of soft law will also strengthen the 'mutual learning process' between supervisors and courts,[169] helping them to interpret the technical aspects of the dispute but leaving national judges with a necessary margin of flexibility to assess the specific issue at stake and will increase the uniform application of the conduct of business rules which are drafted in broad terms

The horizontal indirect effect of ESMA's conduct of business handbook will also contribute to the hybridisation of national private law. National private law should be interpreted in light of conduct of business rules which, in turn, should be read in light of soft-law instruments. For example, ESMA guidelines may offer support to arguments that contractual disclaimers which rule out a firm's liability for the suitability rule should not be enforceable or that compliance with the fair treatment clause should be effective, ensuring the client's understanding of the risks involved in the financial instrument.

To assess the extent to which MiFID II conduct of business rules and ESMA's conduct of business handbook may actually affect private law duties and remedies, the next two chapters will analyse how national ADR bodies and courts have interpreted and enforced conduct of business rules in investment services disputes.

[168] N Moloney, 'Institutional Governance and Capital Markets Union: Incrementalism or a "Big Bang"'? 407.

[169] OO Cherednichenko, 'Contract Governance in the EU, Contract Governance in the EU: Conceptualising the Relationship between Investor Protection Regulation and Private Law' 21(4) *European Law Journal* 500–520 at 515.

4

Civil Law Effects of Conduct of Business Rules in Out-of-Court Proceedings

I. Out-of-Court Retail Dispute Resolution in EU Law

Access to out-of-court dispute resolution mechanisms for retail clients is a key element of the EU retail market regulation.

In 2001 the Commission launched the Financial Services Complaints Network (FIN-NET)[1] to provide consumers with easy access to Alternative Dispute Resolution (ADR) procedures in cross-border disputes, put the consumer in touch with the relevant ADR scheme and provide the necessary information about it.[2] MiFID I encouraged Member States to set up ADR procedures for consumer disputes.[3]

After the global financial crisis, the Organisation for Economic Co-operation and Development (OECD) recommended that in national jurisdictions 'consumers have access to adequate complaints handling and redress mechanisms that are accessible, affordable, independent, fair, accountable, timely and efficient'.[4] Member States have set up ADR procedures within national supervisory authorities and have created special ADR schemes to compensate the losses suffered by retail clients for the mis-selling of particular financial products. MiFID II required Member States to set up out-of-court dispute resolution and other mechanisms to ensure compensation for breaches of MiFID II and MiFIR.[5] MiFID II complements the new legislative framework for consumer ADR procedures laid

[1] Commission, IP/01/152, February 2001.

[2] Commission, Report Brussels, December 2017 FIN-NET activity report 2016. Despite the network's undisputed success since 2001, many consumers and businesses are unaware that it exists. The Commission therefore announced in its Consumer Financial Services Action Plan: Better Products, More Choice (COM(2017) 139).

[3] Art 53 of MiFID I.

[4] OECD, 'G20 High-level Principles on Financial Consumer Protection'. October 2011.

[5] Art 75 of MiFID II.

down in 2013 by the ADR Directive and the ODR Regulation[6] and supports the Commission's initiatives to strengthen ADR mechanisms for investment services disputes.[7]

This chapter explores the role of private law in out-of-court dispute resolution, namely how ADR bodies apply private law concepts in the resolution of retail clients' disputes. Under the ADR Directive, ADR entities are free to choose the legal basis they use to resolve the dispute (ie regulation, private law, equity). However, Article 69(2) of the MiFID II strengthens the law enforcement function of ADR procedures by linking compensation to breaches of MiFID II. In addition, ADR bodies are generally set up within supervisory authorities and may tend to apply regulatory and supervisory standards when resolving a dispute. It will be argued that the application of regulatory principles and private law concepts to resolve disputes will give rise to mixed or hybrid private law duties and remedies, transforming ADR proceedings in mechanisms to ensure the effective application of EU conduct of business rules.

To demonstrate this hypothesis, this chapter illustrates the main innovations of the ADR Directive and MiFID II and examines the institutional features of ADR procedures in the four jurisdictions. It then assesses the impact of regulation and private law in their adjudicative approach. Building on this analysis, the chapter assesses whether the 'law enforcement' function of ADR procedures and the correspondent emergence of a hybrid private law are in line with the ADR Directive and MiFID II as well as with the general principles of EU law and fundamental rights.

II. The EU Regulatory Framework

A. ADR Directive

The ADR Directive harmonises national consumer ADR procedures transforming the principles of the Commission's recommendations 98/257/EC[8] and 2001/310/EC[9] (expertise, independence, impartiality, transparency, effectiveness, fairness, liberty and legality) into minimum binding legal requirements.[10]

[6] Directive 2013/11/EU of the European Parliament and of the Council of 21 May 2013 on alternative dispute resolution for consumer disputes (ADR Directive) [2013] OJ L 165/63 and Regulation (EU) No 524/2013 of 21 May 2013 of the European Parliament and of the Council on online dispute resolution for consumer disputes (ODR Regulation) [2013] OJ L 165/1.

[7] Commission, Green Paper on retail financial services: better products, more choice, and greater opportunities for consumers and businesses. Brussels (COM(2015) 630) and Commssion, Study on the role of digitalisation and innovation in creating a true single market for retail financial services and insurance. June 2016 (FISMA/2015/075D).

[8] Commission Recommendation 98/257/EC of 30 March 1998 on the principles applicable to the bodies responsible for out-of-court settlement of consumer disputes [1998] OJ L 115/31.

[9] Commission Recommendation 2001/310/EC of 4 April 2001 on the principles for out-of-court bodies involved in the consensual resolution of consumer disputes [2001] OJ L 109/56.

[10] Art 2(3) of ADR Directive.

The directive covers cross-border and domestic consumer disputes concerning contractual obligations stemming from sales or services contracts, including in investment service contracts.[11] However, it only applies to consumer disputes, so it should not apply, except as otherwise provided by national law, to disputes regarding a retail client who does not qualify as a consumer.[12]

The directive applies to procedures where the ADR body proposes or imposes a solution or brings the parties together with the aim of facilitating an amicable solution, without prejudice to Directive 2008/52/EC which harmonises mediation procedures.[13] It does not apply to the complaint-handling procedures set up by financial firms to deal with clients' complaints.[14]

ADR bodies may use different legal basis to resolve the dispute (eg legal provisions, considerations of equity, codes of conduct) provided that the types of rules used are made publicly available and the persons in charge of the procedure need have (only) a general understanding of law.[15] Hence, the decision of the ADR body does not need to comply with legal provisions. This model of 'light law enforcement'[16] is mitigated, only for the cases where the ADR procedure imposes a solution, by the fact that that solution will be in line with the level of protection afforded to consumers by national mandatory law.[17] In the context of investment service disputes, this provision entails that adjudicative ADR schemes should comply with the mandatory requirements of national law transposing MiFID II.

Finally, to ensure that ADR entities function properly, the directive requires Member States to designate a competent authority to assess whether the dispute resolution entities qualify as ADR entities and comply with the quality requirements of the directive. In the examined jurisdictions, the supervisory authorities have been designated as competent authorities to monitor compliance of ADR schemes with the directive.

B. MiFID II

MiFID II strengthens the out-of-court resolution of retail financial disputes in two ways.

[11] Art 2(2d,g) and Recital 16 of ADR Directive. Recital 7 of the Commission's proposal included the complaints submitted by traders against consumers in the scope of the directive. Contrary to the Commission's proposal, the final version of the directive excludes complaints filed by traders against consumers or disputes between traders.

[12] Recital No 53 of ADR Directive recommends that Member States strengthen networks of ADR entities, such as the financial dispute resolution network 'FIN-NET' and encourage ADR entities to become part of such networks.

[13] The ADR Directive applies to arbitration, unless it is based on a pre-dispute agreement, in accordance with Art 10(1). See N Reich, A 'Trojan Horse' in the Access to Justice – Party Autonomy and Consumer Arbitration in Conflict in the ADR-Directive 2013/11/EU?' (2014) 10 *European Review of Contract Law* 268.

[14] Art2(2)(b) of ADR Directive.

[15] Art 7(1)(i) and Art 6(1)(b) of ADR Directive.

[16] G Wagner, 'Private Law Enforcement through ADR: Wonder Drug or Snake Oil? (2014) 51 *Common Market Law Review* 177.

[17] Art 11(1) of ADR Directive.

First, Article 75 of MiFID II requires (whilst MiFID I merely encouraged) Member States to set up procedures for the 'out-of-court settlement of consumer disputes concerning the provision of investment and ancillary services provided by investment firms' and to ensure that all investment firms adhere to one or more such bodies implementing such complaint and redress procedures. The European Securities and Markets Authority (ESMA) has been mandated to publish and keep an up-to-date list of all extra-judicial mechanisms on its website.[18] It is worth mentioning that even if Article 75(1) of MiFID II makes reference to 'consumer disputes', the term 'consumer' should not be restricted to natural persons acting outside their business, trade or profession but should be read in a broad sense of 'consumers of financial services', thus including both natural and legal persons. This reading finds support not only in the title of this provision ('Extra-judicial mechanism for *investors'* complaints') but also in Recital No 151 of this directive according to which the objective of out-of-court dispute resolution mechanism is that of 'protecting clients and without prejudice to the right of customers to bring their action before the courts'. This shows that co-legislators intended to ensure the broadest possible access to ADR procedures.

Second, Article 69(2) of MiFID II requires Member States to establish mechanisms to ensure that compensation can be paid or other remedial action be taken in accordance with national law for any financial loss or damage suffered as a result of an infringement of this Directive or of Regulation (EU) No 600/2014.[19] In its initial version, this provision, which was added by the European Parliament to the Commission proposal, granted to the competent authorities a supervisory power to set up mechanisms to compensate clients, akin to FCA's consumer redress scheme.[20] Afterwards, the provision was amended, transforming the supervisory power into an obligation on Member States.[21] This legislative choice reflects the importance given by EU law to the need of resolving clients' disputes while ensuring an effective enforcement of MiFID II.

[18] Art 75(3) of MiFID II.

[19] For more detail on this provision, see F Della Negra, 'The Effects of the ESMA's Powers on Domestic Contract Law' in M Andenas, G Deiprenbrock *Regulating and Supervising European Financial Markets* (Leiden, Springer, 2016) 155.

[20] That provision was originally included by the EU Parliament in Art 72(ha) ('Remedies to be made available to competent authorities') of the Commission MiFID II proposal ('require that compensation be paid or other remedial action be taken to correct any financial loss or other damage suffered by an investor as a result of any practice or conduct that is contrary to this Directive or to Regulation (EU) No … /… [MiFIR].')

[21] Position of the European Parliament adopted at first reading on 15 April 2014 with a view to the adoption of Directive 2014/…/EU of the European Parliament and of the Council on markets in financial instruments and amending Directive 2002/92/EC and Directive 2011/61/EU (recast) (P7_TC1-COD(2011)0298). Available at: www.europarl.europa.eu/sides/getDoc.do;jsessionid=23B19FEA48075723FE08DA114916105A.node1?pubRef=-//EP//TEXT%20TA%20P7-TA-2012-0406%200%20DOC%20XML%20V0//en.

Notwithstanding the legal form of the 'mechanism' envisaged in Article 69(2) (ie private or public fund, consumer redress schemes or ADR procedure), this mechanism can grant compensation only if MiFID II has been breached. The application of MiFID II conduct of business rules to the facts of the dispute is therefore a pre-requisite for compensation. This will strengthen the *effet utile* of conduct of business rules via extra-judicial private enforcement.

Arguably, the impact of Article 69(2) of MiFID II in litigation before national courts is more limited.[22] This provision does not harmonise the civil law consequences for breaches of conduct of business rules. Although it makes reference to the term 'remedial action', this was probably used in the broad sense of 'redress', rather than in narrower sense of 'private cause of action', given that the provision was originally intended to give to supervisory authorities the power to require (to investment firms) to pay compensation or other remedial action. Moreover, according to Article 69(2) of MiFID II, compensation or other remedial action should be taken 'in accordance with national law'. This means that if private law is applied to the resolution of disputes which fall under the scope of Article 69(2), private law should be interpreted in light of the wording and purpose of this provision to ensure its full effectiveness. By contrast, *stricto iure*, this provision does not require national courts to interpret national private law in conformity where private law is applied outside the scope of this provision, namely in a judicial dispute.[23]

III. National Out-of-Court Dispute Resolution Mechanisms

Apart from the MiFID II requirement to set up ADR procedures for investment disputes, in the absence of other EU law provisions it is up to the Member States to define the detailed rules governing ADR procedures within the minimum requirements of the ADR Directive and subject to the principle of equivalence and effectiveness and ensuring the full respect of the fundamental right of effective judicial protection.[24] The next sections give an account of the ADR procedures for investment services disputes operating in the UK, France, Italy and Spain.

[22] See Della Negra, 'The Effects of the ESMA's Powers on Domestic Contract Law' 156.

[23] See instead D Busch and C Van Dam, 'A Bank's Duty of Care: Perspectives from European and Comparative Law' in D Busch and C van Dam (eds), *A Bank's Duty of Care* (Oxford, Hart Publishing 2017) 420 who argue that this provision codifies the principle of effectiveness of EU law and could be used to interpret national law in judicial proceedings.

[24] See, Joined Cases C-317/08, C-318/08, C-319/08 e C-320/08, *Alassini and Others*, ECLI:EU:C:2010:146, paras 47–67 and case C-75/16, *Menini, Rampanelli v Banco Popolare Società Cooperativa*, ECLI:EU:C:2017:457, paras 53–55.

A. The UK

The system of out-of-court dispute resolution in the UK is centred on the Financial Ombudsman Service (FOS).[25] This ADR was set up by the FSMA in 2000, replacing eight dispute resolution schemes organised either on a voluntary or a regulatory basis,[26] with the aim to resolve disputes between firms and clients 'quickly and with minimum formality'.[27] Besides FOS, there are other out-of-court financial dispute resolution managed by private organisations which offer mediation, arbitration and conciliation schemes.[28] The ADR Directive has been transposed by the the Alternative Dispute Resolution for Consumer Disputes (Competent Authorities and Information) Regulations 2015.

(i) The Financial Ombudsman Service

Governance

The Financial Ombudsman Service (FOS) is administered by a body corporate acting as scheme operator (the Financial Ombudsman Service Limited) and is composed of a chair and nine directors appointed by FCA and funded by industry. The scheme operator is responsible for appointing the ombudsmen and the Chief Ombudsman.[29]

Even though FOS is operationally independent from FCA,[30] the latter maintains relevant powers with regard to its governance (eg the appointment and removal of directors of the scheme operator). The two authorities must also cooperate and collaborate to achieve their regulatory objectives on the basis of a Memorandum of Understanding (MoU).[31] Signed on 18 December 2015, this implements the duty, introduced by FSA 2012, to disclose to FCA any information

[25] FOS is regulated by Part XVI and Schedule 17 of the FSMA 2000 (ss 225–234) and by the redress part (DISP) of the FCA Handbook.

[26] The Office of the Banking Ombudsman (OBO), the Office of the Building Societies Ombudsman (OBSO), the Office of the Investment Ombudsman (OIO – for firms regulated by IMRO), the Insurance Ombudsman (IOB), the Personal Insurance Arbitration Service (PIAS), the PIA Ombudsman Bureau (PIAOB), the SFA Complaints Bureau and Arbitration Service (SFA CB) and the (voluntary) FSA Direct Regulation Unit and Independent Investigator.

[27] Section 225 of the FSMA 2000.

[28] See, in particular, the City Disputes Panel (CDP). This is a non-profit organisation created in 1994 with the purpose of resolving disputes in the financial service industry through several ADR procedures to market participants.

[29] See Schedule 17 (the Ombudsman scheme) of FSMA 2000.

[30] Ibid, ss 1B and 225.

[31] See, under FCA' s regime, the MoUs of 1 April 2013 and of 18 December 2015. Under the FSA regime, MoU between the Financial Services Authority and the Financial Ombudsman Service Limited (FOS) (last updated 6 April 2007). Available at: www.fsa.gov.uk/pubs/mou/fsafos.pdf. See also the MoU between FOS and the Information Commissioner's Office, OFT, Pensions Ombudsman, Banking Code Standard Board.

that would assist it in achieving its objectives (FSMA 2000 s 232A) and to inform FCA about serious shortcomings in a firm's complaint handling, concerns about the fitness and propriety of a firm or approved person or other issues that may require action in accordance with its statutory objectives. The FOS has a limited immunity from liability in damages. It can be held liable only if the act or omission is shown to have been in bad faith; or so as to prevent an award of damages made in respect of an act or omission on the ground that the act or omission was unlawful as a result of section 6(1) of the Human Rights Act 1998.[32]

Jurisdiction and Procedure

The FOS is competent for disputes related to any act or omission made by regulated firms in carrying out their regulated activity, including consumer credit contracts and complaints resulting from a determination made by the firm under a consumer redress scheme (compulsory jurisdiction) and for disputes against firms that voluntary joined the scheme (voluntary jurisdictions).[33] According to the 2018 Annual report, the majority of disputes (36%) concern complaints about the sale and advice of PPIs, while only 28 per cent concern investment and pensions.[34]

The FOS resolves *complaints* at the earliest possible stage and by whatever means are deemed most appropriate, including mediation. The procedure is free of charge and complaints do not need to be handled by a lawyer.[35]

A complaint is admissible only if it is brought by qualified persons, such as, in particular, a consumer, or a micro-enterprise with assets of less than £1 million (professional clients and eligible counterparties are not entitled to complain) after it has been submitted to the firm's internal complaint handling.[36] It can only resolve disputes up to an award limit of £150,000.

If these procedural conditions are met, FOS may decide to uphold or dismiss the complaint on its substance or to dismiss it without examining the substance for a number of 'subjective' (eg the complainant has not suffered (or is unlikely to suffer) financial loss) and 'objective' (eg the complaint is frivolous or vexatious or it has already been considered by courts) grounds.[37]

In two instances, which reflect a quasi-supervisory role played by FOS,[38] it may decide not to consider the merits of the case. First, the Ombudsman may – with

[32] See s 225(4) of FSMA 2000 and Sch17, para 10.

[33] See JL Powell and R Stewart (eds), *Jackson & Powell on Professional Liability* (London, Sweet and Maxwell, 2016) 1071. The voluntary jursdiction is subject to the same procedural rules of the compulsory jurisdiction, unless otherwise established (DISP 4.2.4).

[34] FOS, Annual Report and Accounts for the Year Ended 31 March 2018, 12 July 2018, 23. In 2018, FOS resolved approximately 250,000 complaints on PPI.

[35] See DISP 3.7.10.

[36] See DISP 2.7.3 and DISP 2.7.9.

[37] See, in more detail, DISP 3.3.4.

[38] See R James and PE Morris, 'The Financial Ombudsman Service: A Brave New World in Ombudsmary' (2002) *Public Law* 640.

the complainant's consent – decide to refer the case to the court as a 'test case' if the dispute raises an important or novel point of law and would more suitably be dealt with by a court.[39] However, this power has rarely been used because disputes are generally centred on matters of fact and do not turn on matters of law.[40]

Second, if there is an issue that may have 'wider' implications for a relevant number of consumers and firms, FOS but also FCA, or an interested party (consumer or industry body) can start a wider implication case (WIC).[41] In this circumstance, FCA may decide to tackle the issue by means of a specific regulatory or supervisory action. If it decides that this is not the most appropriate way forward, then FOS will consider consulting industry and consumer experts before reaching a decision on individual cases or, if the firm agrees to pay the complainant's legal costs, the ombudsman service will consider whether the issue is more suitable for a 'test case' in the courts. As I will show below, FOS called for a WIC to address the mis-selling of payment protection insurance policies.

Decision

The dispute is resolved depending on FOS' determination of what is 'fair and reasonable in all the circumstances of the case'.[42] To this end, it takes into account the relevant: (i) law and regulations; (ii) regulators' rules, guidance and standards; (iii) codes of practice; and (iv) (where appropriate) what they consider to have been good industry practice at the relevant time.[43] The FOS cannot annul or rescind the contract but it can award compensation up to a certain limit (currently £150,000). In 2012, this limit was increased from £100,000.[44] In 2018, FCA proposed a further increase to £600,000 with the aim of including more than 80 per cent of the approximately 200,000 SMEs who are not currently eligible.[45]

Compensation can include financial, non-financial[46] and consequential losses, provided they are foreseeable. However, if a consumer complains about the

[39] See DISP 3.4.2.

[40] FSA, Consultation Paper, 19/2006, 17. A test case was initiated by the PIA's Ombudsman which referred the decision about the Equitable Life bonus case. The House of Lords, by overturning the judgment of the High Court, decided that the directors' decision to set different criteria of remuneration was contrary to the terms of the policy (*Equitable Life Assurance Society v Hyman* [2000] 3 All ER 961). Another test case was launched in 2007 by FOS, in agreement with the OFT before the High Court to tackle the issue of unauthorized overdraft bank charges. Available at: www.financial-ombudsman.org.uk/news/updates/bank-charges-26-07-07.html.

[41] The WIC is not based on statutory law or regulation but has been developed as a working practice between FCA and FOS. See, in more detail: www.financial-ombudsman.org.uk/publications/ombudsman-news/57/57-wider-implications.htm.

[42] Section 228 of FSMA 2000.

[43] See DISP 3.6.4.

[44] If the FOS considers that fair compensation requires payment of a larger amount, they may recommend that the respondent pays the complainant the balance (DISP 3.7.6).

[45] FCA, Consultation on SME access to the Financial Ombudsman Service and Feedback to DP15/7: SMEs as Users of Financial Services Consultation Paper CP18/3 January 2018, 4.

[46] See DISP 3.7.2.

outcome of the consumer redress scheme, FOS has less discretion as it should decide the complaint by reference to what the determination under the consumer redress scheme should have been.[47]

UK courts have constantly held that FOS is not bound by common law.[48] As Rix LJ put in *R* (*On the application of Heather Moor and Edgecomb Ltd v Financial Ombudsman Service Ltd*) 'the efficient and cost-effective and relatively informal type of alternative dispute resolution should not be stifled by the imposition of legal doctrine; on the other hand transparency, consistency and accessibility as to the principles which inform the ombudsman's determinations remain virtues in this new setting; and that publicity as to those principles and those determinations can assist in that regard'.[49]

Taking into account the need to balance FOS' discretion with minimum consistency in its decision-making, national courts have established that whether correct advice has been given according to the relevant regulatory law or whether causation has been established are not relevant tests for FOS adjudication[50] and it could determine a complaint outside the common law limitation periods.[51] In the same vein, the amount of compensation shall not necessarily correspond to the respondent's liability but to the amount which FOS 'considers subject to the limits of reasonableness, fair compensation for loss or damage falling within section 229(3) of FSMA 2000.[52] The FOS, however, and differently from the courts, should take into account the principles of FCA's Handbook in deciding what would be fair and reasonable and what redress to offer.[53]

Nature and Effects of the Decision

The complainant has the right to refuse or accept FOS' decision. If they reject it, neither party will be bound by it;[54] if they accept, the decision is binding on both parties, enforceable[55] and precludes the parties from bringing a claim based on the same facts in court.[56]

[47] Section 404B(4) of FSMA 2000.

[48] See in particular *R (on the application of IFG Financial Services Ltd) v FOS v Mr and Mrs Jenkins* [2005] EWHC 1153, para 13.

[49] *R (on the application of Heather Moor and Edgecomb Ltd) v FOS* [2008] EWCA Civ 642, para 89. See also *The Queen on the Application of British Bankers Association v FSA, FOS v Nemo Personal Finance Ltd* [2011] EWHC 999 (Admin) para 82.

[50] *R (on the application of Green) v FOS v Gillian & Edward Gunner* [2012] EWHC 1253 (Admin), para 38.

[51] *R (on the application of Bamber & BP Financial Services) v FOS* [2009] EWCA 593.

[52] *R (on the application of IFG Financial Services Ltd) v FOS v Mr and Mrs Jenkins*, para 19.

[53] *R (on the application of British Bankers' Association) v FSA* [2011] EWHC 999 (Admin) para 77. The Court held that the Principles of the FSA's Handbook related to the PPI complaints 'are of the essence of what is fair and reasonable'.

[54] See DISP 3.6.6.

[55] See DISP 3.7.13.

[56] See *Clark & Anr v In Focus Asset Management & Tax Solutions Ltd v FOS* [2014] EWCA Civ 118 and *Andrews v SBJ Benefit Consultants* [2010] EWHC 2875 (Ch)).

The decision is publicly available in full on the FOS website[57] and may be challenged by way of judicial review on the basis that the determination was not, in fact, fair and reasonable or by way of defence (on public law grounds) against an action to enforce the award. However, the scope for judicial review is limited. The court cannot determine whether FOS has correctly decided the issue at stake but can only consider whether its 'opinion as to what is fair and reasonable in all the circumstances of the case is perverse or irrational'.[58] For example, in a case where the High Court annulled FOS' decision, it was decided that there must be a logical connection between the breach found and the redress given to the investor (eg if FOS found that the investors would not have invested as much in the product if correct advice had been given, the redress cannot put the investor in the position in which they would have been had no investment been made).[59]

In *Heather Moor & Edgecomb Ltd v The UK*, the European Court of Human Rights (ECtHR) confirmed that FOS's proceeding is compatible with the right to a fair trial guaranteed by Article 6(1) of the ECHR. The Strasbourg Court held it does not preclude access to justice and does not breach the principle of foreseeability because FOS' discretion is not broad, its decision explained in detail its motivation and there was no sign of arbitrariness.[60]

(ii) Consumer Redress Schemes

FCA may require firms to set up a consumer redress scheme (CRS) to compensate clients.[61] This is a publicly driven private enforcement mechanism which aims to compensate clients and to secure the safety and soundness of firms and the stability of the financial system, reducing the risks of litigation against financial firms and the resulting civil law consequences.[62]

A CRS can be set up if three cumulative conditions are met: (i) there may have been a widespread or regular failure by a firm to comply with regulatory requirements; (ii) as a result, consumers have suffered (or may suffer) loss or damage in

[57] Section 7 of Sch 17. FOS decisions have been published on the FOS website (www.financial-ombudsman.org.uk) since 1 April 2013.

[58] *R (on the application of IFG Financial Services Ltd) v FOS v Mr and Mrs Jenkins*, para 13. See also PE Morris, 'The Financial Ombudsman Service and the Hunt Review: Continuing Evolution in Dispute Resolution' (2008) *The Journal of Business Law* 785.

[59] *R (on the application of Garrison Investment Analysis) v FOS*, para 26.

[60] ECtHR, *Heather Moor & Edgecomb Ltd v the UK* no 1550/09, 14 June 2011, pp 14 and 15.

[61] FCA has set up two CRS against mis-selling of personal protection insurance policies and complex investment products. See FSA, 'Requirements Included in the Firm's Permission at the Request of the Firm under s 44 of the Financial Services and Markets Act 2000' (18 February 2010). Available at: www.fsa.gov.uk/pubs/ other/financial_services.pdf (last accessed 8 January 2013) and FSA, 'Consumer Redress Scheme in Respect of Unsuitable Advice to Invest in Arch Cru Funds./24. December 2012 FSA. Arch Cru Funds Consumer Redress Scheme Instrument 2012. 13 December 2012, FSA 2012/77.

[62] See M Andenas and I Chiu, *The Foundations and Future of Financial Regulation* (Abingdon, Routledge, 2013) 266.

respect of which, if they brought legal proceedings, a remedy or relief would be available; and (iii) FCA deems it appropriate.[63]

FCA is entitled to 'extrapolate reasonably from evidence' (eg FCA's thematic work, enforcement investigations) whether the failure is widespread or regular.[64] The scheme may also be set up for failures of general law and may cover instances where loss is foreseeable but may not yet have crystallised.[65]

Procedurally, CRS requires the firm to investigate internally alleged breaches of rules, ascertain whether the breach caused a loss to the client and (if so) provide redress to the client (retail and non-retail). In comparison to FOS, CRS seems to be linked to a typical private law adjudication. Although the scheme can be set up even if loss is foreseeable but may not yet have crystallised,[66] FCA can give an example of conduct that constitutes a breach only if this would be held by a court to constitute a breach. It may also require firms to gather certain evidence but it 'cannot disregard the normal legal rules on causation or remoteness of loss'.[67] Moreover, unlike FOS, CRS can only be used to require redress in relation to those failures in respect of which a remedy or relief would be available in legal proceedings.[68] Therefore, breaches of FCA's principles or industry guidance confirmed by FCA which do not give rise to a right of action under section 138D of FSMA 2000 are not actionable via a consumer redress scheme.

Consumers can submit a complaint to FOS but its jurisdiction is limited to whether the firm's determination respected the rules laid down by the scheme.[69]

Any person (eg a firm, consumers or their representative) is allowed to challenge the rules setting up CRS by way of judicial review before the Upper Tribunal.[70] Access to the CRS does not, in itself, prevent the consumer's access to courts, but any redress received in court proceedings would be discounted from compensation payable under CRS and vice versa.[71]

[63] The rules on the consumer redress scheme are laid down in FCA CONRED Consumer Redress Schemes sourcebook, amended on 21 April 2016 (FCA 2016/32). The Financial Services Act 2010 gave to FSA (now FCA) the power to set up CRD, without prior authorisation from HM Treasury. The Treasury retains the power to widen the scope of the consumer redress scheme, namely by amending the definition of consumers or firms (s 404G of FSMA 2000). This means that a breach of Principles for Business, which are not actionable in court, cannot be used to require firms to set up CRS under s 404. Instead, such a breach would be actionable before FOS. For more detail, see FSA, Guidance note, 10/2010. 23 July 2010.

[64] Section 1.3.4. and 1.3.5. of the CONRED.

[65] Ibid, Section 1.3.8.

[66] Ibid.

[67] Ibid ss 1.5.10 and 1.5.12.

[68] Ibid s 1.3.16.

[69] The Alternative Dispute Resolution for Consumer Disputes (Competent Authorities and Information) Regulations 2015 (SI 2015/542) limited the possibility for a consumer to appeal the decision of the CRS subject to the prior consent between the parties (Sch 7, introducing s 1A in s 404B of FSMA 2000).

[70] Section 404D of FSMA 2000.

[71] Section 1.5.24 of CONRED.

(iii) Special Redress Scheme for Mis-selling of Interest Rate Hedging Products

In 2012, FSA found that thousands of clients had suffered large losses as a result of mis-selling of interest rate hedging products (IRHPs).[72] As a result, it sought the agreement of the banks involved in the review to set up an internal redress mechanism to compensate unsophisticated retail clients, on the basis of what is fair and reasonable, for losses suffered as a result of mis-selling since 2001. To ensure that outcomes were fair and reasonable, the banks' review of each case was overseen by an independent reviewer, appointed under section 166 of the FSMA. Independent reviewers, selected by the banks and approved by FSA, were in charge of monitoring the correct application of FSA guidance for each of the phases of the review process (assessment of sophistication, assessment of non-compliance, and determination of fair and reasonable redress). When the opinions of the bank and the independent reviewer diverged, the opinion of the latter was to prevail.

According to FSA 'fair and reasonable' redress means 'putting the customer back in the position they would have been in had the regulatory failings not occurred'. In addition to the 'basic redress' (ie the difference between the payments they would have made on the alternative product, compared with the payments they did make), clients could claim consequential losses (the cost of being deprived of money and other losses suffered), which were assessed by reference to established legal principles relating to claims in tort and breach of statutory duty (ie causation, remoteness and evidence) and loss of profits (ie if the money had not been used to make IRHP payments, it would have been available to the customer who could have generated more profits) for which clients needed to prove loss of opportunity.

This special-purpose ADR scheme has been subject to strong criticism. According to Richard Samuel, it gave the banks all they wanted: 'a redress procedure run by themselves, which operated in secret, which did not apply the law, produced no legal precedent, which did not award consequential loss and in which the principle vehicle for compensation was the opportunity to sign up to a new financial product with the same bank'. It failed to treat clients fairly.[73] The Chief Executive Officer of FCA, Dr Andrew Bailey, did admit in front of a Parliamentary Committee that this scheme was 'enormously controversial'.[74] The House of Commons

[72] These products, which include swaps, caps, collars and structured collars, aim to enable the customer to manage fluctuations in interest rates and are typically sold together with a loan.

[73] R Samuel, 'Tools for Culture Change: FCA, Now You Are Listening! Time To Build An Independent, Low Cost Forum for Conduct Dispute Resolution' (2017) 12 *Capital Markets Law Journal* 281. See also R Samuel, 'Tools for Changing Banking Culture: FCA Are You Listening?' (2016) 11 *Capital Markets Law Journal* 129.

[74] Treasury Committee Oral Evidence: Appointment of Andrew Bailey as Chief Executive Officer of the Financial Conduct Authority, HC 568 Wednesday 20 July 2016, reply to Q32. Available at: http://

considered that to treat customers with fair outcomes 'what is needed is not ad hoc compensation schemes, but a long-term, effective and timely dispute resolution mechanism for both regulated and unregulated financial contracts' and called on FCA to create a sustainable platform for commercial financial dispute resolution'.[75]

According to FCA, banks have sent 18,200 redress determinations to customers: 14,700 included a cash redress offer, 3,500 of which confirmed that the IRHP sale either complied with the rules or that the customer suffered no loss; around 95 per cent of offers have been accepted.[76]

(iv) Special Redress Scheme for Mis-selling Payment Protection Insurance (PPI)

PPIs mis-selling is 'the biggest issue of financial mis-selling in recent years'.[77] FCA forced banks to return more than £18 billion to their customers.[78] On 1 July 2008 FOS's chairman warned FSA that the systemic mis-selling of PPI needed a 'wider regulatory action'. In 2010, FSA published a policy statement which required firms to set up an internal mechanism to handle complaints relating to the sale of PPI.[79]

The scheme's rules, included in DISP App 3 of the FCA Handbook, deviate from traditional common law procedural and substantive principles. For instance, if the firm determines that there was a breach, it should consider whether the complainant would have bought the payment protection contract in the absence of that breach. However, it should presume that the complainant would not have bought the payment protection contract.[80] In addition, firms must assess the alleged breach taking into account not only contractual documentation but also the 'true substance' of the complaint and to analyse the root causes of those complaints including concerns raised both at the time of the sale and subsequently and the relevant decisions of FOS.[81]

Since 2011, firms have handled over 18.4 million PPI complaints and paid over £26 billion in redress.

data.parliament.uk/writtenevidence/committeeevidence.svc/evidencedocument/treasury-committee/appointment-of-andrew-bailey-as-chief-executive-officer-of-the-financial-conduct-authority/oral/36229.pdf.

[75] See Samuel, 'Tools for Culture Change: FCA, Now You Are Listening!' 298.

[76] Data available at: www.fca.org.uk/consumers/interest-rate-hedging-products.

[77] See FCA, 'Annual Report 2017/2018', 24. PPI is an insurance against a borrower becoming unable to make credit repayments for specified reasons, such as accidental injury. See in detail E Ferran, 'Regulatory Lessons from the Payment Protection Insurance Mis-selling Scandal in the UK' (2012) *European Business Organisation Law Review* 251.

[78] ESRB, Report on misconduct risk in the banking sector, 6.

[79] The scheme rules were announced in FSA, 'The Assessment and Redress of Payment Protection Insurance Complaints Feedback on the Further Consultation in CP10/6 and Final Handbook', August 2010.

[80] See DISP App 3.1.3.

[81] See DISP App 3.2.2 and App 3.4.1.

The British Bankers' Association, on behalf of affected PPI firms, brought an action for judicial review of the special rules, alleging that they breached section 150 (now s 138D) of FSMA 2000, which prevents the use of a private cause of action in relation to a firm's breach of a principle, and section 404 of FSMA 2000, because this scheme would have circumvented its requirements by setting up a 'special' consumer redress scheme. In *BBA v FSA and FOS*, the High Court dismissed these arguments. The Court held, in the first place, that even if the principles cannot give rise to a private cause of action in a court of law, they can give rise to obligations or compensation. For this reason, FOS must take them into account in its adjudication and they can give rise to 'significant legal consequences as between firms and the FSA', including the setting up of the PPI redress scheme.[82] Moreover, the Court held that this special scheme is different from a consumer redress scheme in a number of respects (ie the payment of compensation to non-complainants is not compulsory, the degree of regulatory oversight is considerably less and the enforcement can only be indirect).[83]

A significant change in PPI redress has been introduced by the landmark judgment of the Supreme Court in *Plevin v Paragon Personal Finance Ltd*.[84] The issue at stake was whether the firm's failure to disclose commission and the failure of the lender to advise on the suitability of the PPI sold by another firm made the relationship unfair. Lord Sumption held that the non-disclosure of the amount of commission made the contractual relationship unfair under section 140A(1)(c) of the Consumer Credit Act 1974. The Judge held that 'a sufficiently extreme inequality of knowledge and understanding is a classic source of unfairness in any relationship between a creditor and a non-commercial debtor' and in the specific case, given that where the borrower was not informed about the fact that more than two-thirds of the premium was going to intermediaries, concluded that 'any reasonable person [...] would be bound to question whether the insurance represented value for money, and whether it was a sensible transaction to enter into'. He therefore concluded that the 'the fact that she was left in ignorance [...] made the relationship unfair'[85] but he held that lender's failure to conduct a suitability assessment of the borrower could not be treated as something done 'by or on behalf of' the insurance firm because the lender was not acting as the firm's agent.[86] Consequently, the Supreme Court decided to reopen the credit agreement and remitted to the first instance court to decide the relief that should be granted to the borrower. This judgment is important because it entails that compensation should be granted even if there was no mis-selling but there was a failure to disclose commission. To provide guidance on the impact of this ruling

[82] *BBA v FSA and FOS* [2011] EWHC 999 (Admin), para 86.
[83] Ibid, paras 237–238.
[84] *Plevin v Paragon Personal Finance Ltd* [2014] UKSC 61.
[85] Ibid, para 18.
[86] Ibid, paras 30–32.

on PPI's dispute resolution, on 1 March 2017, FCA amended the rules on PPI redress scheme but set a deadline of 29 August 2019 to submit a complaint with the aim of bringing the PPI issue to an orderly conclusion and bring finality and certainty for both consumers and firms.[87]

B. France

In France out-of-court dispute resolution mechanisms for investment services disputes are based on public and private mediation schemes. In 2001, the *Loi Murcef* required credit institutions to set up an internal mediation scheme for retail client disputes.[88] Credit institutions have set up internal mediation schemes (*médiation en compte propre*) or have adhered to schemes provided by trade associations, such as the *Fédération bancaire française* (FBF) and the *Association des Sociétés Financières* (ASF) (*médiation en compte commun*).

Whilst in the banking sector ADR procedures are managed and funded mainly by the credit institutions themselves, in the investment services sector they are managed and funded by the supervisory authority. In 2003, AMF's mediation scheme (*Médiation de l'Autorité des Marchés Financiers*)[89] replaced that established by COB in 1997.[90] Since then, it has handled most investment service-related disputes.

The ADR Directive was transposed by Order No 1033/2015 and Decree No 1382/2015.[91] An important provision of the law transposing the ADR Directive is that if a public mediator is competent to resolve it, the dispute shall not give rise to other conventional mediation procedures, unless the two mediators reach an agreement.[92] A new entity, the *Commission d'Evaluation et de Contrôle de la Médiation de la Consommation*, composed of judges from the *Cour de Cassation*

[87] FCA, 'Payment Protection Insurance Complaints: Feedback on CP16/20 and Final Rules and Guidance PS 17/3'. March 2017. On 20 October 2017 the Court of Appeal refused permission to appeal by a compensation claims company (We Fight Any Claim) against the decision of the lower administrative court to refuse the judicial review of FCA's new package of measures in relation to PPI complaints.

[88] Loi n° 2001-1168 du 11 décembre 2001 portant mesures urgentes de réformes à caractère économique et financier ('*Loi Murcef*') (JORF n°288 du 12 décembre 2001 p. 19703 texte n° 1).

[89] Law n° 2003-706 du 1er août 2003 de sécurité financière, which introduced Art 621-19 of the CMF and the *charte de mediation*. The *charte de mediation*, originally drafted in 1997 to regulate the mediation scheme set up within the COB, the AMF's predecessor, was subsequently revised after the establishment of the AMF.

[90] COB, Rapport Annuel COB 1998. 6 May 1999, 91.

[91] See Ordonnance n° 2015-1033 du 20 août 2015 relative au règlement extrajudiciaire des litiges de la consommation (JORF n°0192 du 21 août 2015 p. 14721 texte n° 43) and Décret n° 2015-1382 en date du 30 octobre 2015 relatif à la médiation des litiges de la consommation (JORF n°0253 du 31 octobre 2015 page 20408 texte n° 42).

[92] Art L 152-5 of Decree No 1382/2015. See E Guinchard, 'The Implementation of the Consumer ADR Directive in France' in P Cortés (ed), *The New Regulatory Framework for Consumer Dispute Resolution* (Oxford, Oxford University Press, 2016) 166.

and *Conseil d'Etat*, representatives of consumer associations, representative of business federations, and experts, was set up to monitor compliance with the ADR Directive's requirements.[93]

(i) Médiation de l'AMF

The mediator is appointed by the President of the AMF for a three-year term and must respect the requirements of independence. The mediator cannot receive instructions regarding the resolution of disputes and is responsible for its own budget. The mediator is competent to resolve disputes related to the breach of conduct of business rules for financial services, irrespective of their value. Both retail and non-retail investors can submit a complaint to AMF.[94] To be admissible, the client must have already complained to the firm's internal complaints-handling body and must not have submitted a complaint to court. Differently from the ombudsman scheme, the mediator can consider the case only if both parties agree to the mediation procedure.

The procedure is free of charge for the complainant, will last 90 days, suspends the prescription period and does not prejudice the right of the parties to pursue the claim in court. The mediation procedure is subject to strict confidentiality rules. Statements, opinions and documents used during the mediation procedure cannot be used by parties during judicial proceedings. Mediation is concluded by a non-binding proposal which must be motivated in law and equity.[95] The parties have 30 days to accept or refuse this proposal and they can also mandate the AMF mediator to monitor the execution and enforcement of the mediation agreement. According to the AMF mediator, the parties follow the mediator's proposal in most cases.[96]

The AMF has also the power to submit proposals for legislative reform related to the protection of consumers and clients of financial services but, as noted by ESMA in its 2016 MiFID peer review, information on the complaints the Ombudsman receives is not currently passed to AMF.[97] The AMF publishes an annual report, which contains the aggregate data on the functioning of ADR and must be delivered to the *Collège de l'Autorité des marchés financiers*, the President of the Republic and the parliament. The mediator's proposals are not publicly available.

In 2017, for the first time in five years, the AMF mediator recorded a decline in the number of referrals to 1,361 cases (down from 1,501 in 2016 and 1,406 in 2015).

[93] L615-1 et seq and Arts R615-1 et seq of Code de la consommation. The *Commission d'évaluation et de contrôle de la médiation* replaces the *Comité de la médiation bancaire* introduced by the *Loi Murcef*.

[94] AMF, Annual Report 2014, 10.

[95] Art 5 of Charte de la médiation, in Annual Report 2017, 49.

[96] AMF, Rapport du médiateur 2017, 12 April 2018, 15 (54% of the mediatéur decisions are favourable to claimants and are followed by the parties in 96% of cases).

[97] ESMA, 'MiFID Suitability Requirements', Peer review, para 119.

One of the reasons was the decline in complaints about forex investments,[98] which was due to AMF's prohibition on the marketing of these practices adopted on the basis of the *Loi Sapin 2* judgment.[99] Most complaints concerned bad order execution and incorrect information or advice.[100] There is no limit to compensation. For example, in 2017, in disputes on forex investments, the mediator proposed compensation ranging from €250 to €88,500, allowing investors to recover a total of approximately €1 million.[101] As mediation proposals are not publicly available, it is not possible to fully understand the adjudicative approach here.

(ii) Médiation de Fédération bancaire française (FBF) and Médiation de l'Association française des Sociétés Financières (ASF)

The mediation schemes offered by FBF and ASF are available to consumers and firms that belong to the association.[102] The two mediation schemes are governed by similar rules and procedures.[103] The ASF and FBF mediators can hear disputes regarding securities, banking and insurance contracts. Unlike AMF's mediation, these are available only for consumers (natural persons who act outside their trade, business or profession).

Like AMF mediation, these procedures are free of charge for the complainant, last 90 days, suspend the prescription period and do not prejudice the right of the parties to pursue the claim in court. The mediation is concluded with a non-binding proposal based on law and/or equity.[104] However, the mediator can order the publication of the proposal in the contract between the firm and the client. If the bank does not intend to comply it must give the reason for its non-compliance.[105] The FBF mediator proposes a solution taking into 'strict account' the regulations, the context and the facts of the dispute to determine a solution '*la plus adaptée aux faits et la plus juste*'.[106] The FBF and ASF publish an annual report with the aggregate data of their activity (mediation proposals or their extracts are not publicly available)[107] and ASF also provides that the decision of the mediator must be published on its website and must be mentioned in the contract between the bank and the complainant.[108]

[98] AMF, *Rapport du médiateur* 2015, 19 (228 complaints received in 2015).
[99] Ibid, 2017, 12 April 2018, 7.
[100] Ibid at 15.
[101] Ibid at 19.
[102] 80 investment firms adhere to ASF mediation and 225 credit institutions adhere to FBF mediation.
[103] See *charte de la mediation* FBF and *charte de mediation* ASF.
[104] Charte du service de médiation auprès de la fédération bancaire francaise (Art 1). Available at: www.fbf.fr.
[105] Charte mediation ASF (Art 6).
[106] FBF, 'Annual Report 2017', 26.
[107] Charte de la mediation FBF (Art 7) and Charte de la mediation ASF (Art 9).
[108] Ibid, Art 8; Ibid, Art 8.

In 2017, the ASF mediator received 1,644 complaints (down from 1,669 in 2016, 1,783 in 2015 and 1,755 in 2014) concerning insurance, banking and payment services.[109] In 46 per cent of the eligible complaints, the solution was favourable for the defendant firm. The amounts claimed are rather low, ranging from €1.25 to €27,600.

In 2017, the FBF mediator received 4,864 complaints applications (5,593 in 2016, 4,182 in 2015 and 2,984 in 2014).[110] Around 80 per cent of the complaints concerned banking services (ie payment services) and, as in the ASF mediation, the amounts claimed are rather low (only 79 complaints exceeded €10,000). Notably, in the majority of cases, the mediator proposed a solution in favour of the defendant financial institution.[111]

(iii) Médiation en compte propre

The largest French banking groups (BNP Paribas, Credit Agricole and Société Générale) have set up 'in-house' mediation schemes (*médiation en compte propre*). Mediators are independent and are not remunerated by the banks. These mediation schemes are competent for disputes concerning the bank's credit, financial and insurance services. Access to the procedure is restricted to consumers (natural persons who act outside their trade, business or profession). The parties to the procedure must respect a duty of confidentiality and must not disclose information related to the procedure in the course of subsequent judicial proceedings, unless expressly agreed. The client's recourse to mediation, however, is considered as an express authorisation to waive bank secrecy with regard to the information necessary for the mediation investigation.

An interesting aspect of these mediation schemes is that the disputes related to the policy of the bank (*politique générale*) – including tarifs and refusal of credit – and those related to the performance of financial instruments dependent upon market oscillations fall outside the scope of their mediation.[112] Moreover, the rules of procedure introduce some important restrictions to the complainant's access to the ADR. If a judicial proceeding has already been initiated, the acceptance of the mediation by the mediator suspends the judicial proceeding until the end of the mediation procedure.[113] But inasmuch as mediation suspends any court action

[109] ASF, Rapport annuel 2017, 13.

[110] FBF, Rapport d'activité 2017, 7.

[111] Ibid, 11–12.

[112] Charte de la mediation BNB Paribas. Clientele des particuliers, Juin 2014, Art 1. Available at: www.secure.bnpparibas.net/banque/PA_CanalnetApp/documentum/canalnet/public/PDF/Charte_Mediation_Bancaire_BNP_Paribas_20080523034436.pdf; Charte de la mediation bancaire du credit agricole (31 décembre 2013) Art 3-2. Available at: www.ca-paris.fr/charte-mediation.html; Charte de la médiation. Société Générale, Art 3. Available at: https://static.societegenerale.fr/ass/ASS/Repertoire_par_type_de_contenus/Fichiers_a_telecharger/charte-mediation.pdf.

[113] Charte de la mediation bancaire du credit agricole (Art 8); Charte de la médiation. Société Générale (Art 9). The BNP Paribas mediation scheme, by contrast, provides that mediation cannot be initiated if a judicial proceeding is ongoing (Art 5).

seeking an order for payment or resolution of a contract that interrupts any execution path, the recourse to the mediation does not preclude the bank from adopting precautionary measures (*mesures conservatoires*).[114]

The mediation is free of charge for the consumer and lasts 90 days. It is concluded by the mediator's proposal, which is non-legally binding on the parties. However, unlike the other examined mediation schemes, the rules of procedure give the parties the power to transpose the proposal into a legally binding settlement agreement (*transaction*) which prevents the parties from pursuing the claim in court.[115] Turning now to the effective functioning of these schemes, the data available for the mediation scheme of BNP Paribas shows that, in 2015, the mediator received 5,440 complaints (up from 2,058 in 2014) of which only 699 were examined.[116] Complaints concerned banking contracts but not securities or investment contracts. Only in 24 per cent of the proposals was the complainant successful. Overall, the bank was asked to pay €136.987.75 in compensation; €109,255.05 was for breach of regulations and contractual obligations and €27,732.70 was based on an equitable judgment.[117]

C. Italy

In Italy the out-of-court resolution of securities disputes relies on both public statutory-based ADR and a privately based ADR procedure. The publicly based ADR procedures were established within the supervisory authorities in the aftermath of the bankruptcies of Parmalat, Cirio and the Republic of Argentina to ensure fast, cheap and effective mechanisms for access to justice, thus restoring the confidence of retail investors in financial markets.[118] In addition to ADR procedures established within CONSOB (Arbitro per le controversie finanziarie, which replaced the Camera di conciliazione e arbitrato), the Italian Banking Association set up an ADR entity in 1993 (Ombudsman-giurì bancario) for the resolution of securities disputes. A distinctive feature of the Italian out-of-court system is that the admissibility of actions before national courts regarding commercial

[114] Charte de la mediation BNB Paribas (Art 8); Charte de la mediation bancaire du credit agricole (Art 8); Charte de la médiation. Société Générale (Art 9). Precautionary measures seem to refer to judicial actions aimed at preserving the credit before the declaratory action. See also Recommendation 2013-01 du Comité de la médiation bancaire du 30 avril 2013 relative aux chartes, contrats et documents assimilés portant application des dispositions légales régissant la médiation bancaire (Art 3).

[115] Charte de la mediation BNB Paribas (Art 3); Charte de la mediation bancaire du credit agricole (Art 9).

[116] BNP Paribas, Rapport du médiateur entre BNP Paribas, B*Capital et leurs clients particuliers Année 2015, September 2016, 21.

[117] BNP Paribas, Rapport du médiateur entre BNP Paribas, B*Capital et leurs clients particuliers Année 2015, 33.

[118] Art 27(1) of the Law 262/2005 introduced ADR in the field of banking services, within the Banca d'Italia (Art 29(1)) and delegated the government to establish ADR in the field of investment services (Art 27(1)).

contracts, including financial and banking contracts, is conditional on an attempt to settle the dispute out of court.[119] Italy has transposed the ADR Directive with Legislative Decree 130/2015 and designated CONSOB as the competent authority for ADR procedures in the securities sector.[120]

(i) Ombudsman-giurì bancario (Ombudsman)

The Ombudsman was established in 1993 by the Italian Bank Association. The Conciliatore Bancario Finanziario – Associazione per la soluzione delle controversie bancarie, finanziarie e societarie, an association which includes 1,150 members – made up of banks, investment firms, funds and trade associations – is responsible for a mediation, arbitration and Ombudsman scheme.[121]

The Ombudsman resolves the dispute through a panel composed of a President appointed by the Council of State and four members appointed by the Conciliatore Bancario Finanziario and approved by consumers and banking associations. The panel members must respect requirements of experience, competence and independence.[122] The Ombudsman is competent for investment services disputes concerning both retail and non-retail clients. To be admissible, the complaint must relate to an infringement which has occured within two years of the date of the alleged violation (the time limit is one year for complaints before the ABF and ACF), it must have already been submitted to the firm's internal complaints handling and it must not have been submitted to other ADR entities or courts.

The Ombudsman must make a decision within 90 days. The rules of procedure do not specify whether the Ombudsman must follow legal rules; they only provide that the decision must be taken on the basis of the documentation submitted by the parties. The Ombudsman can grant compensation up to €100,000 and can also declare the contract null and void and order restitution. The decision is not legally binding on the parties and cannot be enforced. However, a firm's failure to comply with the decision is published in the national press at the respondent's expense. The Ombudsman publishes a report on its annual activity which includes the extract of the most relevant decisions.[123]

[119] Art 5(1) of Legislative Decree 28/2010. See also F Della Negra. 'Le controversie in materia consumeristica. Strumenti di composizione: negoziali e non negoziali' in P Gianniti (ed), *Processo civile e soluzioni alternative delle liti tra privati. Verso un sistema di giustizia integrato* (Aracne, 2016) 741.

[120] Decreto Legislativo 6 agosto 2015, n. 130 Attuazione della direttiva 2013/11/UE sulla risoluzione alternativa delle controversie dei consumatori, che modifica il regolamento (CE) n 2006/2004 e la direttiva 2009/22/CE (direttiva sull'ADR per i consumatori) (GU n 191 del 19-8-2015).

[121] Ombudsman-Giurì bancario. Regolamento per la trattazione dei reclami e dei ricorsi in materia di servizi e attività di investimento. Ottobre 2009.

[122] The four members shall be appointed from among the members of the Consumer Association and the Customers Association and two of them from the Italian Banking Association.

[123] Since 2014 the Conciliatore Bancario Finanziario publishes a journal ('repertorio') and the extract of the most important decisions per year ('massimario'). The subsequent references to decisions can be found on the massimario which is available at: www.conciliatorebancario.it/index.php/ombudsman/decisioni.

The statistical data available show a constant increase of the number of complaints submitted to the Ombudsman:[124] between 2010 and 2013 approximately 4,300 complaints were submitted.[125] Almost 2,400 (55%) were dismissed for procedural reasons. Where a decision has been issued, the Ombudsman ruled in favour of the investor in 935 cases (40% of the cases admitted; 21.7% of the total number referred to the Ombudsman).[126] Since the Ombudsman's competence overlaps with that of the new ADR mechanisms set up by CONSOB (ACF), it ceased its activity as of 9 January 2017.

(ii) *Arbitro per le controversie finanziarie* (ACF)

On 9 January 2017, ACF replaced CONSOB's *Camera di conciliazione e arbitrato*, which was established in 2007 to resolve retail clients' disputes through a mediation or arbitration scheme.[127] ACF is based on the model of the *Arbitro Bancario Finanziario* (ABF) set up by Banca d'Italia in 2008 for the resolution of banking contracts,[128] and is responsible for the resolution of disputes between retail clients and financial service providers for the breach of conduct of business of the Italian law transposing MiFID, including cross-border disputes and those arising from online contracts as defined by the ODR Regulation.

The ACF panel is composed of three members appointed by CONSOB and two chosen by the associations of investment firms and retail clients. Panel members must meet the requirements of competence, experience and, unlike the ABF panels, independence. The panel members can be dismissed by CONSOB only for motivated reasons and are supported by a secretariat. The procedure is free of charge for the client[129] and must be concluded within 90 days (60 days for ABF). Previous unsucccessful recourse to the firm's internal complaint handling is a condition of access to ACF.[130]

[124] See G Sangiorgio, 'Problemi della pratica un esempio di giustizia "domestica" alternativa a quella dell'a.g.o.: l'ombudsman – giurì bancario' (2009) 3 *Banca Borsa Titoli di Credito* 344.

[125] 1,079 complaints were submitted in 2013; 1,172 in 2012; 612 in 2011 and 1,491 in 2012 (data provided by the Secretary of the Financial Ombusman).

[126] Decisions in favour of the client were: 108 in 2013; 99 in 2012; 167 in 2011; and 561 in 2010.

[127] Decreto Legislativo 8 ottobre 2007, n. 179, istituzione di procedure di conciliazione e di arbitrato, sistema di indennizzo e fondo di garanzia per i risparmiatori e gli investitori in attuazione dell'articolo 27, commi 1 e 2, della legge 28 dicembre 2005, n. 262. (GU n. 253 del 30 ottobre 2007). The rules of procedure have been laid down in CONSOB Regulation No 16763/2008. As of 17 January 2012, 284 requests for mediaiton had been submitted to the mediaiton chamber (71% in favour of the client), and there had been no requests for arbitration. This ADR procedure was subsequently amended by the CONSOB, Delibera n 18275 del 18 luglio 2012 (Regolamento di attuazione del decreto legislativo 8 ottobre 2007, n 179, concernente la Camera di conciliazione e arbitrato presso la Consob e le relative procedure) (GU n 176 del 30-07-2012).

[128] See in detail on the ABF, AA Dolmetta, *Trasparenza dei prodotti bancari. Regole* (Bologna, Zanichelli, 2013).

[129] The financial firm, instead, must pay a lump sum between €400 and 600 if the client's claim is upheld.

[130] The complaint shall be submitted to ACF, like ABF, within one year from the unsuccessful recourse to the firm's internal complaint handling.

The ACF can grant compensation up to €500,000 (ABF's award limit is €100,000) for losses suffered by the client as a result of the firm's breach of rules, excluding, in line with Article 1223 of the Civil Code, losses which are not a direct consequence of the infringement. The only remedy that can be granted is compensation – the ACF cannot rescind contracts nor declare them null and void. Unlike ABF, ACF cannot grant compensation for non-pecuniary losses and in its proceedings the burden of proof is reversed, in line with Article 23(6) of TUF. Therefore, it is up to the financial firm to prove compliance with the conduct of business rules (fairnesss, transparency and information) owed to the clients.

The ACF shall make its decision on the basis of the legal rules and – importantly – the acts of general application of CONSOB and ESMA and the guidelines of association approved by CONSOB and codes of conduct applicable to the financial firm. The decision of ACF is not legally binding on the parties and cannot be enforced. However, non-compliance is published in national newspapers and on the ACF's website.

Based on its first annual report, ACF received 1,839 complaints, of which 1,469 have been admitted; 779 decisions were adopted, 61.6 per cent were favourable to the client.[131] More than half (57%) of the admitted complaints concerned investment advice, while the remaining complaints were related to execution of orders, the placement of financial instruments and portfolio management. The ACF has granted compensation for a total amount of €5.2 million and awarded €27.175 on average per client.

(iii) Fondi di solidarietà e procedure arbitrali

In 2016, the Italian Government introduced a solidarity fund and a special arbitration procedure to compensate holders of subordinated debt instruments issued by four small Italian credit institutions (Banca Marche, Banca Popolare dell'Etruria e del Lazio, Cassa di Risparmio di Ferrara and CariChieti) which were subject to resolution and compulsory liquidation.[132]

The solidarity fund is managed and funded by the Fondo Interbancario di Tutela dei Depositi (FITD), a deposit guarantee scheme, established in 1987 in the form of a private law consortium, supervised by Banca d'Italia.[133] The solidarity

[131] ACF, Relazione sull'attività svolta. Anno 2017. 26 Marzo 2018.

[132] The resolution plan involved the full write-down of shares and subordinated debt and the transfer of assets and liabilities to four bridge banks and the transfer of bad loans to an asset management vehicle. The four banks were put into resolution following the decision of Banca d'Italia, approved by the Ministry of Economy and Finance, on 22 November 2015 at 22.00. For more information, see the Banca d'Italia notification to the EBA in accordance with Art 83 of the BRRD. See: www.eba.europa.eu/documents/10180/1380023/Notification+from+the+Bank+of+Italy.pdf.

[133] The solidarity fund was established by Art 1, para 855 of the Law 208/2015 (Legge di stabilità per il 2016). The Decreto legge n 59 del 3 maggio 2016, recante *'Disposizioni urgenti in materia di procedure esecutive e concorsuali nonché a favore degli investitori in banche in liquidazione'*, converted into Law 119/2016, conferred on the FITD the task of managing the fund.

fund grants a lump sum amounting to 80 per cent of the purchase price of the subordinated debt to the clients (natural persons or individual businesses) who meet certain criteria related to their income and movable assets and who bought subordinated debt from the four banks before 12 June 2014.[134] The fund assesses whether the client meets the admissibility criteria and grants the lump sum, if the client provides evidence of the direct contractual relationship with the bank (excluding instruments issued by these banks through other intermediaries, including those who were part of the banking group).[135]

The funds used for compensation are taken from a deposit guarantee scheme funded by Italian joint stock credit institutions. As of 29 March 2018, the fund has received 16,038 requests and has awarded compensation in 15,443 cases. The average award is €11,700.[136] The government has extended access to the solidarity fund to clients and natural and legal persons who held subordinated debt of Banca Popolare di Vicenza SpA and Veneto Banca SpA when they were placed into compulsory administrative liquidation.[137]

The clients of the four small credit institutions who purchased subordinated debt, can also submit an application to a special arbitration procedure set up within the national anti-corruption authority (Autorità nazionale anticorruzione, ANAC). Recourse to arbitration is possible only for those clients who did not apply to the solidarity fund; the arbitration precludes access to the solidarity fund and to the courts.[138] Access to arbitration is also possible for clients who purchased subordinated debt after 12 June 2014. The client can be awarded 100 per cent of the purchase price of the securities. Compensation is subject to a determination of the bank's liability for a breach of conduct of business rules of information, fairness and transparency laid down by the Legislative Decree No 58/1998 and the damages should be quantified on the basis of a 'concrete assessment' after the gains received by the client have been substracted.[139] The arbitration award is issued within 120 days and is executed by the FITD. Members of the arbitration bodies are appointed by the government, having heard parliament's commissions, from among persons of impartiality, independence and competence.

[134] The client must prove that his or her personal income in 2014 was lower than €35,000 or that his or her movable assets amounted to less than €100,000 as of 31 December 2015. Law Decree 237 del 23 dicembre 2016, converted into Law 15 del 17 febbraio 2017 broadened the access to the solidarity fund including the spouse and certain relatives of the client.

[135] Regolamento del Fondo di Solidarietà Procedura per l'indennizzo forfettario ai sensi della legge 119 del 30 giugno 2016 e della legge 15 del 17 febbraio 2017 Aggiornamento dell'11 aprile 2017, 9.

[136] Data available at www.fitd.it/Home/FDS_info_attivita.

[137] Art 6 of the Decreto Legge 25 giugno 2017, n 99 Disposizioni urgenti per la liquidazione coatta amministrativa di Banca Popolare di Vicenza SpA e di Veneto Banca SpA convertito in legge n 121 del 31 luglio 2017 (GU n 184 dell'8 agosto 2017).

[138] Art 1, pars 857–860, della Legge di stabilità per il 2016 (Art 9, para 6).

[139] Arts 3(2) and 7(1) of Decree 9 May 2017, n 83 Regolamento disciplinante la procedura di natura arbitrale di accesso al Fondo di solidarieta', di cui all'articolo 1, 857, d), della legge 28 dicembre 2015, n 208 (17G00101) (GU n 135 del 13-6-2017).

As of 3 May 2018, the arbitrator had examined 181 requests for arbitration, upheld 144 of them and awarded €3,765,700 in compensation (63% of the total amount claimed).[140]

D. Spain

In Spain the out-of-court dispute resolution of investment services disputes is based on several public and private mechanisms. Law No 44/2002 required credit, investment and insurance firms to set up internal complaint-handling mechanisms to deal with disputes arising between them and their clients[141] and to set up ADR procedures for Banco de España, the CNMV and the Directorate General Insurance and Pension Funds (*Comisionado para la Defensa del Cliente*).[142] In 2011, this was replaced by the *Servicios de Reclamaciones*, which are part of the consumer protection department of these authorities.[143]

Investment services disputes can also be resolved by way of arbitration or mediation schemes. Law 26/1984 introduced, in accordance with Article 51 of the Spanish Constitution,[144] an arbitration procedure for consumers and clients disputes (*Systema arbitral de consumo*) and Royal Decree Law No 5/2012 introduced a voluntary mediation scheme.[145]

In the wake of the financial crisis, two special ADR procedures were established to compensate retail clients for losses suffered as a result of the mis-selling of *participaciones preferentes* and other hybrid financial instruments and to provide redress to clients who entered into mortgage contracts with unfair floor clauses. Spain transposed the ADR Directive under Law No 7/2017 and designated the CNMV as the competent authority for monitoring compliance with the requirements of the ADR Directive.[146] Importantly, Law No 7/2017 required the legislator

[140] Data available at: www.anticorruzione.it/portal/public/classic/Comunicazione/News/_news?id=2611acce0a7780424bb8ec754dcd660b.

[141] Art 29 of Ley 44/2002, de 22 de noviembre, de Medidas de Reforma del Sistema Financiero (BOE, n 281 de 23 de 1 de Noviembre 2002) required credit and investment firms to establish a *departamento o servicio de atención al cliente* and give them the power to appoint an independent expert to resolve disputes on investment services (*Defensor del Cliente*).

[142] See Art 30(4) of the Ley 44/2002, de 22 de noviembre rules of procedure laid down by Real Decreto 303/2004.

[143] See the fifth transitional provision of the Ley 2/2011, de 4 de marzo, de Economía Sostenible (BOE n 55 de 5 de Marzo de 2011). The order of the Ministry of Economy and Competitiveness ECC/2502/2012 lays down the rules governing the procedures before the Servicios de reclamaciones (BOE-A-2012-14363).

[144] Art 51 requires public bodies (*poderes públicos*) to protect consumers and clients through proceedings that ensure the safety, health and legitimate economic interests of consumers. After a short period of experimentation from 1986 until 1993, the arbitration for consumers' disputes was formally enacted by RDL 636/1993 and recently modified by RDL 231/2008.

[145] Real Decreto-Ley 5/2012, de 5 marzo de mediación en asuntos civiles y mercantiles (BOE n 162, 5/2012).

[146] Ley 7/2017, de 2 de noviembre, por la que se incorpora al ordenamiento jurídico español la Directiva 2013/11/UE, del Parlamento Europeo y del Consejo, de 21 de mayo de 2013, relativa a la

to set up a single ADR scheme for the resolution of disputes in the financial sector, thus replacing the three ADR schemes already in place for banking, securities and insurance contracts disputes.[147]

(i) Servicio de Reclamaciones de la CNMV

Retail clients and both natural or legal persons can submit enquiries (*quejas*), complaints (*reclamaciones*), consultations (*consultas*) in relation to a legal interest or subjective right based on contract terms, financial regulation and good financial practices (*buenas prácticas*).[148] To be admissible, complaints must have already been submitted to the firms' internal complaints handling department (*Departamentos* or *Defensor del cliente*) and must be submitted no later than six years since the time the alleged breach occurred. Since 2012, clients can submit multiple complaints in a single action when the firm's conduct is identical or substantially similar.[149] The procedure lasts four months is free of charge.

The dispute is resolved through a non-binding recommendation (*informe*) that must contain a clear statement on whether the financial firm observed the relevant conduct of business rules.[150] This does not award any compensation or other civil law remedies to the client.[151] When the recommendation is favourable to the complainant, the firm is requested to provide information regarding the follow-up remedial actions taken (eg compensation) within one month.[152] Any firm's failure to respect the recommendation can be taken into account by the authorities in their day-to-day supervision.[153] The decisions of the *Servicios de reclamaciones* are not public, but the CNMV publishes an annual report that contains the aggregate data on the functioning of these ADRs and extracts from the most important decisions.

In 2017, there was a slight decrease in the number of complaints received and finalised, in comparison to the previous two years.[154] 45 per cent of the

resolución alternativa de litigios en materia de consumo (BOE n 268, de 4 de noviembre de 2017, p 105693). Notably, its Art 2(a) extends ADR to legal persons who act outside their business or profession, unless otherwise provided by law.

147 First additional provision of Law No 7/2017.

148 For the definition of *quejas, reclamaciones* and *consultas,* see Art 1(3) of the Real Decreto 303/2004 de 20 de febrero, por el que se aprueba el Reglamento de los comisionados para la defensa del cliente de servicios financieros (BOE n 54, de 3 de marzo de 2004, p 9703).

149 Orden ECC/2502/2012, de 16 de noviembre and CNMV Circular 7/2013 of 25 September 2013 (norma octava).

150 See Servicio de reclamaciones CNMV, Annual Report 2011, 28.

151 CNMV, Memoria reclamaciones 2011, 17.

152 Ministerio de Economía y Competitividad. Orden ECC/2502/2012 and CNMV Circular 7/2013, de 25 de septiembre, de la Comisión Nacional del Mercado de Valores, por la que se regula el procedimiento de resolución de reclamaciones y quejas contra empresas que prestan servicios de inversión y de atención a consultas en el ámbito del mercado de valores (BOE n 262 de 1 de Noviembre de 2013).

153 Banco de España. Memoria de reclamaciones 2015, 35.

154 CNMV, Memoria reclamaciones 2017, 50. In 2017 the CNMV resolved 663 complaints (in comparison to 743 in 2016 and 1,516 in 2015).

recommendations were favourable to the complainant.[155] In 2017, defendant firms complied with the CNMV's recommendations in 58.3 per cent of the cases (in comparison to 45.8% in 2016 and 31.3% in 2015).[156] The low level of firms' compliance with the recommendation cast doubt on the capacity of this ADR procedure to strengthen compliance with MiFID conduct of business rules.[157]

(ii) Systema Arbitral de Consumo

The *Systema Arbitral de Consumo* is managed by public administrations who appoint the members of the panels at both national and local levels. The decision of the arbitrator is legally binding, enforceable and non-appealable.[158] The award can be annulled by national courts only in exeptional circumstances, including any violation of a mandatory rule governing the arbitration. This procedure aims to facilitate the consumer's access to justice: legal assistance is not compulsory, the proceeding must terminate within six months (except for motivated reasons) and the arbitrators decide on the basis of equity, unless the parties agree that the dispute is to be decided on the basis of law. The procedure is confidential (the hearing is private, and parties and arbitrators can be sanctioned if they reveal the contents of the award) and is free for the consumer. Although this arbitration scheme can resolve financial and banking disputes involving consumers, it has so far played a very limited role in financial dispute resolution (in 2007, only 1.3% of arbitration awards dealt with banking or financial contracts).[159] The main reasons for the low uptake of this ADR is because clients used the existing sectoral and specific ADR mechanisms in the Spanish legal system.

(iii) Arbitraje de preferentes y deuda subordinada

After the financial crisis, a special arbitration procedure was set up to resolve disputes on the mis-selling of *participaciones preferentes* and other hybrid financial instruments distributed by credit institutions (Bankia, CatalunyaCaixa, and Novacaixagalicia, or NCG) where the *Fondo de reestructuración ordenada bancaria* (FROB) owned a majority capital stake.[160] One of the conditions of the MoU signed

[155] Ibid, 50.
[156] CNMV, Memoria reclamaciones 2017, 53.
[157] ESMA, Peer review suitability requirements, para 126.
[158] If the parties agree on the proposal of the arbitrator, the dispute can be settled before the final determination.
[159] DG SANCO, Study on the use of Alternative Dispute Resolution in the European Union – Country report Spain, 2009. Available at http://ec.europa.eu/consumers/redress_cons/sp-country-report-final.pdf.
[160] BFA/Bankia, CatalunyaCaixa, NCG Banco and Banco de Valencia. On 18 December 2013 the FROB resolved to sell its entire stake in NCG Banco SA (88, 33%) to Banco Etcheverría, SA /Grupo Banesco.

in 2012 between Spain and the European Commission was the burden sharing between hybrid capital holders and subordinated debt holders in banks receiving public capital.[161] The FROB implemented this requirement by allocating losses on hybrid capital and subordinated debt holders. The special arbitration procedure was set up to ensure a fast, effective and cheap redress for holders of hybrid capital and subordinated debt and to determine the amount of client's losses that would ultimately be paid by the FROB and thus fall on taxpayers.[162]

To ensure transparency and accountability of this arbitration procedure, Royal Decree No 6/2013 set up a commission of inquiry (*Comisión de seguimiento de instrumentos híbridos de capital y deuda subordinada*), composed of senior representatives from the CNMV and the Banco de España.[163] The arbitration scheme was only available for retail clients holding *participaciones preferentes* and other defined complex instruments up to €10,000 (417,490 retail clients were covered for a total amount of €7,940 million).[164] The dispute was decided on the basis of the criteria established by Commission of inquiry.[165] These included private law-derived concepts, such as the lack of capacity to contract, and regulatory-derived factors such as the incorrect information provided about the product features, the risks involved and the volume of the transaction. The arbitration, however, had no duty to apply regulatory or private law rules.

The procedure comprised two phases. First, an independent expert appointed by the banks, assessed the merits of each claim and calculated the maximum recoverable compensation.[166] The independent expert then issued an opinion, followed by a proposed covenant to submit the claim to arbitration. If the client accepted the covenant, they must sign an 'Arbitration Agreement', waiving the right to pursue the dispute before a court of justice. The second phase of the procedure is thus managed by the *systema arbitral de consumo* which decided the dispute through a legally binding and enforceable award. The arbitration was in law and the opinion of the expert served to support evidence.[167] The awards are not publicly available so it is not possible to fully understand the impact of private and case law on this procedure.

According to the most recent data published by the *Comision de seguimento*, 79 per cent of eligible clients (328,059) submitted an application for arbitration

[161] MoU, para 17.

[162] See CFA Institute, *Redress in Retail Investment Markets. International Perspectives and Best Practices*. January 2015, 47.

[163] Real Decreto-ley 6/2013, de 22 de marzo, de protección a los titulares de determinados productos de ahorro e inversión y otras medidas de carácter financiero (BOE n 71, de 23 de marzo de 2013, p 22901).

[164] Comisiòn de seguimento de instrumentos hybridos de capital y deuda subordinada. Séptimo informe trimestral sobre la comercializaciòn de instrumentos hibridos de capital y deuda subordinada. Enero 2015.

[165] FROB, Publicidad de los criterios básicos determinados por la Comisión de Seguimiento de Instrumentos Híbridos de Capital y Deuda Subordinada. Nota de prensa, 17 Abril 2013. Available at: www.frob.es/es/Lists/Contenidos/Attachments/319/20130417_PREFERENTES.pdf.

[166] PWC for Nova Galicia Banco, Ernst & Young, for Catalunya Banc and KPMG for Bankia.

[167] See CFA Institute, *Redress in Retail Investment Markets*, 51.

for a total amount of €5,188 billion.[168] The independent expert issued a positive opinion in 75 per cent of cases. Among them, 73 per cent (282,414 clients) received a favourable arbitration award for a total amount of almost €3 billion (€2,988 million). Therefore, each arbitration award has, on average, provided €10,580 in compensation. To have a better understanding of the impact of this arbitration scheme on financial disputes in Spain, it is important to contrast these figures with those related to judicial disputes. Over the same period of time, 29,461 lawsuits were filed with national courts totalling almost €1,830 billion.[169] As of January 2015, the first instance courts had ruled in favour of clients in 89.4 per cent of cases and had awarded €530 million in compensation. The average award per judgment was thus €60,000.[170] As I will show below, the positive outcome, in terms of compensation, is primarily driven by the purposive interpretation of national private law in light of conduct of business rules.[171] However, since this pro-investor case law 'transfers' money from the publicly owned FROB (and not from the banks) to clients, the deterrent-effect of these judgments could be limited: at the end of the day, compensation for misconduct of publicly owned credit institutions is 'funded' by the public budget both in arbitration and litigation.

(iv) ADR Scheme for Disputes on Floor-clauses in Mortgage Contracts

Another special out-of-court dispute resolution mechanism was set up in 2016 to compensate clients who suffered losses as a result of unfair floor clauses (*cláusulas suelo*) included in mortgage contracts. The origin of this ADR scheme is in the landmark *Francisco Gutiérrez Naranjo et al* judgment,[172] where the CJEU held that the limitation of the retroactive effect of the nullity (eg restitutionary effects) of floor clauses, in accordance with the case law of the Spanish Supreme Court,[173] is in contrast with Article 6(1) of Directive 93/13. The main purpose of this special ADR scheme is to avoid creating a backlog resulting from the large amounts of

[168] Comision de seguimento de instrumentos híbridos de capital y deuda subordinada. Séptimo informe trimestral.

[169] This data includes the disputes against Bankia, Catalunia caxia and NGC Banco.

[170] Spanish courts handed down 8,717 judgments in favour of clients and 1,043 judgments in favour of credit institutions. Data available on Aranzadi Información Legal, Thomson Reuters.

[171] See Chapter 5.

[172] Joined cases C-154/15, C-307/15 and C-308/15, *Francisco Gutiérrez Naranjo et al*, ECLI:EU:C:2016:980. See for more detail Chapter 8.

[173] STS, 9 May 2013, n. 241, in particular, para 211. The Plenary Session of the Supreme Court, in a dispute between a consumer association and many credit institutions, held that the floor clauses breached the transparency requirement of Directive 1993/13 because even if they were clear in the text (*transparencia documental*) they did not ensure that the consumer effectively understood the material consequences of their application (*transparencia real*). However, the court limited the retroactive effect of the declaration of nullity to avoid serious economic repercussions for creditors and the financial system.

claims for the restitution of the sums unduly paid due to the unfair floor clauses.[174] Access to the scheme is voluntary. The credit institution makes a proposal for the amount to be returned to the consumer. If the consumer accepts the proposal, they cannot make the same claim in a court.[175] A commission, composed of the Vice Governor of the Banco de España as chair together with seven other members from different government ministries and organisations representative of social interests (including consumers, advocates and the judiciary), will monitor and assess compliance by credit institutions with the rules governing this ADR procedure.[176]

As of 20 September 2017, 1,052,789 claims have been submitted to the credit institutions and 63 per cent have been declared admissibile.[177] 87 per cent of the admitted complaints have been settled with an agreement which awarded, on average, €4.354,23 for each client. Only 37.5 per cent of affected customers have reached an agreement with the banks throughout this system.

It is noteworthy that, to increase the efficiency of judicial resolution of disputes over floor clauses, on 25 May 2017, the Spanish General Council of the Judiciary (*Consejo General del Poder Judicial*) put in place an extraordinary measure mandating 54 first instance courts (at least one per province) to decide disputes on floor clauses in mortgage contracts.[178] In the overwhelming majority of judgments (98.3% out of 9,326) courts ruled in favour of the consumers.[179]

IV. Adjudicative Approach

The next sections examine how (ie on the basis of which rules) the Italian Ombudsman, ACF, the CNMV's Complaints Service and FOS – the only ADR mechanisms for which the full text or extracts of the decisions were available – have decided the disputes submitted to them. To facilitate the comparison between different

[174] Real Decreto-ley 1/2017, de 20 de enero, de medidas urgentes de protección de consumidores en materia de cláusulas suelo (BOE n 18 de 21 de enero de 2017).

[175] The parties can agree to suspend ongoing proceedings on the same matter to start this extra-judicial process and the judicial proceedings on the same subject matter can be suspended during the procedure, at the parties request, during this process.

[176] See ECB, Opinion of 26 May 2017 on the Commission for the monitoring of alternative dispute resolution procedures and the reserve funds of banking foundations (CON/2017/19).

[177] Comisión de seguimiento, control y evaluación prevista en el Real Decreto-Ley de 20 de Enero, de medidas urgentes de protección de consumidores en materia de cláusulas suelo. Prime informe semestral, Noviembre 2017.

[178] The measure was in force from 1 June until 31 December 2017. See www.poderjudicial.es/portal/site/cgpj/menuitem.65d2c4456b6ddb628e635fc1dc432ea0/?vgnextoid=3b96a92cf8f3c510VgnVCM1000006f48ac0aRCRD&vgnextlocale=en&vgnextfmt=default&vgnextchannel=a64e3da6cbe0a210VgnVCM100000cb34e20aRCRD&lang_choosen=en.

[179] Data available at: www.poderjudicial.es/cgpj/es/Poder-Judicial/En-Portada/El-98-3-por-ciento-de-las-mas-de-9-000-sentencias-dictadas-en-2017-por-los-juzgados-especializados-en-clausulas-abusivas-fueron-favorables-al-cliente.

adjudicative approaches, ADR bodies' decisions are examined on the basis of the type of conduct of business rule whose infringement was alleged and the type of remedy granted to investors.

A. Fair Treatment Clause

MiFID's duties to act honestly, fairly and professional and in the best interest of the clients were recurrently used as a legal basis to provide redress to retail clients especially where firms did not ensure a substantial or effective compliance with more specific conduct of business rules.

In the UK, FOS has decided a high number of disputes where the client challenged the outcome of the review conducted by the redress scheme on IRHPs. In many cases it has concluded that the bank, despite the positive outcome of its review, had not properly informed clients on the break cost of the hedging product and awarded compensation to the client.[180] In one case, FOS concluded that even if the bank had communicated to the client information about the operation of the various hedging options of the swap, the information on break costs was not sufficiently clear to enable a customer (who was an experienced businessman) to understand the magnitude of the risk. FOS came to this conclusion by assessing the client's comments from phone call transcripts, which showed he could not quantify the costs of the different hedging options.[181]

In Italy, the Ombudsman has often decided a dispute based on a literal interpretation of the contractual documentation submitted by the parties. For example, it decided that the fact the contract specified the risks of a debt instrument and documented the (positive) outcome of the suitability and appropriateness test excludes a liability of the firm for breach of conduct of business rules.[182] The ACF has taken a less formalistic approach by pointing out, in several decisions, that investment firms must ensure an effective and concrete compliance with their information duties: the client's declaration that he received the information is not sufficient to prove firm's compliance with its duties.[183] In disputes concerning the sale of illiquid debt securities, ACF held that the firm is liable for its failure to provide the information set out in the CONSOB Communication n 9019104/2009 on illiquid financial instruments.[184] It is, however, for the client to provide information to prove the illiquid nature of the instrument, the fact that the issuer is not listed is not sufficient.[185] In disputes concerning Lehman Brothers' securities, ACF confirmed that the firm cannot limit disclosure to the rating of the security but

[180] Ref DNR1087405, ref DNR1544213, DRN2008922.
[181] Decision March 6, 2014 ref DRN7540587. See also Decision DRN1631455.
[182] Decision of 31 May 2016, n 899/2015, in Annual Report, 2016, 67.
[183] Decisions nn 11, 34, 155/2017 in Annual Report 2017, 96.
[184] Decisions n 16, 25, 26, 54, 61, 71,107/2017 in Annual Report 2017, 62.
[185] Decisions n 36, 38, 90/2017 in Annual Report 2017, 62.

must also provide any relevant information which can offer an updated view about the risks of the instrument and help the client to take a more informed investment decision.[186]

In Spain, the CNMV Complaints Service has emphasised, like the Italian ACF, the need for effective compliance with MiFID's conduct of business rules. For example, it consistently held in disputes on *participationes preferentes* and subordinated debt, that the firm does not meet its information obligations on the features and inherent risks by simply referring to the content of its prospectus available on CNMV's registers.[187] The CNMV also found a breach of pre-contractual disclosure rules where the clients had signed the prospectus summary on a date later than that of the subscription order, which implied that the entity had not provided them with the information prior to contracting the mandatory exchangeable subordinated bonds.[188] More recently, in numerous decisions on the mis-selling of *participaciones preferentes* the CNMV noted that the firms did not provide adequate information, either because the information was contradictory and thus misleading for the client, or because key information on the technical features of the product were missing.[189] Similarly, the CNMV has recently stressed the importance of detailed precontractual information on the risks of the CFDs and options.[190]

B. Suitability Rule

In the UK, FOS decided a high number of securities disputes concerned the question as to whether the firm gave advice to the client or whether it provided an execution-only service. To consider this question, it mainly took into account the concrete circumstances of the case and the documentary evidence available (eg e-mail exchanges between the parties, declaration of the client in the MiFID questionnaire). In one case, FOS concluded that a firm could not make implicit recommendations or advice to clients in the absence of an advisory contract because this could place the client in a more precarious situation that they would have been without the advice.[191] In another case, quoting CESR and *Rubenstein v HSBC* ([2012] EWCA Civ 1184), it concluded that advice can be given even if the adviser made comments which gave the impression that a product was suitable.[192]

[186] Decision n 116/2017, in line with Cass 18 May 2017, n 12544 in Annual Report 2017, 63,

[187] CNMV, Annual report 2016, 98 (complaint R/143/2016).

[188] Ibid, 2017, 97 (R/856/2015).

[189] CNMV, Memoria reclamaciones 2014, 47 and Memoria reclamaciones 2017, 115.

[190] Ibid, 2017, 117 (R/150/2017, R/751/2016, R/752/2016, R/151/2017, R/149/2017, R/174/2017, R/176/2017 y R/297/2017).

[191] FOS, ref DRN7123282.

[192] FOS, ref DRN8682889/2017.

The FOS generally adheres to regulatory requirements of COBS rules, for example, assessing whether correct information was provided about the affordability and capacity for loss.[193] In addition, FOS emphasised that the suitability test should allow the firm to obtain 'as much information as is necessary to understand the essential facts about the client' and that a questionnaire cannot attempt to abrogate the responsibility of the firm to get to know its client, passing on the consumer the responsibility to assess his suitability.[194]

In several decisions, regarding the alleged mis-selling of contracts for difference (CfD), distributed under execution-only agreements, FOS undertook a complete assessment on whether the firm had respected the appropriateness rule (COBS 10.2). It concluded that the warning that the product was not appropriate for the client could not be considered as an 'oxymoric clause' and the firm could not be held responsible for the loss suffered by the client.[195] In a strand of cases regarding the mis-selling of IRHPs, FOS decided that advice was given to client and dismissed the banks' argument that, in line with the judgments in *Green and Rowley v Royal Bank of Scotland*, the bank's breach of suitability rule did not give rise to a remedy in common law.[196] FOS stressed that this judgment 'focused on the application of common law duties, rather than an analysis of the bank's adherence to the Conduct of Business (COB), and other, regulatory rules [and] the judgment was not an assessment of what is fair and reasonable.[197] Also, in disputes concerning complaints for unsuitable advice or portfolio management, FOS undertook a concrete examination of the facts at stake (ie whether the sum invested was proportionate in comparison to the total amount of investor's portfolio)[198] to decide whether the financial service was suitable for the risk profile and professional experience of the client. In some cases, FOS also took into account the suitability rule (COBS 9.2) and examined whether the firm had observed all the procedural steps prescribed by that rule, irrespective of whether it complied with its duties at common law.[199]

In Italy, the Ombudsman has taken a quite formal approach in assessing compliance with the suitability rule and has consistently held that the firm meets the suitability rule in transactions involving illiquid debt securities when the client declares in the MiFID questionnaire that he has sufficient knowledge and experience in financial instruments and accepts the risks connected to illiquidity.[200]

[193] FOS, ref DRN0703177/2018 (in the case at stake, FOS concluded that sufficient information was given).

[194] FOS, ref DRN9083640/2016.

[195] FOS, ref DNR8042618 and DNR5067630. See also FOS, ref DRN1036921/2018.

[196] *Green and Rowley v Royal Bank of Scotland plc* [2012] EWHC 3661 (QB) and *Green and Rowley v Royal Bank of Scotland Plc* [2013] EWCA Civ 1197.

[197] Ref DNR7426826 and ref DNR7432617.

[198] Ref DRN0990618 and ref DRN3529093.

[199] Ref DRN0627149 and ref DNR7476955 (where FOS applied Principle 6 from the FSA's Handbook according to which a 'firm must pay due regard to the interests of its customers and treat them fairly').

[200] Decision n 159/2016, in Annual Report, 2016, 77.

By contrast, ACF has assessed the practical and factual dimension of the firm's conduct, by evaluating if the firm has effectively informed the client about the risks of the financial instruments. In particular, it held, in line with the settled case law of the Italian Supreme Court, that the firm cannot simply inform the client about the unsuitability of the investment but it must also explain why it is unsuitable by referring to the specific risks of the instrument.[201] If the firm comes to the conclusion that the financial instrument is unsuitable it should give the client enough time to reflect on whether, in spite of that assessment, he still would like to execute the order.[202] ACF has also taken into account the concrete circumstances of the case, including the client's profile. For instance, it held that a firm failed to conduct its suitability test by recommending illiquid instruments to a client who was 80 years old with no experience in financial markets.[203] In the same vein, ACF has decided, making reference to the 2012 ESMA Guidelines on Suitability (ESMA/2012/387) that clients are bound by their declaration, but firms should assess the reliability of information received to reduce the risk of self-assessment and should have adequate tools in place to make this assessment.[204]

In Spain the CNMV's Complaints Service recommended that firms should determine the client's risk profile on the basis of its internal product governance rules and make sure that this classification is consistent with the client's profile emerging from the MiFID questionnaire as well as the advice or portfolio management contract.[205] The CNMV's Complaints Service stressed in numerous recommendations that it is not good practice for firms to include generic disclaimers in their contractual documentation as evidence of compliance with informational requirements.[206] It also decided that, irrespective of whether an advisory contract was concluded, the service may constitute advice[207] if (i) it is offered through private banking, rather than the retail or commercial segment of the firm (private banking services are usually provided by qualified staff); (ii) the client received a MiFID questionnaire in response to his question about the best options for investing; (iii) the client recognised that they have received advice; (iv) there are e-mails, telephone recordings and other elements on durable media that make it possible to verify that the entities performed more-or-less explicit investment recommendations with regard to one or several products; and (v) the financial instrument is offered to recover losses suffered in another previously acquired product with similar characteristics.

[201] Decision n 116/2017 in Annual Report 2017, 67.
[202] Ibid, Decision n 61/2017, 67.
[203] Ibid, Decision n 138 and 150/2017, 68.
[204] Ibid, Decision 10, 13, 62, 115, 116/2017, 164.
[205] CNMV, Memoria reclamaciones 2010, 26. The CNMV also noted that firms provide wrong classification of investment products, such as the classification of subordinated debt securities in the '*risk free*' bracket (CNMV, Memoria reclamaciones 2012, 29).
[206] See, in particular, CNMV, Memoria reclamaciones 2013, 38 where the CNMV laid down recurrent types of terms which should not be included in financial contracts.
[207] CNMV, Memoria reclamaciones 2011, 26. See also 2017, 112.

C. Appropriateness Rule

FOS assessed the appropriateness rule in light of the regulatory requirements (COBS 10.2.1). Interestingly, given that this test focuses only on whether the investor has sufficient knowledge and experience to understand the risks involved in the service or instrument offered and complainants were generally experienced investors buying complex financial instruments, FOS, in several cases, concluded that this test was not breached or that the firm was not under the obligation to perform it.[208]

In Italy, while ACF has not yet expressly considered claims regarding the breach of appropriateness rule, the Italian Ombudsman has consistently held that the clients' declaration that he has knowledge and experience in investment services, shields firms from civil liability.[209] A warning as to the lack of appropriateness of the financial instrument can be validly given to the client who purchased securities on an internet platform even if that warning is transmitted via a pop-up.[210]

In Spain, the CNMV's Complaints Service issued a catalogue of recommendations on when a financial product should be considered appropriate (eg when the client has actual investment experience in products with similar characteristics, an academic qualification in finance, or when a finance department or chief financial officer is making investment decisions on their behalf).[211] In this respect, CNMV recommended that the warnings on the lack of appropriateness should be clearly visible and introduced in separate documents to make sure that the client is effectively informed.[212] It has also stressed that firms must comply with the requirement of Circular 3/2013 providing the proper warnings to clients if the financial instrument is not suitable.[213]

D. Remedies for Breaches of Conduct of Business Rules

In the UK FOS has consistently held that compensation should leave the client in the same position as if they had not been given unsuitable advice. This is calculated by comparing the actual investment performance with what could have been achieved from more appropriate types of investment.[214] The causal link between the conduct and the breach is assessed using less strict criteria than the ones

[208] FOS, ref DRN9077503/2015; ref DRN9813068/2017; ref DRN7720848/2018; ref DRN6031301/2018 and ref DRN8994666/2018.

[209] Decision of 27 January 2016, n 786/2014; decision of 27 October 2014, n 548/2013.

[210] Decision of 5 July 2016, n 94/2016, in Annual Report 2016, 78.

[211] CNMV, Memoria reclamaciones, 2010, 24.

[212] Ibid, 2012, 29 (R/880/2015 and R/44/2016(R/416/2016).

[213] Ibid, 2017, 87 (R/752/2016, R/149/2017 and R/151/2017).

[214] FOS ref DRN4404806.

courts would probably use in similar circumstances. For example, in a case where unsuitable advice was given, FOS held that it was 'fair and reasonable' to give compensation, notwithstanding arguments about a break in the chain of 'causation' and the 'remoteness' of the loss from the (poor) advice given, because the consumer would not have invested in the first place had it not been for the unsuitable advice.[215]

In disputes concerning Lehman Brothers products, sovereign bonds and illiquid products, the Italian Ombudsman has consistently held that the lack of suitability[216] or appropriateness[217] test determines the absolute nullity of the contract and the consequent restitution of the purchase price of the financial instrument to the client. Notably, the Ombudsman has also taken this decision after the landmark judgments of the Supreme Court of 19 December 2007, n. 26724 and 26725, which denied that the breach of conduct rules causes the contract to be null and void.[218] Instead, when the suitability or appropriateness test has not been properly carried out (ie because some information has not been given or requested by the client), the Ombudsman has decided to compensate the client for the difference between the value of the securities at the purchase and their value at the moment of submission of the complaint, since it is not possible to determine whether they would have bought the securities had the bank complied with its conduct of business rules.[219] However, the Ombudsman has not compensated non-economic losses deriving, in particular, from 'pain and suffering'[220] or 'loss of time' due to research done by the client to understand information provided by the intermediary[221] or to the time needed to prepare the complaint[222] or the delay in the redemption of units.[223]

In line with the Ombudsman, ACF has decided that compensation shall amount to the difference between the value of the financial instrument at the time of the purchase and the value obtained from the sale of that instrument, or at the time when the client was aware, with due skill and care, about the riskiness of that instrument, excluding the dividends or coupons received.[224] However, where the sale of the financial instrument is legally or practically not possible (ie for illiquid instruments), the compensation should also include the loss of value of the instrument which took place after this moment and until the time of the award of compensation.[225] Where the defendant firm did not promptly execute

[215] FOS, ref DRN8682889/2017. See also FOS, ref DRN6024919/2015.

[216] Decision of 26 June 2013, n 119/2013, n 175/2013, decision of 25 January 2013 n 875/2012.

[217] Decision of 13 February 2012, n 1029/2012 and decision of 15 March 2012, n 352/2013.

[218] See Chapter 6.

[219] Decision of 27 January 2016,. 653/2015; decision of 27 January 2016, ricorso n 568/2015 in Annual Report 2016, 128.

[220] Decision of 25 January 2013, n 677/2012.

[221] Decision of 28 June 2012, n 427/2012 and n. 299/2012; decision of 10 October 2012, n 299/2012.

[222] Decision of 26 February 2013, n 876/2012.

[223] Decision of 25 January 2013, n 677/2012.

[224] Decisione n 21/2017 in Annual Report 2017, 72.

[225] Decisions n 35, 71/2017 in Annual Report 2017, 73.

the order to sell instruments issued by Banca Popolare di Vicenza SpA and Veneto Banca SpA, ACF compensated the loss of chance equal to the amount that the client would have received, had the firm promptly executed the sale order.[226]

V. A Comparative Assessment

A. 'Supervisory ADR Procedures'

The paragraphs above shown a general increase in the number of complaints submitted to ADR bodies for domestic retail client disputes. The data collected by ESMA on complaints submitted to NCAs confirms a general trend towards the 'de-judicialisation' of retail client disputes. From 2014 to 2018 clients submitted at least 1,000 complaints in every quarter of the year for mis-selling, reaching 3,500 complaints in 2Q/2015, 2,500 complaints in 2Q/2016 and 2,000 complaints in 2Q/2017.[227] The number of cross-border disputes, remains quite low.[228]

The creation of ADR bodies within supervisory authorities might have favoured the de-judicialisation of retail client disputes. 'Supervisory ADR procedures' leverage the resources, expertise and reputation of these authorities, thus incentivising clients to rely on out-of-court dispute resolution mechanisms. This has also shown that 'supervisory ADR procedures' make an important contribution to ensuring the effectiveness of EU conduct of business rules.

This type of ADR procedure does not simply produce 'a settlement for the parties' but determines how regulatory duties and supervisory expectations should be interpreted and, in this sense, they truly complement the investors' protection mandate of supervisory authorities.[229] Even if these ADR schemes are not legally required (and will not be required under the ADR Directive) to apply legal rules when resolving disputes, they rely on such rules to resolve disputes. There is a difference in the type of 'legal rules' used to decide the dispute. The examined data show that the Italian ACF relies on private law rules and case law,

[226] Decisions n 1, 3, 4, 38, 70, 98, 99, 120, 123, 141, 153/2017 in Annual Report 2017, 73.

[227] ESMA, *Report on Trends, Risks and Vulnerabilities* n 1/2018, 20. However, in 2015, ESMA reported that, in 2013, on average 27% of all individuals reporting problems did not lodge a complaint (ESMA, *Report on Trends, Risks and Vulnerabilities* No 1/2015, 35).

[228] FIN-NET handled 2,571 complaints in 2016, of which only 514 concerned investment services contracts. See also Special Eurobarometer 446, July 2016. Available at: http://ec.europa.eu/COMMFrontOffice/PublicOpinion/index.cfm/Survey/getSurveyDetail/instruments/SP ECIAL/surveyKy/2108.

[229] See H-W Micklitz, The Transformation of Enforcement in European Private Law: Preliminary Consideration (2015) 4 *European Review of Private Law* 502 and M Cantero Gamito 'Dispute Resolution in Telecommunications: A Commitment to Out-of-Court' (2017) 2 *European Review of Private Law* 387. For a different opinion based on the UK system: Samuel, *Tools for Culture Change: FCA, Now You Are Listening*! 285. However, the ADR product is only that: a settlement for the parties. ADR does not produce what a court produces: clarification of the law for the benefit of the market as a whole. In fact, it does not even apply the law, but does what seems to be reasonable.

whereas the UK FOS[230] and the Spanish CNMV's ADR scheme make their decisions or recommendations based on their fair and equitable judgment and by relying on financial regulatory standards.

Similarly, the type of remedy granted to investors (which is generally compensation for damages) is determined by the applicable private law rules. The degree of influence of private law in out-of-court dispute resolution is higher in Italy than in the UK where FOS does not generally apply the common law, although some of its positions (ie on the measure of damages) reflect those of national courts. The Spanish supervisory ADR does not rely on private law concepts to resolve disputes, but this could be explained by the fact that this ADR scheme proposes a non-binding solution to the parties.

Therefore, although ADR entities do not apply strictly legal rules, they refer to regulatory principles to assess firms' conduct and they take private law concepts (ie causation, measure of damages) to award compensation to clients. The emergence of hybrid private law in ADR should be positively welcomed because this ensures that these bodies strengthen the effectiveness of conduct of business rules and increase the increase the foreseeability of adjudication.[231]

Finally, the publication of decisions and the sufficient degree of independence of the persons in charge of the procedure strengthens the law enforcement function of these ADR schemes, ensuring compliance with the principle of legality in the ADR Directive and Article 69(2) of MiFID II.

B. 'Special Purpose ADR Procedures'

In addition to 'supervisory ADR procedures' in Italy, Spain and the UK, several specific out-of-court procedures have been set up to compensate investors for the widespread detriment caused by mis-selling, to lighten the burden on national courts and to prevent the potential negative impact of court litigation on financial stability. Lack of publicity around the decisions makes it difficult to assess the potential role played by regulation and private law. This increases the risk of legal uncertainty, since complainants are unable to understand how their dispute might be decided. However, anecdotal evidence indicates that regulatory and private law principles have played a role in the Spanish arbitration on *participaciones preferentes* and in the UK consumer redress schemes, although in neither scheme were ADR bodies under an obligation to apply legal rules.

The extraordinary nature of these ADR procedures raises, nevertheless, several key legal issues in relation to the principles of the ADR Directive[232] as well

[230] *BBA v FSA and FOS*, para 77.

[231] See, for this risk especially, O O Cherednichenko, 'Public and Private Enforcement of European Private Law in the Financial Services Sector' (2015) 4 *European Review of Private Law* 640.

[232] The examined special purpose ADR procedures would qualify as ADR procedures under and Recital No 20 of the ADR Directive given that, even if they are set up on *ad hoc* basis, they do not

as the fundamental rights laid down in Article 47 of the Charter. Full compliance of out-of-court dispute resolution with the fundamental right to an effective judicial protection is key to ensure public trust in the effectiveness and fairness of these procedures.[233]

In the landmark *Alassini* judgment, the CJEU held that the Italian law requiring an out-of-court settlement as a mandatory condition for admissibility before the courts might restrict the principle of effective judicial protection but that it corresponded to an objective of general interest (ie to lighten the burden on the court system) and was not disproportionate, given that there is no less restrictive alternative to the implementation of a mandatory procedure and it is not evident that any disadvantages caused by the mandatory nature of the out-of-court settlement procedure are disproportionate to those objectives.[234] Hence, if the CJEU were to follow the approach of *Alassini*, it is likely that the application of Article 47 of the Charter would need to strike a balance between the individual right to an effective procedure and the public interest in the quick and less-expensive resolution of disputes.[235]

The aspects that raise doubts about the compatibility of the special purpose ADR procedures with the ADR Directive and EU fundamental rights relate to the independence of those in charge of the procedure, the publicity, the procedural fairness and the legality of this procedure.

To begin with, in some of the examined special purpose procedures those in charge (ie the skilled person in the UK IRPH scheme) or involved (ie the independent expert in the Spanish arbitration for *participationes preferentes*) in the procedures were appointed by the defendant firms, subject to the approval of a public authority (in the UK, the IRPH scheme), or were the defendant firms themselves (in Spain, the ADR scheme for floor clauses; in the UK, the redress scheme for PPI). The directive acknowledges that 'procedures where the natural persons in charge of dispute resolution are employed or receive any form of remuneration exclusively from the trader are likely to be exposed to a conflict of interest'[236] but it allows Member States to establish these procedures if the specific requirements of its Article 6(3) are met. However, none of the special purpose ADR procedures examined above appear to be in line with these requirements. From a fundamental

concern a single dispute but potentially a very high number of disputes on the same matter. For that reason it could be concluded that they are set up on durable basis under Art 4(1)(h) of the ADR Directive.

[233] Recital No 61 of the ADR Directive states that it respects fundamental rights and observes the principles recognised by the Charter of Fundamental Rights of the European Union, specifically Arts 7, 8, 38 and 47 thereof.

[234] Joined Cases C-317/08, C-318/08, C-319/08 and C-320/08, *Alassini*, paras 64 and 65.

[235] See C Mak, 'Rights and Remedies. Art 47 EUCFR and Effective Judicial Protection in European Private Law Matters' in H-W Micklitz, *Constitutionalisation of European Private Law* (Oxford, Oxford University Press, 2014) 246.

[236] Recital No 22 and Art 2(2)(a) of the ADR Directive.

rights perspective, it should be noted that a body established to determine a limited number of disputes is, in principle, compatible with the fundamental right to a fair trial.[237] However, the CJEU has held on several occasions that the independence requirement not only requires that the body should not receive instructions or is not subject to any hierarchical constraint,[238] ('external independence') but also that it exercises its functions having no interest in the outcome of the proceedings apart from the strict application of the rule of law ('internal independence').[239] In this regard, it is doubtful that the special purpose ADR schemes where the person in charge of resolving the dispute is the defendant firm or one of its employees can actually ensure an impartial resolution of the dispute.

Another aspect observed in special purpose ADR procedures is that the decisions of these special purpose ADR entities (in Spain, the UK and Italy) remain confidential (only the complainant has access to them) and not even extracts are publicly available. Lack of publicity about the decisions makes it difficult for complainants to foresee what could be the outcome of their dispute and when adjudicators deviate from legal or regulatory principles which may conflict with the fundamental right to a fair trial. Publicity around legal proceedings is one of the requirements that ensures the right to a fair trial. In *Heather Moor & Edgecomb Ltd v the UK*,[240] the ECtHR held that lack of publicity around FOS' decision violates, in principle, the right to a fair trial protected by Article 6(1) of the ECHR, given that there was no compelling reason not to publish the FOS's decision. It is likely that the same approach would be followed by the CJEU in the interpretation of Article 47(2) of the Charter.[241]

In addition, special purpose ADR procedures limit the rights of defence of the complainant. In both the Spanish arbitration for *participaciones preferentes* and in the UK IRPH scheme procedures the possibility for the client to defend himself were limited. In the Spanish procedure, the client could not state its case before the

[237] ECtHR, *Lithgow and Others v the United Kingdom*, n 9006/80, 9262/81, 9263/81, 9265/81, 9266/81, 9313/81 and 9405/81, 8 July 1986, para 201.

[238] Case C-53/03, *Syfait and Others*, ECLI:EU:C:2005:333, para 31 where the CJEU held that the Greek competition authority cannot be considered as either a court or tribunal because, even if its members had personal and operational independence, there were no specific guarantees in place regarding their dismissal or the termination of their appointment. *Contra*, opinion AG Jacobs who argued that admitting a reference from this body would allow the reference to be made at the earliest possible stage and would also ensure that a reference to the CJEU is made by a specialised entity rather than a generalist court charged with the review of an administrative decision at a later stage.

[239] Case C-503/15, *Panicello v Pilar Hernández Martínez*, paras 37 and 38.

[240] ECtHR, *Heather Moor & Edgecomb Ltd v the UK*, p 15. On the facts the Strasbourg Court found that in the specific case that right was not breached given that in subsequent judgments of domestic courts, proceedings brought for the review of FOS' decision, quoted at length from FOS's final decision, thus achieving the purpose of Art 6(1) of the ECHR.

[241] See, in more detail, on the relationship between Art 47 of the Charter and Arts 6, 13 of the ECHR, S Prechal, 'The Court of Justice and Effective Judicial Protection: What Has the Charter Changed?' in CH Paulussen, T Takacs, V Lazic, B van Rompuy (eds), *Fundamental Rights in International and European Law* (The Hague, Springer, 2015) 154.

arbitrator (if the opinion of the independent expert was negative);[242] in the IRPH scheme, the client did not have access to all the material on the basis of which the decision was taken.[243] These procedural constrains do not seem to be in line with the fairness' principles of the ADR Directive[244] and with the principle of equality of arms, which implies that each party must be afforded a reasonable opportunity to present his case and that any document submitted to the court can be examined and challenged by any party to the proceedings.[245] In this regard, a situation where the ADR body (like the banks involved in the UK IRPH scheme) can decide the dispute based on its own evidence that is not disclosed to the other party alters the balance between the parties to proceedings, placing the complainant at a substantial disadvantage.

A further aspect that could be scrutinised by the CJEU is whether national ADR procedures grant a level of protection in line with the mandatory rules laid down by MiFID II and strengthen its effectiveness.[246] While supervisory ADR procedures seem to ensure the effectiveness of this directive, because they apply its standards to dispute resolution, it is unfortunately not possible to assess, given the confidential nature of their decisions, whether special purpose ADR procedures actually apply MiFID II and can afford to complainants the level of protection warranted by mandatory rules.[247]

Finally, except for Italy (where consumers have the duty to bring their dispute to an ADR procedure before going to court), participation in ADR procedures (supervisory and special purpose) is voluntary; therefore they are, in principle, in line with the fundamental right to an effective remedy and to a fair trial.[248] In some of them (eg Spanish arbitration on *participationes preferents*), the consumer may decide to accept the proposal or award of the ADR body; in this case the ADR procedure prevents the consumer from bringing the case in court. This form of 'quasi-arbitration' appears to be in line with the ADR Directive, which precludes only arbitration clauses that deprive the consumer of their right of access to a court[249] but accepts that the solution imposed on the parties is binding if they specifically accepted this.

[242] CFA Institute, *Redress in Retail Investment Markets. International Perspectives and Best Practices*, 66.
[243] In *Holmcroft Properties Ltd, R (on the application of) v KPMG LLP & Ors* [2016] EWHC 323 (Admin) the High Court dismissed the challenge for judicial review against the bank's decision not to award consequential losses on the basis of material not disclosed to the client because the bank did not have the obligation to disclose the full records available or even those records on which the bank has relied but it was enough that the bank fairly summarises the reasons why it has reached the decision in circumstances where the customer has a proper opportunity, and is sufficiently informed, to be able to respond to, and if appropriate take issue with, those reasons.
[244] See in particular Art 9(1)(a) of the ADR Directive.
[245] Case C-199/11, *Europese Gemeenschap v Otis NV*, ECLI:EU:C:2012:684, paras 71–72.
[246] The CJEU assessed this aspect in Joined Cases C-317/08, C-318/08, C-319/08 and C-320/08, *Alassini*, para 45.
[247] Art 11(1) of the ADR Directive.
[248] See also Reich, A 'Trojan Horse' 278.
[249] Art 10 of ADR Directive.

VI. Preliminary Conclusion

After the crisis the EU and Member States broadened access to out-of-court dispute resolution mechanisms for retail clients.

MiFID II requires Member States to set up ADR procedures for investment services disputes and mechanisms to compensate clients for infringements of its conduct of business rules. Member States introduced two types of ADR procedures: 'supervisory ADR procedures', set up within supervisory authorities on a permanent basis and 'special purpose ADR procedures', set up by legislators or supervisory authorities to react to widespread mis-selling of financial products.

Since access to ADR procedures is generally not mandatory (ie consumers may decide not to use them) and the outcome of the procedure is not binding (ie firms may decide not to comply with it), ADR procedures can achieve these goals only if both sides trust the procedural and substantive fairness of the procedure.

Procedural fairness is mainly a function of the independence, fairness and transparency of the procedure. While supervisory ADR procedures provide sufficient safeguards in this regard, special-purpose ADR procedures have revealed some deficiencies particularly regarding the independence requirement. Lack of independent adjudication (as shown by the experience of the UK IRPH scheme) undermines the credibility of dispute resolution, the investors' confidence in financial markets and the trust in the supervisory authority involved in the procedure.

Substantive fairness depends on the right balance between ensuring 'justice' in the individual case and securing a sufficient level of predictability and consistency in the decisions. A crucial factor is the role of regulatory and private law principles. On the one hand, the imposition of detailed legal rules and doctrine would stifle ADR bodies and reduce the benefits of an informal, efficient adjudication for retail clients.[250] On the other hand, informal, non-legalistic forms of dispute resolution may give excessive discretion to ADR bodies, undermining out-of-court dispute resolution.

Article 69(2) of MiFID II, made a choice in favour of a law-enforcement-driven out-of-court dispute resolution, establishing a (necessary) link between compensation and breach of conduct of business rules. This provision could indeed strengthen the enforcement of conduct of business rules 'out of courts'. While decisions of supervisory ADR procedures are often informed by regulation and private law (and therefore safeguard MiFID standards of client protection) and give rise to a form of 'administrative enforcement of private law',[251] it was not possible, due to lack of publicity around the decisions, to establish the role played by regulation and private law in the 'special purpose ADR procedures'.

[250] *BBA v FSA and FOS*, para 82.

[251] Micklitz, 'The Transformation of Enforcement in European Private Law' 498.

It has been argued that the use of private law and regulation to grant remedies to clients in out-of-court dispute resolution creates a hybrid private law, which shapes private law remedies on the client's need for protection.

Hybrid private law could implement the MiFID II requirement of a law enforcement-driven ADR procedure and could achieve the right balance between 'discretion and consistency'.[252] Regulatory principles (ie suitability) and private law concepts (ie causation) allow ADR bodies to deviate from the strict application of legal rules where necessary to ensure a fair outcome in the individual case but ensure that decisions comply with regulatory duties and that outcomes are fairly predictable for retail clients as well as investment firms.

The next chapter examines whether and to what extent a hybrid form of private law is also emerging in mis-selling litigation before national courts.

[252] The Hunt Review, The Independent Review of the Financial Ombudsman Service. Opening up, reaching out and aiming high. An Agenda for Accessibility and Excellence in the Financial Ombudsman Service. The Report of an Independent Review of the Financial Ombudsman Service by Rt Hon Lord Hunt of Wirral MBE, 18.

5

Civil Law Effects of Conduct of Business Rules before National Courts

I. Mis-selling Litigation: An EU Law Issue

The tension between regulation and private law has originally arisen in litigation before national courts. The issue across continental jursdictions and the UK was whether, in the absence of an EU law provision, general private law should have been 'adjusted' to provide remedies for breaches of special or sectoral rules falling outside civil codes and common law. Until the global financial crisis, the 'civil law effects' of conduct of business rules was mainly a national (private) law issue concerning the relationship between general private law and special regulations.[1] The failure of Lehman Brothers transformed this national law issue into an EU law and investor protection issue. Thousands of retail investors who suffered unexpected losses due to the credit and investment firms' bankruptcies and the drop of interest rates which affected derivative contracts claimed compensation alleging that pre-MiFID and MiFID I conduct of business rules have been breached.

MiFID I, which became applicable one year before the outbreak of the crisis, offered these investors the chance to put forward new (civil law) claims, based on lack of suitability and appropriateness assessments. A general defence of investment firms and credit institutions was that conduct of business rules do not concern the private law relation between firm and client but only the public law relation between supervisory authorities and firms, therefore, in the absence of an express contractual agreement or a legislative provision, they do not produce civil

[1] For an overview of the debate see especially D Mazeaud, 'Droit commun du contrat et droit de la consommation. Nouvelles frontierès?' in *Études de droit de la consommation. Liber amicorum Jean Calais-Auloy* (Paris, Dalloz, 2004) 697; U Breccia, 'La parte generale fra disgregazione del sistema e prospettive di armonizzazione' in E Navarretta (ed), *Il diritto europeo dei contratti fra parte generale e norme di settore* (Milano, Giuffré, 2008) 31. With special regard to financial regulation, see G Alpa, 'Gli obblighi informativi precontrattuali nei contratti di investimento finanziario. Per l'armonizzazione dei modelli regolatori e per l'uniformazione delle regole di diritto comune' (2008) *Contratto e Impresa* 914; F Annunziata, *Regole di comportamento degli intermediari e riforme dei mercati mobiliari – L'esperienza francese, inglese e italiana* (Milano, 1993) 423; A Hudson, *The Law of Finance* (London: Sweet & Maxwell, 2013)14–15.

law effects. National courts were faced with the question of whether the 'special' investor protection conduct of business rules can produce effects in private law relations, enabling clients to claim compensation or other private law remedies for their violation.

Against this backdrop, this chapter examines the civil law effects of pre-MiFID and MiFID I conduct of business rules in the four selected jurisdictions. In particular, it aims to show how the EU conduct of business rules, as transposed by national law, have influenced the national courts' interpretation of national private law duties (ie duty of care and good faith) and remedies (ie compensation for damages and avoidance of contracts). Specific features of national private laws (ie the role of freedom of contract and good faith,[2], the rules for compensation of pure economic losses,[3] the meaning of 'rights' and 'remedies'[4]) and judicial interpretative techniques[5] have a crucial impact in determining the civil law consequences of conduct of business rules. However, it is beyond the scope of this study to conduct a dogmatic examination of these private law aspects. The main focus of this chapter will be on how the case law of national courts has given effect (or enforced) conduct of business rules before and after the global financial crisis.

To this purpose, the chapter will first illustrate the impact played by conduct of business rules on private law duties, both in advised and non-advised transactions.[6] Second, it will examine the type of remedy have been granted to investors for breaches of conduct of business rules. Finally, it will assess the different judicial approaches emerged across continental jurisdictions and between these jurisdictions and the UK.

II. National Judicial Approaches

A. Private Law Duties in Advised and Non-advised Transactions

(i) The UK

Before the global financial crisis, disputes arose due to a breach of the pre-FSMA conduct of business rules in the distribution of complex financial products; after

[2] See H-W Micklitz, 'On the Intellectual History of Freedom of Contract and Regulation' (2015) 4 *Penn State Journal of Law & International Affairs* 1.

[3] See B.S Markesinis, 'An Expanding Tort Law – The Price of a Rigid Contract Law' (1987) 103 *Law Quarterly Review* 354.

[4] See C van Dam, 'European Tort Law and the Many Cultures of Europe' in T Wilhelmsson (ed), *Private Law and the Many Cultures of Europe* (The Hague, Kluwer Law International, 2007) 57.

[5] See especially H-W Micklitz, *The Politics of Judicial Co-operation in the EU Sunday Trading, Equal Treatment and Good Faith* (Cambridge, Cambridge University Press, 2005) 35

[6] See, for this methodology, also OO Cherednychenko, *Fundamental Rights, Contract Law and the Protection of the Weaker Party* (Sellier, European Law Publishers, 2007) 390. Advised transactions will include investment advice and portfolio management transactions; non-advised transactions will include transactions governed by the appropriateness rule and execution-only transactions.

the crisis they concerned breaches of COB and COBS rules mostly in connection to the distribution of Lehman Brothers securities and interest rate swaps.

The Notion of Investment Advice

The examination on the impact of conduct of business rules on private law duties is particularly relevant in the UK. In this country, the most relevant hurdle faced by plaintiffs in compensation claims is to prove that the firm owed a duty of care to provide investment advice.[7] The centrality of the duty of care in mis-selling litigation is a consequence of the limitations imposed by common law to the compensation of pure economic losses.

Traditionally, pure economic losses, like investment losses, could be recovered only under contract law. Tort law was restricted to the compensation of personal injury or physical damage to property.[8] In the landmark case *Hedley Byrne v Heller*, the House of Lords for the first time held that if the defendant assumed implicitly or explicitly responsibility for what he said and did vis-à-vis the claimant (so called 'assumption of responsibility test')[9], pure economic loss may be recovered through tort law rights of action.[10] Subsequently, English courts developed other tests to establish when a duty of care under tort law exists for pure economic losses ('three-fold-test' and 'incremental test').[11] Without examining the implications stemming from these different liability tests, it should be noted that, as Lord Bingham held in *Her Majesty's Commissioners of Customs and Excise v Barclays Bank plc*, irrespective of the test applied to achieve that outcome, courts have to examine 'the detailed circumstances of the particular case and the particular relationship between the parties in the context of their legal and factual situation as a whole'.[12]

That said in general, the issue whether a bank or investment firm owes duty of care vis-à-vis the investor was thoroughly investigated in *JP Morgan Chase*

[7] See, in detail, K Alexander, 'England and Wale's in D Busch and C van Dam (eds), *A Bank's Duty of Care* (Oxford, Hart Publishing, 2017) 261.

[8] See C Van Dam, *European Tort Law*, 2nd edn (Oxford, Oxford University Press, 2013) 213.

[9] *Hedley Byrne & Co Ltd v Heller & Partners Ltd* [1964] AC 465, para 510. The House of Lords overrulled the prcedent *Candler v Crane, Christmas & Co* [1951] 2 KB 164, by expressly upholding the dissenting opinion delivered by Denning LJ in this judgment. However, *Hedley Byrne v Heller* the House of Lords decided, on the facts, that the bank effectively disclaimed any assumption of a duty of care.

[10] *Hedley Byrne & Co Ltd v Heller & Partners Ltd* para 510. The House of Lords overruled the prcedent *Candler v Crane, Christmas & Co* [1951] 2 KB 164, by expressly upholding the dissenting opinion delivered by Denning LJ in this judgment. However, *Hedley Byrne v Heller* the House of Lords decided, on the facts, that the bank effectively disclaimed any assumption of a duty of care.

[11] See, in detail, on the different tests JL Powell and R Stewart (eds), *Jackson & Powell on Professional Liability* no 2.033.

[12] *Her Majesty's Commissioners of Customs and Excise v Barclays Bank plc* [2007] 1 AC 181 para 189; [2006] UKHL 28, para 4 *per* Lord Bingham. See also *Property Alliance Group Ltd v The Royal Bank of Scotland plc* [2018] EWCA Civ 355, para 62 where the Court of Appeal said that these tests are complementary and should not be considered in isolation from each other.

Bank v Springwell Navigation Corp,[13] where a financial firm (Springwell) brought several claims against Chase for loss suffered in connection with the purchase of 'GKO-Linked Notes' concluded under the pre-FSMA regulatory framework. The High Court and the Court of Appeal dismissed all the claims.[14]

In the first instance judgment, Gloster J came to the conclusion that the absence of any written advisory agreement 'is a significant pointer against the existence of an advisory obligation'.[15] The Judge made an important distinction between giving advice and assuming responsibility for that advice.[16] Giving advice via 'normal recommendations' is an activity that can be done also by a salesperson and does not give rise to a duty of care of providing advice which specifically applies to investment advisers.[17] Only an assumption of responsibility for that advice can give rise to a correspondent duty of care which is actionable at common law.[18]

Under this restrictive notion of investment advice (which is, in practice, centred on an advisory agreement), personal recommendations do not constitute advice. This view was upheld in subsequent judgments on mis-selling cases under the COB[19] and COBS[20] rules. However, in a more recent strand of judgments, the High Court has accepted that an advisory relationship can also be based on a recommendation. In particular, in *Rubenstein v HSBC Bank Plc* concerning a mis-selling of a AIG bond to a retail sophisticated investor under the COB regime, His Honour Judge Havelock-Allan QC held that 'the key to the giving of advice is that the information is either accompanied by a comment or value judgment on the relevance of that information to the client's investment decision, or is itself the product of a process of selection involving a value judgment so that the information will tend to influence the decision of the recipient. In both these scenarios the information acquires the character of a recommendation. If a client asks for a recommendation, any response is likely to be regarded as advice unless there is an express disclaimer to the effect that advice is not being given'.[21] While *Rubenstein v HSBC Bank Plc* paved the way for other judgments that adopted its

[13] *JP Morgan Chase Bank and Others v Springwell Navigation* [2008] EWHC 1186 (Comm). Previously, the 'pragmatic approach' to assess the duty of care was considered in *Bankers Trust International PLC v PT Dharmala Sakti Sejahtera* [1996] CLC 518, para 534.

[14] *Springwell Navigation Corporation (a Body Corporate) v Jp Morgan Chase* [2010] EWCA Civ 1221.

[15] *JP Morgan Chase Bank and Others v Springwell Navigation*, para 440.

[16] Ibid, para 452.

[17] Ibid, para 374.

[18] Ibid. However, Gloster J did not exclude that in other cases a duty of care could also arise where a recommendation is made (para 454). See also *Standard Chartered Bank*, para 544.

[19] *Wilson v MF Global UK Limited* [2011] EWHC 138 (QB) para 94.

[20] *Bank Leumi (UK) plc v Wachner* [2011] EWHC 656 (Comm), para 198; *Standard Chartered Bank v Ceylon Petroleum Corporation* [2011] EWHC 1785 (Comm), para 508; *Grant Estates Limited v RBS*, para 73.

[21] *Rubenstein v HSBC Bank Plc* [2011] EWHC 2304 (QB), para 81. The Court referred to *Martin v Britannia Life Limited* [1999] EWHC 852 (Ch) para 5.2.5. and *Walker v Inter-Alliance Group plc* [2007] EWHC 1858, para 30.

'regulatory driven' notion of advice,[22] in some recent swap mis-selling judgments the High Court re-affirmed the traditional view that a recommendation is not sufficient to give rise to a duty of care to advise.[23]

Non-advised Transactions

When the investor is unable to prove that the financial instrument was provided on advisory basis, the issue is whether the firm owes further duties than the *Hedley Byrne v Heller's* duty not to mis-state and whether regulatory duties may influence the content of these duties. In *Bankers Trust International PLC v PT Dharmala Sakti Sejahtera*, a swap mis-selling case decided in the pre-MiFID regulatory framework, Mance J held that 'if the bank does give an explanation or tender advice, then it owes a duty to give that explanation or tender that advice fully, accurately and properly' and that when a bank makes a representation to the other party it has the duty 'to present the terms and effects of each swap accurately and fairly'. This wording imposed on firms a 'positive' duty to state facts fairly and accurately which went beyond the duty not to mis-state.[24] On the facts, nevertheless, this duty was held to be lacking, given that the investors were experienced in financial matters and should have understood the risks of the swap.[25]

However, in *Green and Rowley v Royal Bank of Scotland plc*,[26] another swap mis-selling case, Tomlison LJ, upholding the judgment of the High Court,[27] held that only a duty to take reasonable steps not to mislead (included in COB Rule 2.1.3) is comprised within the common law duty, whereas the duty to take reasonable steps to communicate clearly or fairly (also included in that rule) goes beyond 'the accuracy of what is said which is the touchstone of the *Hedley Byrne* duty'.[28] In addition, the Judge held that the duty imposed by COB Rule 5.4.3 to take reasonable steps to ensure that the counterparty to a transaction understands its nature goes beyond *Hedley Byrne*'s duty not to mis-state and rejected the view that this COB rules give rise a co-extensive duty of care at common law because a common law duty does not arise by reason of the imposition of the statutory duty but out of the relationship so created.[29]

A more open approach was followed in *Crestsign Limited v National Westminster Bank Plc*, where the Judge, quoting *Bankers* and distinguishing the

[22] *Green and Rowley v RBS* [2012] EWHC 3661 (QB), para 48; *Zaki v Credit Suisse (UK) Ltd.* [2011] 2 CLC 523, para 83–85; *Crestsign v Royal Bank of Scotland* [2014] EWHC 3043 (Ch) 88 at 89; *Haider Abdullah and others v Credit Suisse (UK) Limited and Credit Suisse Securities (Europe) Limited* [2017] EWHC 3016 (Comm), paras 167–168.

[23] *Thornbridge Ltd v Barclays Bank Plc* [2015] EWHC 3430 (QB), para 96; *Marz Ltd v Bank of Scotland Plc* [2017] EWHC 3618 (Ch), para 220; *London Executive Aviation Ltd v The Royal Bank of Scotland Plc* [2018] EWHC 74 (Ch), para 171.

[24] See K Alexander, 'England and Wales' in D Busch and C van Dam (eds), *A Bank's Duty of Care* 254.

[25] *Bankers Trust International Plc v PT Dharmala Sakti Sejahtera* [1996] CLC 518, para 555.

[26] *Green and Rowley v Royal Bank of Scotland plc* [2012] EWHC 3661 (QB), para 82.

[27] Ibid [2013] EWCA Civ 1197.

[28] Ibid, para 17.

[29] Ibid, paras 23–29.

case from *Green and Rowley* held that in an execution-only relationship, the bank not only has a duty not to mis-state but also has a duty 'to explain fully and accurately the nature and effect of the products in respect of which he chose to volunteer an explanation'.[30] This duty did not extend to 'a duty to educate in the sense of giving a comprehensive "tutorial" and satisfying "itself" that [the claimant] understood every aspect of each product nor to a duty to explain other products that the client might have wanted to purchase but the bank did not want to sell'.[31]

Crestsign Limited v National Westminster is important also because, even if there was no advisory relationship and the plaintiff could not rely on the private cause of action for the breach of statutory duty, the Judge held that 'COBS duties are likely to be relevant in determining the standard of care required of a reasonably careful and skilled adviser, since a reasonably skilled and careful adviser would not fall short of the standard required to meet relevant regulatory requirements'.[32] Nevertheless, as the Judge himself noted, this conclusion was 'a Pyrrhic victory of principle but a defeat on the facts' because the bank did not give misleading information and succesfully disclaimed its responsibility for negligent advice.[33]

In several recent swaps mis-selling cases,[34] English courts have refrained from recognising the 'intermediate duty' set out in *Crestisgn* – between the duty not to mis-state and a duty to advise – to fully explain the financial product to the client in execution-only transactions.

A different approach was followed in *Thomas v Triodos Bank*,[35] where the claimants complained that the bank did not provide information about the financial consequences of the redemption of commercial borrowing facilities. His Honour Havelock-Allan QC held that the bank did not owe an advisory duty but nevertheless was under an intermediate information disclosure duty, namely to explain in plain English the financial implications of fixing the rate, more specifically of what this entailed and what the consequences were.[36] While this judgment moves away from the *caveat emptor* approach that underpinned *Green and Rowley v Royal Bank of Scotland plc*,[37] it should be noted it concerned a loan agreement (and not swap contracts) and that the bank subscribed to the Business Banking Code which required it to disclose clear information about the features of the services offered to clients. In fact, in *Property Alliance Group Limited v RBS*, the Court of Appeal,

[30] *Crestsign Limited v National Westminster Bank Plc* [2014] EWHC 3043 (Ch), para 153.

[31] Ibid, para 154.

[32] Ibid, paras 127 and 146.

[33] Ibid, para 177. The Judge also added that 'while the result may seem harsh to some, it is not the role of the common law and this court to act as a regulator'.

[34] *Thornbridge Ltd v Barclays Bank Plc*, paras 125–128 and *Marz Ltd v Bank of Scotland Plc*, para 239.

[35] *Thomas v Triodos Bank* [2017] EWHC 314 (QB).

[36] Ibid, para 81.

[37] See, in this sense, P Reynolds and A Collins, 'Non-advised sales of financial products: an end to caveat emptor?' (2018) Journal of International Banking Law and Regulation, 1.

in a judgment handed down on 2 March 2018, upheld the High Court's decision to dismiss a mis-selling swap claim and firmly reaffirmed that firms do not owe, in principle, an intermediate duty vis-à-vis clients.[38]

Advised Transactions

If the parties entered into an advisory relationship, English courts have accepted that the content of that duty of care, in both contract and tort law, would be informed by the regulatory duties.

The High Court has first affirmed this principle in three judgments concerning disputes litigated under the pre-FSMA rules.[39]

In *Loosemore v Financial Concepts*, His Honour Judge Jack QC held that 'the skill and care to be expected [from the firm] would ordinarily include compliance with the [conduct of business] rules' (FIMBRA suitability rule).[40] In *Seymour v Caroline Ockwell & Co*, His Honour Judge Havelock-Allan QC held that 'whilst the ambit of the duty of care owed by a financial adviser at common law is not necessarily co-extensive with the duties owed by that adviser under the applicable regulatory regime (FIMBRA suitability rule), the regulations afford strong evidence as to what is expected of a competent adviser in most situations'.[41] Similarly, in *Shore v Sedgwick Financial Services Ltd*, the Judge held that 'the skill and care to be expected of a reasonably competent financial adviser ordinarily includes compliance with the relevant regulatory rules (IMRO's suitability rule) [...] and "the regulations afford strong evidence as to what is expected of a competent adviser in most situations" [...]'.[42]

This approach has also been endorsed under the COB and COBS rules. In particular, in *Rubenstein v HSBC Bank plc*, the High Court held that 'in an advisory relationship the scope of the duty which Mr Marsden owed to Mr Rubenstein in contract and in tort embraced the relevant requirements of COB, in particular as to the suitability of the product he or she was recommending him'[43] and held that the firm breached the duty of care, the clear, fair and not misleading requirement (COB 2.1.3R) and the suitability rule (COB 5.3.5(2)R).

In *Al Sulaiman v Credit Suisse Securities (Europe) Ltd*, the High Court reiterated that the reasonable steps required under COB and COBS correlate with the exercise of reasonable care required in contract and tort to achieve the same ends

[38] *Property Alliance Group Limited v the Royal Bank of Scotland* paras 67–68 (the Court of Appeal stated 'the expression "mezzanine" duty or intermediate duty, first coined in *Crestsign*, is best avoided. It appears to reflect the notion that there is a continuous spectrum of duty, stretching from not misleading, at one end, to full advice, at the other end').

[39] See also *Gorham and others v British Telecommunications Limited Plc* [2000] 1 WLR 2129, 2141.

[40] *Loosemore v Financial Concepts* [2001] Lloyd's Rep PN 235, para 241.

[41] *Seymour v Caroline Ockwell & Co* [2005] EWHC 1137 (QB) para 76.

[42] *Shore v Sedgwick Financial Services Ltd* [2007] EWHC 2509 (QB), para 161. The appeal against this judgment was dismissed (*Shore v Sedgwick Financial Services Ltd* [2008] EWCA Civ 863).

[43] *Rubenstein v HSBC Bank plc* [2011] para 87 and [2012] para 46.

but dismissed the damages' claims.[44] In the same vein, in *O'Hare & Ors v Coutts & Co*, where an experienced businessman claimed damages for losses suffered in relation to five investments for £8 million made on the advice of the defendant bank, it was confirmed that 'the regulatory regime is strong evidence of what the common law requires [from a financial adviser]' but, on the facts, the Judge found that this duty was not breached.[45] This judgment offers more guidance on how the suitability rule could influence the duty of care.

According to Kerr J, neither the authorities nor the COBS rules prohibit

> a private banker using persuasive techniques to induce a client to take risks the client would not take but for the banker's powers of persuasion, provided the client can afford to take the risks and shows himself willing to take them, and provided the risks are not – avoiding the temptation to use hindsight – so high as to be foolhardy. The authorities include mention of the adviser sometimes having to save the client from himself, but also of the principle that investors take responsibility for their investment decisions including mistaken ones. The duty of care must reflect a balance between those two propositions, which pull in opposite directions'.[46]

Therefore, the duty of care is breached when the investment firm encourages foolhardiness (ie advising him to hazard all he has in a high-risk product) but not where the client takes up a higher risk than he would have done without the advice.[47]

Later on in *Haider Abdullah v Credit Suisse*, a case where members of a wealthy Kuwaiti family complained that they were sold investment products that entailed a higher level of risk than they were prepared to take,[48] Andrew Baker J agreed with Kerr J in that the duty of care is not breached for the fact that the client is 'taking risk or trading beyond the [previously] agreed objective', provided that 'in so advising the private banker must take reasonable steps to ensure that the client appreciates that that is what he is being advised to do'.[49] Notably, the Judge held that the standard-form risk warnings and disclaimers in term sheets or product descriptions may not be enough to explain the magnitude of that risk in the market and other circumstances in which the investment is proposed.[50] For this reason, when a riskier product is offered to the client, the nature of that product should be 'brought squarely to the client's attention and explicit confirmation being obtained from him (and preferably documented) that he is content to be exposed to the greater level of risk'.[51] In this case, it was found that the bank breached its suitability rule and the High Court awarded damages for the breach of section 138D of FSMA.

[44] *Al Sulaiman v Credit Suisse Securities (Europe) Ltd & Anor* [2013] EWHC 400 (Comm), para 18.
[45] *O'Hare & Ors v Coutts & Co* [2016] EWHC 2224 (QB) para 207.
[46] Ibid, para 218.
[47] Ibid.
[48] *Haider Abdullah v Credit Suisse* [2017] EWHC 3016 (Comm).
[49] Ibid, para 170.
[50] Ibid, para 168.
[51] Ibid, para 218.

(ii) France

Financial litigation in France has mostly focused on the breach of conduct of business rules in financial derivatives transactions. Apart from disputes on the mis-selling of interest rate swaps, a typical pattern of litigation concerns the firms' breach of the duty, now set out in the AMF General Regulation, to ensure that clients' debt positions in short-selling transactions conducted on the regulated markets (*service de règlement ou de livraison différé*) are sufficiently covered by collateral.[52] As a preliminary point, it is also worth noting that on 1 October 2016, Order No 2016-131 reforming the French Civil Code provisions on contract law and the general regime and proof of obligations, came into force.[53] The provisions of the civil code indicated in this study refer to the old civil code, which has been the subject of any litigation so far.

Non-advised Transactions

While English courts are careful about expanding common law duties via regulatory duties, French courts have shaped general private law duties to inform (*óbligation de renseignement*), to warn (*óbligation mise en garde*) and to advise (*óbligation de conseil*) on the basis of applicable regulatory framework.[54] In comparison to UK courts, French courts give lesser importance to the type of contractual relationship (advised or non-advised) between firms and clients to determine the private duties of investment firms. Ever since the so called *arrêt Buon*, handed down on 5 November 1991,[55] the Supreme Court held that whatever the contractual relationship between the client and the bank, the bank has a duty to warn the client about the risks incurred in speculative financial operations. The Supreme Court came to this important conclusion based on the Decree of 3 January 1968, which required firms to ensure that client's positions in short-selling transactions are appropriately covered and Article 1147 cc.[56] Notably, at the time the transactions took place (between 1980 and 1982) there was no express legislative duty for firms to warn clients about investment risk. For this reason, it has been argued that this duty was a 'judicial creation'.[57]

On 26 February 2008 the Supreme Court, overturning the judgment of the Court of Appeal and previous settled case law,[58] held, on the basis of Article 1147 cc

[52] See Chapter 2.

[53] Ordonnance n° 2016-131 du 10 février 2016 portant réforme du droit des contrats, du régime général et de la preuve des obligations (JORF n°0035 du 11 février 2016 texte n° 26).

[54] See M Fabre-Magnan, *De l'obligation d'information dans les contrats* (Paris, LGDJ, coll. Bibl. dr. privé, 1992) n° 467 ss; M. Storck, *Le particularisme de l'obligation d'information en matière de gestion d'instruments financiers* (2006) *Revue trimestrielle de droit commercial* 157.

[55] Cass, com, 5 November 1991, *Bull* 1991, n 327, pourvoi n 89-18.005.

[56] Under the new civil code, Art 1231 lays down conditions for contractual liability.

[57] See, in more detail, T Bonneau, 'France' in Busch and van Dam, *A Bank's Duty of Care* 115.

[58] Cass, com, 2 December 1997, n 95-17.594, *Bull* 1997, IV, no 314; Cass, com, 8 July 2003, n 00-18.941, *Bull* 2003, IV, no 118; Cass, com, 8 July 2003, n 00-18.941 and Cass, com, 14 December 2004, n 02-13.638.

and Article 533-4 CMF, that a breach of the firms' duty to ensure that the client debt position is covered makes the firm liable for contractual damages because the rules on the duty to cover debt positions not only aim to protect the effiency and stability of the financial system but also the clients who make a buy or sell order through an intermediary firm.[59]

In other judgments, the Supreme Court clarified that, even if a firm has the power to require higher collateral than that provided for by the AMF Regulation (Article 516-4(2)), the amount must be proportionate to the risks of the transaction[60] and that a firm's failure to require the client to provide collateral renders it liable for the aggravation of the loss suffered by the client.[61]

The Supreme Court extended the duty to warn beyond failure to cover client positions. On 12 February 2008 the Supreme Court, in a dispute on breach of information duties on execution-only transactions concluded before MiFID,[62] held that whatever the contractual relationship between the client and the bank, the financial institution not only has a duty to warn the client but it also has a duty to assess its financial situation, thus extending to execution-only transactions the duty that MiFID had previously established for advised transactions.

However, even before the entry into force of MiFID, the Supreme Court clarified that the duty to warn only applies if the transaction concerns speculative products and a non-expert client.[63] The Supreme Court has followed a case-by-case approach to identify speculative transactions. It has held that speculative transactions include short-selling practices[64] and options,[65] while non-speculative transactions include an interest rate swap concluded for hedging purposes,[66] the purchase of units in UCITS[67] and a life insurance contract.[68]

The distinction between non-expert (*opérateur profane*) and expert clients (*opérateur averti*), introduced in the pre-MiFID regulatory framework, is based on the concrete level of knowledge and experience of the client, based on their

[59] Cass, com, 26 February 2008, *Bull* 2008, IV, n°42, pourvoi n. 07-10.761. See also Cass, com, 4 November 2008, n 07-21.481, *Bull* 2008, IV, no 185; Cass, com, 13 October 2009, n 08-13.878; Cass, com, 24 November 2009, n 08-13.295.

[60] Cass, com, 18 May 2010, n 09-67.102. See M.Storck, *Disproportion du montant de la couverture avec le risque spéculatif* (2012) 4 *Revue de Droit bancaire et financier* 162.

[61] Cass, com, 22 May 2012, n 11-17.936.

[62] Art 3-3-5 du Règlement Général du Conseil des marchés financiers.

The same principle has been reiterated under Art 10 of décision n° 99-07 du Conseil des marchés financier (Cass, com, 4 November 2008, *Bull* 2008, IV, n°185, pourvoi n°07-21.481) and after MiFID entered into force (Cass, com, 16 February 2016, n° 14-25.104 (confirming that the duty to warn the client on the complexity and high risks of the the financial instrument shall be respected also in execution only transactions in accordance with Art 533(13) of the CMF).

[63] See recently, with regard to transactions conducted under the MiFID's regulatory framework: Cass, com, 10 February 2015, 13-28483 and Cass, com, 8 November 2017, n 15-22672.

[64] Cass, com, 12 February 2008, D 2008. 689, obs.X Delpech.

[65] Cass, com, 23 February 1993, D 1993. 424, note I. Najjar.

[66] Cass, com, 24 May 2018, n 17-14697.

[67] Cass, com, 19 September 2006, JCP 2006 II 10201; Cass, com, 12 October 2010, n° 09-16.961, D 2011 472.

[68] Cass, com, 20 March 2007, JCP E 2007 1819.

previous transactions,[69] irrespective of the legal status of the client as a natural or legal person. For example, French courts held that a client who has worked in a stock exchange[70] or for an insurance company[71] or an engineering company[72] or an old lady with previous experience in securities markets[73] have sufficient knowledge to understand the risks of financial transactions, but a lawyer or expert in the field of financial regulation is not deemed to be a professional client.[74]

If the transaction is not speculative and/or does not concern a non-expert client, firms have only a private law duty to inform the client, in both non-advised and advised transactions, about the characteristics of the financial instrument. The Supreme Court has derived this duty from Article 1147 cc, Article 58 of Law 597/1996[75] and Article 533(4) of the CMF pre-MiFID.[76] Firms do not comply with this duty if they just provide clients with an information notice on financial instruments approved by the supervisory authority without giving specific information about their specific charateristics.[77]

Advised Transactions

According to the settled case law, financial firms do not have a general duty to advise clients (*óbligation de conseil*);[78] this duty can be enforced only if its is expressly laid down by law or the contract.[79] The frequent nature of financial transactions does not indicate *per se* that the client is fully aware of the risks,[80] but it is a factor that could provide evidence of the client's expertise, together with the expertise acquired by the client during the contractual relationship.[81] The Supreme Court has stressed in several judgments that the suitability rule requires firms to conduct a thorough assessment of clients' experience, knowledge and objectives and this cannot be complied with by simply asking the client to conduct a

[69] Cass, com, 27 May 2014, 09-13803.

[70] Cour d'Appel de Paris, 26 April 2000, *Moritz c/ SA Oppenheim-Pierson-Melendes.*

[71] Cour d'Appel de Paris, 29 October 1999, *SA Wargny c/ Moreau.*

[72] Cass, com, 7 April 1998, *Savour club c/ BFCE et Cie AGF*, RTD com. 1998 p 637.

[73] Cass, com, 18 October 2017, n 16-10271.

[74] Cass, com, 26 March 2008, *Bull* 2008, IV, n 07-11.554.

[75] Cass, com, 10 January 2012, n 10-28800.

[76] See, in particular, Cass, com, 19 septembre 2006, n° 05-14.343, 05-14.344 et 05-15.304, *Bull* 2006, IV, n 185, 186 and 187.

[77] Cass, com, 24 June 2008, n 06-21.798 (with regard to an information notice approved by the Commission des opérations de bourse on collective investment funds). See also Cass, com, 24 juin 2008, n 06-21.798.

[78] See, in particular, J Attard, 'Du champ d'application du devoir de conseil du banquier' (2011) *Revue trimestrielle de droit commercial* 11.

[79] See Cass, com, 14 January 2016, n 14-27.001. See also A Prum, 'Le dilemme de la jurisprudence: protege' (2015) *Droit & Patrimonie* 85.

[80] Cour d'Appel de Paris, 26 November 1999, *Chaumet c/ SA Wargny*, RD bancaire et financier 2000, no 79.

[81] Cass, com, 6 December 2005, Juris-Data n. 031396.

self-assessment of their competence.[82] However, in a recent judgment concerning the alleged breach of the suitability rule, the Supreme Court considered the fact that the client, while retail and non-experienced, had communicated to the bank that his investment objective was to make a speculative investment. Based on this, the Court concluded that no breach could be imputed to the firm.[83]

In portfolio management transactions, the Supreme Court requires the financial firm to hold a higher standard of skill and care than in non-advised transactions.[84] The Supreme Court applies the rules of the contract of mandate and therefore considers this contract as involving an *obligation de moyen* but requires the financial firm to have a general duty to supervise the client (*obligation générale de vigilance*) not only before the conclusion of the contract but also during its performance, by disclosing all the circumstances that might change the initial relationship and which may impact on the investment.[85]

(iii) Italy

In Italy, most securities disputes have arisen for mis-selling of securities issued by the Republic of Argentina (Argentina bonds), the Cirio Group (Cirio bonds) and the Parmalat Group (Parmalat bonds) between 2000 and 2003.[86] These securities, typically bonds, were distributed to unsophisticated retail clients without investment advice, prospectus and rating, before their issuance (in the so called 'grey market'). The bankruptcy of these issuers caused losses to thousands of clients and triggered an unprecedented wave of disputes that are still being decided by the Italian Supreme Court. After the global financial crisis, a high number of disputes concerned the mis-selling of Lehman Brothers' bonds and interest-rate swaps.

Non-advised Transactions

One of the most recurrent claim concerns the breach of the pre-MiFID suitability rule (Article 29(3) of Consob Regulation No 1152/1998). In 2008, the Supreme Court held that this suitability rule imposes stricter requirements than the principle of pre-contractual good faith and also applies to execution-only services and to all non-professional clients, even if they have previously invested in risky securities.[87] The Supreme Court came to this conclusion based not only

[82] Cass, com, 27 May 2014, 09-13803; Cass, com, 27 May 2014, 09-13804; Cass, com, 13 May 2014, 09-13805.

[83] Cass, com, 26 April 2017, n. 15-27731.

[84] Cass, com, 5 May 2009, pourvoi n 08-14.983 and 23 June 2009, n 07-22.032.

[85] Cass, com, 8 November 2005, Juris-Data n 030874.

[86] See in detail on this case law A Perrone and S Valente, 'Against All Odds: Investor Protection in Italy and the Role of Courts' (2012) 13 *European Business Organization Law Review* 31.

[87] Cass, 25 June 2008, n 17340. See also Cass, 17 February 2009, n 3773 and Cass, 7 June 2016, n 15269. The judgments of Italian courts are available at: www.ilcaso.it and www.dejure.it.

on the letter of CONSOB Regulation No 10943/1997, applicable at the time of the purchase, but also on the purpose of conduct of business rules to protect investors.

The Supreme Court has subsequently clarified the intensity of the (pre-MiFID) suitability requirements. In a dispute over the mis-selling of Argentina's bonds in 2000, the Supreme Court held that even if a firm provided information and warnings about the unsuitability of the investment but not in written form, the burden of proof of compliance with these duties remains with the firm.[88] More importantly, the Court stressed that the specific purpose of this rule is to enable the client to make an informed decision: therefore the firm must inform the client not only about the illiquid nature of the financial instrument, connected to the fact that it is not listed, but also about the specific reasons that make the investment unsuitable for them (specifically: the risk of the effective redemption of the instrument at the maturity date).[89]

In addition, according to the settled case law, the information to be provided to the client under the pre-MiFID suitability rule must be concrete and effective – the information cannot be standardised[90] or contain technical jargon or complicated syntax (eg obscure sentences, use of subordinated sentences).[91] The warning that the financial instrument is not suitable cannot be provided in a generic, standardised sentence but must explain the specific risks to allow the client to make an informed decision.[92]

However, the lower Italian courts are divided as to whether the firms' failure to inform clients about the counterparty risk of Lehman Brothers Group is a breach of the suitability rule. Some Tribunals held that firms could not be expected to provide this information,[93] given that its securities were rated as 'very high' by financial advisers (eg 'Consorzio Patti Chiari'). Other Tribunals, by contrast held that even if a financial intermediary could have foreseen Lehman's collapse, it should have informed the client taking into account not only the rating of the securities but also the deteriorating financial situation of the Lehman Brothers Group after 2007, the amount of money the client had invested, and the nature of the client.[94]

[88] See also Cass, 23 September 2016, n 18702.

[89] See also Cass, 18 May 2017, n 12544. See also Cass, 27 April 2016, n 8394; Cass, 21 April 2016, n. 8089; Cass, 17 November 2016, n 23417; Cass, 26 January 2016, n 1376; Cass, 15 November 2016, n 23268.

[90] See Cass, 18 May 2017, n 12544 and Cass, 16 February 2018, n 3914.

[91] See Cass, 3 April 2014, n 7776.

[92] See Cass, 18 May 2017, n 12544.

[93] See, in particular, Trib Monza, 24 February 2014, n 605; Trib Firenze, 20 February 2014, Trib Roma, 8 November 2013, n 898; Trib Roma, 6 September 2013, n 17856; Trib Torino, 20 November 2012; App. Trieste, 11 May 2012; Trib Venezia, 5 November 2009; Trib Palermo, 5 April 2011.

[94] See in particular Trib Salerno, 20 October 2012 which underlined that already in 2007 Lehman Brothers had fired about 1,200 employees, in 2008 accumulated losses on mortgage securities by $ 2.8 billion and by the end of August 2008, Lehman shares had lost 73% of their value. See also App Trieste, 18 December 2014; Trib Verona, 19 March 2013; Trib Modena, 15 July 2011, n 1190; Trib Torino, 22 December 2010, n 7674. See Trib Massa, 22 October 2015.

In a judgment handed down in 2016, concerning a dispute about Cirio's bonds, the Supreme Court held that even if the applicable law *ratione temporis* allowed the firm to proceed with the transaction if the client gave a written order, the firm has a duty not to carry out an unsuitable transaction.[95] In such a case, the firm should withdraw from the contract of mandate concluded with the client, given that the unsuitable nature of the transaction represents a justified reason for withdrawal under general contract law (Article 1722(1)(3) and Article 1727(1) cc). Therefore, in this case, the Supreme Court used general private law to impose on the firm the 'duty to refuse' introduced by MiFID I.

At any rate, the client's declaration that the financial instrument is adequate does not ensure full compliance with the suitability rule because this provision aims to protect them against the risk of not being adequately informed and cannot be used by the bank to disclaim its civil liability.[96]

With regard to MiFID I conduct of business rules, the Tribunal of Verona, in a dispute about the mis-selling of shares of Banca Popolare di Vicenza SpA, held that the bank's failure to inform their client about the risks deriving from the illiquid nature of the securities was a breach of the appropriateness rule.[97] Making express reference to the CONSOB communication on illiquid financial instruments, the Tribunal stressed that the bank should have assessed the effective capacity of the client to understand the risks involved in these securities which were more similar to OTC derivatives (in respect of which the client had declared to have not sufficient knowledge and experience) than shares in listed companies.

Advised Transactions

In general, there are fewer judgments on advised transactions and the Supreme Court has not yet handed down a judgment on transactions concluded under MiFID I.

Several judgments of the Supreme Court concern the breach of pre-MiFID conduct of business rules in portfolio management services. The Supreme Court, in disputes concerning the pre-MiFID framework, decided that the contract law rule under which the delay of the principal (mandante) to approve the transaction of the agent (mandatario) determines the tacit approval of the transaction (Article 1712(2) cc) does not apply to the portfolio management contract because this service aims to provide a 'surplus of protection' to the client and is not compatible with the private law rule of tacit approval of the transaction.[98]

For the same reason (ie to ensure an effective protection of clients) the Supreme Court has reiterated in several cases that the client has the right to be

[95] Cass, 9 August 2016, n 16828.

[96] Cass, 25 September 2014, n 20178 and Cass, 6 August 2014, n 17726.

[97] Trib Verona, 21 March 2017.

[98] Cass, 24 February 2014. Compare it with Cass, 5 February 2013, n 2736, which noted that the 'investment contract' aims to protect clients by including in its scope financial instruments that would not be regualted by the civil code.

properly informed and advised during the entire contractual relationship in light of the principle of good faith and fair dealing laid down in Articles 1175 and 1375 cc.[99]

In another case where two unsophisticated retail investors invested a large sum of money (€32 million) in bonds issued by an Icelandic bank, nationalised after the banking crisis, the Supreme Court decided that even if the bank is generally bound by the instructions given by the client (Article 24(1)(b) of Legislative Decree No 58/1998), the firm has the duty to refuse to carry out the transaction and to withdraw from the portfolio management contract, if the investment is not suitable.[100] This is because a firm, given its professional expertise, should always assess whether the client's instruction is adequate and suitable for their profile.

With regard to the MiFID suitability rule, the Court of Appeal of Milan decided that a firm had failed to assess the suitability of the interest rate swap, inter alia, because of the disproportion between the amount of the swap (notional amount: €3 million) and the client's debt (€540,000).[101] The Court upheld the termination of contract decided by the tribunal.

(iv) Spain

In Spain, the largest number of securities disputes arised after the global financial crisis concerned the mis-selling of *participaciones preferentes* and subordinated debt instruments to unsophisticated retail clients. Firms distributed these instruments among large numbers of retail clients to raise cheap capital, typically through non-advised services, without informing investors of their characteristics and risks. After the crisis, where some issuing banks were recapitalised (Bankia, NGC Banco, Catalunia Caxia), investors suffered huge losses. This triggered an unprecedented number of compensation claims. Special out-of-court procedures were set up specifically to deal with disputes against the failed banks. To give some idea of the impact these claims had on the Spanish judicial system, by July 2013, around 6,400 lawsuits had been brought against the banks accounting for a total amount of €430 million.[102] As in France and Italy, other strands of case law concerned the mis-selling of Lehman Brothers' bonds and interest-rate swaps which were offered by credit institutions in conjunction with mortgage loans to offset the (expected) upward trend of the mortgage variable interest rate.[103]

[99] Cass, 24 February 2014, n 10306; Cass, 3 April 2014, n 7776 and Cass, 12 April 2018, n 15936.

[100] Cass, April 2015, n 7922, p 30.

[101] App Milano, 26 May 2016.

[102] Comision de seguimento, first trimestral report, September 2013.

[103] See, inter alia, JG Pascual, 'La protección de consumidores y usuarios en la contratación de permuta financiera o swap' (2013) *Revista Doctrinal Aranzadi Civil-Mercantil* 9; C Martinez Escribano, 'Delimitacion del error en los contractos de swaps' (2013) *Revista de Derecho Bancario y Bursátil* 130.

Non-advised Transactions

The majority of disputes concern a firm's alleged failure to comply with general information duties and the pre-MiFID suitability rule (Article 4(1) of the Annex to the Royal Decree No 629/1993) which applied to both advisory and non-advisory services. In several judgments the Supreme Court held that, given the information asymmetry between the retail client and the firm, even in the pre-MiFID regulatory framework, firms must provide clients with specific information as to the characteristics of a product and its risks.[104]

The need to provide a client with detailed information on risk, both in non-advised and advised services, arises not only from regulatory duties but also from the duty of good faith in negotiations. As the Supreme Court ruled in cases concerning the mis-selling of Lehman Brothers' bonds, this private law duty expands the firm's regulatory duties requiring it to inform clients about the risk of losing their entire investment capital due to the potential insolvency of the issuer.[105] According to the Supreme Court, the economic function (*función económico-social*) of contracts concluded in securities markets presupposes that clients receive detailed information about the risks involved.[106] For this reason, conduct of business rules require firms to meet standards of information that are higher than those required by national private law.

However, lack of pre-contractual information could not be alleged where the investor is sophisticated. In a judgment on the mis-selling of Lehman Brothers' bonds, the Supreme Court upheld the decision of the Court of Appeal and dismissed the claim because the investors acted through a professional financial intermediary, who negotiated the terms of the purchase, having complete knowledge of the characteristics and risks of the products, therefore lack of information could not be alleged.[107]

Advised Transactions

A recurrent issue in the litigation on interest rate swaps sold after the entry into force of MiFID I is whether advice was given to the client and therefore whether the firm was required to conduct a suitability test. It is settled case law that to understand whether advice was given it is necessary to conduct a concrete assessment of the service provided by the firm and it is not necessary that an advisory agreement has been concluded.[108] Liability for investment advice cannot be excluded

[104] See, in particular, STS, 21 July 2015, n 3228. The Supreme Court held that even if Law No 47/2007 granted firms a period of six months to adapt their internal processes to MiFID transposition laws, this did not exempt firms from compliance with MiFID information duties, given that they essentially replicate their pre-MiFID duties: STS, 13 June 2015, n 3221.

[105] STS, 30 September 2016, n 4282.

[106] STS, 7 October 2016, n 614.

[107] STS, 18 April 2013, n 243/2013 recurso: 2353/2011.

[108] STS, 25 February 2016, n 610; STS, 17 June 2016, n 2894; STS, 30 November 2016, n 5288. See also, for the reference to the CJEU judgment: Audiencia Nacional, 15 July 2013, n 3163.

by contract terms because conduct of business rules have a mandatory nature and cannot be derogated by the parties.[109] The written and signed declaration that the suitability test was conducted, does not disclaim the firm from liability under private law.[110]

In numerous swap mis-selling disputes, the Supreme Court held that compliance with the pre-MiFID or MiFID conduct of business rules cannot be ensured just by delivering contractual documentation to the client or by giving information 'about what it is obvious', but requires complete information about the risks deriving from the oscillation of the interest rates.[111] In contrast to the case law of English courts, the Spanish Supreme Court held that unless the client is a professional investor, the information duties cannot be met by the content of the contract and the firm has a positive obligation to facilitate the understanding of clients about the risks of the financial instrument.[112] Whereas the firm cannot be asked to predict the future evolution of interest rates,[113] it shall provide a complete information, sufficient and understandable about the consequences of an increase or decrease of interest rates.

In a judgment concerning the mis-selling of a Lehman Brothers' bonds to a married couple, the Plenary Session of the Supreme Court held that firms have a reinforced duty of information, especially when the bank concluded a portfolio management contract.[114] The Supreme Court clarified that it is for the bank to identify the inconsistency between the risk profile chosen by the client (very low) and the financial instruments (extremely complex). It is also noteworthy that, in this case, the Supreme Court affirmed that the pre-MiFID framework should be interpreted in light of MiFID I, even if this directive had not yet been transposed into national law.

B. Remedies for Breaches of Conduct of Business Rules

(i) The UK

Compensation for Breach of Contract

In the UK, investors can rely on contractual, tortious and statutory rights of action to obtain compensation for investment losses. A financial advisory contract implies a duty to use reasonable skill and care when recommending investments.[115]

[109] STS, 16 November 2016, n 5109.

[110] STS, 13 July 2015, n 3221.

[111] See, in particular, STS, 4 December 2015, n 4948; STS, 1 February 2016, n 317; STS, 16 May 2017, n 1895.

[112] STS 5111/2016.

[113] STS, 7 July 2014, n 2660 and STS, 26 February 2015, n 756.

[114] STS, 18 April 2013, n 244/2013 recurso: 1979/2011.

[115] *Investors Compensation Scheme Ltd v West Bromwich Building Society* [1999] Lloyd's Rep PN 496. See in more detail JL Powell and R Stewart (eds), *Jackson & Powell on Professional Liability* 1095.

The duty of care in contract law, is co-extensive to that imposed by tort law and should be informed by regulatory requirements. Traditionally, courts have held that the duty of care requires a professional to act as a 'reasonably competent practitioner in the relevant sector of the profession'.[116] However, in *O'Hare & Ors v Coutts & Co*, the High Court held that when financial advice is provided, the adviser should act with a higher standard of care which entails 'proper dialogue and communication between adviser and client', including the duty to ensure that 'the client understands the advice and the risks attendant on a recommended investment'.[117]

The fact that regulatory duties should inform the common law duty of care does not mean that regulatory duties become contractual duties.[118] English courts have generally declined to treat regulatory duties as contract duties because the client may enforce these regulatory duties with a statutory cause of action, so there is no need to treat these duties as contract duties.[119] It is not sufficient for courts to find that an implied term would have been adopted by the parties as reasonable men if it had been suggested to them, 'it must have been a term that went without saying, a term necessary to give business efficacy to the contract, a term which, though tacit, formed part of the contract which the parties made for themselves'.[120] Following this view, the High Court firmly rejected the plaintiff's claims that COBS rules can be incorporated, by implication, into contracts.[121]

Tort of Negligence

A claim for compensation for breach of the duty care under the tort of negligence can be successful if the defendant owes a duty of care to the claimant, the breach of the duty of care caused damage to the claimant and there is a causal link between the breach and the damage.[122] As mentioned, the duty of care at common law, whilst not co-extensive, should be informed by the applicable regulatory duties

[116] *Bolam v Friern Hospital Management Committee* [1957] 1 WLR 582.

[117] *O'Hare & Ors v Coutts & Co*, para 204 (Kerr J followed the reasoning of *Montgomery v Lanarkshire Health Board* [2015] AC 1430 where the Court held that, in the medical sector, the duty to explain the risks to a person to whom advice is given goes beyond the so-called *Bolam* test).

[118] Only in a few previous judgments had English courts accepted that regulatory duties can be implicitly incorporated into contracts: *Larussa-Chigi v CS First Boston Ltd* [1998] CLC 277 and *Brandeis Brokers Ltd v Black* [2001] 2 Lloyd's Rep 359 (with regard to Securities and Futures Authority rules).

[119] See *Clarion Ltd v National Provident Institution* [2000] 1 WLR 1888, p 6 (with regard to the Securities and Investments Board's Statements of Principle); *Bear Stearns Bank Plc v Forum Global Equity Ltd* [2007] EWHC 1576 (Comm), para 147 (with regard to the Loan and Market Association standard contract terms).

[120] See, in particular, *Trollope & Colls Ltd v North West Metropolitan Regional Hospital Board* [1973] 1 WLR 601, 609 per Lord Pearson.

[121] *Thornbridge Ltd v Barclays Bank Plc*, para 137; *Wilson v MF Global UK Ltd*, para 15; *Bailey & Anor v Barclays Bank Plc* [2014] EWHC 2882 (QB), para 55 and *Grant Estates Limited v RBS*, para 67.

[122] See, in particular, AC Johnston, B Markesinis and S Deakin *Markesinis and Deakin's Tort Law*, 7th edn (Oxford, Oxford University Press, 2012) 99. A Hudson, *The Law of Finance*, 767.

where there is an advisory relationship. Particular attention should now be devoted to the causation requirement and the measure of damages.

In securities litigation, English courts rely upon the traditional 'but-for' clause or *condicio sine qua non* theory to establish the causal link; these ascertain whether, had the investors been properly advised or informed, they would have purchased the same financial instrument at the same conditions.[123]

In advisory transactions, the plantiff should be able to prove that if the correct advice had been given, he would have purchased a different investment product.[124] In cases where the investor was deemed to have a sufficient level of expertise and experience, courts rejected the claim that they would have not purchased the product, had they received correct advice.[125] In non-advisory relationships, plaintiffs should be able to prove that the information they received did, in fact, determine their choice of investment.[126]

This principle was applied by the High Court in three judgments where an investment firm (Camerata) claimed damages against Credit Suisse for the mis-selling of structured notes related to Lehman Brothers for the amount of $25 million. The plaintiff alleged that if he had been correctly informed about the Lehman Brothers' risk of default he would have sold the note.[127] In the first judgment,[128] while the the judge accepted this statement, he held that such advice 'would have been more pessimistic than would have been reasonable and proper' and that the correct advice, which should have been limited to the worsening of the Lehman's rating and some speculation about its position in the press, would not have led the investor to make a different investment decision.[129]

This reasoning was confirmed in the second and third 'Camarata' judgments where the High Court decided that there was no causal link between the alleged breach of the duty of care and COBS suitability rule and the loss because the investor, given his knowledge, experience and attitude to risk, would not have made a different investment, even if the correct advice had been given.[130]

The causal link between the breach of duty of care and the loss can be broken, however, if the investor decides not to provide additional collateral to support

[123] See, in particular, Johnston, Markesinis and Deakin *Markesinis and Deakin's Tort Law*, 106 and R McCormick and C Stears, *Legal and Conduct Risk in the Financial Markets* (Oxford, Oxford University Press, 2018) 464.

[124] *Beary v Pall Mall Investments* [2005] EWCA Civ 415 at para 38. The Court of Appeal rejected the view that the principles of causation established in *Chester v Afshar* UKHL 41, [2005] 1 AC 134, a medical liability case, where the court departed from the traditional 'but for test' to state that a fair remedy for the loss suffered by the patient can be extended to securities litigation.

[125] *Zaki & Ors v Credit Suisse (UK) Ltd* [2011] EWHC 2422 (Comm), para 133.

[126] *JP Morgan Chase Bank and Others v Springwell Navigation*, para 639.

[127] *Camerata Property Inc v Credit Suisse Securities (Europe) Ltd* [2011] EWHC 479 (Comm).

[128] Ibid, para 238.

[129] Ibid, para 239.

[130] *Camerata Property Inc v Credit Suisse Securities (Europe) Limited* [2012] EWHC 7 (Comm) 2012 WL 14689, para 88 and *Camerata Property Inc v Credit Suisse Securities (Europe) Limited* [2013] EWHC 29 (Comm) 2013 WL 128088, para 4.

his/her leveraged investment positions. In *Al Sulaiman v Credit Suisse Securities (Europe) Limited, Plurimi Capital LLP*, where the investor did not provide a margin call within the timescale stipulated by the bank with a consequent loss of the capital invested, Cooke J noted that, had the investor been informed about the risk of margin call of $5 million, she would not have changed her investment strategy given her high attitude towards risk.[131] Hence, he found that on the particular facts of the case, the investor had made an irrational and unreasonable decision not to put up a margin call and this decision had broken any chain of causation.[132] However, in *Haider Abdullah v Credit Suisse*, the judge found on the facts of the case that the investor's decision not to meet Credit Suisse's margin call in late October 2008, leading inevitably to the closing out of his portfolio, with the loss of $26 million did not break the causal link because it was motivated by the concern that further funds could have been lost had the call been made.[133] Therefore, it seems that the assessment of the causal link is fundamentally dependent on the specific facts of the case and is not influenced by regulatory-driven considerations.

The measure of damages is determined on a case-by-case basis. In *Seymour v Caroline Ockwell & Co*, the court compensated the amount invested (the purchase price)[134] while in *Shore v Sedgwick Financial Services Ltd*, it only compensated the difference between the purchase price and the price the investor would have paid in the absence of misconduct (so-called 'out-of-pocket')[135] and in *Rubenstein v HSBC Bank Plc*, the damage was calculated as if the bank had given the correct advice (expectation damages).[136] Notably, in calculating the amount of damages the court alleviated the investors' burden of proof because the investor cannot be asked to assess what the most suitable investment would have been because in that specific case 'he would have invested in whatever [the adviser] advised him to invest in'.[137]

To estimate the measure of damages, courts examine whether the plaintiff contributed to the damage,[138] whether the financial instrument had any residual value which should be considered at the time of the litigation[139] and whether the

[131] *Al Sulaiman v Credit Suisse Securities (Europe) Limited, Plurimi Capital LLP* [2013] EWHC 400 (Comm) 2013 WL 617348, para 164.

[132] *Al Sulaiman v Credit Suisse Securities (Europe) Limited, Plurimi Capital LLP*, para 210.

[133] *Haider Abdullah v Credit Suisse* [2017] EWHC 3016 (Comm), paras 239–243.

[134] *Seymour v Caroline Ockwell & Co* para 168.

[135] *Shore v Sedgwick Financial Services Ltd*, para 204. See also *Haider Abdullah v Credit Suisse*, para 246.

[136] *Rubenstein v HSBC Bank Plc* [2011] para 124. See also *O'Hare & Ors v Coutts & Co*, para 253.

[137] *Rubenstein v HSBC Bank Plc* [2011] para 126.

[138] See *Spreadex Limited v Sanjit Sekhon* [2008] EWHC 1136 (Ch) 2008 WL where the amount of damages was reduced due to the contributory negligence of the plaintiff.

[139] *Camarata Property Inc v Credit Suisse Securities (Europe) Ltd* [2011] EWHC 479 (Comm) 2011 WL 674989, para 241.

investor was in the position 'to take a truly independent trading decision' to avoid or reduce the amount of the loss.[140] Another fundamental criterion adopted by UK courts to limit the potential extent of the recoverable damage is the remoteness of the loss. In *Rubenstein v HSBC Bank plc* while the first instance Judge found that the loss was too remote because it derived from the 'extraordinary and unprecedented financial turmoil' caused by the Lehman Brothers' collapse,[141] the Court of Appeal held that the loss was not too remote and that the remoteness test should take into account the purpose of the statutory rules which, in this case, aimed to protect consumers (ie the consumer protection objective of section 2 of FSMA 2000 and the COB rules).[142]

Tort of Deceit

The tort of deceit (or the tort of fraudulent misrepresentation) can be successful if (a) the defendant makes a false representation;[143] (b) the defendant knows that the representation is false, alternatively he is reckless as to whether it is true or false; (c) the defendant intends that the claimant should act in reliance on it; and (d) the claimant does act in reliance on the representation and suffers loss.[144]

In comparison to the tort of negligent misrepresentation, the tort of deceit has several advantages for the investor (ie compensation includes any losses, including lost profits,[145] the plaintiff does not need to prove the firm owed an advisory duty and the defendant cannot claim that the plaintiff contributed to the loss).[146] However, these must be weighed against the significant burden of proof placed on the plaintiff. The most problematic elements that need to be proved are that the defendant made a representation on which the claimant relied and whether this representation was intentional (ie whether the plaintiff knew that the representation was not true).

The proof that the bank made a statement that amounts to a representation is particularly difficult because English courts allow banks and investment firms,

[140] *Cassa Di Risparmio Della Repubblica Di San Marino Spa v Barclays Bank Ltd* [2011] EWHC 484 (Comm), para 560. The High Court decided that the investor remained to a significant extent 'locked into' the investment because the financial instruments were not readily marketable assets and it was unlikely that anyone other than the defendant bank would have been willing to buy them at a realistic price.

[141] *Rubenstein v HSBC Bank plc*, para 116 (only nominal damages were awarded).

[142] Ibid [2012] EWCA Civ 1184 paras 123–124 and *Haider Abdullah v Credit Suisse*, para 211. See also *O'Hare & Ors v Coutts & Co*, para 253 (where concurrent causes of action in tort and contract arise, the test of remoteness should be the more restrictive contract test).

[143] A representation can be based an express or implied statement. In an express statement, courts consider what a reasonable person would have understood from the words used in the context in which they were used; in an implied statement, courts consider what a reasonable person would have inferred was being implicitly represented by the representor's words and conduct in their context (silence by itself cannot found a claim in misrepresentation). See *Raiffeisen Zentralbank Osterreich AG v The Royal Bank of Scotland Plc* [2010] EWHC 1392 (Comm), paras 82–83.

[144] *ECO3 Capital Ltd and Others v Ludsin Overseas Ltd* [2013] EWCA Civ 413, para 77.

[145] *Parabola Investments Ltd v Browallia Cal Ltd* [2009] EWHC 901 (Comm), para 159.

[146] See Powell and Stewart, *Jackson & Powell on Professional Liability* 1098.

particularly in the context of complex financial transactions with sophisticated investors, to disclaim liability for misrepresentation.[147] In this case, the investor is contractually estopped from denying the existence of the facts and matters agreed, unless in the context of fraud.

This principle was affirmed in *Peekay Intermark Limited, Harish Pawani v Australia and New Zealand Banking Group Limited*, where an investment firm claimed damages for misrepresentation under section 2(1) of the Misrepresentation Act 1967 for the mis-selling of a structured product linked to the Russian GKO. In the first instance, the High Court upheld the claim because, even if the claimant did not carefully read the contractual documentation, given the 'considerable confidence' placed by the claimant in its bank, the claimant had no reason to think that the terms and conditions they were expecting to receive would relate to a fundamentally different product from that which had been described to him.[148]

The Court of Appeal overturned the High Court judgment. The reason is that a sophisticated investor 'who signs a document knowing that it is intended to have legal effect is generally bound by its terms, whether he has actually read them or not'.[149] According to Lord Justice Moore-Bick, this is 'an important principle of English law which underpins the whole of commercial life; any erosion of it would have serious repercussions far beyond the business community'.[150]

In the same vein, in *Raiffeisen Zentralbank Osterreich AG v RBS*, the High Court stressed that it cannot be assumed that a sophisticated investor (in this case, a credit institution) does not understand that the information memorandum on the complex financial instrument negotiated did not contain any representation that could be relied upon.[151]

It should be noted that section 2 of the Unfair Contract Terms Act 1977 (UCTA) and section 3 of the Misrepresentation Act 1967 prohibit a person from excluding or restricting liability for negligence and misrepresentation unless the contract clause satisfies the requirement of reasonableness. Several English judgments have reiterated that limitations of liability are reasonable between commercial parties and cannot be challenged by way of these statutory instruments.[152]

Even if the investor demonstrates that a representation was made, he must prove that the defendant knew that it was false. In *Cassa di Risparmio della*

[147] *Peekay Intermark v Australia and New Zealand Banking Group* [2006] EWCA Civ 386, paras 56 and 57; *Springwell Navigation v JP Morgan Chase Bank* [2008] EWHC 1186 (Comm), para 556; *Reifeissen*, paras 314–315; *San Marino*, para 508. See in more detail, J Braithwaite, 'The Origins and Implications of Contractual Estoppel' (2016) *Law Quarterly Review* 1.

[148] *Peekay Intermark Limited, Harish Pawani v Australia and New Zealand Banking Group Limited* [2005] EWHC 830 (Comm), para 37.

[149] Ibid, para 43.

[150] Ibid.

[151] *Raiffeisen Zentralbank Osterreich AG v RBS* [2010] EWHC 1392 (Comm), para 97.

[152] See *Springwell Navigation Corporation (a Body Corporate) v JP Morgan Chase* [2008] para 603; *Titan Steel Wheels Limited v The Royal Bank of Scotland Plc*, para 99; *IFE v Goldman Sachs* [2006]

Repubblica di San Marino SpA (CRSM) v Barclays Bank Ltd, CRSM claimed damages for negligent and fraudulent misrepresentation in connection with the purchase of a series of collateralised debt obligations (CDOs).[153] The Judge held that the bank, to increase its profits, deliberately selected entities for inclusion in the reference portfolios of the CDOs with high spreads for their ratings,[154] but concluded that the bank expressed its views with reasonable grounds for belief in their truth. For this reason, the fraud was excluded. In fact, what it is required is dishonest knowledge, in the sense of an absence of belief in truth and this was not proved by the plaintiff.[155] In this vein, in *Grant Estates Limited v RBS*, the Scottish Court of Session emphasised that 'a clear and specific basis for the inference of dishonesty' is necessary to prove fraud[156] because 'allegations of dishonesty can have very serious consequences for people, particularly those engaged in regulated professions, and can blight careers, at least temporarily, even if they are eventually not substantiated'.[157]

Misrepresentation Act 1967

The requirements for a claim for damages under section 2(1) of the Misrepresentation Act 1967 are the same as for a claim in deceit except for the fact that the person making the misrepresentation is liable even if the misrepresentation was not made fraudulently, unless he proves that he reasonably believed the facts represented to be true.[158] In addition, damages include any loss flowing from the representation, as in the tort of deceit, but even if the representation had been made fraudulently.[159] However, given the broad measure of damages available, courts held that 'where there is room for an exercise of judgement, a misrepresentation should not be too easily found'.[160] Like in the tort of deceit, this claim can be estopped by contract clauses and plaintiffs must prove that they would have entered into the transaction, had the misrepresentation not been made. It is not sufficient for the representee merely to show that he was supported or encouraged in reaching his decision by the representation in question.[161]

EWHC 2887 (Comm), para 71 and *Grant Estates Limited vs RBS*, para 87; *Raiffeisen Zentralbank Osterreich AG v RBS*, para 314.

[153] *Cassa di Risparmio della Repubblica di San Marino SpA v Barclays Bank Ltd* [2011] EWHC 484 (Comm), para 312.

[154] Ibid, para 314.

[155] Ibid, para 227.

[156] *Grant Estates Limited vs RBS*, para 89.

[157] Ibid, para 93. See also *Standard Chartered Bank v Ceylon Petroleum Corporation*, para 572.

[158] *Cassa di Risparmio della Repubblica di San Marino SpA v Barclays Bank Ltd*, para 213.

[159] *Royscot Trust Ltd v Rogerson & Anor* [1991] EWCA Civ 12.

[160] *Avon Insurance Plc v Swire Fraser Limited* [2000] 1 All ER (Comm) 573, para 200 and *Raiffeisen Zentralbank Osterreich AG v The Royal Bank of Scotland Plc* [2010] EWHC 1392 (Comm), para 85.

[161] *Cassa di Risparmio della Repubblica di San Marino SpA v Barclays Bank Ltd*, para 467.

Tort of Breach of Statutory Duty

The tort of breach of statutory duty is distinct from the tort of negligence.[162] The principles of causation, foreseeability and/or remoteness of damage apply as prescribed by tort law but they may operate in different ways, depending on the purpose of the conduct of business rule that was breached.[163]

Section 138D of FSMA (previously, FSMA, s 150) allows a private person who suffers loss as a result of a rule breach a right of action for damages. The current formulation of the rule is the result of a legislative evolution that has gradually restricted the scope of this right of action.[164] While the FSA 1986 granted the right of action to a 'person', the Companies Act 1989 (s193) restricted it to 'private investors'; eventually, FSMA 2000 narrowed it down to a 'private person'. This cause of action is limited to the breach of a 'rule'; it is not available for the breach of 'relevant requirement', 'principles for business', 'statements of principles', 'evidential provisions' and 'guidance'.[165] The FSA endorsed the restriction of the statutory right of action in section 62 of the 1986 Act and the decision to make the breach of the SIB's principles immune from civil liability. This was 'the deliberate creation of an interpretative community'[166] motivated by fear that the consistent interpretation of the principles with the body of FSA's rules 'might be put at risk if civil litgation between private parties were to become the engine driving the interpretation of the Principles'.[167]

The most vexed issue with regard to this statutory cause of action concerns the meaning of 'private person'. According to the Rights of Action Regulations 2001, a 'private person' is a natural and legal persons unless they suffered the loss in the course of carrying on business of any kind.[168]

In *Titan Steel Wheels Ltd v Royal Bank of Scotland plc*,[169] a case where a company creating steel wheels (Titan), claimed damages under section 150 of FSMA for the mis-selling of two derivative products. The Judge, having stressed

[162] See Hudson, *The Law of Finance*, 689.

[163] See also *SAAMCO v York Montague Ltd* [1997] AC 191, para 212 and *Rubenstein v HSBC Bank Plc* [2012], para 45.

[164] See E Lomnika 'Private Damages Claims for Breaches of Securities Regulation Law' in R Plender (ed), *Legal History and Comparative Law. Essays in Honour of Albert Kiralfi* (London, Frank Cass, 1990) p 133 and, more recently, SK Afghan, 'What is the purpose of section 138D of the FSMA 2000 (as amended)?' (2018) Journal of International Banking Law and Regulation, 163 ss.

[165] See R Smerdon and G Morse, *Palmer's Company Law. The Protection of Investors and the Regulation of Financial Services. Civil Liability for Certain Breaches of the FSMA 2000 Regime*, Vol 3 (London: Sweet and Maxwell, 2017) s 10.

[166] J Black, *Rules and Regulators* (Oxford, Clarendon Press, 1997) 107–108. See also EE Avgouleas, *The Mechanics and Regulation of Market Abuse: A Legal and Economic Analysis* (Oxford, Oxford University Press, 2005) 471.

[167] FSA, 'The FSA Principles for Business. Consultation paper' n 13, October 1998, para 23.

[168] See Department of Trade and Industry, Consultation Paper 'Defining the Private Investor', September 1990, para 52. This notion was then included in the FSA 1986 (Restriction of Right of Action) Regulations 1991 (SI 1991 No 489) and in the FSMA 2000 (Rights of Action) Regulations 2001 ('the 2001 Regulations') (SI 2001 No 2256).

[169] *Titan Steel Wheels Limited v The Royal Bank of Scotland Plc* [2010] EWHC 211 (Comm) 2010 WL 442366.

that the legislator, as shown by the legislative history of this provision, aimed to limiting strategical litigation, dismissed the claim for a statutory duty because the notion of 'in the course of carrying on business of any kind' must be interpreted broadly as including not only the the financial transactions that form an integral part of the business but also the transactions that are 'incidental', if the scale and frequency of the hedging is well sufficient to satisfy any requirement of regularity. The Judge therefore accepted that this statutory cause of action has very limited relevance for non-individual plaintiffs. In subsequent judgments, English courts denied the right to standing under section 150 of FSMA to the wife of a private investor,[170] a corporation with a sole shareholder,[171] an investment company[172] and property developing companies.[173]

In *Grant Estates Limited v RBS*, where a venture company claimed damages for breach of COBS rules, breach of contract, negligent advice and misrepresentation in relation to the mis-selling an interest rate swap,[174] the Scottish Court of Session, confirmed that the narrow scope of the statutory cause of action and dismissed the claim that section 150 of FSMA should be interpreted in light of MiFID I because MiFID I did not require Member States to establish a private cause of action and the private cause of action under section 150 was not introduced to transpose EU law.[175] In *Green & Rowley v RBS*, Tomlinson J reiterated that an extention of the notion of 'private person' would be 'an invitation to the court to drive a coach and horses through the intention of Parliament to confer a private law cause of action upon a limited class'.[176]

Breach of Fiduciary Duties

In several cases investors claimed that a firm has breached its fiduciary duties. A fiduciary duty is 'the duty undertaken by a person (fiduciary) to act on behalf of or for the benefit of another, often as an intermediary with a discretion or power which affects the interest of the other who depends on the fiduciary for information and advice'.[177] Fiduciary duties, however, have limited application in the financial sector and, more generally, in commercial relationships[178] because, in these transactions, 'the parties are expected to be the authors of their own rights

[170] *Gorham v British Telecommunications Plc* [2000] 1 WLR 2129.

[171] *Diamantides v JP Morgan Chase Bank* [2005] EWCA Civ 1612, [2005] All ER (D) 323 (Dec).

[172] *Camerata Property Inc v Credit Suisse Securities (Europe) Ltd Q* [2012] EWHC 7 (Comm) paras 94–98.

[173] *Nextia Properties Limited v The Royal Bank of Scotland plc, National Westminster Bank plc* [2013] EWHC 3167 (QB) para 104; *Grant Estates Ltd v RBS* [2012] CSOH 133, para 62.

[174] *Grant Estates Limited v RBS* CA152/11.

[175] Ibid, para 47.

[176] *Green & Rowley v RBS*, para 30. See recently: *London Executive Aviation Ltd v RBS*, para 166.

[177] Law Commission 'Fiduciary Duties and Regulatory Duties' December 1995, Law Com No 236.

[178] See Law Commission, 'Fiduciary Duties of Investment Intermediaries' June 2014, Law Com No 350, 195.

and obligations'[179] and because firms are allowed to disclaim their liability for fiduciary duties.[180] At any rate, to understand whether a the firm-client relationship gives rise to a fiduciary duty, English courts focus on the specific nature of the relationship between the parties.[181] In *Brandeis (Brokers) Limited v Herbert Black et al*, the High Court found that a broker owed a fiduciary duty to his clients because the substance of the relationship revealed that the contractual relationship was essentially an agency relationship which is 'by its nature a form of fiduciary relationship [because] otherwise an agent would be free to make a profit from his or her position behind the principal's back'.[182] In *Springwell v JP Morgan*, however, where there was no advisory relationship between the parties, Gloster J rejected the plaintiff's view that the defendant had a fiduciary obligation to the investor because 'the mere fact that one party to a commercial relationship "trusts" the other does not predicate a fiduciary relationship' and the plaintiff could not expect that the defendant would subordinate its own interests.[183]

(ii) France

The Nullity of Contracts for Mistake or Fraud

In France, national courts have rarely declared contracts null and void for breach of information duties. In a recent case, a client claimed the annullment of a swap contract for mistake (Article 1110 cc) and compensation for contractual liability. However, the Tribunal of Paris rejected both claims.[184] According to the Tribunal, the fact that the swap was risky cannot be considered as a false representation of facts (mistake) and that the financial firm did not breach an information duty, taking into account the fact that the firm had negotiated the IRS on their own behalf, without advice.

In another case, the Supreme Court, in a dispute on the mis-selling of a swap concluded by a corporation, held that, under Article 1116 cc, a fraud can be committed by omitting information (*simple silence*) but, on the basis of the facts of the case, the investment firm could not know, before the conclusion of the contract, that the interest rates would have been as low as they were.[185] For the

[179] Ibid at 195.

[180] *London Executive Aviation Ltd v RBS*, para 58.

[181] See Law Commission, 'Fiduciary Duties of Investment Intermediaries', 197.

[182] *Brandeis (Brokers) Limited v Herbert Black, American Iron and Metal Company Incorporated, Lito Trade Incorporated Representation* 2001 WL 513189, para 43. See, however, *Diamantis Diamantides v JP Morgan* [2005] EWCA, para 43 where the Court of Appeal decided that the bank did not owe fiduciary duty to the investor, who was the sole owner of an investment vehicle with whom the bank had concluded a derivative contract on an advisory basis.

[183] *JP Morgan Chase Bank and Others v Springwell Navigation*, paras 573 and 574.

[184] TGI Paris, 9e ch, 3e sect, 29 January 2015, n 11/09601, *Syndicat Intercommunal pour la Destruction des Résidus Urbains (SIDRU) c/ DEPFA Bank Public Limited Company enseigne* 'DEPFA Bank').

[185] Cass, com, 2 June 2015, n 14–18.999. See also Cass com, 11 March 2014, n 12-29.506 (the Supreme Court rejected the claim for the annullment of the contract for fraud because of lack of fraud in the concrete case).

same reason, the Supreme Court rejected the claim for absolute nullity for lack of cause (Article 1131 cc) because there was no evidence that the financial firm had known in advance that the interest rate would have been low, thus frustrating the 'aleatory nature' of the contract. Finally, the Supreme Court rejected the client's claim for contractual liability because the financial firm did not breach any information duties.

In another case regarding the mis-selling of a swap to a corporation, the Supreme Court rejected a claim for the annullment of a contract on the ground of mistake but held the financial firm liable for breach of contract under Article 1147 cc because of the breach of duty to warn the client, in particular, about the renegotiation of the swap.[186] However, the Supreme Court held that the financial firm, who acts on their own behalf, does not have the duty to inform its counterparty (the client) about the profits (and the methodology to calculate them) that it would make from the transaction.

Breach of Contract and Compensation for Damages

The private law remedy that French courts have most frequently granted to clients is compensation for breach of contract under Article 1147 cc.[187] Courts use this provision as a general rule to affirm the civil liability of investment firms, irrespective of the type of service (advised or non-advised), regulatory framework in place (pre-MiFID or post-MiFID) and time of the breach (before or after the conclusion of the contract). The 'universal' nature of this remedy indicates that French courts, differently from those in England, consider that conduct of business rules have contractual nature and their breach can lead to damages for breach of contract.[188] It is for the firm to prove that it has complied with its duty to inform, warn and advise.[189] The client must prove the causal link between the breach of duty and the loss but thay do not need to prove the negligence of the financial firm.[190] The firm's negligence (*faute*) is implicit in the breach of the conduct of business rules.

The Supreme Court seems to resort to the traditional 'but for test' doctrine to establish the causal link between the firm's breach and the client's loss. In a recent judgment, concerning the alleged breach of information duties in a portfolio management transaction, the Supreme Court held that the firm's failure to

[186] Cass, com, 17 March 2015, n 13-25.142.3.

[187] Ordonnance n° 2016-131 du 10 février 2016 portant réforme du droit des contrats, du régime général et de la preuve des obligations.

[188] See, in this regard, X Delpech, Obligation de couverture en matière d'opérations financières: revirement de jurisprudence (2008) *Recueil Dalloz* 778 who considers these judgments as 'arrêts 'politiques' because the Supreme Court aims to influence the behaviour of certain categories of market participants.

[189] Cass, civ, 25 February 1997, n 94-19685; Cass, Civ, 15 May 2002, n 99-21521.

[190] Cass, com, 4 February 2014, n 13-10-630 (with regard to the breach of duty to advice in portfolio management services).

assess the financial situation of the client, his experience and objectives cannot, in itself, lead to compensation for damages unless the damage was exclusively caused by this failure.[191]

According to the settled case law, the recoverable damages resulting from the financial firm's breach of duty to warn, inform or advise amounts to the loss of a chance that a less-risky investment would have been made, had the firm complied with its duties.[192] The loss of chance also includes the loss of opportunity to choose a less-risky investment.[193] Therefore, clients do not generally obtain full compensation (ie loss suffered and loss of profits).[194]

The rationale for the recourse to the 'loss of chance theory' is that conduct of business rules impose *obligations de moyens* and do not require the firm to ensure that the client makes a profitable investment.[195] Therefore, it cannot be demonstrated that in the absence of breach, the client would not have suffered the same loss. However, in a recent judgment, the Supreme Court held that compensation can include, in addition to the loss of chance, non-pecuniary damages (*préjudice moral*) when the amount of the loss is considerable and caused serious financial difficulties for the client.[196]

In disputes regarding the client's obligation to cover positions on financial markets, the Supreme Court held that the contributory negligence of a retail client[197] – where the client fails to provide collateral – does not discharge the firm from its obligation to liquidate his or her debit position in time and cannot reduce the amount of compensation due to the client.[198] The firm's duty to require collateral and liquidate exposure is a mandatory duty of public policy (*ordre public*) which must be respected notwithstanding the client's opposition or failure to provide sufficient collateral.

(iii) Italy

Nullity of Contracts for Breach of Mandatory Rules of Public Order

Like in France, since Italian law does not provide for a statutory private law remedy for losses suffered as a result of breaches of conduct of business rules, national

[191] Cass. com, 3 May 2018, n 16-16809.

[192] See, in particular, Cass. com, 15 September 2009, n 08-14.398; Cass com, 9 March 2010, n 08-21.547; Cass com, 12 June 2012, n 11-20303; Cass com, 9 December 2014, n 13-23673.

[193] Cass com, 26 June 2012, n 11-11450.

[194] The breach of best execution obligations gives rise to a full compensation: Cass, com, 24 June 2014, n° 614 F-D, pourvoi n° M 13-17.772, *Bendali v CRCAM Brie Picardie*.

[195] Cour d'Appel de Paris, 23 March 2006, Médikéo c/ BNP Paribas: *Bull* Joly Bourse, mai-juin 2006.

[196] Cass, com, 4 February 2014, n 13-10-360, comment by X Delpech, 'Responsabilité du prestataire de services d'investissement et préjudice réparable'.

[197] See, instead, Cass, com, 14 December 2004, n 02-13.638, which held that a non-retail sophisticated client cannot invoke the failure to inform to discard his fault.

[198] See in particular, Cass, com, 26 June 2012, n 11-11.450 and Cass, com, 26 March 2013, n 293 F-P+B, *Lanes v Société Dubus*, Bull Joly Bourse juin 2013.

courts must rely on general private law to provide redress to clients. This has given rise to a variety of different remedial solutions.[199]

Between 2004 and 2007 several Tribunals decided, in disputes concerning the mis-selling of Parmalat, Cirio and Argentina bonds, that, since these conduct of business rules qualify as imperative rules of economic public policy, in light of Article 47(1) of the Italian Constitution, which 'encourages and safeguards savings in all its forms', their breach determines the absolute nullity of the contract under Article 1418(1) cc and triggers the restitution of the sums paid by the client.[200] In some judgments, Tribunals decided to annul the contract for mistake pursuant to Article 1428 cc or fraud under Article 1439 cc.[201]

By contrast, other courts, while considering these rules as mandatory, did not regard them as imperative rules of economic public policy[202] and decided that their breach can only give rise to pre-contractual (Article 1337 cc) or contractual liability (Article 1218 cc)[203] and, if the breach is sufficiently serious, the termination of the contract (Article 1453 cc)[204] which, like the nullity, triggers restitutionary effects.

Given these significant divergences arisen in the case law of lower courts, the Plenary Session of the Supreme Court was called upon to clarify the civil law effects of the breach of conduct of business rules.[205] In two landmark judgments handed down in 2007 the Supreme Court held that the breach of the pre-ISD conduct of business rules (which were applicable to the dispute at stake) cannot determine the absolute nullity of the contract but only the pre-contractual or contract liability of the firm or the termination of contract. These judgments were grounded on the dogmatic distinction between rules affecting the validity of contracts ('*regole di validità*') and rules regulating the conduct of the parties ('*regole di comportamento*').[206] While acknowledging that conduct of business rules are mandatory for

[199] See, in more detail, V Roppo, 'La tutela del risparmiatore fra nullità, risoluzione e risarcimento (ovvero, l'ambaradan dei rimedi contrattuali)' (2005) *Contratto e Impresa* 902; A Bertolini, Risparmio tradito: una riflessione tra teoria generale del contratto e disciplina dei mercati (2010) 2 *Nuova Giurisprudenza Civile Commentata* 337; F Greco, 'Informazione pre-contrattuale e rimedi nella disciplina dell'intermediazione finanziaria' (Milano, Giuffrè, 2010).

[200] On Argentina bonds see: Trib Ferrara, 25 February 2005; Trib Mantova, 10 December 2004; Trib Mantova, 22 March 2007. On the Cirio bonds, see: Trib Palermo, 14 January 2010; Trib Trani, 31 January 2006; Trib Novara, 10 January 2006; Trib Reggio Emilia, 22 December 2005; Trib Roma, 3 December 2005. On the Parmalat bonds see: Trib Venezia, 16 February 2006; Trib Venezia, 29 September 2005; Trib Parma, 13 April 2005.

[201] See Trib Pinerolo, 14 October 2005; Trib Lanciano, 30 April 2007; Trib Ancona, 12 April 2007.

[202] See Cass, 29 September 2005, n 19024, in *Foro it.* 2006, I, 1105 ss.

[203] In general, the contracts for the purchase of bonds were preceeded by a master agreement which states the general rights and obligations. Based on this framework agreement parties further conclude executions orders to sell or buy securities.

[204] See, for the Cirio bonds: Trib Verona, 23 December 2008; Trib Como, 7 February 2007; Trib Rimini, 7 December 2006.

[205] Cass Sez Un, 19 December 2007, n 26724, 26725. See, for a comment, D Maffeis, *Dopo le Sezioni Unite: l'intermediario che non si astiene restituisce al cliente il denaro investito* (2008) *Contratti* 555.

[206] On the distinction between *regole di validità* e *regole di comportamento*, see G D'Amico, *Regole di validità e principio di correttezza nella formazione del contratto* (Napoli, ESI, 1996). This distinction has

investment firms, the Supreme Court decided that they do not qualify as rules on the validity of contracts, given the absence of an express legislative provision, and can only constitute rules of conduct. Breaches of these rules can affect only the parties' rights and obligations but not the contract as an act. Therefore, the only remedies available for investors are compensation for pre-contractual liability (if the breach is commited before concluding the contract) or contractual liability (if it is committed after the conclusion of the contract) or, if the breach of conduct of business rule is sufficiently serious, to its termination.[207] The 2007 judgments have been subject to strong criticism. It has been argued that the distinction between the *regole di validità* and *regole di comportamento* is excessively formalistic and may weaken the effective protection of investors.[208] Undoubtedly, from a remedial perspective, these judgments have made it more difficult for the investor to obtain the restitution of the purchase price of the security in case of breach of conduct of business rules. This is now possible only if the investor proves that the breach is sufficiently serious. However, from a broader European perspective, it is noteworthy that neither the 2007 judgments, nor the subsequent case law of Italian courts, which has adhered to the 2007 judgments, have called into question the contractual nature of conduct of business rules and their civil law effects.[209] It remains to be seen, however, whether breaches of MiFID I's duty to refuse a transaction – which has not yet been the object of a Supreme Court's judgment – will be regarded as a rule of conduct, even if it has a clear impact on the content of the private law relation between firms and clients.[210]

Nullity of Swap Contracts for Lack of Cause

As I said, Italian courts have generally adhered to the Supreme Court's judgments of 2007, refusing to declare investment contracts null and void for breaches pre- and post-MiFID conduct of business rules. However, in a recent strand of judgments, lower courts have declared financial derivative contracts null and void because they lacked a rational allocation of risks between the two parties. The leading case is a judgment of the Court of Appeal of Milan handed down in 2013. The Court held that lack of pre-contractual information about the negative mark-to-market (Mtm) of the swap made it impossible for the client to know what they would have to pay to the bank on termination of that contract to offset

been criticised by part of the legal doctrine. See G Vettori, 'Contract Without Numbers and Without Adjectives. Beyond the Consumer and the Weak Enterprise' (2013) 9 *European Review of Contract Law* 233.

[207] See also Cass, 17 February 2009, n 3773, in *Danno e resp*, 2009, p 503 ss.

[208] See Vettori, 'Contract without numbers and without adjectives' 233.

[209] See Cass, 7 June 2016, n 11641 according to which breaches of conduct of business rules are 'violazione di obbligo endocontrattuale', p 5.

[210] See, in this sense, A Tucci, Il contratto inadeguato e il contratto immeritevole (2017) *Contratto e Impresa 921* and D Imbruglia, *La Regola di Adequatezza e il Contratto* (Milano, Giuffré, 2017) 500–505.

its initial negative Mtm.[211] Since the Mtm is unilaterally determined by the bank, it is, in practice, possible for the bank to design the contract to decide how much the client would pay on its termination. For that reason, the information about the formula and value of the Mtm – as recommended also by CONSOB[212] – is key for the client to decide whether to enter into the transaction. On this basis, the Court of Appeal held that lack of pre-contractual disclosure on the Mtm did not allow the client to assess the effective costs of the swap and to assess whether the returns between the two parties of the derivative are allocated in a rational manner. Therefore, the Court declared the swap null and void for lack of cause, given that the allocation of risk and return, which is an essential element of the swap, was ultimately left to the discretionary choice of one contractual party.[213] In several other judgments, lower courts have confirmed this line of reasoning, declaring the nullity of swap contracts for lack of cause and ordering the firm to pay back to the client the sums initially paid to enter into the swap.[214] Notably, the duty to disclose the Mtm and specific costs of interest rate swaps has not been based on MiFID's disclosure duties or conflict of interest rules[215] but on the basis of general private law and, in particular, the concept of cause of the contract.[216]

Breach of Contract and Compensation for Damages

After the two landmark Supreme Court judgments of 2007, breach of conduct of business rules may give rise either to the termination of the contract, if the breach is sufficiently serious, or to the compensation for damages based on pre-contractual or contractual liability.[217] To determine if a breach is sufficiently serious, courts must focus their assessment on the type of client, their level of expertise and the complexity of the financial instrument. In this regard, the breach

[211] App Milano, 18 September 2013. The first instance court awarded only pre-contractual damages to the investor. See for a comment, D Imbruglia,La creazione razionale dell'alea nei derivati OTC e la nullità dello swap per vizio di caus (2013) *Persona e Mercato* 332.

[212] CONSOB, Comunicazione n 9019104/2009, para 1.2.

[213] See, in more detail, on the doctrine of the cause in concrete (causa in concreto), Vettori, Contract Without Numbers and Without Adjectives 237.

[214] See in particular Trib Torino, 17 January 2014; App Torino, 22 April 2016; Trib Milano, 7 July 2016; Trib Treviso 26 August 2015; Trib Roma, 8 January 2016; Trib Milano, 9 March 2018 n 2807; App Milano, 25 September 2018. See also Cass, 31 July 2017, n 13013, which required the judge to take into account the sectoral conduct of business rules when assessing the legality of the swap contract.

[215] See the judgments of the German Federal Supreme Court dated 22 March 2011, file no XI ZR 33/10 and 28 April 2015, file no XI ZR 378/13. For a comment: JD Jansen, 'Passion to Inform – BGH Expands Banks' Advisory Duties' (2011) 12 *German Law Journal* 1504.

[216] See instead L Enriques and M Gargantini, 'The Expanding Boundaries of MiFID's Duty to Act in the Client's Best Interest' (2017) *The Italian Law Journal* 405 who argue that this duty is based on MiFID's duty to act in the client's best interest.

[217] Traditionally, in Italy pre-contractual liability qualified as a *species* of tortious liability. However, more recently, the Supreme Court held that it should qualify as a form of contractual liability (Cass, 20 December 2011, n 27648). See, for an overview of this case law, F Della Negra, 'La natura della responsabilità precontrattuale: la quiete dopo la tempesta?' (2013) 7 *Danno e responsabilità* 754.

of the suitability rule may not be deemed to be sufficiently serious if the client, in light of his experience and attitude to risk, would have purchased the financial instrument even if the bank had properly conducted the suitability test.[218]

If the breach is not sufficiently serious, the investor has to rely either on the firm's pre-contractual liability or its contractual liability to obtain compensation.

A first issue is the standard to determine the causal link. In this regard, the recent case law of the Supreme Court has revealed three main approaches.[219]

In some judgments, the Supreme Court required the client, in accordance with the traditional theory of *conditio sine qua non*, to demonstrate that if the firm had complied with its conduct of business rules, he would not have carried out the transaction.[220] In other judgments the Court decided that the causal link can be established when it is likely, based on the regular behaviour of a rational investor (*id quod plerumque accidit*), that the client would not have purchased the same security had the firm provided the correct information.[221] In a third strand of judgments, the Supreme Court went a step further and held that the causal link between the breach of conduct of business rules and the client's loss can be presumed if the firm failed to comply with the conduct of business rules.[222] The rationale being that since compliance with these rules ensures that clients can take informed decisions, non-compliance is an indicator that the client could not take such a decision, so the loss suffered cannot be fully attributed to the client but should be causally ascribed to the firm. It is also noteworthy that the Supreme Court pointed out that the misconduct does not need to be the exclusive cause of the loss and that the causal link cannot be broken by showing the high-risk attitude of the investor because the investor cannot be required to accept unknown risks.[223]

A second issue is the measure of damages. In its landmark judgments in 2007, the Supreme Court held that in a pre-contractual breach of regulatory duties, damages should also include economic loss, expressed either in the less advantageous investment ('*minor vantaggio*') or in the increased economic burden ('*maggior aggravio*') caused by the breach of conduct of business rules, in addition to the losses that are a direct and immediate consequence of the breach.[224] If the breaches occur after the conclusion of the contract, damages will include both the loss suffered and any lost profits.

[218] See Imbruglia, *La Regola di Adequatezza e il Contratto*, 325.

[219] See, in more detail, A Mager, 'Oltre la violazione dei doveri informativi nei servizi di investimento. La cassazione e il nesso di causalità' (2018) 6 *Rivista di diritto bancario* 41.

[220] See Cass, 25 October 2017, n 25335. The speculative nature of the investment may reveal that, even if he receives correct information about the risks, it is likely that he still wants to proceed with the investment and in this case a causal link cannot be established.

[221] See Cass, 3 June 2016, n 11466.

[222] See Cass, 18 May 2017, n 12544; Cass, 16 February 2018, n 3914; Cass, 20 March 2018, n 6920.

[223] See Cass, 28 February 2018, n 4727.

[224] See Cass, Sez. Un, 19 December 2007, n 26724, 26725. See also, before, Cass, 29 September 2005, n 19024.

In 2011 the Supreme Court specified the criteria to be used to quantify the measure of damages. The damages should reflect the risk that that a well-informed client would not reasonably have taken or not to the same degree, had the firm provided accurate information.[225] Therefore, in principle, the damage should correspond to the difference between the value of securities at the time of purchase and their value at the time of the dispute. However, if before filing the lawsuit, the client became aware of the risks of the securities but decided not to sell them, compensation would be a proportionate reduction of the loss of value of the securities from the purchase to the moment where the investor became aware of these risks. It is interesting to note that these criteria substantially reflect those used by the ACF to determine the measure of damages in out-of-court disputes.[226] In line with the 'case law' of the ACF, Italian courts also decided that if the securities are illiquid and therefore cannot easily be sold, compensation can be equal to their purchase price.[227]

The amount of compensation, however, cannot be reduced due to a client's contributory negligence, unless his behaviour is exceptionally imprudent or accomodates the violation of rules committed by the financial firm.[228] The client's failure to inform themselves about the risks of the financial instrument cannot be a reason to reduce compensation due to the firm's breach of conduct of business rules.[229]

(iv) Spain

Nullity of Contract for Mistake

Just as in France and Italy, in the absence of a special statutory private law remedy, the remedies for breach of conduct of business rules are based on general contract law.

Spanish courts have rarely declared contracts null and void for illegality (the breach of the mandatory rules of public order under Articles 6(3) and 1255 cc)[230] or for the lack of consent or the object or the cause of the obligation (Article 1261 cc).[231] A distinguishing feature of Spanish case law is that in the

[225] See Cass, 29 December 2011, n 29864 p 24 and Cass, 11 June 2010, n 14056 regarding the issuer's liability for a misleading prospectus and Cass, 12 December 2013, n 27875, regarding the joint liability of the issuer and intermediary for mis-selling of Cirio bonds. See F Della Negra, 'Il concorso di colpa tra società emittente ed intermediario finanziario: la recente pronuncia della Suprema Corte' (2014). Available at: www. giustizia.civile.com.

[226] See Chapter 4.

[227] Tribunale di Verona, 21 March 2017.

[228] See Cass, 22 September 2015, n 18613.

[229] See Cass, 29 December 2011, n 29864 and Cass, 12 April 2018, n 15936, para 2.4.

[230] STS, 30 June 2015 n 323 (the breach of pre-contractual information duties cannot lead, per se, to the nullity of contracts).

[231] JPI, O Porriño, 26 March 2013, n 416. The Tribunal dismissed the claim for absolute nullity for lack of consent because, on the facts, the Court decided that consent had been given but declared the contract null and void for error and fraud.

overwhelming majority of cases where the investor's claim has been upheld, courts declared the contract null and void for mistake or error, in accordance with Articles 1265 and 1266 cc.

A client's mistake (ie a false representation of the legal or factual reality) determines the nullity of the contract if three conditions are met.[232] First, the mistake must be essential: it must concern the subject matter of the contract (ie the termination costs of a swap contract).[233] Second, it must be inexcusable in the circumstances: it cannot be based on the client's negligence. The client's mistake is excusable even if they themselves could have checked the information made available by the CNMV because the firm has an active obligation to inform and the client has a legitimate expectation to receive correct information.[234] Third, there must be a causal link between the incorrect information and the misconceived representation of the factual or legal reality behind the conclusion of the contract. Lack of information on the risks deriving from a lowering of the Euribor or the costs of termination of the swap is normally considered to be the cause of a legally relevant mistake.[235]

A recurrent question arising in the case law is whether the breach of the regulatory duties can, in itself, lead to a mistake. In a landmark judgment handed down on 20 January 2014, the Supreme Court held that a lack of suitability test, while it does not indicate in itself the existence of the mistake, entails a presumption that the client entered the contract due to an essential and excusable error. Here, the error is essential because it concerns regulatory duties and is causally determined by the breach of information duties (*error heteroinducido*).[236] Notably, the omission of relevant information determines the excusable character of the mistake because regulatory duties, derived from EU law, indicate the legislator's intention to ensure an enhanced protection to the client.[237] While the Supreme Court did not provide a systematic doctrine as to when the firms can revert the presumption, it once decided that the presumption cannot hold where the firm has proved that, in a sale of *participaciones preferentes* through an advisory service, all the information was delivered to clients.[238]

If the client is a sophisticated investor, Spanish courts undetake a concrete assessment on the excusability of the mistake. In several judgments the Supreme Court overturned the judgment of the Court of Appeal, which had declared the nullity of the IRS, because the purpose of the retail client (a company) was to speculate and therefore the investor was supposed to assume the risk of losing

[232] See, in more detail, A Carrasco Pereira, 'Aventuras, inventos y mixtificationes en eld debate relative a las participationes preferentes' (2014) 133 *Revista de Derecho Bancario y Bursatil* 39.

[233] STS, 15 October 2015, n 4271.

[234] STS, 16 September 2015, n 4004.

[235] STS 1339/2017.

[236] STS, 20 January 2014, n 354; STS, 10 September 2014, n 4339; STS, 11 March 2016, n 985.

[237] STS, 17 June 2016, n 2894.

[238] STS, 20 April 2017, n 1497 and STS n 1295/2017.

its investment.[239] However, in some recent judgments, the Supreme Court has decided that the mistake is excusable, based on the circumstances of the case, even if the client is experienced.[240] It clarified that it cannot be presumed that a company is an expert client because the expertise and knowledge required to understand complex financial instruments does not derive from its normal business with credit institutions. The error committed by the company is excusable because its board of directors cannot be required to have specific knowledge of complex financial products.[241]

Termination of Contract and Compensation for Damages

The other private law remedies granted for the breach of conduct of business rules are the termination of the contract, where the breach of contract is sufficiently serious (Article 1124 cc)[242] and the compensation for damages for pre-contractual or contractual liability.

Banks and investment firms should comply with a higher standard of care than other commercial parties.[243] In addition, like in France and in Italy, regulatory duties are treated as contractual duties and therefore breach of regulatory duties may be actioned by contract law remedies.[244] Remedies for breach of contract are generally a 'second-best' option for investors (after the nullity for mistake): even if the action for the termination of contract can be exercised five years after the conclusion of the contract (instead of four years for the action for annullment),[245] the plaintiff must prove that the breach is sufficiently serious and that the breach of duty occurred after the conclusion of the contract.

In a recent judgment concerning the mis-selling of *participaciones preferentes* under the pre-MiFID regulatory framework, the Supreme Court held, differently from the first instance court, which declared the contract terminated, that termination cannot be warranted because the breach of duties took place before the conclusion of the contract and decided that since the client's consent was affected, the contract is null and void for error.[246] Therefore, whilst nullity of contract for

[239] STS, 21 November 2012, n 843; STS, 17 February 2014, n 1353/2014.

[240] See, however, STS, 11 May 2017, n 1854 and STS, 20 January 2014, n 354.

[241] STS, 12 May 2017, n. 1861.

[242] See, for a general overview, MF Benavides, 'Participaciones preferentes: aproximación al problema y primeras respuestas de la jurisprudencia civil' (2012) *Revista CESCO de Derecho de Consumo* 17; C Guerrero, 'Las acciones y participaciones preferentes: acciones judiciales y estrategias de defensa' (2012) 6 *Revista Aranzadi Doctrinal*.

[243] F Zunzunegui Pastor, 'Aproximación a la responsabilidad contractual de los prestadores de servicios de inversión (2016) 35 *Revista de derecho bancario y bursátil*' 142.

[244] The integration of regulatory duties into contractual duties is based on Art 259 of the commercial code which requires agents to observe the laws and regulations and provides a liability for contravention of these regulations. See F Zunzunegui Pastor, Aproximación a la responsabilidad contractual de los prestadores de servicios de inversión 144.

[245] Law No 42/2015, reforming Law No 1/2000 has amended Art 1964 cc reducing the prescription period for personal private law actions (*acciones personales*) from 15 years to five years.

[246] STS, 13 September 2017, n 491.

mistake or fraud can be declared when the breach of conduct of business rules affected the consent of the investor (ie before concluding the contract) the termination of a contract is a remedy available only for serious breaches of contractual obligations or regulatory duties that apply during the performance of the contract. The reason is that conduct of business rules integrate the content of contracts, therefore their breach can give rise to claims for breach of contract.[247]

In actions for damages, clients can obtain full compensation, in light of Articles 1106 and 1107 cc, for the loss suffered and loss of profits.[248] However, compensation is calculated on the amount that the client would have received from selling the security, had he been informed about the adverse situation of the issuer or, for interest-rate swaps, the sum paid on early termination.[249] The Supreme Court has assessed the causal link on a case-by-case basis. In some cases, the compensation claims were dismissed because the contract was concluded more than one year before the Lehman Brothers' failure and the firm was not required to inform the client about the risk.[250] In others, the Supreme Court decided that a causal link existed because firms have a duty to inform their clients about the risks of their investment including unforseeable risks such as bankruptcy.[251] It seems however, that the failure to conduct a suitability test can be a cause of the damage because it led the client to take on a risk that they would not have taken, had the bank conducted this test.[252]

III. A Comparative Assessment

A. Private Law Duties

In the examined continental jurisdictions, national courts impose on investment firms private law duties that are stricter than disclosure and distribution rules. A similar trend has also been observed in the Netherlands[253] and in Germany.[254]

[247] STS, 18 April 2013, n 244.

[248] See STS, 13 July 2015, n 3221 and STS, 14 November 2016, n 5108. For more detail, see YB Sainz de Baranda, 'El caso Lehman Brothers en la jurisprudencia española. Alcance de la responsabilidad de las entidades bancarias y de las empresas de servicios de inversión' (2012) 128 *Revista de Derecho Bancario y Bursátil* 211.

[249] L Sánchez, M Ángel, E Valpuesta Gastaminza, PJ Bueso Guillén, J Noval Pato, 'Spain' in Busch and van Dam (eds), *A Bank's Duty of Care*, 195.

[250] STS, 18 April 2013, n 3016.

[251] STS, 16 September 2015, n 4004 (with regard to bonds issued by the Landbanski Island).

[252] STS, 13 June 2015, n 3221.

[253] See judgment of the Dutch Supreme Court dated 5 June 2009, NJ 2012, 182, 183 and 184. In this regard, see Cherednychenko, 'Contract Governance in the EU: Conceptualising the Relationship between Investor Protection Regulation and Private Law' (2015) 21(4) *European Law Journal* 500–520 at 514.

[254] See judgment of the German Federal Supreme Court dated 7 July 1993, BGHZ 123, 126 and, more recently, the Higher Regional Court Düsseldorf 16 December 2010, *WM* 2011, 399, 400. See, in this

In particular, courts require investment firms to provide information about the specific risks of the individual financial instrument offered to clients, whereas Article 19(3)(4)(5) of MiFID I (likewise the corresponding provisions of MiFID II) requires firms to provide information only about the 'specifc type' of instrument offered.[255] In addition, courts have stressed that disclosure should be clear and personalised, so firms do not automatically comply with MIFID I disclosure rules if they provide only standardised information or warnings. Notably, firms are also subject to these duties in non-advised transactions.

The legal basis for these additional duties is the pre-contractual duty of good faith or the duty of care under general contract law. In the examined continental jurisdictions, conduct of business rules are treated as 'special' contract law mandatory duties (even if they are located outside civil codes), that cannot be derogated by the parties. Therefore, general contract law assists courts in imposing stricter duties where this is necessary to compensate an imbalance of information asymmetry and bargaining power between firms and clients. The court's assessment indeed focuses on the substantive aspects of the transaction (ie experience and expertise of the client in financial matters) rather than on its formal or contractual aspects (ie advised or non-advised). For this reason, conduct of business rules set a 'floor' and not a 'cap' for client protection.

This judicial approach affords a high level of retail client protection, especially in transactions where the boundaries between advised and non-advised services might become blurred by the firm's 'generic recommendations'.

Case law in the the UK offers a rather different picture of the interplay between conduct of business and private law duties. In the UK, courts emphasise the need to protect the freedom of contract of market participants and the principle of *caveat emptor*. As a consequence, the type of contract and the specific contract terms negotiated by the parties become a crucial indicator to determine whether the firm's conduct is capable of attracting the obligations and duties of care of an investment advisor or whether it should be governed by tort law.

Where the investor proves the existence of an advisory relationship (which fundamentally depends on the existence of an advisory contract, given that a personal recommendation is generally not deemed to be sufficient) courts have accepted that contract or tort law duties should be interpreted in light of pre-MiFID I and MiFID I transposed provisions.[256] In this instance, UK courts have held, not differently from continental courts, that information needs to be personalised and cannot be generic.[257] However, a breach of conduct of business

regard, J-H Binder, 'Germany' in Busch and van Dam *A Bank's Duty of Care* 68 and P Mülbert, 'The Eclipse of Contract Law in the Investment Firm–Client Relationship: The Impact of the MiFID on the Law of Contract from a German Perspective' in G Ferrarini and E Wymeersch (eds), *Investor Protection in Europe: Corporate Law Making: The MiFID and Beyond* (Oxford, Oxford University Press, 2006) 317.

[255] See, in France, Cass, com, 24 June 2008, n 06-21.798; in Italy: Cass, 18 May 2017, n 12544; in Spain: STS, 7 October 2016, n 614.

[256] See *Al Sulaiman v Credit Suisse Securities (Europe) Ltd & Anor*, para 18.

[257] See *Haider Abdullah v Credit Suisse*, para 168.

rule is not necessarily a breach of duty of care: 'if an investment is in fact suitable for the client, then it does not ultimately matter if there have been failings in the process'[258] and a duty of care could not be breached simply because an unsuitable financial instrument was recommended, unless the firm 'encouraged foolhardiness'.[259]

A major difference in comparison to continental jurisdiction is that firms are allowed, based on the doctrine of estoppel, to disclaim their liability for negligent advice and misrepresentation. This type of disclaimer is, in practice, a major hurdle for investors to obtain compensation. In fact, where the firm successfully disclaims its liability or no advisory relation or was demonstrated, investors' claims have been dismissed and courts have reached the firm conclusion that regulatory duties can influence common law duties. Notably, this conclusion was reached even after the entry into force of the COBS rules which introduced the appropriateness rule for non-advised transactions. Although in some interest swap mis-selling judgments, some courts recognised that firms should fully explain the nature and effect of the financial instruments,[260] in most of them, courts held that firms have only the negative duty not to carelessly mislead their clients.[261] The underlying rationale for treating non-advised sales differently from advised sales is that in a commercial relationship between sophisticated parties, 'if a buyer of a product does not understand the product, it should obtain proper advice and pay for it'.[262] This reasoning reveals a 'pragmatic and commercially sensible approach'[263] to contractual interpretation. While continental judges interpret general private law in a purposive way (ie to ensure a high level of client protection) in the UK, judges adopt a textualist interpretative approach, based on what 'parties might reasonably have been thought to mean rather than a subjective method based on 'the court deciding what the parties true intention actually was'.[264] Textualist interpretative techniques ensure certainty in commercial transactions,[265] but obfuscate the EU law duty of conform interpretation and the principle of effectiveness. The protection of investors in financial transactions ultimately depends on their bargaining power to conclude an advisory contract and/or to reject liability disclaimers rather than the firm's application of conduct of business rules.

[258] Andrew Smith J in *Camerata Property Inc v Credit Suisse Securities (Europe) Ltd* [2011] 2 BCLC 54, para 99; *Al Sulaiman v Credit Suisse Securities (Europe) Ltd*, para 19 and *Zaki & Ors v Credit Suisse (UK) Ltd*, para 82.

[259] *O'Hare v Coutts & Co*, para 218.

[260] See *Crestsign Limited v National Westminster Bank Plc*, para 153. See, for a detailed analysis of this case-law, P Reynolds and A Collins, 'Non-advised sales of financial products: an end to caveat emptor?' (2018) Journal of International Banking Law and Regulation, 1.

[261] See, recently, *Property Alliance Group Limited v Royal Bank of Scotland*, para 67.

[262] *JP Morgan Chase Bank and Others v Springwell Navigation*, para 489, Gloster J, quoting PR Wood, *Regulation of International Finance*, 1st edn (London, Sweet & Maxwell, 2007).

[263] *London Executive Aviation Ltd v The Royal Bank of Scotland Plc*, para 166.

[264] See also McCormick and Stears, *Legal and Conduct Risk in the Financial Markets* 428.

[265] M Bridge and J Braithwaite, 'Private Law and Financial Crises' (2013) 13 *Journal of Corporate Law Studies* 361.

B. Private Law Remedies

The most striking aspect observed in the examined continental jurisdictions is that, despite the absence of an express private law remedy for breaches of conduct of business rules, French, Italian and Spanish courts often grant it.

In these countries, retail clients can rely on contract law remedies, namely liability for damages or avoidance of contracts. Avoidance of contracts has not only been based on defects in consent (in Spain) but also on lack of cause, due to the 'irrational' allocation of risks determined by the contract terms (in Italy). Interestingly, a breach of the conduct of business rules is not always a necessary or sufficient element to grant compensation or other remedies to investors. The remedial response is determined by the concrete knowledge, experience and expertise of the investor and general private law doctrines. In France, the investor should prove that a less risky investment would have been made, had the firm complied with its duties. In Spain, the breach grounds a presumption of a legally relevant mistake but the firm is allowed to rebut that presumption. In Italy, the breach must be sufficiently serious, or, in derivative contracts, it should 'reveal' an irrational contractual allocation of the risks between the parties. Conceptually, this suggests that there is no substitution of national private law with regulatory concepts but rather a synthesis or hybridisation between the two. It remains to be seen how the executive remedial conditions (ie causation, measure of damages) should be interpreted to ensure their compliance with the principle of equivalence and effectiveness.

In the UK, investors can make use of a statutory right of action in addition to common law rights of action to obtain redress. However, since this is available only for losses suffered by individual investors outside a business activity, its role in compensating investors was rather limited.[266] Common law claims based on deceit and misrepresentation have failed because investors found it difficult to prove fraud or because of the contractual disclaimers which contracted-out liability for misrepresentation. Claims based on common law succeded only where they were based on negligent advice (although in these cases, investors also brought claims on breach of statutory duty).[267] This shows that the existence of an advisory relation – a feature that has much less relevance in the examined continental jurisdictions – was, *de facto*, a pre-condition to obtain compensation. Another relevant aspect is the factual background of these cases. Where the courts granted compensation, claimants were individuals with a low or medium degree of sophistication[268] who purchased mixed financial-insurance products,

[266] To our knowledge, only in *Haider Abdullah v Credit Suisse*, para 247 compensation was expressly based on s 138D.

[267] *Loosemore v Financial Concepts, Seymour v Caroline Ockwell & Co, Shore v Sedgwick Financial Services Ltd, Rubenstein v HSBC Bank plc, Thomas v Triodos Bank*. See, in more detail, P Reynolds, 'Selling Financial Products' (2014) 29(5) *Journal of International Banking Law* 269.

[268] A nurse (*Loosemore v Financial Concepts*), farmers (*Seymour v Caroline Ockwell & Co*), manager of a pension fund (*Shore v Sedgwick Financial Services Ltd*), lawyer (*Rubenstein v HSBC Bank plc*).

pension schemes[269] or a loan.[270] In swap mis-selling disputes concerning sophisticated clients, compensation claims were generally dismissed.[271] The 'inequality of knowledge and understanding' that continental courts consider as the rationale for the investor-friendly interpretation of liability standards may play a role before English courts only if it is 'sufficiently extreme' and does not concern commercial transactions.[272]

Finally, regulatory duties inform not only the scope of the duty of care but also the remoteness requirement[273] whereas the causation requirement and the measure of damages are assessed on a case-by-case approach and are less influenced by regulatory principles. This also shows that, in the UK, private law remedies are subject to a process of hybridisation, although this is in limited instances where a duty of care in common law was established.

IV. Preliminary Conclusion

The above analysis has shown similarities across the examined continental jurisdictions and important divergences between continental jurisdictions and the UK. In continental Europe, conduct of business rules produce civil law effects and give rise to contract law remedies, notwithstanding the absence of an express statutory remedy. In the UK, conduct of business rules produce civil law effects and, in practice, give rise to a private law remedy only in advisory transactions, despite the presence of a statutory remedy for breaches of conduct of business rules. In the UK, therefore, conduct of business rules were judicially enforced only where the investor could prove the existence of an advisory transaction.

The different intensity of civil law effects of conduct of business rules derives from both legal and factual differences. In the UK, the lack of a principle of pre-contractual good faith, the doctrine of estoppel and the textualist interpretative approach of English courts prevent regulatory, 'investor-friendly', standards from influencing or changing the contractual allocation of rights and duties. Only in advised transactions did English courts allow plaintiffs to rely on regulatory standards to determine the content of the duty of care in common law. By contrast, in continental jurisdictions, the purposive interpretation of general

[269] In *Loosemore v Financial Concepts, Seymour v Caroline Ockwell & Co* and *Rubenstein v HSBC Bank plc,* the financial instrument was a mixed financial-insurance product, whereas in *Shore v Sedgwick Financial Services Ltd* it was a pension scheme.

[270] See *Thomas v Triodos Bank.*

[271] The exception is *Haider Abdullah v Credit Suisse*, where, nevertheless, English courts upheld a compensation claim by a sophisticated individual investor who entered into a financial derivative transaction.

[272] *Plevin v Paragon Personal Finance Ltd*, para 18.

[273] *Rubenstein v HSBC Bank Plc*, para 123 and *Haider Abdullah v Credit Suisse*, para 211.

contract law doctrines (ie good faith, cause of contracts) in light of the investor protection's objective of financial regulatory duties has facilitated the synthesis (or the hybridisation) between general private law and the conduct of business rules. This does not clearly eliminate the differences that also exist in continental jurisdictions in relation to some executive remedial conditions, but it ensures that MiFID I, and in a forward-looking perspective, MiFID II conduct of business rules produce civil law effects before national courts.

From an EU law perspective, it could be concluded that continental courts broadly respect the principle of conform interpretation and ensure the effectiveness of conduct of business rules. Instead, in the UK these EU law principles have been overshadowed by general private law doctrines and by the need to respect the freedom of contract of sophisticated financial market participants. However, these different judicial approaches may be influenced by the factual background of the disputes. Whereas in continental jurisdictions the plaintiff is generally a unsophisticated retail client (or a prudent saver), in the UK the plaintiff is often a sophisticated retail client (high net worth individuals or SMEs) or a professional client. Hence, in the UK, the strong emphasis on the principle of *caveat emptor* and the use of 'market-friendly standards of liability'[274] reflects the fact that the financial disputes that end up in court involve sophisticated investors. It is in this regard significant that in most of the cases where English courts upheld the investors' compensation claims, plaintiffs were natural persons who did not enter into speculative transactions. In addition, the 'investor-friendly' standards of liability that in continental jurisdictions are warranted by judicially driven hybrid private law, in the UK are ensured by extra-judicial enforcement mechanisms (FOS's adjudication and consumer redress schemes) that are not bound by common law.

The difference in the level of client protection between continental jurisdictions and the UK arises for retail sophisticated clients or retail clients who are legal persons, like SMEs. While in continental jurisdictions, they generally benefit from the standard of protection that courts grant to retail clients who are natural persons, in the UK they might not be permitted to bring a claim to FOS, due to the award limits, and would not qualify as private persons under section 138D of FSMA, because they are legal persons acting in the course of their business.[275] Hence, they have to seek redress in court and thus must jump serious hurdles (in particular, the proof of an advisory transaction) to obtain compensation.

The difficulty that this type of client faces to obtain an effective remedy for a breach of the conduct of business rules not only impairs the deterrent effect of conduct of business rules and the confidence of important market actors, such as SMEs, in the financial markets, but it also raises doubts on the compatibility of

[274] R La Porta, F Lopez-De-Silanes, A Shleifer, 'What Works in Securities Laws?' (2006) 28 *The Journal of Finance* 28.

[275] See Afghan, 'What is the purpose of section 138D of the FSMA 2000 (as amended)?', 166.

UK law with the EU law principle of effectiveness, as well as with the fundamental right of effective judicial protection.

In the examined continental jurisdictions, investors have been granted access to judicial remedies. However, the conditions to exercise these remedies often diverge and it is therefore necessary to assess how the EU principle of effectiveness and equivalence, which applies by virtue of the procedural autonomy that Member States enjoy in this area, could affect the interpretation of these executive remedial conditions.

To this purpose, in the next chapter the analysis will examine the compatibility of hybrid private law and the limitations to the access to justice rights of investors, with the general principles of EU law and fundamental rights.

6

The Emergence of Hybrid Private Law in Retail Financial Markets: Foundations and Legitimacy

I. Anchoring Hybrid Private Law to EU Law

The previous chapters have shown a process of hybridisation between general private law and sectoral regulatory duties. Hybridisation has different institutional drivers and intensity. In Italy, France and Spain, hybridisation is driven by national courts, which recognise civil law effects of conduct of business rules and grant clients a private law remedy for breaches of these rules, notwithstanding of the absence of an express statutory right of action. In the UK, hybridisation is primarily driven by FOS and consumer redress schemes. The national courts' role in hybridisation is limited to advisory transactions. In non-advised transactions courts support a model of separation between regulatory and private law duties, refusing to grant investors a remedy based on common law for breach of regulatory duties or to interpret the duty of care in light of these duties.

The emergence of hybrid private law shows the essential role of general private law in protecting investors in the EU and the fact that statutory rights of action are neither necessary nor a sufficient pre-requisite to strengthen the judicial enforcement of conduct of business rules. However, the judicial creation of private law duties that are stricter than regulatory duties and the conferral on investors of private law remedies not expressly laid down by EU and national law may raise doubts as regards the compatibility of hybrid private law duties and remedies with EU law. It could be argued that hybrid private law oversteps the boundaries of EU law, imposing a civil law burden on investment firms that is not foreseen by law.

In addition to this, hybrid private law has different forms and intensity across jurisdictions. There are important divergences, also within continental jurisdictions, as regards the type of influence of regulatory duties on private law duties and the type of remedy for breaches of conduct of business rules. The limited involvement of the CJEU in the interpretation of MiFID conduct of business rules, in comparison to other areas of EU (ie consumer) law has not facilitated the building of a harmonised law of remedies for breaches of conduct of business rules.

To understand the EU law foundations of hybridisation and provide guidance on how remedial conditions should be interpreted in light of EU law, this chapter seeks to assess the compatibility of hybrid private law duties and remedies with the general principles of EU law and the relevant case law of the CJEU. It is argued that, despite the absence of an express EU law provision, the doctrine of horizontal effects of EU legal acts and the principles of equivalence and effectiveness require national courts to grant civil law effects to MIFID II's conduct of business rules.

The chapter is organised as follows. It starts by analysing the nature of hybrid private law duties and the limits on the imposition of stricter private law duties than than those laid down in conduct of business regulations. It then examines hybrid private law remedies, focusing on how the compensation for damages and the avoidance of contracts – the two types of remedies mostly granted to investors by courts and ADR bodies – should be interpreted to comply with the principle of effectiveness. Finally, it considers the effect of the horizontal application of EU fundamental rights in retail securities disputes.

II. Hybrid Private Law Duties

In continental jurisdictions, national courts and ADR bodies refer to conduct of business rules to reinforce the private law duty of care. This gives rise to stricter (ie hybrid) duties than the regulatory duties in both advised and non-advised transactions. While in advised transactions, there is some homogeneity between the continent and the UK – in both cases courts accept that regulatory duties have civil law effects – in non-advised transactions there is a clear difference between the UK and other courts, given that in the UK, contrary to continental jurisdictions, regulatory duties do not produce effects in these relationships. It is therefore necessary to see whether the approach of the continental courts is in line with EU law.

A. Horizontal Direct and Indirect Effects of MiFID II Conduct of Business Rules

Under MiFID I, regulatory duties could produce only horizontal indirect effects, via the duty to conform interpretation and the theory of exclusionary effects. Under MiFID II, regulatory duties may also produce horizontal direct effects via the Commission MiFID II Regulation. This is a directly applicable act; its provisions, which are normally clear, precise and unconditional, may be invoked against a firm in a civil proceeding.[1] Although it is not possible to examine the horizontal

[1] See Chapter 2.

effects of all MiFID II's conduct of business rules, one important application of the doctrine of horizontal direct effects concerns financial derivative contracts. The horizontal direct effects of the duty to act in the client's best interest, in conjunction with the duty to communicate to clients one-off and ongoing charges related to the financial instrument, including swap fees, should entail that investment firms disclose the breakage costs of the swaps even if they are acting as contractual counterparty of the client.[2] The invocability of Commission MiFID II Regulation may also serve as a defence against the enforcement of a contract concluded in breach of the duty to refuse a transaction or the duty to conclude a written client agreement.

While the horizontal direct effect of MiFID II might have little impact in Italy, Spain and France, where *de facto* regulatory duties have already been translated into private law duties, it might have a strong impact both in the UK especially in non-advised transactions and in Germany where courts have accepted that regulatory duties may inform the content of private law duties but did not go as far as to hold that the two duties are co-extensive.[3]

MiFID II, like MiFID I, will also produce horizontal indirect effects, particularly through the instrument of conform interpretation. Its most important application concerns the fair treatment and best interest duties which largely overlaps with the duty of pre-contractual good faith (firms shall 'act honestly and fairly') and the duty of care (firms shall 'act professionally') in the performance of contracts. However, it differs from general private law concepts because it requires firms to customise the duty of fairness, honesty and professional diligence, based on the type of client, to achieve their best interests. As I will show below, this requires firms to adopt a reinforced standard of care in contractual or tortious relationships with clients.

An EU law issue that will also arise with regard to MiFID II is whether national courts can impose private law duties that are stricter than the regulatory duties contained in MiFID II. Some scholars argued that the answer should be negative because MiFID I is a maximum harmonisation directive, so duties going beyond it should not be accepted.[4] Others argued that stricter private law duties should be accepted because MiFID I does not provide for a maximum harmonisation of conduct of business rules.[5] Irrespective of the level of harmonisation, the crucial aspect, in our view, is the scope of harmonisation of MiFID I and MIFID II. Since private law does not fall within the harmonisation scope of these

[2] Arts 65(1)(2) and 50(2) of Commission MiFID II Regulation and Annex II of Commission MiFID II Regulation.

[3] See, in more detail, J-H Binder, '*Germany*' in D Busch and C van Dam (eds), *A Bank's Duty of Care* (Oxford, Hart Publishing, 2017) 61.

[4] See PO Mülbert, 'The Eclipse of Contract Law in the Investment Firm-Client-Relationship' in G Ferrarini and E Wymeersch *Investor Protection in Europe: Corporate Law Making, The MiFID and Beyon* (Oxford, Oxford University Press, 2014) 317.

[5] See OO Cherednychenko, 'Contract Governance in the EU: Conceptualising the Relationship between Investor Protection Regulation and Private Law' 21(4) *European Law Journal* 500–520 at 507.

directives (therefore limits to harmonisation do not apply to private law rules) national courts are, in principle, free to interpret domestic private law to impose stricter private law duties on investment firms. In addition, national courts can use the flexibility provided by the fair treatment clause, without necessarily referring to national private law, to introduce 'hybrid duties' that are stricter than the detailed disclosure and distribution rules.[6] For this reason, it would be in line with MiFID II to require firms in both advised and non-advised transactions to provide individualised, concrete and effective information about the risks and costs of the specific financial instrument (eg the mark to market (Mtm) of a swap) where this is necessary to ensure client's protection.

B. Limits to the 'Judicial Gold-plating': *Nationale-Nederlanden v Van Leeuwen*

Yet, is there any limit to the stricter private law duties than MiFID II's standards ('judicial gold-plating')?[7] A similar question was examined in *Nationale-Nederlanden v Van Leeuwen* where a Dutch court asked the CJEU whether Article 31(3) of the Third Life Assurance Directive, precludes an obligation on the part of a life assurance provider based on national 'open and/or unwritten rules', such as the reasonableness and fairness which govern the (pre)contractual relationship and/or a general and/or specific duty of care, to provide policyholders with more information on costs and risks of the insurance policy'.[8] While the directive provided for minimum harmonisation, Article 31(3) allowed Member States (a) to impose stricter information duties on insurance firms only if that information enabled the policyholder to understand the essential elements of the commitment and (b) to restrict the additional information which may be required from insurance companies by the Member State to what is necessary to achieve that end. Dutch law transposed this provision and left the option to provide additional information to the requirement of reasonableness and fairness under Article 6:2 of the civil code.

The CJEU held that the 'open and/or unwritten rules' of national private law could result in information duties that are stricter than those laid down in the national law transposing the directive, provided that the additional information required is clear, accurate and necessary for the policyholder to understand the essential characteristics of the commitment and it ensures a sufficient level of legal certainty.

[6] Busch, van Dam, *A Bank's Duty of Care* 413.

[7] Legislative goldplating should respect the conditions of Art 24(12) of MiFID II.

[8] See also Case C-51/13, *Nationale-Nederlanden Levensverzekering*, ECLI:EU:C:2015:286, para 34. See for a comment, Busch, Van Dam, *A Bank's Duty of Care*, 409.

This judgment confirms, in our view, that general private law duties may contain additional, more stringent duties than MiFID II's duties for investment firms. There are, however, three limitations to judicial gold-plating. First, the reinforced private law duties must be clear and specific, even if they derive from a general duty. Second, they must achieve the result sought by the investor protection objective and do not go beyond that purpose (ie requiring firms to give a personalised warning could be disproportionate if that warning had already been given in that form). Third, the additional duties must ensure a sufficient degree of legal certainty. This entails that the aggrieved party should be able to reasonably foresee the content of its additional obligations when entering into the transaction. However, a firm could not rely on the principle of legal certainty to redress a situation caused by its own failure to comply with a regulatory requirement,[9] nor to argue that a provision cannot be interpreted in a manner that is consistent with MiFID II because it had already consistently been interpreted in a manner that is incompatible with EU law.[10] In addition, it should be noted that firms are in a better position than their retail client to assess the risks and characteristics of the financial instruments and services they offer. Therefore, they should be able to calibrate the amount of pre-contractual information that needs to be given to each client on the basis of their specific situation.[11]

III. Hybrid Private Law Remedies

A. Individual Rights to Investors: Conditions

The pre-condition to enforce conduct of business rules with a private law remedy is that that rule confers an individual right on the client. To determine whether an EU law provision confers rights on individuals, it is necessary that 'the respective legal duty was imposed, if not exclusively, at least *also* for the sake of the individual' who claims protection.[12] As has been already argued, the emphasis placed by MiFID II on extra-judicial enforcement of conduct of business rules is a strong, indicator of the legislative intention to create rights of action for breach of conduct of business rules.[13] A second indicator is the investor protection purpose of these rules.

[9] Case C-209/12, *Walter Endress v Allianz Lebensversicherungs AG*, para 30.

[10] C-441/14, *Dansk Industri v Estate of Karsten Eigil Rasmussen*, ECLI:EU:C:2016:278, paras 33–34.

[11] See Case C-51/13, *Nationale-Nederlanden Levensverzekering Mij NV v Hubertus Wilhelmus van Leeuwen*, para 30.

[12] See T Eilmansberger, 'The Relationship between Rights and Remedies in EC Law: In Search of the Missing Link' (2004) 41 *Common Market Law Review* 1199 at 1242.

[13] C Hadjiemmanuil, 'The Banking Union and Its Implications for Private Law: A Comment' 16(3) *European Business Organization Law Review* 383–400 at 389.

The scope of this investor protection purpose is defined by the level of detail and/or the transactional nature of the rule. The more detailed the requirement, the stronger the legislative's intention to fix in advance the interest that the individual is entitled to enforce via that requirement and the narrower the margin of manoeuvre left to national private law.[14] However, the detailed nature of a requirement may neither be sufficient nor necessary to grant a right to investors. On the one hand, some requirements, like the fair treatment and best interest duties, may be able to confer rights on the investors even if they are generally framed. On the other hand, there are very detailed requirements, such as prudential requirements, but they are unable to confer a right on the investors against the firm.

It is argued that the requirement at stake should also have a 'transactional nature': it must entail or facilitate an investors' decision concerning whether, how and on what terms they enter into a financial transaction ('transactional decision').[15] In our view, disclosure, distribution and the product governance rules that impose requirements for the sake of the client, a potential client or the end client (target market identification obligation) entail or facilitate a client's decision, including a decision not to enter in the transaction.[16] This also holds true for the general fair treatment and best interest duties that presuppose the existence (at least) of a pre-contractual relation between two identified or identifiable parties with a view of entering into a financial transaction. Unlike more detailed conduct of business rules, these general rules make reference to standards (ie fairness, best interest) to leave courts, adjudicators and supervisory authorities free to determine on the basis of the circumstances of each case, whether a certain conduct is in line with the regulatory requirements. This legislative technique strengthens the 'anti-elusive' purpose of these rules, enhancing the protection of investors in financial transactions.

General rules that protect individual interests should be differentiated from detailed rules that protect general or diffuse interests.[17] For example, as previously mentioned, prudential capital requirements[18] are very detailed and prescriptive but they protect a general interest in the safety of individual credit and investment firms and, in fact, apply irrespective of a financial transaction between the

[14] Case C-101/08, *Audiolux SA ea v Groupe Bruxelles Lambert SA (GBL) and Others*, ECLI:EU:C:2009:626, para 62. See also Case C-131/88, *Commission v Federal Republic of Germany* ECLI:EU:C:1991:87, para 7.

[15] The notion of 'transactional decision' is laid down in Art 2(k) of Directive 2005/29/EC of the European Parliament and of the Council of 11 May 2005 concerning unfair business-to-consumer commercial practices in the internal market and amending Council Directive 84/450/EEC, Directives 97/7/EC, 98/27/EC and 2002/65/EC of the European Parliament and of the Council and Regulation (EC) No 2006/2004 of the European Parliament and of the Council ('Unfair Commercial Practices Directive') [2005] OJ L 149/22.

[16] See Chapter 2.

[17] See F Wilman, *Private Enforcement of EU Law Before National Courts* (Cheltenham: Edward Elgar, 2016) 490.

[18] Part Three of the CRR.

aggravied firm and third parties. Investor and depositors' protection is only an indirect purpose of these requirements. For that reason, as the CJEU held in *Peter Paul*, the existence of prudential requirements and the fact that the protection of depositors is one of the objectives of the requirements, is not sufficient to confer a right on these individuals.[19]

The transactional nature is also missing in MiFID II's organisational requirements. The primary objective of these requirements is to allow the firm, as an organisation, to fulfil its conduct of business duties vis-à-vis its clients at the point of sale of financial instruments. A breach of the duty to have in place adequate product governance arrangements does not automatically result in a loss for the client and does not affect his transactional decision.

It should also be noted that private enforcement would be unsuitable to enforce prudential and organisational requirements. Their infringement is not easily observable and any damage may not be quantified and causally linked to a conduct.[20] For this reason, the effectiveness of these requirements relies almost exclusively on the supervisory and public enforcement actions of competent authorities. To conclude, MiFID II disclosure, distribution and product governance requirements are generally capable of conferring rights on individual investors, thus empowering them to enforce these requirements via a private law remedy in a judicial or extra-judicial proceeding.

B. *Genil v Bankinter*: Towards an Implied Private Law Remedy?

Where EU law grants a right to individuals but does not confer a remedy to enforce this right, national law must ensure that the individual has an equivalent and effective remedy to enforce that right before a national court. EU law is not generally concerned about the legal form of the remedy (tortious or contractual) but requires in light of the principle of *ubi jus ibi remedium*, embodied in Articles 6 and 13 of the ECHR and Article 47 of the Charter, that an individual can effectively action a remedy to enforce a right through the judicial process.[21]

The question of whether breaches of conduct of business rules should give rise to a civil law consequence has been examined for the first, time by the CJEU in *Genil v Bankinter*.[22] In the case at stake, an investor (an SME) claimed that the interest rate swap it had concluded with a bank was null and void due to the bank's failure to conduct the suitability and/or appropriateness test prescribed by

[19] Case C-222/02, *Peter Paul*, paras 40 and 41.

[20] See Hadjiemmanuil, *The Banking Union and Its Implications for Private Law*, 396.

[21] See W Van Gerven 'Of Rights, Remedies and Procedures' (2000) 37(3) *Common Market Law Review* 501–536 at 525 and V Tresjack and E Beysen, 'European Consumer Protection Law: Curia Semper Dabit Remedium?' (2011) 48 *Common Market Law Review* 105.

[22] Case C-604/11, *Genil v Bankinter*, ECLI:EU:C:2013:344.

national law transposing MiFID I. The Spanish referring court asked the CJEU several questions about the correct interpretation of MiFID I provisions on investment advice, in particular whether the omission of the suitability or appropriateness tests must cause the contract between the investor and the investment institution to be void *ab initio*. The CJEU answered as follows:

> 57 It should be noted that, although Article 51 of Directive 2004/39 provides for the imposition of administrative measures or sanctions against the parties responsible for non-compliance with the provisions adopted pursuant to that directive, it does not state either that the Member States must provide for contractual consequences in the event of contracts being concluded which do not comply with the obligations under national legal provisions transposing Article 19(4) and (5) of Directive 2004/39, or what those consequences might be. In the absence of EU legislation on the point, it is for the internal legal order of each Member State to determine the contractual consequences of non-compliance with those obligations, subject to observance of the principles of equivalence and effectiveness (see, to that effect, Case C-591/10 Littlewoods Retail and Others [2012] ECR, paragraph 27 and the case-law cited).[23]

Two years later, in *Banif Plus Bank Zrt v Márton Lantos*, a Hungarian court sought guidance from the CJEU on whether the circumvention of Article 19(4) and (5) of MiFID I leads to the annulment of the loan agreement. The CJEU reiterated this paragraph in *Genil v Bankinter*, thus leaving it for the national court the task to determine the civil law consequences of breaches of conduct of business rules.[24]

The 'deferent approach' adopted by the CJEU in these two judgments leaves open key questions about the civil law effects of conduct of business rules.[25] Yet, in our view, these two judgments have important implications that should not be underestimated. The CJEU confirmed that the suitability and appropriateness rules are right-conferring provisions and require Member States to determine the contractual consequences of conduct of business rules within the boundaries of the principle of equivalence and effectiveness. Specifically, the national legislative discretion is limited to determining the contractual consequences of non-compliance with those obligations and does not extend to the choice of whether a contractual consequence should be given at all. The CJEU carved out the latter 'choice' from the principle of procedural autonomy with the consequence that this should be an obligation for Member States based on the full

[23] Case C-604/11, *Genil v Bankinter*, para 57.

[24] Case C-312/14, *Banif Plus Bank Zrt v Márton Lantos*, ECLI:EU:C:2015:794, para 79. In the case at stake, the CJEU decided that foreign currency denominated loan agreement does not qualify as an investment service and therefore established that the MiFID I conduct rules were not applicable to this transaction. The CJEU reiterated para 57 of *Genil v Bankinter*

[25] See, for the distinction within preliminary rulings between outcome, guidance and deference cases T Tridimas, 'The ECJ and National Courts: Dialogue, Cooperation and Instability', in D Chalmers and A Arnull (eds), *The Oxford Handbook of European Union Law* (Oxford, Oxford University Press, 2015) 409.

effectiveness of MiFID I.[26] This reading of the judgment not only reflects the letter of the judgment but also the the principle of *ubi jus, ibi remedium*. If suitability and appropriateness rules give rise to an individual right, a private law remedy should be, in principle, available to enforce this right.[27] Only its executive conditions should be governed by the principle of equivalence and effectiveness. It follows from this interpretation that these two judgments apply not only to contractual consequences (which were mentioned by the CJEU in response to the narrow formulation of the questions referred for a preliminary ruling) but also tortious and statutory consequences stemming from an violation of MiFID I and MiFID II conduct of business rules.

C. The Judicial Reactions to *Genil v Bankinter*: Dialogue and Resistance

Overall, the impact of *Genil v Bankinter* and *Banif Plus Bank Zrt v Márton Lantos* on national case law was rather limited. Only the Supreme Spanish Court has made express reference to this judgment on several occasions, mainly to justify its interpretation of national private law provisions on avoidance of contracts in light of MiFID I's investor protection objective. French, Italian and English courts, by contrast, did not make reference to these judgments.

In Germany, *Genil v Bankinter* played a minor role. This is demonstrated by a recent judgment of the German Federal Supreme Court,[28] handed down soon after *Genil v Bankinter*, on the civil law effects of MiFID I rules on inducements.[29] The Supreme Court held that these rules may be relevant to determine the content and scope of pre-contractual and contractual advisory obligations but cannot give rise to an autonomous tort law remedy, given that they have a public law nature. At the heart of the Court's reasoning is the fact that MiFID I does not require Member States to set out such a remedy and that had the legislators wanted to include it, they would have done so expressly. Another argument of the Court is that administrative sanctions ensure compliance with national law on the principle of effectiveness and are sufficient to achieve the investor protection objective of MiFID I.[30] It is doubtful whether this judicial approach, which has been confirmed

[26] Compare the first and the second sentence of para 57: in the second sentence the CJEU held that only the determination of the contract law consequences falls within the procedural autonomy of Member States.

[27] See M Andenas and F Della Negra, 'Between Contract Law and Financial Regulation: Towards the Europeanisation of General Contract Law' 28(4) *European Business Law Review* 499–521 at 511 and S Grundmann, 'The Bankinter Case on MiFID Regulation and Contract Law' (2013) 9 *European Review of Contract Law* 267. For a more dubitative view on the meaning of this paragraph, see Cherednychenko, 'Contract Governance in the EU' 505.

[28] BGH, 17 September 2013 – XI ZR 332/12, para 24.

[29] Section 31d(2) of the German Securities Trading Act (Wertpapierhandelsgesetz, WpHG).

[30] BGH, 17 September 2013 – XI ZR 332/12, para 36. In the same sense, see also BGH, 19 February 2008 – XI ZR 170/07; BGH 27 September 2011, XI ZR 178/10; BGH 27 September 2011, XI ZR 182/10.

by subsequent case law,[31] is in line with the CJEU's case law: the dogmatic qualification of conduct of business rules as rules of public law nature is not a relevant criterion to determine, under EU law, the civil law effects of these duties and may ultimately obfuscate the need to ensure the effectiveness of MIFID conduct of business rules.

Be that as it may, the case law of the German Federal Supreme Court offers the opportunity to examine two objections to the claim that MiFID I and MiFID II conduct of business rules should give rise to a civil law remedy.

The first objection is that, had EU legislators wanted to grant a civil law remedy for breaches of conduct of business rules, they should have done so expressly. Additionally, one may argue, the rejection of the Commission's proposal to introduce a principle of civil liability in MiFID II shows that EU legislators did not want to grant such a remedy to investors. These arguments, in our view, are not conclusive. The rejection of the Commission's proposal may prove that co-legislators did not want, at that stage, to create an harmonised regime for civil liability but cannot prove that MiFID II's conduct of business rules do not either produce civil law effects or give rise to a private law remedy. The reason is that the general principles of EU law, consolidated in the settled case law of Union courts, ensure that a remedy is warranted whenever an EU law provision confers a right on individuals. If the legislators wanted to achieve the objective of pre-empting national private law remedies, they should have done so expressly, as they did in respect of the EMIR (Article 12(3)). The absence of such an express provision in MiFID II means that the legislators have implicitly accepted that its conduct of business rules, like the pre-MiFID and MiFID conduct of business rules, may continue to give rise to civil law effects.

A second potential objection is that private law remedies are not necessary to ensure the effectiveness of MiFID II because this could also be achieved by out-of-court dispute resolution mechanisms and/or supervisory authorities.[32] This objection does not seem convincing. First, lack of private enforceability undermines the *effet utile* of MiFID II. Supervisory authorities do not have sufficient resources to investigate and sanction all potential infringements of MiFID II conduct of business rules and need to prioritise their actions focusing on the most relevant or serious infringements.[33] ADR bodies and consumer redress schemes afford fast and cheap redress to clients but they are not generally bound to respect MiFID II standards and to grant full compensation to clients. Furthermore, the fact that it is impossible to enforce the breach of conduct of business rules through a private law remedy in a judicial process may infringe the fundamental right protected by Article 47(1) of the Charter. Given that, in EU law, ADR procedures

[31] BGH 3 June 2014, XI ZR 147/12, no 35.

[32] For the interpretation of this provision, see Chapter 4 above. See also Recital No 22 of the PRIIPs Regulation.

[33] See VD Tountopoulos, 'Market Abuse and Private Enforcement' (2014) 3 *European Company and Financial Law Review* 312.

cannot express a final (ie irrevocable) determination (and cannot preclude access to courts), if clients were to be prevented from obtaining judicial redress, they would be, in practice, 'forced' to accept a non-judicial decision on matters affecting individual rights. Such an outcome would infringe the fundamental right to an effective remedy before a court.

D. Upgrading National Private Law Remedies via the Principles of Equivalence and Effectiveness

(i) The Principle of Equivalence

Genil v Bankinter left unanswered the question of what private law remedies would be in line with the principles of equivalence and effectiveness. To provide more guidance in this regard, it is first necessary to highlight the main features of these two principles.

To begin with, the principle of equivalence, which is an expression of the general principle of equal treatment, prescribes that national private law remedies and procedures for the breach of EU law shall not be less favourable than those governing similar domestic situations.[34] This requires national courts to compare objectively and in the abstract the actions for infringement of EU law-derived rights with that of the infringement of national law, taking into account the purpose and the essential characteristics of allegedly similar domestic actions.[35] The principle of equivalence may produce a strong impact on national private law, 'questioning the overall coherence of national choices about remedies and procedures'.[36] On several occasions, the CJEU held that national courts have the duty to assess *ex officio* the unfairness of contract terms where this duty would apply to domestic situations where the infringed rule ranked as a rule of public policy.[37] Hence, in so far as MiFID II conduct of business rules are mandatory rules of public policy,[38] national remedies and procedures applicable for the breach of mandatory rules (ie absolute nullity, ex officio application) should also apply to conduct of business rules, as transposed by national law.

[34] See Wilman. *Private Enforcement of EU Law Before National Courts*, p 30.

[35] See case C-261/95, *Palmisani v INPS*, ECLI:EU:C:1997:351, para 39.

[36] M Dougan, 'The Vicissitudes of Life at the Coalface: Remedies and Procedures for Enforcing Union Law' in P Craig and G de Burca (eds), *The Evolution of EU Law* (Oxford, Oxford University Press, 2011) 423.

[37] Case C-126/97 *Eco Swiss*, ECLI:EU:C:1999:269, para 35; case C-168/05 *Mostaza Claro* ECLI:EU:C:2006:675, para 35; case C-40/08, *Asturcom Telecomunicaciones SL*, ECLI:EU:C:2009:615, paras 53–54.

[38] See M Tison, The Civil Law Effects of MiFID in a Comparative Law Perspective: Challenging the Prudential Supervisor: Liability, Financial Law Institute, WP 2010-05, p. 13 who qualifies conduct of business rules as EU 'ordre public' and Busch and Van Dam, 'A Bank's Duty of Care' in *A Bank's Duty of Care*, 420. In some Member States however, the qualification of conduct of business rules as mandatory rules of public policy order is questioned (eg see Italy).

(ii) The Principle of Effectiveness

The principle of effectiveness prescribes that national law shall not make it either impossible in practice or excessively difficult to enforce the rights conferred on individuals by EU law.[39]

To assess whether national law makes the application of EU law impossible or excessively difficult account must be given to 'the role of that provision in the procedure, its progress and its special features, viewed as a whole, before the various national instances' (contextual criterion) and 'the basic principles of the domestic judicial system, such as protection of the rights of defence, the principle of legal certainty and proper conduct of procedure' (balancing criterion or procedural rule of reason).[40] However, the CJEU also takes into account the factual and practical dimension of effectiveness related to the specific situation at stake.[41]

The case law on the Directive 1993/13 on unfair contract terms provides a meaningful example of the *ad hoc* application of effectiveness and offers useful guidance to interpret national private law in retail securities disputes which, like consumer disputes, are generally characterised by an asymmetry of information and bargaining power between clients and firms.

In this case law, the CJEU held that the enforcement of consumer rights is excessively difficult where there is a 'significant risk' that a remedy is not exercised in practice, even if national law formally granted that remedy. For example, the rapidity of the enforcement proceedings and/or the cost of legal proceedings in relation to the amount of the disputed debt or consumers' ignorance of their rights, may dissuade consumers from defending themselves, thus showing that enforcing their rights is excessively difficult.[42] To ensure adequate protection of consumer rights, the CJEU required national courts to assess of their own motion (*ex officio*) the unfairness of contract terms in several situations where national law either did not allow[43]

[39] In Case 33/76, *Rewe-Zentralfinanz and Rewe-Zentral*, ECLI:EU:C:1976:188 the CJEU made reference to the 'impossible in practice' test. Afterwards, in Case C-199/82, *Amministrazione delle Finanze dello Stato* v *SpA San Giorgio*, ECLI:EU:C:1983:318 the CJEU raised the threshold by introducing the test of 'impossible or excessively difficult'-effectiveness. This test is now included in Recital No 11 of Directive 2014/104/EU of 26 November 2014 on certain rules governing actions for damages under national law for infringements of the competition law provisions of the Member States and of the European Union ('Antitrust Damages Directive') [2014] OJ L 349/1). For the development of the principle of effectiveness in the case law, see Dougan, 'The Vicissitudes of Life at the Coalface: Remedies and Procedures for Enforcing Union Law, 408.

[40] Joined Cases C-430-431/93, *Van Schijndel*, EU:C:1995:441, para 19 and Case C-312/93, *Peterbroeck*, EU:C:1995:437, para 14.

[41] Case C-453/00, *Cofidis SA v Jean-Louis Fredout*, ECLI:EU:C:2002:705, para 37. See F Cafaggi, P Iamiceli, (2017) 'The Principles of Effectiveness, Proportionality and Dissuasiveness in the Enforcement of EU Consumer Law' 3 *European Review of Private Law*' 575–618 at 578.

[42] Case C-618/10, *Banco Español de Crédito SA*, ECLI:EU:C:2012:349, para 54 and case C-415/11, *Mohamed Aziz*, ECLI:EU:C:2013:164, para 58.

[43] Joined cases C-240/98 to C-244/98, *Océano Grupo Editorial and Salvat Editores*, para 25; Case C-168/05 *Mostaza Claro*, para 25; case C-40/08 *Asturcom Telecomunicaciones* para 29; case C-137/08 *VB Pénzügyi Lízing* para 47; case C-243/08, *Pannon GSM* para 31; case C-618/10, *Banco*

or prohibited the courts from so doing[44] or to suspend a mortgage enforcement proceeding to ascertain the unfairness of the term upon which the enforcement had been initiated.[45]

This case law confirms the theory that the principle of effectiveness not only removes procedural obstacles to protection but also sets requirements to improve the substantive protection of consumers.[46] The 'remedial shaping function' of the principle of effectiveness was driven by the need to ensure the effective judicial protection of consumers,[47] particularly where they and their family were exposed to the risk of an irreversible loss of their mortgaged property.[48]

This risk and its connected social implications might not be present in a typical mis-selling dispute, but the criterion of 'significant risk' adopted by the CJEU in consumer disputes could also be used in retail client disputes where there is a concrete 'need for protection' of the retail client.[49] The main factors to be taken into account in this context include the clients' knowledge, experience and expertise in financial markets, their bargaining power (ie to what extent they have the power to individually negotiate contract terms), their ability to appreciate the risk of their investments, the type of financial instrument (ie complex or non-complex, liquid or illiquid), the type of investment service (ie advised or non-advised) and the volume of the investment in comparison to their economic situation.

For instance, in the UK, in the examined circumstance where retail clients may not have found full redress before FOS (eg because their loss exceeds the award limit of £150,000) and would not qualify as a private person under section 138D of the FSMA (ie because they are legal persons acting in the course of their business) and would not be able to prove the existence of a duty of care at common law (ie because no advisory agreement could be proven) there is a significant risk that these clients will be unable to exercise their rights before their national court.

Español de Crédito SA v Joaquín Calderón Camino, ECLI:EU:C:2012:349; Case C-32/12, *Soledad Duarte Hueros v Autociba SA, Automóviles Citroën España SA*, ECLI:EU:C:2013:637, para 43. See, in more detail on this case law, H-W Micklitz and N Reich. 'The Court and Sleeping Beauty: The Revival of the Unfair Contract Terms Directive' (UCTD) (2014) 51 *Common Market Law Review* 804.

[44] Case C-453/00, *Cofidis SA v Jean-Louis Fredout*, para 39.

[45] Case C-415/11, *Mohamed Aziz*, para 53 and comment by H-W.Micklitz, 'Unfair Contract Terms – Public Interest Litigation before European Courts', in E Terryn, G Straetmans and V Colaert (eds), *Landmark Cases of EU Consumer Law. In Honour of Jules Stuyck*, (Cambridge, Intersentia, 2013) 648, who speaks of the 'hidden constitutionalization of private law'.

[46] See in particular, N Reich, *General Principles of EU Civil Law* (Cambridge Intersentia, 2013) 97.

[47] Joined Cases C-222/05 to C-225/05, *J van der Weerd and Others v Minister van Landbouw, Natuur en Voedselkwaliteit*, ECLI:EU:C:2005:79, para 40.

[48] See Case C-415/11, *Mohamed Aziz*, ECLI:EU:C:2013:164, para 61. Case C-169/14, *Sanchez Morchillo*, ECLI:EU:C:2014:2099, para 43 and Case C-34/13, Kušionová, ECLI:EU:C:2014:2189, para 63. See for a comment F Della Negra, 'The Uncertain Development of the Case Law on Consumer Protection in Mortgage Enforcement Proceedings: Sánchez Morcillo and Kušionová' (2015) 4 *Common Market Law Review* 1999–1032 at 1020.

[49] See Recital No 104 of MiFID II.

Having said this, the next sections will examine, in light of the principle of effectiveness, the two most frequent remedies granted to retail clients for breaches of conduct of business rules, namely the avoidance of contracts and compensation for damages.

IV. The Design of Effective Private Law Remedies

A. Avoidance of Contracts

In several continental jurisdictions (Italy, Spain and Austria) breaches of conduct of business rules may determine the avoidance of financial investment contracts due to mistake (Spain and Austria[50]) or lack of essential elements of the contract (Italy).

(i) Hirmann v Immofinanz AG

Avoidance or invalidity removes from the market an act of private autonomy in contrast with the legal order and requires the parties to restore the *status quo ante* via restitution. This is the most favourable remedy for the investor and the most intrusive remedy for the firm. In competition law, public procurement and consumer law the EU has introduced rules to harmonise remedies for avoidance of contracts.[51] In some recent judgments the CJEU has addressed the question of whether the avoidance of a contract for breach of regulatory duty and the consequent restitutionary effects are compatible with the principle of effectiveness.

The question has arisen in *Hirmann v Immofinanz AG* where an investor claimed the cancellation of a contract for the purchase of shares on grounds of mistake and damages because the prospectus contained information which was incomplete, false or misleading.[52] The Austrian referring court asked several questions to the CJEU for a preliminary ruling aiming to assess, in essence, whether the private law remedy of the cancellation of a share purchase contract and the restitution of the purchase price is in line with the Second Council Directive 77/91/EEC[53] and the Prospectus, Transparency and Market Abuse Directives. The CJEU recalled that, in the absence of any EU law provision for the award of damages and the possibility of an award of punitive damages, it is for the

[50] See J Ring and M Spitzer, 'Austria' in Busch and van Dam, *A Bank's Duty of Care*, 104.

[51] See in more detail Wilman, *Private Enforcement of EU Law Before National Courts* 303.

[52] Case C-174/12, *Hirmann v Immofinanz AG*, ECLI:EU:C:2013:856.

[53] Second Council Directive 77/91/EEC of 13 December 1976 on coordination of safeguards which, for the protection of the interests of members and others, are required by Member States of companies within the meaning of the [second paragraph of Art 48 EC], in respect of the formation of public limited liability companies and the maintenance and alteration of their capital, with a view to making such safeguards equivalent (OJ 1977 L26, p1), as amended by Council Directive 92/101/EEC of 23 November 1992 (OJ 1992 L347, p64) ('the Second Directive'),

domestic legal system of each Member State to set the criteria to determine the extent of the damages, provided that the principles of equivalence and effectiveness are observed.[54] With specific regard to the national regime which required the the company concerned to repay to the purchaser a sum equivalent to the purchase price of the shares and to redeem those shares, the CJEU held that:

> 'the civil liability regime provided for in the national legislation at issue in the main proceedings constitutes an appropriate remedy for the harm suffered by the investor and for the failure of the issuing company to comply with the information requirements. Further, it is capable of deterring issuers from misleading investors'.[55]

The CJEU considered also whether the restitutionary effect of this remedy was compatible with EU law. It distinguished this case from the *Friz* judgment. In that case the CJEU held that the Council Directive 85/577/EEC on contracts negotiated away from business premises does not require Member States to give *ex tunc* effects to the consumer's withdrawal from a membership with a real estate fund and thus to release the consumer from all the consequences resulting from the exercise this right.[56] This conclusion was motivated by the fact that, in accordance with the general principles of civil law, a satisfactory balance should be struck between offering the consumer the possibility to cancel their contract and to recover their holding, while taking on a proportion of the risks inherent to any capital investment of the type at issue in the main proceedings.[57] However, in *Hirmann*, the CJEU held that this reasoning does not apply. Whereas in *Friz*, the consumer's renunciation of the contract was based on the exercise of a right granted by the Council Directive 85/577, in *Hirmann* the cancellation of the contract was solely based on the irregular conduct of the issuing company which was the cause of harm to the purchaser.[58] Therefore, the CJEU concluded that the retroactive effect of the remedy was compatible with EU law.

In contrast to *Genil v Bankinter*, in *Hirmann* the CJEU interpreted Directives (Prospectus and Transparency Directives) that, unlike MiFID I and II, contain a minimum harmonisation of civil liability for breaches of regulatory duties. Nevertheless, *Hirmann* is significant because it shows that in securities disputes the CJEU could take into account the deterrent effect of a private law remedy to assess its compliance with the effectiveness principle.

(ii) Francisco Gutiérrez Naranjo

The importance of the deterrent effect of private law remedies has also been emphasised in *Francisco Gutiérrez Naranjo*. The case originates from two judgments

[54] Case C-174/12, *Hirmann v Immofinanz AG*, para 40.
[55] Ibid at para 43.
[56] Case C-215/08, *Friz GmbH*, ECLI:EU:C:2010:186. In *Schulte* the CJEU accepted that notification of the cancellation has the effect, both for the consumer and for the trader, of restoring the *status quo ante* (case C-350/03, *Schulte* ECLI:EU:C:2005:637, para 88).
[57] Case C-215/08, *Friz GmbH*, para 48.
[58] Case C-174/12, *Hirmann v Immofinanz AG*, ECLI:EU:C:2013:856, para 62.

of the Spanish Supreme Court handed down in 2013 and 2015 where the Court declared that the 'floor' clauses contained in consumer mortgage loan contracts were unfair, but decided to limit the temporal effects of its judgments because there was a risk that restitution would trigger serious economic repercussions.[59] However, three Spanish lower courts doubted that this case law was compatible with EU law and therefore asked the CJEU if Article 6(1) of Directive 93/13 precludes a national case law which limits the restitutory effects deriving from the declaration of nullity of floor clauses contained in mortgage loan agreements.[60]

In his opinion, Advocate General Mengozzi held that this case law is compatible with the directive. According to the Advocate General, the need for legal certainty advanced by the Spanish Supreme Court '[...] on account of the many legal situations which are potentially affected and which could undermine the stability of an economic sector – is a concern shared by the EU legal order' and exceptionally justifies the limitation of the temporal effects of the declaration of invalidity of unfair terms.[61] In particular, the Advocate General held that such limitation does not infringe the principle of effectiveness given that consumer protection is not absolute and that a consumer who had concluded a loan agreement containing a 'floor' clause could easily repay one loan using another from a different bank and the floor clause would not have led to a substantial change in the monthly amount payable by consumers.[62]

The CJEU (Grand Chamber) did not follow his opinion. According to the CJEU, even if the directive does not expressly regulate the civil law effects of the unfairness of contract terms – a point emphasised by the Advocate General[63] – 'the determination by a court that such a term is unfair *must*, in principle, have the consequence of restoring the consumer to the legal and factual situation that he would have been in if that term had not existed'[64] because 'the absence of such restitutory effect would be liable to call into question the dissuasive effect' of this directive.[65] Consequently, the CJEU decided that the referring courts must disapply the temporal limitation of invalidity of unfair contract terms because that limitation is not compatible with EU law.

In line with *Hirmann* and previous case law on Directive 1993/13[66] the CJEU stressed that the deterrent effect is an essential component to ensure the

[59] STS, 1916/2013, No 241/2013 of 9 May 2013 (concerning a collective action for an injunction brought by a consumer association against several credit institutions) and judgment No 139/2015 of 25 March 2015 (ES:TS:2015:1280) (with regard to an individual action brought by a consumer against a bank).

[60] Joined cases C-154/15 and C-307/15, *Francisco Gutiérrez Naranjo*, ECLI:EU:C:2016:980.

[61] Opinion of the Advocate General Mengozzi Joined cases C-154/15 and C-307/15, *Francisco Gutiérrez Naranjo v Cajasur Banco* SAU ECLI:EU:C:2016:552, para 74.

[62] Opinion of AG Mengozzi in Joined cases C-154/15 and C-307/15, *Francisco Gutiérrez Naranjo*, para 73.

[63] Ibid at para 63.

[64] Joined cases C-154/15 and C-307/15, *Francisco Gutiérrez Naranjo*, at para 61.

[65] Ibid at para 63.

[66] See also Case C-618/10, *Banco Español de Crédito* EU:C:2012:349, para 69 and, recently, Case C-26/13, *Árpád Kásler, Hajnalka Káslerné Rábai v OTP Jelzálogbank Zrt*, ECLI:EU:C:2014:282, para 83.

effectiveness of EU law and also the fundamental right to an effective judicial protection.[67] An interesting feature is that the CJEU did not refer in its judgment to the need to balance the protection of consumers with the need of ensuring financial or economic stability. This could be an indication that financial stability concerns invoked by the firms, and not supported by legal provisions, do not justify a reduction of the standard of protection for retail clients.

(iii) Avoidance of Contracts for Breach of Suitability and Other Conduct of Business Rules

The CJEU has given an important deterrent function to invalidity of unfair contract terms as well as securities contracts concluded in breach of regulatory duties.[68] However, it has recalled the need to use this remedy only where necessary to neutralise an unfair advantage of one party to the detriment of the other to preserve confidence in the contractual relationship.[69] Although MiFID II does not contain a provision such as Article 6(1) of Directive 1993/13, the rationale of the examined case law, given the similarities between consumer disputes (often involving mortgages contracts) and retail securities disputes, offer some guidance to shape an effective invalidity remedy in retail disputes.

In this regard, distinction should be made between breaches of suitability rule and other conduct of business rules.

Where a contract is concluded in breach of the firm's duty to refuse a transaction or without a suitability test, the invalidity of that contract (or its contract terms if it can remain effective without that term), would be justified in light of the principle of effectiveness.[70] MiFID II prohibits the firm from carrying out a transaction where a financial instrument is unsuitable. If, in breach of this prohibition, a transaction is executed, there is a significant risk that the client purchases an instrument that is unsuitable and incurs unforeseen losses. The nullity of the contract and the consequent restitution of the purchase price neutralises, *ex post*, this risk, restoring the pre-contract situation in which the client would have been, had no contract been concluded. This type of remedy also ensures the deterrent effect of the suitability rule, so that the party better placed to prevent the breach of the rule (i.e. the investment firm) internalises the cost of its non-compliance.

By contrast, invalidity and restitution could be disproportionate to sanction breaches or omissions of the fair treatment clause, disclosure and appropriateness rule. In these cases, MiFID II accepted that, given the more limited role of the firm in the client's decision making, a transaction should remain in place even if these

[67] See also case C-483/16, *Zsolt Sziber v ERSTE Bank Hungary Zrt.*, ECLI:EU:C:2018:367, para 55.

[68] See F Cafaggi and P Iamiceli, 'The Principles of Effectiveness, Proportionality and Dissuasiveness in the Enforcement of EU Consumer Law: The Impact of a Triad on the Choice of Civil Remedies and Administrative Sanctions' (2017) 25 *European Review of Private Law* 609.

[69] Case C-453/10, *Jana Pereničová, Vladislav Perenič v SOS financ spol. s r. o.*, ECLI:EU:C:2012:144.

[70] See also D Imbruglia, *La Regola di Adeguatezza e il Contratto*, 504.

conduct of business rules are breached. The client may decide 'at his own risk' to enter into an inappropriate transaction. Therefore, any remedy that would put the client in the same position as if no contract had been concluded would grant the client an advantage vis-à-vis the firm and create legal uncertainty.[71] Therefore, compensation for damages, which should place the client in the same position he would have been had the firm given him the correct information, seems to better reflect the purpose of these conduct of business rules.

B. Liability for Damages

In the examined jurisdictions, compensation for losses suffered as a result of breaches of conduct of business rules is the minimum remedy granted by national courts on the basis of pre-contractual, contractual or tortious liability. However, there are significant differences among jurisdictions with regard to the legal standard to ascertain the breach of the duty of care, the factual and legal causation, the measure of damages and the burden of proof.

(i) Breach of Duty of Care

The first condition to establish the tortious and contractual liability of the defendant firm is that the investment firm breached its duty of care. In Italy, France and Spain, a breach of conduct of business rules, both in advisory and non-advisory transactions, is a breach of the general duty to perform the obligation with skill and care; in the UK, however, this does not automatically give rise to a breach of a duty of care in common law, although it should help courts in shaping the firm's duty of care in advisory relations.

The duty of conform interpretation does not require courts to replace the general duty of care with the specific regulatory duties or to hold that regulatory duties and duty of care are co-extensive, but to interpret the general duty of care in light of the overriding duty to act honestly, fairly and professionally in the best interests of its clients. Conceptually, EU law does not require a substitution of the general duty of care with detailed regulatory duties but rather the hybridisation or synthesis between these different duties. In practice, hybridisation means that the firm should adopt the standard of skill and care that it could reasonably be expected to exercise towards clients, commensurate with the market practice in the firm's field of activity. In comparison to the general duty of care in general private law, which is generally based on the nature of professional activity,[72] MiFID's standard of care should also be calculated based on the client's interest, both in advisory and non-advisory relationships.

[71] See Opinion AG Trstenjak in case C-453/10, *Jana Pereničová, Vladislav Perenič v SOS financ, spol Sro*, ECLI:EU:C:2011:788, paras 65–67.

[72] See eg, Art 1176(2) of the Italian Civil Code.

More specifically, in advisory relationships, the firm should ensure that the client understands the risks (risk comprehension), is able to absorb them (risk capacity) and is willing to run these risks (risk tolerance). As the UK High Court clearly held in *Haider Abdullah v Credit Suisse,* the greater the risk to which the adviser exposes his client, the stronger the need for the adviser to ensure by way of specific documentation that the client is fully aware of the risks he is taking.[73]

In non-advisory relations, the duty of conform interpretation cannot be limited to a duty not to mis-state facts or not to give false or misleading information. It requires the firm to ensure that the retail client fully understands the risks of the product. The legal basis for this is the fair treatment and the best interest duty and, where applicable, the appropriateness rule. This type of duty does not go so far as to require firms to assess the client's risk capacity and tolerance but to prepare the pre-contractual documentation in such a way that the product's risk and return are clearly explained. The riskier or more complex the product, the stronger the need to explain it to the client. The firm's duty of care should be informed by the clients' best interest. If the circumstances of the case reveal that the client was put in a particularly difficult position (ie because he was offered self-placed instruments without advice) national courts should be allowed to require firms to also assess risk capacity and risk tolerance, even if this goes beyond the appropriateness test.[74]

Finally, it is important to note that advisory and non-advisory relations should be distinguished based on whether a personal recommendation was given and not whether an advisory contract was concluded.[75] If the protection granted by MiFID II to retail clients is made dependent on the conclusion of a contract, the *effet utile* of conduct of business rules would be substantially reduced given that, in retail client transactions, the client does not have the power to individually negotiate contract terms so cannot influence the way the contracts are drafted. Taking into account the ESMA guidelines on suitability, the client should be entitled to claim that the suitability rule was breached wherever the firm gave a personal recommendation, notwithstanding the absence of an advisory agreement.

(ii) Factual Causation

A 'but for test' or *conditio sine qua non* seems to be the general model used to select factual causes in the examined jurisdictions, although more innovative causation theories based on the balance of probabilities or increase of risk have been adopted in certain jurisdictions (eg Italy and France). These innovative theories respond to the need to overcome the difficulties posed by the *conditio sine qua non* theory

[73] See also *Haider Abdullah v Credit Suisse* [2017] EWHC 3016 at para 168.
[74] In this case, the conditions for the 'judicial gold-plating', examined above, should be respected.
[75] See also Case C-604/11, *Genil v Bankinter*, para 53.

in demonstrating a causal link based on a hypothetical, counter-factual scenario. This theory requires the judge to compare an actual fact (the investment decision made by the client) with a hypothetical scenario (what the client would have done, had the firm complied with the conduct of business rule). The firm's conduct is the factual cause of the loss only if the client would not have suffered the same loss, had the firm provided correct information under the hypothetical scenario. Legally, to conduct this counter-factual analysis, it is necessary to understand whether the firm's conduct should either be an exclusive or a contributory cause of the loss, the client's role in the causal link and what standard should be adopted to prove that the client would have acted differently in the absence of the breach of conduct of business rule.

To begin with, it should be noted that, Article 69(2) of MiFID II indicates the need to establish a causal link between the firm's conduct and the loss (the loss should be 'the result' of the infringement) but it does not specify how the standard of causation should be determined. It is for Member States to define the detailed rules on the application of the concept of a 'causal relationship', provided that the principles of equivalence and effectiveness are observed.[76] Useful guidance on how the causal requirement should be interpreted in light of the principle of effectiveness was provided by the CJEU in the *Kone* judgment,[77] a case on the actions for damages resulting from umbrella pricing caused by a cartel.[78] The CJEU held that the full effectiveness of Article 101 of TFEU would be undermined by a national law which makes a claim for compensation subject to the existence of a 'direct causal link' between the breach and the loss and excludes compensation when the loss is the result of a cartel which distorted the price formation mechanisms governing competitive markets.[79]

In our view, the adoption of a theory of contributory causation, embraced by the CJEU in this competition law case, would also be appropriate in retail disputes and would be legally justified by the principle of effectiveness. The price of financial instruments traded on secondary markets is determined by many inter-related factors (ie a capital issuance launched by a firm's competitor, the corporate restructuring of the issuer or any supervisory/enforcement action) and retail clients have scarce resources to monitor these markets in advance before making an investment. This means that, in principle, the firm's conduct can be causally relevant even if it is not the exclusive cause of the loss. In advised services, where the firm

[76] Joined cases C-295/04 to C-298/04, *Manfredi*, see also case C-199/11, *Europese Gemeenschap v Otis NV*, ECLI:EU:C:2012:684, para 43.

[77] Case C-557/12, *Kone AG and Others*, ECLI:EU:C:2014:1317. In the national proceeding, the injured party claimed damages by alleging that the price paid for the purchase of an elevator from a manufacturer not involved in the cartel, was nevertheless set under the protection of the elevator cartel and was thus higher than would otherwise have been expected under competitive conditions. Austrian courts dismissed the claim because of the lack of causation between the cartel and the loss suffered by the customer.

[78] See in more detail, I Lianos, 'Causal Uncertainty and Damages Claims for the Infringement of Competition Law in Europe' (2015) 34 *Yearbook of European Law* 170.

[79] Case C-557/12, *Kone AG*, para 33.

plays a greater role in determining a client's decision, it could be presumed that the breach of the conduct of business rule led to a recoverable damage. In non-advised services, it is necessary to assess the level of knowledge, experience and expertise of the client.

This brings us to the second causation problem mentioned above. If the investor is sophisticated (ie experienced in financial matters), their willingness to bear risk may point to the fact that they would have purchased the financial instrument even if the firm had complied with its conduct of business rules.[80] If the investor is unsophisticated, the fact that they were willing to bear risk does not mean that they were aware of or informed about it.[81]

Finally, given the counterfactual nature of the causal assessment, so as not to make the compensation of damages either excessively difficult or impossible in practice, it should be sufficient for the investor to prove, by way of presumption and building on their previous 'investment history' that it would have been 'more likely than not' that they would have taken a different decision in the absence of misconduct.

(iii) Legal Causation

The examined jurisdictions have introduced several mechanisms (ie foreseeability, remoteness) to limit the potential far-reaching effects of factual causation.[82] The first mechanism is to restrict recoverable damages to those which reflect a detriment to the persons who are protected by the scope of the rule at stake.[83]

Moreover, as the CJEU has held in the *Kantarev* judgment, 'it is a general principle common to the legal systems of the Member States that the injured party must show reasonable diligence in limiting the extent of the loss or damage, or risk having to bear the loss or damage himself'.[84] However, the CJEU specified that 'it is clear from the case-law that it would be contrary to the principle of effectiveness to oblige injured parties to have recourse systematically to all the legal remedies available to them even if that would give rise to excessive difficulties or could not reasonably be required of them'.[85] In light of this case law, retail clients have a general duty to prevent the damage before it occurs (eg by selling their securities before their portfolio further deteriorates) but this duty should take into account the specific characteristics of the client (ie their capacity inform themselves about market developments and the financial instrument (eg if is still liquid)).[86]

[80] See, in this sense, the judgment of the Dutch Supreme Court of 27 November 2009, JOR 2010/43. For more details, see Busch and Van Dam, *A Bank's Duty of Care*, 427.

[81] See, in this sense, Cass, 28 February 2018, n. 4727.

[82] See C van Dam, *European Tort Law* (Oxford: OUP 2013) pp 308 & 309.

[83] Opinion of the Advocate General Kokott, in case C-557/12, *Kone AG*, para 41.

[84] C-571/16, *Nikolay Kantarev v Balgarska Narodna Banka*, para 141.

[85] Ibid at para 142.

[86] See also case C-497/13, *Faber v Autobedrijf Hazet Ochten BV*, ECLI:EU:C:2015:357, para 63 (the consumer cannot be required, given his weak position vis-à-vis the seller as regards the

(iv) Quantification of Damages

In the examined jurisdictions the measure of damages oscillates between the out-of-pocket and restitutionary measure – 'the competing paradigms of damages in securities law'.[87]

The 'out-of-pocket' measure is the difference between the purchase price of the securities and their value had there been no breach of conduct of business rules. It places the plaintiff in the position they would have been in had the firm given correct information and generally corresponds to a tortious or pre-contractual measure of damage (ie reliance interest or negative interest).

Restitutionary damages award to the plaintiff the purchase price of the security and restores the parties' pre-contract situation, placing the investor in the position they would have been in had no contract been concluded. It is generally awarded by invalidity or rescissionary remedies.

National courts have rarely awarded 'benefit-of-the-bargain' damages (ie the difference between the represented value of the security as purchased or sold and the fair value of the security on the date of the trade). These damages place the plaintiff in the position they would have been had the reality been as represented. It represents a contractual measure of damages equal to the expectation created by the firm's conduct.[88]

Since EU law does not establish rules on the measure or quantification of damages, it is for Member States to govern this matter, subject to the principles of equivalence and effectiveness. In *Manfredi*, however, the CJEU held that national law would breach the principle of effectiveness if compensation does not include, in addition to the actual loss (*damnum emergens*), the loss of profit (*lucrum cessans*) and interest. The Court also added that the total exclusion of loss of profit, especially in the context of economic or commercial litigation, would be such as to make reparation practically impossible.[89] In *Hirmann*, the CJEU, held that a restitutionary measure of damages is, in principle, compatible with EU law and would ensure the deterrent effect of regulatory duties.

Article 69(2) of MiFID II specifies that compensation should be given for 'any loss' and thus confirms that, in principle, damages should comprise both actual loss and loss of profit plus interest.[90] That said, in principle, the loss suffered by

information relating to the qualities of those goods, to furnish evidence that a lack of conformity adversely affects the goods that he has purchased (here, a second-hand vehicle) because this would make it impossible or excessively difficult for the consumer to exercise the rights which he derives from Directive 1999/44).

[87] FH Easterbrook and DR Fischel, Optimal Damages in Securities Cases (1985) 52(3) *University of Chicago Law Review* 611–641 at 634.

[88] Against compensation of loss of profits and consequential damages, see Easterbrook and Fischel, *Optimal Damages in Securities Cases* 633.

[89] Joined cases C-295/04 to C-298/04, *Manfredi*, para 92. See also case C-536/11, *Donau Chemie and Others*, ECLI:EU:C:2013:366, paras 25–27.

[90] See, in general, in EU law Reich, *Horizontal Liability in EC Law*, 730.

the client reflects the fact that, due to the breach of conduct of business rules, the client purchased the financial instrument at a price that was higher than its real value.[91] Since the market value of financial instruments continuously changes over time, once the causal link between the firm's conduct and the loss has been established, the measure of damage should amount to the difference between the purchase price of the financial instrument and its price at the time of the dispute.[92] From the amount resulting from this difference it is necessary to deduct the potential gains obtained after its purchase.[93] Compensation should be reduced by the amount that the client would have 'saved' by selling the financial instrument from the time he became aware or could have reasonably realised the loss suffered. This avoids the risk that the client keeps the financial instrument in their portfolio, thus increasing the amount of the loss. It is clear, however, that the burden on the client to take measures to prevent a worsening of the loss should be assessed using the type of financial instrument (ie liquid or illiquid) and their experience and expertise in financial matters.

(v) Burden of Proof

Finally, a relevant issue for retail investors is the burden of proof in compensation claims. In the examined jurisdictions, courts lighten the burden for the proof of the breach of duty of care (because they consider sufficient the proof of a breach of regulatory duty) but require the client, in conformity with the ordinary contractual evidential rules, to prove the damage and generally the causal link between the damage and the conduct. In the UK, the burden of proof is heavier because clients also need to prove that a duty of care at common law has been breached and often that an advisory contract was concluded.

It is for Member States to provide rules for the burden of proof, in accordance with the principle of equivalence and effectiveness.[94] Whether evidential rules make the enforcement of MiFID II's rights impossible or excessively difficult will clearly depend on the specific factual circumstances of the case. However, from a legal perspective, evidential rules should be interpreted to take into account the asymmetry of information and the bargaining power between firms and clients. Given that retail clients have very limited bargaining powers, contractual documentation cannot be, in itself, a sufficient element to discharge a firm's liability.

[91] See G Afferni, *Il quantum del danno nella responsabilità precontrattuale* (Torino, Giappichelli, 2008) 154.

[92] If the security is illiquid and cannot be sold, the value at the time the claim is brought should be taken into account.

[93] It is assumed that the breach is not intentional. If it is, to strengthen the deterrent, the value of the instrument could be calculated at the time the claim is brought. See, in more detail, F Sartori, *Le regole di condotta degli intermediari finanziari. Disciplina e forme di tutela* (Milano, Giuffré, 2004) 399.

[94] See, in particular, Case C-3/17, *Sporting Odds Ltd v Nemzeti Adó- és Vámhivatal Központi Irányítása*, ECLI:EU:C:2018:130, para 56. See also the Opinion AG Kokott in Case C-176/17, *Profi Credit Polska SA v Biel*.

Likewise, MiFID questionnaires should be supplemented by other factors (ie disproportion between the value of the security and the client's available income or economic resources) that reveal the lack of suitability or appropriateness of the security. Non-documentary evidence (ie witness declarations) as well as acts of supervisory authorities, where they can be disclosed in accordance with professional secrecy obligations,[95] could be important tools to prove a breach of conduct of business rules.

V. Horizontal Application of EU of Fundamental Rights

A. Retail Clients' Fundamental Rights

MiFID II, unlike MIFID I, declares that its provisions respect fundamental rights and must be implemented in accordance with those rights and principles.[96] National courts must interpret national law and EU law in light of EU fundamental rights.[97] In retail client disputes, fundamental rights may have different functions and applications given that both clients and firms may invoke fundamental rights to obtain an interpretation of the applicable law in conformity with these rights.

In particular, from the retail client's perspective, the principles of effective judicial protection and a high level of consumer protection contained in Article 38 of the Charter may be of relevance. The principle of effective judicial protection, enshrined in Article 47 of the Charter and Articles 6 and 13 of the ECHR, is an 'umbrella principle'[98] which comprises the right to an effective remedy, the rights of the defence, the principle of equality of arms, the right of access to a tribunal and the right to be advised, defended and represented.[99]

Although Article 47 of the Charter is not intended to create new remedies,[100] it can upgrade national remedies, thus creating hybrid remedies to ensure the

[95] See Chapter 7.

[96] See Recital No 166 of MiFID II.

[97] See, in particular, C-275/06, *Promusicae*, ECLI:EU:C:2008:54, para 68 and Case C-579/12 RX-II, *Commission v Strack*, ECLI:EU:C:2013:570, para 40. For the lack of horizontal direct effects of fundamental rights see the opinion of AG Trstenjak in Case C-282/10, *Dominguez* ECLI:EU:C:2011:559, paras 80–83.

[98] S Prechal, 'The Court of Justice and Effective Judicial Protection: What Has the Charter Changed?' in C Paulussen, T Takacs, V Lazic, B van Rompuy (eds), *Fundamental Rights in International and European Law* (The Hague, TMC Asser Press, 2015) 149.

[99] Case C-199/11, *Europese Gemeenschap v Otis NV and Others*, ECLI:EU:C:2012:684, para 48.

[100] Case C-583/11, *P Inujt Tapirirt Kanatami*, ECLI:EU:C:2013:625, paras 97 and 103 and Case C-432/05, *Unibet*, ECLI:EU:C:2007: para 40.

effective protection of EU rights.[101] The CJEU has given shape to 'constitutional hybrids' in several preliminary rulings on Directive 1993/13 in disputes concerning the compatibility of national mortgage enforcement proceedings with EU law. In one case, the CJEU held that the principle of effectiveness 'implies a requirement of effective judicial protection guaranteed by Article 47 of the Charter'[102] and concluded that national mortgage enforcement proceedings were in contrast with the principle of equality of arms.[103]

However, in other judgments, where national mortgage enforcement proceedings were at stake, the CJEU interpreted national procedural law in light of Articles 7, 34(3), 38 and 47 of the Charter, but came to the conclusion that national procedural law was, in principle, compatible with these provisions. The CJEU pointed out that neither the principle of effectiveness nor Articles 47 and 38 of the Charter can be invoked to fully compensate for the total inertia on the part of the consumer concerned[104] nor where national law imposes additional requirements to actionate a remedy.[105] It is also noteworthy that while in an increasing number of cases national courts have asked the CJEU to assess the compatibility of national procedural law with Article 47 of the Charter, only in few cases has it actually conducted this assessment.[106]

What, then, are the implications of this case law for the protection of retail clients in securities disputes?

This case law shows that the horizontal effects of fundamental rights may vary significantly, depending on the specific factual and legal context of the dispute.[107] The cautious approach followed by the CJEU in consumer law matters suggests that in retail financial disputes, fundamental rights will lead to the creation of hybrid private law remedies only where essential procedural guarantees are infringed and

[101] N. Reich, 'The Principle of Effectiveness and EU Private Law' in U Bernitz, X Groussot and F Schulyok (eds), *General Principles of EU Law and European Private Law* (Kluwer Law International, 2013) 308. See also C Mak, 'Rights and Remedies: Article 47 EUCFR and Effective Judicial Protection in European Private Law Matters', in H-W Micklitz (ed), *Constitutionalization of European Private Law* (Oxford, Oxford University Press, 2014) 253.

[102] Case C-539/14, *Sánchez Morcillo, María del Carmen Abril García*, ECLI:EU:C:2015:508, para 50. See also case C-483/16, *Zsolt Sziber v ERSTE Bank Hungary Zrt*, ECLI:EU:C:2018:367, para 49.

[103] See, in more detail, Della Negra, 'The Uncertain Development of the Case Law on Consumer Protection in Mortgage Enforcement Proceedings: Sánchez Morcillo and Kušionová' 1027.

[104] Case C-470/12, *Pohotovosť sro v Miroslav Vašuta*, ECLI:EU:C:2014:101, paras 52–53 and case C-34/13, *Monika Kušionova v SMART Capital as*, ECLI:EU:C:2014:2189, 56.

[105] C-483/16, *Zsolt Sziber v Erste Bank Hungary Zrt*, para 51.

[106] See for instance Case C-433/11, *SKP ks v Kveta Polhošová*, ECLI:EU:C:2012:702; Case C-92/14 *Tudoran v SC Suport Colect* ECLI:EU:C:2014:2051; Case C-49/14, *Finanmadrid EFC SA v Jesús Vicente Albán Zambrano*, ECLI:EU:C:2016:98, para 57. Case C-7/16, *Banco Popular Español SA, PL Salvador SARL v María Rita Giráldez Villar*, ECLI:EU:C:2016:523.

[107] See, with reference to consumer law, AML van Duin, 'Metamorphosis? The Role of Article 47 of the EU Charter of Fundamental Rights in Cases Concerning National Remedies and Procedures under Directive 93/13/EEC', Centre for the Study of European Contract Law Working Paper Series No 2017-05, 11.

access to judicial remedies is undermined (eg because clients do not have the same procedural right as the firms[108] or legal aid is not made available for clients who lack sufficient resources[109]).

A situation like that examined in the UK, where certain investors (ie SMEs) may be prevented from obtaining full compensation for breaches of conduct of business rules raises doubts about the compatibility of relevant national laws not only with the principle of effectiveness but also with the right to an effective judicial protection because in such a case there would be no remedy available to provide redress to these clients. By contrast, it seems unlikely, although legally possible, that fundamental rights grant hybrid private law remedies to investors where national private law rules (eg on causation or the measure of damages) make it excessively difficult.[110] In these situations, the principle of effectiveness, which should be applied examining whether there is a 'significant risk' that the client will not be able to action the remedies or procedures formally available under national law, would provide a more appropriate legal basis to upgrade national private law.

This begs the question whether in practice the horizontal application of the right to an effective remedy would bring any added value to the retail client in comparison to the principle of effectiveness. Conceptually, the fundamental right to an effective remedy shifts the judicial scrutiny from the balancing between the objectives of EU law and the procedural autonomy of Member States to the assessment of whether the individual litigant has effective (ie actual) possibilities to enforce his rights.[111] Moreover, the assessment conducted on the basis of Article 47 of the Charter should not only consider the protective purpose of EU law provisions but also the criteria set out by the ECtHR to assess the litigant's situation under the ECHR. For these reasons, where procedural rights are violated or access to a court is precluded in practice, the fundamental right of effective judicial protection provides for a stronger safeguard than the principle of effectiveness for retail clients, because it allows and requires national courts to take into account a broader set of factual circumstances to prove that the fundamental rights of the client have been breached.

B. Investment Firms' Fundamental Rights

The added value of the fundamental right of effective judicial protection, in comparison to the principle of effectiveness, is also clear where the fundamental rights of the investment firm are at stake. In two judgments concerning the interpretation of the Directive 1993/13 the CJEU has stressed the importance of

[108] Case C-169/14, *Sánchez Morcillo and Abril García*, EU:C:2014:2099, para 49.
[109] Case C-470/12, *Pohotovosť sro v Miroslav Vašuta*, para 53.
[110] See, for more optimistic view, see OO Cherednychenko. 'Fundamental Rights, European Private Law and Financial Services', in H-W Micklitz (ed), *Constitutionalization of European Private Law*, 205.
[111] See Chapter 1.

safeguarding the rights of defence (in particular, the principle of *audi alteram partem*) of the seller or supplier in consumer disputes.[112]

While the rights of defence enshrined in Article 47(2) of the Charter may constitute a limit to the effectiveness of MiFID conduct of business rules,[113] it seems unlikely that the freedom to conduct a business or the right to property, enshrined in Articles 16 and 17 of the Charter, could be used to reduce the protection enjoyed by investors on the basis of MiFID II. The question of a potential contrast between EU 'consumer-protective' legislation and these fundamental rights has arisen in *McDonagh v Ryanair*,[114] a case regarding the right to compensation for flight cancellations under Regulation 261/2004 on passengers' rights. In the civil proceeding, Ryanair claimed that the obligation to provide care to passengers imposed on air carriers following a cancellation of the flight would deprive air carriers of part of the fruits of their labour and of their investments. The national court asked whehter Articles 5(1)(b) and 9 of Regulation No 261/2004 are invalid in light of Articles 16 and 17 of the Charter, as well as the principle of proportionality. The CJEU noted that Article 38 of the Charter should also be taken into account for the assessment and that 'the importance of the objective of consumer protection, which includes the protection of air passengers, may justify even substantial negative economic consequences for certain economic operators'.[115] For this reason, the CJEU held that the obligations imposed by that Regulation on air carriers for flight cancellations were not disproportionate. This judgment shows that when balancing the fundamental rights of firms and retail clients, the fundamental rights of the latter, in light of the investor protection purpose of MiFID II, will, as a principle, outweigh the need to ensure a firm's freedom to conduct business or the right of property.[116]

VI. Preliminary Conclusion

Hybrid private law is one the manifestations of regulatory private law which has emerged in various fields of the internal market.[117] It reflects the transformation

[112] Case C-472/11, *Banif Plus Bank*, EU:C:2013:88, para 29 (the CJEU held that the national court which has found of its own motion that a contractual term unfair must inform the parties to the dispute of that fact and to invite each of them to set out its views on that matter, with the opportunity to challenge the views of the other party) and Case C-119/15, *Biuro podróży 'Partner'*, ECLI:EU:C:2016:987, para 27 (the CJEU held that a contract term cannot be held to be unlawful and sanctioned by a fine solely because an equivalent term has been entered in the national registry of unlawful standard contract terms, without that seller or supplier having been a party to the proceedings culminating in the entry of such a term in that register).

[113] See, in general, M Safjan, 'A Union of Effective Judicial Protection: Addressing a Multi-level Challenge through the Lens of Article 47 CFREU' (2014) *Yearbook of European Law* 5.

[114] See case C-12/11, *Denise McDonagh v Ryanair Ltd*, ECLI:EU:C:2013:43, para 63.

[115] Ibid para 48.

[116] See Recital No 57 of MiFID II.

[117] See, in particular, Micklitz, Comparato and Svetiev, *The Regulatory Character of European Private Law*, 67.

of private law from an instrument to ensure the parties' autonomy to 'a synthesis that combines both its traditional concerns about corrective justice between individuals and instrumental ambitions about steering markets towards distributive justice'.[118]

This chapter has shown that hybrid private law is not a creature of judicial interpretation but has strong normative basis in EU law. The doctrine of horizontal effects requires courts to interpret general private law in light of MiFID II's duties and the principles of equivalence and effectiveness require courts to grant an effective remedy wherever a conduct of business rule grants a right to individual clients. Due to their level of detail and their transactional nature, disclosure, distribution and product governance rules confer rights to clients and they form the basis for the conferral of a private law remedy.

The case law of the CJEU on consumer and competition law offers valuable guidance for interpreting the conditions for the exercise of this remedy. This must be defined in light of the principle of equivalence and effectiveness. The key criterion to determine whether a private law rule makes it excessively difficult or impossible in practice to enforce investors' individual rights is to determine whether there is a 'significant risk' that the investor would not exercise its formal rights due to economic and legal constraints. This should also be assessed based on the factual and practical condition of the investor vis-à-vis the firm. MiFID II's conduct of business rules, supplemented by the ESMA's 'conduct of business handbook' provides the criteria to assess the investor's weaknesses and should therefore drive the interpretation of national private law to ensure that it achieves the investor protection objective of regulation.

The emergence of hybrid private law duties and remedies may also be triggered by the horizontal application of EU fundamental rights. The case law of the CJEU, however, shows that fundamental rights, in particular Article 47 of the Charter, may not be invoked simply to increase the protection of the weaker contractual party or fill the gaps in national private law. A strong justification, based on the risk of infringement of essential procedural guarantees, appears to be necessary to 'upgrade' national law remedies and procedures.

[118] H Collins, 'Governance Implications for the European Union of the Changing Character of Private Law' in F Cafaggi and H Muir-Watt (eds), *Making European Private Law: Governance Design* (Cheltenham, Edward Elgar, 2008), 269, 278

7

Hybrid Enforcement Mechanisms: Future Perspectives

I. Private Enforcement of Conduct Regulation in the EU: Unexpected Importance and Limitations

The most important finding of the previous chapters is that MiFID II and general principles of EU law empower investors to enforce EU conduct of business rules, notwithstanding the absence of an express EU law provision. This shows the unexpectedly important role that general private law and private enforcement are playing to compensate clients and ensure the deterrent effect of conduct regulation in retail financial markets.

While it has been generally argued that, due to the public law nature of conduct of business rules private enforcement played a marginal role in EU financial markets especially when compared to the US,[1] the case law of national courts and ADR bodies and the theory of hybrid private law shows that MiFID I and II, despite the absence of an express private law remedy, do, in fact, enhance the private law enforcement of conduct of business rules. Detailed conduct of business rules have indeed created new possibilities for the private enforcement of securities regulation thus favouring a system of regulation through litigation.[2] Furthermore, in certain jurisdictions, court and out-of-court private enforcement has delivered better outcomes, in terms of compensation and deterrence, than public enforcement.[3] In this vein, ESMA's stakeholder group has indeed acknowledged that 'in many Member States private enforcement is even more important than fines and other measures by NCAs'.[4]

[1] See, recently, A Marcacci, *Regulating Investor Protection under EU Law: The Unbridgeable Gaps with the US and the Way Forward* (Houndmills, Palgrave Macmillan, 2018) 4.

[2] See RD Kelemen, *Eurolegalism The Transformation of Law and Regulation in the European Union* (Cambridge MA, Harvard University Press, 2011) 115.

[3] See A Perrone and S Valente, 'Against All Odds: Investor Protection in Italy and the Role of Courts' (2012) 13 *European Business* 42 (the authors show that the overall amount of damages awarded in individual private enforcement actions outweighted the overall amount of fines imposed by CONSOB for breaches of conduct of business rules between 2005 and 2009).

[4] ESMA 'Securities and Markets Stakeholder Group, Investor Protection Aspects of the Consultation Paper on MiFID II and MiFIR', 4.

This 'judge-made' form of private enforcement of conduct regulation can thus effectively ensure the effectiveness of EU securities regulation, assisting investors in overcoming obstacles (on causation, measure of damages, burden of proof) that may make it excessively difficult to obtain compensation for breaches of MiFID II conduct of business rules.[5] However, hybrid private law may not be enough to help investors to overcome procedural-related obstacles. As is well known, the initiative of private litigants may be limited by rational apathy linked to litigation costs and free riding.[6] These problems are all-the-more-acute in retail financial markets. Although the harm caused by misconduct, on aggregate, may be significant, the low value of the harm suffered by individual investors may not justify the cost of seeking legal redress.[7] The risk of under-enforcement may be increased by the fact that retail clients are not best positioned to detect wrongdoing and might lack sufficient knowledge of their rights when deciding whether to bring a civil action.

Out-of-court dispute resolution mechanisms, by reducing litigation costs, minimise rational apathy but may not ensure that full compensation is granted and/or EU fundamental rights are fully respected. Collective redress mechanisms, by aggregating small-value claims, mitigate free riding but they are still underused in the examined jurisdictions.[8] In addition, private enforcement mechanisms alone do not ensure that the expertise and experience of supervisory authorities, which are often better placed than retail clients to identify wrongdoing, contribute to the effective enforcement of conduct of business rules.

Against this backdrop, this chapter seeks to understand how regulation should be designed to ensure that private enforcement effectively achieves its goals in retail financial markets. It is argued that enhanced co-ordination between private and public enforcement actors and mixed forms of private-public enforcement would incentivise retail clients to bring a claim for misconduct, increasing the likelihood that meritorious claims are pursued, therefore ensuring both the compensation and the deterrence objectives of private enforcement.

[5] In the EU, see especially OO Cherednychenko, 'Public and Private Enforcement of European Private Law in the Financial Services Sector' (2015) 4 *European Review of Private Law* 633. In the US, see especially NS Poser, 'Why the SEC Failed' (2009) 3 *Brooklyn Journal of Corporate Financial and Commercial Law*, 289–324 at 321.

[6] See H Jackson and M Roe, 'Public and Private Enforcement of Securities Laws: Resource-based Evidence' (2009) 93 *Journal of Financial Economics* 207.

[7] See S Issacharoffand and I Samuel, 'The Institutional Dimension of Consumer Protection' in F Cafaggi and H-W Micklitz (eds), *New Frontiers of Consumer Protection. Interplay between Private and Public Enforcement* (Cambridge, Intersentia, 2009) 14.

[8] See, for an overview, Commission, REPORT on the implementation of the Commission Recommendation of 11 June 2013 on common principles for injunctive and compensatory collective redress mechanisms in the Member States concerning violations of rights granted under Union law (2013/396/EU) (COM (2018) 40). On 11 April 2018, the Commission put foward a proposal for a Directive of the European Parliament and of the Council on representative actions for the protection of the collective interests and repealing Directive 2009/22/EC (COM(2018) 184).

The chapter is organised as it follows. It first illustrates the goals and the risks of private enforcement in retail financial makrets. It then discusses how to better design the incentives for retail clients to pursue meritorious claims, taking into account the obstacles that generally affect access to justice. Finally, it provides an overview of the mechanisms that have already been put in place by EU and national law to co-ordinate public and public enforcement and concludes that these should be taken into account also in retail financial regulation.

II. The Goals of Private Enforcement

Private enforcement of conduct of business rules, via courts or ADR bodies, is key to ensure a more efficient financial market, to provide compensation for clients' loss, to secure the deterrent effect of conduct of business rules and investors' confidence in financial markets.

A. Efficiency

Private enforcement and civil liability play a central role in ensuring the efficiency of securities markets. Imposing civil law liability on issuers and those responsible for drawing up the prospectus ensures the effectiveness and deterrent effect of disclosure rules and this ensures an accurate price formation, thus enabling investors to take informed decisions.[9] Civil liability ensures allocative efficiency in secondary markets because misconduct in financial transactions increases the cost of funding for financial institutions, leading to potentially negative consequences for the economy and society as a whole.[10] National courts play a central role in ensuring the efficiency of financial markets not only because they can craft liability standards that are 'less open to subversion by industry influence than regulatory prescriptions'[11] but also because publicly available judgments enhance disclosure and accuracy of price formation, indicating to investors the risks involved in certain financial transactions.[12]

[9] See JC Coffee Jr 'Reforming the Securities Class Action: An Essay On Deterrence and Its Implementation' (2006) 106 *Columbia Law Review* 1534; JM Glover, 'The Structural Role of Private Enforcement Mechanisms in Public Law' (2012) 53 *William and Mary Law Review* 1162; LE Mitchell 'The "Innocent Shareholder": An Essay on Compensation and Deterrence in Securities Class Actions' (2009) 243 *Wisconsin Law Review* 287.

[10] See Coffee Jr, 'Reforming the Securities Class Action' 1576.

[11] See J Armour and JN Gordon, 'Systemic Harms and Shareholder Value' (2014) 6 *Journal of Legal Analysis*, 62.

[12] JP Braithwaite, 'OTC derivatives: The Courts and Regulatory Reform' (2012) 7(4) *Capital Markets Law Journal* 364–385 at 378.

B. Compensation

In retail markets there are several 'institutions' that ensure compensation for losses suffered as a result of misconduct: national courts, ADR bodies, NCAs, via consumer redress scheme and specific private enforcement powers, and regulators, by setting up compensation funds. The fragmentation of compensation across different extra-judicial enforcement mechanisms could be regarded as one of the elements of the 'transformation of enforcement' that Micklitz has observed in EU law.[13] In retail markets, de-judicialisation of disputes may further increase in next years due to new mis-selling risks to which retail clients are exposed, such as product complexity, regulatory developments and digitalisation.

The European Securities and Markets Authority (ESMA) has held on several occasions that the structured retail products, which have become a significant vehicle for household savings, expose retail clients to the risk of unforeseen losses due to their high complexity. Although the volumes of outstanding structure retail products in the EU has recently declined, the share of products without capital protection (and therefore, riskier) has reached more than 99 per cent of the total products issued.[14] The main reason is the low interest rate environment and the consequent search for higher yield which push clients towards riskier products.

In addition, the pressure on financial firms to comply with requirements introduced after the global financial crisis (ie MREL) may push them to broaden their target market for these products to unsophisticated retail clients or to undertake aggressive distribution practices (eg self-placement). The growth in the number of client complaints about hybrid and debt securities reflects the increased risk deriving from this type of instrument.[15]

Finally, new risks derive from the rise of digitalisation and automation of investment services. In particular, the practice of robo-advice exposes clients to the risk that, due to the lack of face-to face interaction, their profile is not correctly identified and their objectives and needs are not correctly assessed.[16]

The main challenge for extra-judicial enforcement mechanisms will be to ensure full compensation of losses, as required by EU law, while ensuring a minimum level of legal certainty to secure the participation clients and firms in this type of dispute resolution. Increasing the award limits of ADR bodies and broadening access for SMEs could be options to mitigate the risks of undercompensation and restore investors' confidence in financial markets.[17]

[13] See H-W Micklitz, 'The Transformation of Enforcement in European Private Law: Preliminary Considerations' (2015) 4 *European Review of Private Law* 497.

[14] ESMA, 'Report on Trends, Risks and Vulnerabilities' n 2/2018, p 56.

[15] Ibid, pp 25–27. The number of complaints has risen in the first quarter of 2018 (reaching 1,500) in comparison to the previous quarter. Execution of orders (32%) and investment advice remain the two primary causes of complaints.

[16] ESAs, 'Joint Committee Report on the Results of the Monitoring Exercise on "Automation" in Financial Advice' 5 September 2018 (JC 2018-29).

[17] See FOS in the UK and ACF in Italy.

C. Deterrence

While 'compensation is a backward looking exercise, seeking to remedy a loss investors have suffered in the past, deterrence is a forward-looking exercise, seeking to provide incentives for future compliance'.[18] Deterrence has traditionally been associated with public administrative and criminal enforcement.[19] However, private enforcement actions and private law remedies, as the CJEU held in several occasions,[20] also strengthen the deterrent effect of regulation. In retail financial markets, deterrence is crucial to enhance the credibility of conduct regulation and to avoid the risk that widespread small-scale gains due to misconduct translate into a very substantial gain at relatively low cost to each consumer (so called 'democratised theft').[21]

Hybrid private law remedies contribute to increase the deterrent effect of conduct of business rules by allowing retail clients to enforce regulatory duties and by ensuring that the measure of damages takes into account the seriousness of the infringement, the injurer's state of mind, the magnitude of the potential harm, and the probability of detection.[22] However, a major hurdle to ensure the deterrent effect of conduct of business rules is the cost of legal proceedings which, compared with the often low value of the claim, prevents retail clients from enforcing their rights.[23] Another problem is that judicial proceedings are often very slow so do not afford an effective response to the needs of justice.[24] In some jurisditions, it can take up to ten years to obtain a final judicial decision.[25] This problem could be remedied not only by setting up special-purpose ADR procedures but also by creating special judicial proceedings to channel financial disputes.

D. Investors' Confidence in Financial Markets

As the CJEU held in *Alpine Investments BV*, 'the smooth operation of financial markets is largely contingent on the confidence they inspire in investors [... and]

[18] P Davies, 'Damages Actions by Investors on the Back of Market Disclosure Requirements' in D Busch, E Avgouleas and G Ferrarini, *Capital Markets Union in Europe* (Oxford, Oxford University Press, 2018) 333.

[19] See AM Rose, 'Public Enforcement: Criminal versus Civil' in JN Gordon and WG Ringe, *The Oxford Handbook of Corporate Law and Governance* (Oxford, Oxford University Press, 2018) 946.

[20] Case C-453/99, *Courage Ltd*, ECLI:EU:C:2001:465, para 27; Case C-295/04, *Manfredi*, ECLI:EU:C:2006:461, para 27; Case C-174/12, *Hirmann v Immofinanz AG*, ECLI:EU:C:2013:856; Case C-618/10, *Banco Español de Crédito SA*, ECLI:EU:C:2012:349, para 69.

[21] Issacharoff and Samuel, 'The Institutional Dimension of Consumer Protection' 14.

[22] Cafaggi and Iamiceli (2017) 25(3) 'The Principles of Effectiveness, Proportionality and Dissuasiveness in the Enforcement of EU Consumer Law' 575–618 at 607.

[23] S Shavell, 'The Fundamental Divergence between Private and Social Incentive to Use the Legal System' (1997) 16 *The Journal of Legal Studies* 575 and, recently, F Weber and M Faure (2015) 'The Interplay between Public and Private Enforcement in European Private Law: Law and Economics Perspective' 4 *European Review of Private Law* 533.

[24] IOSCO, 'Credible Deterrence in the Enforcement of Securities'. regulation, 10.

[25] For example, in Italy it could take from 10–15 years for the investor to receive a definitive judgment.

that confidence depends in particular on the existence of professional regulations serving to ensure the competence and trustworthiness of the financial intermediaries on whom investors are particularly reliant'.[26] The role of private enforcement, in this respect, should not be underestimated.[27] By providing compensation for investment losses, private enforcement reassures individual investors that wrongs can be rectified. Private enforcement also enhances the confidence of financial firms and the market as a whole. It is generally acknowledged that misconduct has profound and far-reaching consequences for all levels of society.[28] Unsophisticated retail clients may not differentiate between banks which behave well and those which behave badly and even one mis-selling case can create the perception that all banks behave badly. Systemic effects may be amplified by so-called 'peer-effects', namely firms' tendency to engage in financial misconduct increases with the misconduct rates of neighbouring firms. In addition, mis-selling practices may increase the cost of equity for financial institutions. The perceived higher risks related to a specific firm or financial sector leads investors to demand higher returns.[29] The increased cost of funding may, in turn, create distortions for the economy as a whole (ie decline of GDP or a rise in unemployment), thus affecting not only investors but also citizens throughout society. These factors can be mitigated by promoting the initiative of private individuals and firms to enforce regulatory duties.

III. The Risks of Private Enforcement

Private enforcement of regulatory duties can also create negative third-party effects or social costs,[30] which include sub-optimal levels of deterrence, vexatious litigation and systemic risks.

A. Sub-optimal Deterrence

It has been argued that private enforcement may lead to sub-optimal deterrence because, in secondary markets, 'the plaintiffs and defendants tend to overlap heavily' therefore compensation results in a wealth transfer between different

[26] Case C-384/93, *Alpine Investments BV v Minister van Financiën*, 995 ECR 1-1141, para 42.

[27] See, instead, for a critical view of private enforcement: MR Götz, TH Tröger 'Should the Marketing of Subordinated Debt be Restricted/Different in One Way or the Other? What to Do in the Case of Mis-selling?, March 2016, 16.

[28] See ESRB, 'Report on Misconduct Risk in the Banking Sector', 4 and IOSCO, 'Credible Deterrence in the Enforcement of Securities Regulation' 6.

[29] See Coffee Jr, 'Reforming the Securities Class Action: An Essay on Deterrence and Its Implementation' 1576.

[30] Shavell, 'The Fundamental Divergence between the Private and the Social Motive to Use the Legal System' 599.

shareholders and 'in each transfer a significant percentage of the transfer payment goes to lawyers and other agents'.[31] Moreover, plaintiffs prefer to sue the individual's employer (eg the intermediary firm) who has much deeper pockets than the responsible officers or managers. Therefore, private litigation may not deter misconduct because compensation costs shift from the individuals responsible for corporate decisions to the firm and its shareholders.[32]

However, this problem can be remedied by special regulatory regimes, such as the Senior Managers's regime in the UK,[33] which may ensure that the individuals who take decisions are fully responsible for their actions.

Sub-optimal deterrent effects may also be caused by over-deterrence. This could be caused by the design of substantive law (ie punitive damages) or procedural rules (ie collective redress mechanisms), or by 'remedial overkill' (ie duplication of liability due to the combination of several private enforcement mechanisms).[34] To avoid these risks in the field of competition law, the Antitrust Damages Directive allows national courts seised of an action for damages to suspend their proceedings for up to two years where the parties are involved in consensual dispute resolution about a claim covered by that action for damages and to consider compensation paid as a result of a consensual settlement and prior to its decision to be a mitigating factor.[35]

B. Vexatious Litigation

Vexatious litigation is where plaintiffs commence or threaten to commence a civil proceeding with the sole intention of extracting economic value from unmeritorious litigation. The abuse of civil litigation can cause serious damage to the efficient functioning of financial markets. For example, in the US, experience has shown that threatening high-value damages to push defendant firms to a settlement was used as a strategic device to 'compensate' future trading lossess.[36] The perceived risks of vexatious litigation have driven the reform of section 62 of

[31] Coffee Jr., 'Reforming the Securities Class Action' 1578.

[32] JC Coffee Jr, 'Law and the Market: The Impact of Enforcement' (2007) 156 *University of Pennsylvania Law Review* 305.

[33] See s 66A(5) of FSMA 2000 which introduced, with effect from 10 May 2016, a special statutory 'duty of responsibility' for Senior Managers of credit institutions. PRA and FCA to prove a contravention of a regulatory requirement by the firm, and that the Senior Manager was responsible for the management of any activities in their firm in relation to which the contravention occurred. The burden of proof lies with the regulators to show that the Senior Manager did not take such steps as a person in their position could reasonably be expected to have taken to avoid this happening. For a comment, Bank of England, 'Strengthening the Link between Seniority and Accountability: The Senior Managers and Certification Regime', *Quarterly Bulletin* 2018 Q3.

[34] See Glover, 'The Structural Role of Private Enforcement Mechanisms in Public Law' 1189.

[35] Article 18(2)(3) of the Antitrust Damages Directive.

[36] E Avgouleas, *The Mechanics and Regulation of Market Abuse: A Legal and Economic Analysis* (Oxford, Oxford University Press, 2005) 474. This type of abuse led the US Congress to introduce several restrictions on the securities class action.

FSA 1986, which, as I have shown above, has narrowed down the scope of the statutory right of action.

However, in retail markets, the risks of vexatious litigation are rather low given that retail clients have generally little incentive to bring lawsuits. In addition, neither EU nor national law offers investors the 'toxic cocktail' (class actions and punitive damages) that could facilitate abuses of civil ligation.[37] Moreover, national courts have developed several tools (ie causation theories, limits to compensation, contributory negligence) to dismiss non-meritorious lawsuits (eg claims brought because the price of the security dropped after purchase) and to ensure that plaintiffs bear the losses caused by their own conduct. Therefore, in our view, general private law provides sufficient safeguards to avoid the risk of creating a 'compensation culture'[38] where investors believe that for every ill there must be a remedy.

C. Systemic Risks

Ensuring the stability of the financial firms and/or the financial system and protecting clients against misconduct are mutually reinforcing objectives: a stable financial market should 'increase the social utility of financial services and instruments for investors'[39] and effective enforcement of conduct of business rules should increase investors' confidence in these markets, incentivising citizens to access to financial markets.

However, these two objectives may also come into conflict. For example, the distribution of complex debt securities may help credit institutions to meet their own requirements but may pose a risk of unforeseen losses for unsophisticated retail clients.[40] Compensation and other civil law remedies might affect the solvency of the defendant firm, creating a need for a recapitalisation that may be difficult where the confidence of investors has been hit by large mis-selling. It has also been argued that litigation against credit institutions subject to resolution measures is problematic because it may further aggraviate their financial distress.[41] Tensions may also arise between ensuring full compensation of mis-sold clients and the objectives of resolution and courts may 'intervene' too late to avoid consumer detriment. In addition, courts have limited capacity to assess the third-party or systemic effects of private litigation given that a typical mis-selling dispute

[37] F. Wilman, *Private Enforcement of EU Law Before National Court:* The EU Legislative Framework (Cheltenham, Edward Elgar, 2015) 489.

[38] R McCormick and C Stears, *Legal and Conduct Risk in the Financial Markets* (Oxford, Oxford University Press, 2018) 450.

[39] Andenas and Chiu, *The Foundations and Future of Financial* Regulation 266.

[40] See Chapter 3.

[41] MR Götz, THTröger 'Should the Marketing of Subordinated Debt be Restricted/Different in One Way or the Other? What to Do in the Case of Mis-selling?, White Paper Series, March 2016, p 14.

does not generally involve consideration of systemic effects on financial markets and civil procedural law generally leaves little room for courts to investigate on their own motion facts that fall outside those brought by the parties.[42]

To limit negative third-party effects of litigation in the context of resolution, it is therefore crucial that conduct of business rules are fully respected where bail-inable is distributed to retail clients and that resolution authorities take into account, as much as possible, retail client protection's concerns in resolution and resolution planning.[43] Minimum denomination limits for issuing bail-inable debt would also reduce the exposure of retail clients to this type of instrument.[44]

More generally, ongoing supervision and regulation could mitigate the negative third-party effects of private litigation. In the annual supervisory review and evaluation process (SREP) supervisory authorities assess, as part of the operational risk's assessment, the credit institution's exposure to conduct risk deriving, inter alia, from mis-selling practices and breaches of conduct of business rules.[45] This may lead to the imposition of additional own funds requirements to mitigate exposure to conduct risks.

Third-party spillovers may also be reduced by specific prudential requirements. In this vein, the AIFM Directive expressly requires alternative investment funds to have additional funds to cover potential liability risks arising from professional negligence orto have professional indemnity insurance against liability arising from professional negligence which is appropriate to the risks covered.[46]

It should be clear, however, that supervisory and regulatory efforts may produce desired outcomes only if supported by an adequate level of financial education. Initiatives to strengthen retail investors knowledge and awareness on financial instruments, markets and risks should be a key complement to investor protection regulatory and supervisory strategies.

[42] On the inadequacy of courts in financial markets, but essentially for their lack of expertise and incentives, see E Glaeser, S Johnson, A Shleifer, 'Coase versus the Coasians' (2001) 116 *Quarterly Journal of Economics* 854. See also RJ Gilson, CF Sabel and RE Scott, 'Contract and Innovation: The Limited Role of Generalist Courts in the Evolution of Novel Contractual Forms' (2013) 188 *New York University Law Review* 171.

[43] EBA and ESMA, 'Statement on the Treatment of Retail Holdings of Debt Financial Instruments', paras 17–18. As of Q3 2017, retail investors in the euro area held €262.4 billion (12.7%) of the EU bank debt securities issued to euro area investors. Senior unsecured debt constituted 81% of retail held debt securities, whereas 19% was represented bysubordinated debt. Italy has the largest amount (€132.3 billion), followed by Germany (€49.4 billion) and then France (€ 31.7 billion).

[44] In Spain, the 13th additional provision of Law 9/2012 limited issuances of participationes preferentes and hybrid financial instruments to €100,000. See, in this sense, EBA and ESMA, 'Statement on the Treatment of Retail Holdings of Debt Financial Instruments', para 18, ECB Opinion of 8 November 2017 on revisions to the Union crisis management framework (CON/2017/47), para 2.11 and D Nouy, Reply to Mr Sven Giegold,Member of the European Parliament, 19 April 2018. Available at: www.bankingsupervision.europa.eu/ecb/pub/pdf/ssm.mepletter180419_Giegold.en.pdf?49516fbe3c129718 2687d57abfe04aab30/05/2018.

[45] EBA, Guidelines on Common Procedures and Methodologies for the Supervisory Review and Evaluation Process (SREP) 19 December 2014 (EBA/GL/2014/13), paras 253–256.

[46] Article 9(7) of AIFMD.

Once a mis-selling dispute arises in the context of resolution or where the defendant firm has financial difficulties, it remains to be seen whether financial stability-related concerns could be invoked by the firms to avoid civil liability or reduce the amount of compensation. Judgments like *Francisco Gutiérrez Navarro* show that, when a financial firm breached its conduct of business rules, national courts have a primary duty to ensure the effectiveness of EU law and the fundamental right to an effective judicial protection. Only exceptional circumstances determined by the specific facts of the case (generally linked to the systemic nature of the risks involved) might lead to restrict the availability of civil law remedies.[47]

IV. The Incentives' Design in Retail Clients' Litigation

A traditional system of private enforcement, based on courts and general private law, may not be enough to achieve private enforcement goals.

The rise of mis-selling due to product complexity, product innovation and regulatory developments requires the increasing involvement of extra-judicial enforcement mechanisms. However, these mechanisms may not always ensure that meritorious claims are upheld and provide full compensation for losses and that retail clients have sufficient incentives to enforce (and thus identify) meritorious claims.[48] In addition, due to the complex functioning of financial instruments and the fact that investors may become aware of misconduct only after the contract has concluded, they may not have accurate facts at their disposal to bring a (meritorious) claim. The defendant firms generally have better information than the plaintiff about the financial instruments they issue and/or distribute, they generally have better resources to deal with legal risks.

Taken together, these factors may impinge the effectiveness of private enforcement and ultimately affect the credibility of the conduct of business rules.

An optimal private enforcement regime should ensure that civil proceedings are initiated by the party (private or public) with better access to the factual information relevant to the alleged wrongdoing and with the best incentive to bring a civil proceeding.[49] Access to information and incentives to bring a claim may vary depending on whether the plaintiff is a sophisticated or unsophisticated investor.

In wholesale markets, where clients are generally sophisticated investors who have the economic resources to manage legal and litigation risks and can negotiate individual contract terms it may be supposed that they have better knowledge than

[47] See case C-526/14, *Kotnik and Others*, EU:C:2016:570, paras 50 and 91.

[48] G Wagner, Private Law Enforcement through ADR: Wonder Drug or Snake Oil?' (2014) 51 *Common Market Law Review* 165–194 at 182.

[49] See Glover, 'The Structural Role of Private Enforcement Mechanisms in Public Law' 1180.

a public authority as to when a breach of contract or regulatory duties occurred. By contrast, in retail markets, investors generally lack the knowledge and experience to know when and what contract or regulatory duties have been breached. It may be very difficult to prove a breach of suitability requirements where firms distribute products with intense *ad hoc* personalised recommendations but without concluding an advisory contract. It is also particularly challenging to prove that, in the absence of the misconduct, the client would have bought another financial instrument or the same instrument but under different conditions given that retail clients have generally no bargaining power and have little knowledge of alternative and appropriate investments. In these circumstances, the expert knowledge of the supervisory authority would help retail clients to identify misconduct. On-site and off-site supervisory activities (ie thematic reviews or benchmarking exercises) could reveal 'red flags' such as a high concentration of client investment in the firm's products, massive re-profiling of clients before product distribution and loans granted to finance the purchase of securities.[50]

As regards to the party with better incentives to start a civil proceeding, it seems that whilst in wholesale markets investors are best placed to detect violations and best incentivised to bring a lawsuit, in retail markets information advantages and incentives to act tend to diverge. In this context, supervisory authorities are, in principle, better placed than retail clients to understand when a regulatory duty has been breached and to gather evidence to prove the violation, but they may not be sufficiently motivated to start administrative or private law proceedings (when they are competent) to enforce the breach regulatory duties. In that situation, it has been argued that, where fact-finding requires specific technical knowledge or where misconduct gives rise to 'multitude of small-scale gains that in aggregate could represent a substantial harm',[51] some involvement of supervisory authorities in private enforcement actions should be considered, to encourage retail investors to enforce breaches of conduct of business rules.[52] However, from a legal perspective, the involvement of supervisory authorities should take into account the need to respect their professional secrecy obligations which impose limitations on divulging confidential information about supervised entities.

V. Connecting Public and Private Enforcement: Towards Hybrid Enforcement Mechanisms?

Given that in retail markets there is a divergence between the party with better information to start a civil proceeding (the supervisory authority) and the party

[50] See F Weber and M Faure, 'The Interplay Between Public and Private Enforcement in European Private Law: Law and Economics Perspective' (2015) 5 *European Review of Private Law* 534.

[51] S. Issacharoff and I. Samuel, The Institutional Dimension of Consumer Protection 14.

[52] See Weber and Faure, The Interplay Between Public and Private Enforcement in European Private Law 544.

with stronger motivation to do so (the retail client), there should be better coordination between supervisory authorities and plaintiffs.

Even if the CJEU has recognised that private parties play a fundamental role in supplementing the enforcement actions of competent authorities in several fields of law (competition, consumer and securities regulation), in EU law public and private enforcement are 'largely unconnected in legal-procedural terms'.[53] Forms of connection between private and public enforcement have been introduced mostly in competition law and range from mechanisms to channel securities disputes through specialised judicial proceedings, to exchange of information duties between ADR bodies and supervisory authorities, to conformation duties of national courts to prior decision of competent authority to forms of hybrid enforcement where public authorities are granted private enforcement powers.

A. Specialised Judicial Procedures

The first mechanism to increase the efficiency of private enforcement is to create specialised courts or tribunals to handle financial disputes. Professor J B Golden proposed the creation of a world court with specialised judges, based on the WTO, to adjudicate complex financial disputes.[54] This specialised court would ensure that judges have the technical knowledge to examine complex facts and would mitigate the risks that (incorrect) judicial decisions create in a global and highly interconnected marketplace.

This proposal led to the creation, in 2012, of the Panel of Recognized International Market Experts in Finance (PRIME Finance), a permanent body for the arbitration and mediation of international financial disputes composed of 130 international specialists.[55] Arbitration is based on the rules of law designated by the parties or the arbitral tribunal shall apply the law which it determines to be appropriate, taking into account the international and/or financial nature of the transaction and/or dispute. Awards are confidential, unless the parties agree otherwise.[56]

[53] See Wilman, *Private Enforcement of EU Law Before National Courts* 417. See also case 28/67, *Firma Molkerei-Zentrale Westfalen/Lippe GmbH v Hauptzollamt Paderborn*, ECLI:EU:C:1968:17, p 153 where the CJEU held that: 'Such actions are different from the exercise of the powers conferred on the Community authorities under the Treaty, in particular by Articles 95 and 97, together with Articles 155 and 169. In fact proceedings by an individual are intended to protect individual rights in a specific case, whilst intervention by the Community authorities has as its object the general and uniform observance of Community law.'

[54] See JB Golden, 'The Courts, the Financial Crisis and Systemic Risk' (2009) 4(1) *Capital Markets Law Journal* S141.

[55] See JJ Dalhuisen, *Dalhuisen on Transnational Comparative, Commercial, Financial and Trade Law* (Oxford, Hart Publishing, 2010) 426.

[56] PRIME Finance Arbitration and Mediation Rules.

Although evidence shows that in the wake of the global financial crisis general courts have developed strong expertise on these matters,[57] arbitrators, in comparison to ordinary judges, will generally be more aware of international practice and have more flexibility to reach an up-to-date and higher-quality decision.[58]

Some authors proposed the creation of specialised tribunals for financial disputes in the UK, to develop specialist jurisprudence in areas where 'traditional private law actions of contract and negligence are increasingly being dovetailed with regulatory duties anyway'.[59] The UK judiciary introduced the 'Financial List' to ensure the 'public interest in the just resolution of commercial disputes', promote access to the courts and the expertise of trial judges and ensure the efficiency of financial markets and strengthening international confidence and trust in the UK judiciary. The List, which became operational on 1 October 2015 and is maintained by the Chancery Division and the Commercial Court, ensures that high-value disputes (those over £50 million) or disputes that raise issues of general importance to the financial markets are heard by a Judge with specialist knowledge and experience in financial markets and through special procedural rules.[60]

In addition to the Financial List, in the UK a 'Financial Markets Test Case Scheme' has been piloted from 1 October 2015 to 30 September 2020 to allow the Court to grant declaratory relief for financial list claims which raise issues of general importance in relation to which immediately relevant authoritative English law guidance is needed.

Another fast-track procedure has been introduced in Spain where the government established that claims related to the avoidance of floor clauses in mortgage contracts are to be dealt with by a designated number of first instance civil courts.

In conclusion, even if specialised judicial procedures do not reduce, per se, problems related to litigation costs for retail clients they should be positively welcomed to increase the efficiency of dispute resolution and strengthen the expertise of generalist courts in financial law matters.

B. Information Exchange between Competent Authorities

The exchange of information between competent authorities is essential to strengthen the effectiveness of private and public enforcement actions. The ADR

[57] See eg, the Chancery Division and the Commercial Court of the High Court of Justice in the UK and the Tribunale ordinario di Milano in Italy.

[58] See Dalhuisen, *Dalhuisen on Transnational Comparative, Commercial, Financial and Trade Law* 425–426. The author proposed the creation of an international commercial court to supervise international aribtration with responsibilities, inter alia, for the appointment, independence, expertise of arbitrators and matters of enforcement of arbitration awards.

[59] See Andenas and Chiu, *The Foundations and Future of Financial Regulation* 188 who argue in favour of developing the Upper Tribunal for Tax and the Chancery which already hears appeals from decisions of the FCA. See also R Samuel, *Tools for Culture Change: FCA, now you are listening!* (2017) 12 (3) 277–279 at 297 who argues for the creation of a new chamber for financial services disputes which would operate under the Courts, Tribunals and Enforcement Act 2007 (CTEA 2007), using the same model as Employment Tribunals.

[60] Civil Procedure (Amendment No 4) Rules 2015 (SI 2015/1569), entered into force 1 October 2015.

Directive requires ADR bodies and supervisory authorities to exchange information on practices in the specific business sectors where consumers have repeatedly lodged complaints. In particular, supervisory authorities, in so far as they are competent authorities for the ADR Directive, shall provide 'technical assessment and information' where this assessment or information is necessary to handle individual disputes and is already available.[61] However, this duty should respect the obligation of professional secrecy. In accordance with Article 76(1) of MiFID II, supervisory authorities may divulge confidential information about supervised entities only in summary or aggregate form, such that individual investment firms, cannot be identified. Only where an investment firm has been declared bankrupt or is being compulsorily wound up, can confidential information which does not concern third parties be divulged in civil or commercial proceedings if necessary (MiFID II, Art 76(2)).[62]

Outside bankruptcy or liquidation of the defendant firm, the plaintiff does not have the right to obtain confidential information from the supervisory authority to be used against that firm in a civil proceeding.[63]

ADR bodies will provide NCAs with detailed information about the number, type or any systematic or significant problem that frequently occurs and can lead to a dispute, subject to professional secrecy obligations laid down by national law.[64] The ADR body shall also submit its recommendations as to how such problems can be avoided or resolved in future.[65] Although ADR does not require its bodies to exchange this information on continuous basis – only every two years – this should be positively welcomed as it will allow supervisory authorities to monitor emerging risks and trends in retail financial markets and become aware of potential infringements. Going forward, national courts should also be required to periodically inform the competent authorities about levels and types of litigation and should be given the power to request relevant documentation from the supervisory authority. In France, Article 141 of Law No 244/2014 granted national courts the power to request the AMF to transmit any documentation (*procès-verbaux et les rapports d'enquête ou de contrôle*) which may be useful to solve the dispute.[66]

C. Conforming Judgments to Supervisory Acts

EU law requires national courts to take into account soft law instruments in their adjudication. However, there is no express duty for national courts to interpret

[61] Article 17(2) of ADR Directive.

[62] See in this regard Case C-594/16, *Enzo Buccioni v Banca d'Italia*, ECLI:EU:C:2018:717, para 40.

[63] See, with regard to the notion of confidential information under MiFID I, case C-15/16, *Bundesanstalt für Finanzdienstleistungsaufsicht v Ewald Baumeister*, ECLI:EU:C:2018:464, para 46.

[64] Article 17(4) of ADR Directive.

[65] Ibid, Article 19(3).

[66] Article L621-12(1) of CMF.

national or EU law in light of soft law, nor to conform their judgments to binding legal decisions adopted by EU and national supervisory authorities.

EU law has introduced 'conformation' mechanisms into competition law. Regulation No 1/2003 allows national courts to ask the Commission to transmit information concerning the application of EU competition rules and prohibits national courts from ruling on agreements, decisions or practices under Articles 81 or 82 of the Treaty. They cannot take decisions running counter to those adopted by the Commission and must also avoid giving decisions which would conflict with a decision contemplated by the Commission in proceedings it has initiated.[67] In the same vein, the Antitrust Damages Directive requires Member States to ensure that an infringement of competition law found by a final decision of a national competition authority or by a review court is deemed to be irrefutably established for the purposes of an action for damages brought before their national courts under Articles 101 or 102 of TFEU or under national competition law.[68]

Article 85(3) of the Bank Recovery Resolution Directive (BRRD) requires national courts, in proceedings for the appeal of a crisis management measure, to use the complex economic assessments of the facts carried out by the resolution authority as a basis for their own assessment. Conformation, in this case, does not concern the outcome of the administrative measure but its factual assessment. This type of 'conforming mechanism' would ensure that the judicial decision is in line with the assessments of facts provided by the party with better expertise and information (ie supervisory or resolution authority), without prejudice of the national courts' right to provide a different interpretation of the law applicable to these facts.[69] Supervisory authorities, therefore, would not 'impose' their interpretation of legal requirements onto national courts but would assist them with their technical expertise.

This conformation mechanism would indirectly incentivise retail clients to bring legal action against firms,[70] easing their burden of proof for retail clients in relation to conducts or practices that have already been subject to a supervisory measure (ie product intervention).[71] Conformation mechanisms should also

[67] Article 15 of the Council Regulation (EC) No 1/2003 of 16 December 2002 on the implementation of the rules on competition laid down in Articles 81 and 82 of the Treaty [2003] OJ L 1/1.

[68] Article 9(1) of Antitrust Damages Directive.

[69] See also M Andenas and I Chiu, *The Foundations and Future of Financial Regulation* (Abingdon, Routledge, 2013) p 331.

[70] See JD Cox and RS Thomas, 'SEC Enforcement Heuristics: An Empirical Inquiry' (2003) 53 *Duke Law Journal* 777. The authors observe that where both a SEC action and a private action proceed for the same misconduct, private recoveries are statistcally larger and settled more quickly than when there is no parallel SEC action.

[71] See ESAs Board of Appeal, *Investor Protection Europe sprl v ESMA*, 10 November 2014 (BoA 2014 05), para 23 where the appellant, contesting ESMA's lack of action against CSSF for breach of EU law, argued that lack of action by the CSSF against the firm would weaken the investors' position in the civil proceeding against the same firm. However, the BoA dismissed the appeal as inadmissible. CSSF neither intervened nor concluded that there was a breach.

aim to avoid the duplication of remedies and/or administrative sanctions. The risk of so-called 'remedial overkill' is all the greater where private litigants can enforce regulatory (not just contract law) duties via a civil proceeding. To reduce this risk, judicial decisions should take into account, in light of the proportionality principle, the amount of any administrative fine imposed by the competent authority on the defendant firm for the same breach, when calculating the measure of damages.[72]

D. Hybrid Enforcement Mechanisms

Public and private enforcement may also be mixed, either by granting quasi-public enforcement powers to private litigants, or by granting private enforcement powers to public authorities ('hybrid enforcement').[73] EU law has granted quasi-public enforcement powers to private litigants. For example, Directive 2004/48/EC on the enforcement of intellectual property rights empowers national courts to grant *ex parte* search orders to preserve relevant evidence concerning the alleged infringement.[74] The Antitrust Damages Directive, empowers national courts to order the disclosure of relevant evidence to the defendant firm.[75] Similar measures in retail financial regulation could be justified by the need to increase the information advantages of investors vis-à-vis firms, although appropriate safeguards are required to preserve the fundamental rights of the defendant firm.[76]

EU law has not granted private enforcement powers to EU and national supervisory authorities. This type of powers has been granted in the US and in the UK. In the US, the Securities and Exchange Commission can commence civil proceedings against firms to ask for example injunctions and disgorgement of profits in favour of investors. Similarly, as I have shown above, the UK FCA may start civil proceedings on behalf of investors, or can set up a consumer redress scheme. Although evidence shows that these authorities used their administrative enforcement powers more than their private enforcement powers,[77] these reflect the rationale to ensure that the party with better information has the power to enforce breaches of the rules and enhance their deterrent effect.

It has also been proposed to grant public authorities the power to pre-vet litigation for breaches of regulatory duties in the wholesale financial markets to 'filter

[72] See Cafaggi and Iamiceli, 'The Principles of Effectiveness, Proportionality and Dissuasiveness in the Enforcement of EU Consumer Law' 613.

[73] See Wilman, *Private Enforcement of EU Law Before National Courts* 492–495.

[74] Article 7 of Directive 2004/48/EC of the European Parliament and of the Council of 29 April 2004 on the enforcement of intellectual property rights (OJ L 195, 2.6.2004, p 16).

[75] Ibid, Art 5(1).

[76] See Wilman, *Private Enforcement of EU Law Before National Courts* 504.

[77] See Cox and Thomas, 'SEC Enforcement Heuristics' 749 and FCA, 'Enforcement Annual Performance Report 2017/18', 8.

out obviously vexatious or ill-motivated litigation, promoting litigation that serves as a force for discipline'.[78] According to this proposal, an investor should submit possible civil actions to the regulator to obtain approval. The regulator's approval, however, would not mean substantive approval of the merits of the case, but may simply act as a mechanism to filter out obviously vexatious or unjustified litigation, promoting litigation that serves as a force for discipline.

However, this mechanism risks transposing onto private enforcement the same risks as regulatory capture, which could affect public enforcement[79] and would put a significant budgetary, administrative, accountability and liability burden on public authorities who would inevitably become liable for restricting the private rights of action of market players.[80] Even if the prior approval were to be conceived as a non-binding opinion, questions may be raised about the extent to which public authorities should serve the interests of private litigants[81] in terms of budgetary resources, accountability and responsibility.

VI. Preliminary Conclusion

Traditional private enforcement structures based on general private law and courts are ill-suited to address the mis-selling and misconduct risks for retail clients. Although general courts have provided significant redress to retail clients in the wake of the global financial crisis, particularly in continental jurisdictions, the mis-selling risks to which retail clients are exposed and the broadening of financial products offered to a wider range of unsophisticated clients call for a more central role for extra-judicial private enforcement mechanisms. However, these are not a panacea for retail clients. As the previous chapters have shown, they might not ensure full compensation and might not respect fundamental procedural rights. Taken together, these factors may prevent private enforcement from achieving its goals and supporting the public enforcement and supervisory actions of competent authorities.

This chapter argued that to facilitate access to justice for retail clients it is necessary to strengthen the co-ordination between supervisory authorities, on the one hand, and national courts and ADR bodies, on the other because, in retail markets, information advantages and incentives to bring a civil action in court tend to diverge. Supervisory authorities are, in principle, better placed than retail clients to understand when a regulatory duty has been breached and to gather evidence

[78] Andenas and Chiu, *The Foundations and Future of Financial* Regulation, 187.

[79] See DF Engstrom, *Public Regulation of Private Enforcement: Empirical Analysis of DOJ Oversight of Qui Tam Litigation under the False Claims Act* (2013) 107 *Northwestern University School of Law Review* 1690.

[80] See Wilman, *Private Enforcement of EU Law Before National Courts*, 497.

[81] See Commission, Cooperation notice, OJ 2004, C 101/54, para 19.

to prove the violation but they may not be sufficiently motivated to commence administrative or private enforcement actions.

To exploit the public-driven fact finding and the private-driven incentive to bring civil law actions, regulatory mechanisms should be introduced at EU level to coordinate public and private enforcement. The mechanisms introduced in other fields of EU law (ie competition law) may provide useful guidance to design similar tools in retail securities markets. The examined tools (ie exchange of information, conformation duties) may also be combined, taking into account the need to respect the principle of proportionality (avoiding 'remedial overkill') and the professional secrecy obligations of EU and competent national authorities.

Enhanced co-ordination between public and private enforcement would achieve several positive outcomes. First, court and out-of-court dispute resolution provides valuable information which allows supervisory authorities to identify trends and vulnerabilities in the retail markets.[82] Second, supervisory assessments used to impose binding legal decisions on market participants could help national courts to assess the factual context of the dispute, leaving the courts free to make their own interpretation of the legal requirements. This would increase the courts' ability to understand technical aspects of financial disputes and would ease the client's burden of proof, particularly where breaches are linked to financial products' design features. Third, granting private enforcement powers to supervisory authorities could be a way to increase the deterrent effect of the conduct of business rules, and at the same time strengthen investors' confidence in financial markets.

[82] ESMA is already collecting this information based on the complaints received from investors by the NCAs.

General Conclusions

This book has examined the civil law effects of MiFID II conduct of business rules from a comparative and institutional perspective. Building on an analysis of the case law and decisions of ADR bodies in the UK, France, Italy and Spain and on the case law of the CJEU, two main arguments have been developed.

The first argument has a descriptive value in that it shows that the EU's conduct of business rules have already produced civil law effects before national courts and ADR bodies. In practice, this means that, even if MiFID I was silent on private law duties and remedies, investment firms have been subject to stricter private law duties than the applicable regulatory duties and breaches of these duties have given rise to a private law remedy.

These duties and remedies have a hybrid nature because they are based on national law, but they have been crafted taking into account the investor protection objective of MiFID. However, there are differences across these jurisdictions as regards the drivers and intensity of hybridisation. In the examined continental jurisdictions, hybrid private law is driven by national courts and ADR bodies. They have imposed stricter private law duties on investment firms, in both non-advised and advisory transactions and have granted a private law remedy (eg compensation or avoidance of contracts) to investors. In the UK, the creation of hybrid private law duties and remedies is mainly driven by out-of-court dispute resolution mechanisms. Here, national courts are more careful about importing regulatory principles in private law adjudication. In particular, whilst in advised transactions, courts have accepted the civil law effects of regulatory duties, interpreting the firm's duty of care in light of the suitability rule, in non-advised transactions, they refuse to grant civil law effects to conduct of business rules. This judicial approach has, to a large extent, limited the possibilities for investors to be successful in their compensation claims. However, the *caveat emptor* principle that allows firms to disclaim their liability for negligent advice and misrepresentation thus making it particularly burdensome for sophisticated investors to claim damages for mis-selling, has been mitigated by the adjudication of the UK FOS which decides disputes based on what is 'fair and reasonable'. The FOS makes use of regulatory principles to resolve disputes; in this sense it creates hybrid private law duties both in advised and non-advised transactions.

The second argument of the book is that MiFID II's conduct of business rules should give rise to civil law effects and enable investors to action private law remedies for breach of these rules. The general principles of EU law, as well as fundamental rights, require, under certain circumstances, national courts and ADR bodies to ensure the effectiveness of conduct of business rules and the effective protection of clients. Conceptually, this entails a form of instrumentalisation of general private law, traditionally aimed at protecting freedom of contract of market participants, to achieve regulatory goals. Instrumentalisation, however, does not mean 'substitution' or 'replacement' of national private law traditions with EU law. Rather, it means synthesis or hybridisation between general private law and EU sectoral regulation. This normative argument builds on the doctrine of horizontal effects of EU law acts and the principle of procedural autonomy.

The duty of conform interpretation requires national courts to interpret general private law duties in light of the wording and purpose of MiFID II conduct of business rules. Conform interpretation may impose stricter duties on firms than those set out in MiFID II. This is legitimate from an EU law perspective because private law duties (and remedies) are not harmonised by MiFID II, so courts should be allowed to impose stricter private law duties on firms based on general private law (ie duty of care and pre-contractual good faith) when this is appropriate in the specific circumstances of the case. Regulatory duties, therefore, should be a 'floor' but not a 'cap' for investor protection.

In addition, it has been argued that, even if MiFID II does not harmonise private law remedies for breaches of conduct of business rules, private law remedies should respect the principle of equivalence and effectiveness, as well as EU fundamental rights. EU law does not express a preference for the nature (contract or tort law) or type (compensation or avoidance of contract) of the remedy but requires national courts and ADR bodies to ensure that a remedy is granted to 'enforce' breaches of the right-conferring rules. In this regard, disclosure, distribution and product governance rules, unless they are setting out organisational requirements, grant individual enforceable rights to clients. Breach of these rules should therefore allow investors to action a private law remedy against the firm, nothwistanding the absence of an express EU or national law provision. The detailed rules governing remedies should be interpreted in light of the principle of effectiveness. This entails that private law rules should not make it excessively difficult to enforce investors' rights. The case law of the CJEU indicates that a 'significant risk' to actioning a remedy (eg due to the cost of legal proceedings) is sufficient to 'upgrade' private law remedies in light of the effectiveness principle. In practice, this should ensure that the national rules on the duty of care, the causal link and the clients' measure of damages take into account the information and bargaining power asymmetry between firms and clients. With Brexit, the force of these EU law arguments may be reduced for the UK. However, the need to ensure an effective judicial protection for some categories of retail clients, particularly SMEs, would still need to be safeguarded under Articles 6 and 13 of the ECHR.

The normative claim of this book (ie that EU conduct of business rules should produce civil law effects) has also been supported by an analysis of the horizontal effects of the ESMA's 'conduct of business handbook'. Indeed, a major contribution of this book is to take a broader institutional view of the interplay between conduct regulation and private law, considering not only the civil law effects of regulation but also quasi-regulatory or soft-law supervisory acts. National courts have a duty to take into account soft law, when interpreting national law. This helps to strengthen the hybridisation of private law, allowing investors to rely not just on regulatory, but also on quasi-regulatory, acts to claim the firm's liability for breaches of MiFID II. This will be particularly important where general conduct of business rules (fair treatment and best interest duties) are at stake. These duties need to be interpreted taking into account ESMA's detailed guidance, expressed in guidelines, Q&As and other soft-law instruments.

The main corollary of this study is that retail clients should be allowed to enforce conduct of business rules in judicial or extra-judicial proceedings, via national private law. Conceptually, this sheds new light on the debate about the role of private enforcement in EU financial regulation. The theory of hybrid private law – and the actual emergence of hybrid private law in national case-law and out-of-court dispute resolution – shows the need to reconsider the doctrinal understanding that the private enforcement of securities regulation has a marginal role in the EU. The reason is that in the EU legal order, detailed regulatory duties (eg conduct of business rules) may confer rights on individuals; in this case, the principle of *ubi jus, ibi remedium*, requires national courts to grant an adequate remedy to protect these rights. Therefore, a lack of a pan-EU private law remedy for breaches of conduct of business rules does not mean that these rules do not produce civil law consequences. It only means that they should be determined by national private law subject to the principles of equivalence and effectiveness. The analysis pointed out that the application of these principles before national courts has a far-reaching effect on general private law, giving rise to a form of hybrid private law.

The key role that the EU 'judge-made' law of remedies could play to increase investor protection against misconduct suggests that potential legislative interventions harmonising the civil law consequences of breaches of conduct of business rules would not only be, in practice, very difficult given the differences between national private laws but also would not necessarily protect investors. Hybrid private law already provides investors with adequate protection, benefitting from the capacity of general private law standards (ie duty of care and good faith) to calibrate the investment firm's obligations on the concrete facts of the case. EU legislative harmonisation in this field will not necessarily achieve greater uniformity given that the detailed remedial conditions of private law remedies (ie causation, measure of damages) would most likely remain embedded in national private law traditions and would continue to be subject to national procedural autonomy. Therefore, in our view, a careful application of the general principles of EU law to national private law could ensure a high level of investor protection in financial transactions and could increase consistency in the civil law consequences of breaches of EU conduct of business rules.

Finally, the book has discussed the impact of hybrid private law on the private enforcement of conduct of business rules. Hybrid private law overcomes substantive law obstacles determined by national evidential rules, causation and measure of damages that would prevent clients from obtaining an effective remedy. It therefore enhances the deterrent effect of conduct of business rules and strengthens investors' confidence in financial markets.

However, access to justice and judicial remedies in retail financial markets may be difficult, in practice, due to the high cost of legal proceedings and the low value of the harm suffered by individual investors which may not justify the cost of seeking legal redress. As in other sectors of the internal market, in the financial sector, private enforcement has undergone an important transformation. Courts have lost centrality, whereas ADR bodies, often set up within supervisory authorities, have achieved a prominent role, giving rise to an administrative enforcement of private law. These ADR bodies – called 'supervisory ADR bodies' – have adjudicated disputes fairly and effectively, applying regulatory and private law standards. After the global financial crisis, Member States have also developed special out-of-court dispute resolution mechanisms to compensate clients for losses suffered as a result of mis-selling practices. However, these *ad hoc* ADR schemes have raised concerns as regards their independence, transparency and fairness.

With the emergence of new risks for retail clients it would be utopian to rely only on courts to compensate clients' losses. Mis-selling should be tackled not only *ex post* via litigation but also *ex ante* through appropriate regulatory choices and supervisory action. In this regard, it has been suggested that, in the current EU institutional context, where soft-law and administrative rule-making have gained increasing importance in shaping the content of EU regulatory requirements, it would be appropriate to exploit the technical expertise of ESMA and NCAs to facilitate the private (judicial and extra-judicial) enforcement of conduct of business rules. EU law has already adopted mechanisms, especially in the field of competition law, to ensure greater coordination between public and private enforcement. A duty to exchange information between ADR bodies, courts and supervisory authorities, combined with a duty for national courts to take into account the assessments made by supervisory authorities, would enhance the capacity of courts to understand the technical aspects of financial disputes and would ease the client's burden of proof in compensation claims.

BIBLIOGRAPHY

Afferni G, *Il quantum del danno nella responsabilità precontrattuale* (Torino, Giappichelli, 2008).

Alexander K, 'Bank Civil Liability for Mis-selling and Advice' in D Busch and C Van Dam (eds), *A Bank's Duty of Care* (Oxford, Hart Publishing, 2017) 253.

Alpa G, 'Gli obblighi informativi precontrattuali nei contratti di investimento finanziario. Per l'armonizzazione dei modelli regolatori e per l'uniformazione delle regole di diritto comune' (2008) *Contratto e Impresa* 889.

Andenas M, 'Rules of Conduct and the Principle of Subsidiarity' (1994) 15 *Company Lawyer* 60.

—— 'Who is Going to Supervise Europe's Financial Markets' in M Andenas and Y Avgerinos (eds) *Financial Markets in Europe: Towards a Single Regulator?* (London, The Hague, New York, Kluwer Law International, 2003) xv–xxvi.

—— 'Harmonising and Regulating Financial Markets' in M Andenas and C Baasch Andersen (ed), *Theory and Practice of Harmonisation* (Cheltenham, Edward Elgar, 2012) 1–29.

—— 'European Monetary Law', in R Wolfrum (ed), *Max Planck Encyclopedia of Public International Law*. Oxford University Press 2012.

Andenas M and Chiu I, *The Foundations and Future of Financial Regulation: Governance for Responsibility* (London and New York, Routledge, 2013).

Andenas M and Della Negra F, 'Between Contract Law and Financial Regulation: Towards the Europeanisation of General Contract Law' (2017) 4 *European Business Law Review* 499.

Annunziata F, *Regole di comportamento degli intermediari e riforme dei mercati mobiliari - L'esperienza francese, inglese e italiana* (Milano, EGEA, 1993).

Arena A, 'Exercise of EU Competences and Pre-emption of Member States' Powers in the Internal and the External Sphere: Towards "Grand Unification"?' (2016) 35 *Yearbook of European Law* 28.

Armour J and Gordom JN, 'Systemic Harms and Shareholders Value' (2014) 6 *Journal of Legal Analysis* 6.

Attard J, 'Du champ d'application du devoir de conseil du banquier' (2011) *Revue trimestrielle de droit commercial* 11.

Avgouleas E, *The Mechanics and Regulation of Market Abuse: A Legal and Economic Analysis* (Oxford, Oxford University Press, 2005).

Benavides MF, 'Participaciones preferentes: aproximación al problema y primeras respuestas de la jurisprudencia civil' (2012) *Revista CESCO de Derecho de Consumo* 17.

Bertolini A, 'Risparmio tradito: una riflessione tra teoria generale del contratto e disciplina dei mercati' (2010) 2 *Nuova Giurisprudenza Civile Commentata* 337.

Binder J-H, 'Germany' in D Busch and C Van Dam (eds), *A Bank's Duty of Care* (Oxford, Hart Publishing, 2017) 61.

Black J, 'The Rise, Fall and Fate of Principles Based Regulation', *LSE Law, Society and Economy Working Papers* 17/2010.

Black J, *Rules and Regulators* (Oxford, Clarendon Press, 1997).

Bonneau T, 'France' in D Busch and C van Dam, *A Bank's Duty of Care* (Oxford, Hart Publishing, 2017) 115.

Braithwaite JP, 'Standard Form Contracts as Transnational Law: Evidence from the Derivatives Markets' (2012) 75 *The Modern Law Review* 779.

——'OTC Derivatives, the Courts and Regulatory Reform' (2012) 7 *Capital Markets Law Journal* 364.

Bridge M and Braithwaite JP, 'Private Law and Financial Crises' (2013) 13 *Journal of Corporate Law Studies* 361.

Busch D, 'A Bank's Duty of Care: Perspectives from European and Comparative Law' in D Busch and C van Dam (eds), *A Bank's Duty of Care* (Oxford, Hart Publishing, 2017) 373.

—— 'Agency and Principal Dealing under MiFID I and MiFID II' in D Busch and G Ferrarini (eds). Regulation of the EU Financial Markets. MiFID II & MiFIR (Oxford, Oxford University Press, 2017) 227.

——'Product Governance and Product Intervention under MiFID II/MiFIR', in D Busch and G Ferrarini (eds), *Regulation of the EU Financial Markets. MiFID II & MiFIR* (Oxford, Oxford University Press, 2017) 154.

—— 'The Private Law Effect of MiFID I and MiFID II' in D Busch and G Ferrarini (eds), *Regulation of the EU Financial Markets. MiFID II & MiFIR* (Oxford, Oxford University Press, 2017) 176.

——'A Stronger Role for the European Supervisory Authorities' in D Busch, E Avgouleas and G Ferrarini (eds), *Capital Markets Union in Europe* (Oxford, Oxford University Press, 2018) 28.

Busch D and van Dam C, 'Conduct-of-Business Rules under MiFID I and II' in D Busch and C van Dam (eds), *A Bank's Duty of Care* (Oxford, Hart Publishing, 2017) 16.

Cafaggi F and Iamiceli P, 'The Principles of Effectiveness, Proportionality and Dissuasiveness in the Enforcement of EU Consumer Law: The Impact of a Triad on the Choice of Civil Remedies and Administrative Sanctions' (2017) 25 *European Review of Private Law* 609.

Capriglione F, 'La nuova finanza: operatività, supervisione, tutela giurisdizionale. Il caso «Italia». Considerazioni introduttive' (la finanza post-crisi: forme operative e meccanismi di controllo) (2017) *Contratto e Impresa* 75.

Carrasco Perera A, 'Aventuras, inventos y mixtificationes en eld debate relative a las participationes preferentes' 133 *Revista de Derecho Bancario y Bursatil* (2014): 39.

Cassese S, 'Quattro paradossi sui rapporti tra poteri pubblici ed autonomie private' (2000) 2 *Rivista Trimestrale di Diritto Pubblico* 389.

Cherednychenko OO, *Fundamental Rights, Contract Law and the Protection of the Weaker Party* (Munich, Sellier, 2007).

—— 'The Regulation of Retail Investment Services in the EU: Towards the Improvement of Investor Rights?' (2010) 33 *Journal of Consumer Policy* 403.

—— 'Full Harmonisation of Retail Financial Services Contract Law in Europe: A Success or a Failure?', in S Grundmann and Y M Atamer (eds), *Financial Services, Financial Crisis and General European Contract Law: Failure and Challenges of Contracting* (Alphen aan den Rijn, Wolters Kluwer, 2011) 243.

——'Fundamental Rights, European Private Law and Financial Services', in H-W Micklitz (ed). *Constitutionalization of European Private Law* (Oxford, Oxford University Press, 2014) 176.

—— 'Public and Private Enforcement of European Private Law in the Financial Services Sector' (2014) 4 *European Review of Private Law* 641.

——'Public Supervision over Private Relationships: Towards European Supervision Private Law?' (2014) 1 *European Review of Private Law* 37.

——'Contract Governance in the EU: Conceptualising the Relationship between Investor Protection Regulation and Private Law' (2015) 21 *European Law Journal* 500.

Chiu I, 'Regulatory Duties for Directors in the Financial Services Sector and Directors' Duties in Company Law: Bifurcation and Interfaces' (2016) 6 *Journal of Business Law* 489.

Choi J and Mitu Gulati G, 'Contract as Statute' (2016) 104 *Michigan Law Review* 1146.

Coffee JC Jr, 'Reforming the Securities Class Action: An Essay On Deterrence and Its Implementation' (2006) 106 *Columbia Law Review* 1534.

—— 'Law and the Market: The Impact of Enforcement' (2007) 156 *University of Pennsylvania Law Review* 305.

Cohen SB, 'The Suitability Rule and Economic Theory' (1971) 80 *Yale Law Journal* 1604.

Colaert V, 'MiFID II in Relation to Other Investor Protection Regulation. Picking Up the Crumbs of a Piecemeal Approach' in D Busch and G Ferrarini (eds). *Regulation of The EU Financial Markets*, 600.

Collins H, 'On the Incompatibility of Human Rights Discourse and Private Law', in H-W Micklitz (ed), *Constitutionalization of European Private Law* (Oxford, Oxford University Press, 2014) 49.

Craig P, 'The Legal Effect of Directives: Policy, Rules and Exceptions' (2009) 34 *European Law Review* 352.

Cruickshank S, 'Is There a Need to Harmonise Conduct of Business Rules', in G Ferrarini (ed), *European Securities Markets – The Investment Services Directive and Beyond* (London–Den Haag–Boston, Kluwer Law International, 1998) 131.

D'Ambrosio R, 'La borsa e la finanza' in E Galanti, R D'Ambrosio, A V Guccione (eds), *Storia della legislazione bancaria finanziaria e assicurativa Dall'Unità d'Italia al 2011* (Venezia, Marsilio Editori, 2012), 235.

—— 'The temporary intervention powers of the European Banking Authority and the European Securities and Markets Authority: content and limits' ERA Forum 2018.

D'Amico G, *Regole di validità e principio di correttezza nella formazione del contratto* (Napoli, 1996).

Dale R, *International Banking Deregulation* (Oxford, Blackwell, 1992).

Dalhuisen JH, *Dalhuisen on Transnational Comparative, Commercial, Financial and Trade Law. Financial Products, Financial Services and Financial Regulation*, vol 3 (Oxford, Hart Publishing, 2016).

Davies G, 'Democracy and Legitimacy in the Shadow of Purposive Competence' (2015) 21 *European Law Journal* 2.

De Lariosere J, 'Report' Brussels. February 2009.

Della Negra F, 'La natura della responsabilità precontrattuale: la quiete dopo la tempesta?' (2013) 7 *Danno e responsabilità* 754.

—— 'Il concorso di colpa tra società emittente ed intermediario finanziario: la recente pronuncia della Suprema Corte' (2014) in www.giustizia.civile.com.

—— 'The Private Enforcement of the MiFID Conduct of Business Rules. An Overview of the Italian and Spanish Experiences' (2014) 10 *European Review of Contract Law* (2014): 571.

—— 'The Uncertain Development of the Case Law on Consumer Protection in Mortgage Enforcement Proceedings: Sanchez Morcillo and Kušionova' (2015) 52 *Common Market Law Review* 1020.

—— 'Diritto alla tutela giurisdizionale effettiva e diritti dei consumatori' in P Gianniti (ed), *La CEDU e il ruolo delle corti, Commentario del codice civile e codici collegati Scialoja-Branca-Galgano*, a cura di G De Nova (Bologna, Zanichelli, 2015) 1567.

—— 'Le controversie in materia consumeristica. Strumenti di composizione: negoziali e non negoziali', in P Gianniti (ed). Processo civile e soluzioni alternative delle liti tra privati. Verso un sistema di giustizia integrato (Aracne, 2016) 741.

—— 'The Effects of the ESMA's Powers on Domestic Contract Law' in M Andenas, G Deipenbrock (eds), *Regulating and Supervising European Financial Markets* (Springer, 2016) 139.

Delpech X, 'Obligation de couverture en matière d'opérations financières: revirement de jurisprudence' (2008) *Recueil Dalloz* 778.

Dolmetta AA, *Trasparenza dei prodotti bancari. Regole* (Bologna, Zanichelli, 2013).

Dougan M, 'Minimum Harmonization and the Internal Market' (2000) 37 *Common Market law Review* 853.

—— 'The Vicissitudes of Life at the Coalface: Remedies and Procedures for Enforcing Union Law' in P Craig and G de Burca (eds), *The Evolution of EU Law* (Oxford, Oxford University Press, 2011) 424.

Easterbrook FH and Fischel DR, 'Optimal Damages in Securities Cases' (1985) 52 *University of Chicago Law Review* 613.

Eilmansberger T, 'The Relationship between Rights and Remedies in EC Law' (2004) 41 *Common Market Law Review* 1241.

Engstrom DF, 'Public Regulation of Private Enforcement: Empirical Analysis of DOJ Oversight of Qui Tam Litigation under the False Claims Act' (2013) 107 *Northwestern University School of Law Review* 1690.

Fabre-Magnan M, *De l'obligation d'information dans les contrats* (LGDJ, coll. Bibl. dr. privé, 1992).

Ferran E 'Regulatory Lessons from the Payment Protection Insurance Mis-selling Scandal in the UK' (2012) 3 *European Business Organization Law Review* 264.

—— 'The Existential Search of the European Banking Authority' (2016) 17 *European Business Organization Law Review* 290.

Gentile M, Linciano N and Soccorso P, 'Financial Disclosure, Risk Perception and Investment Choices. Evidence from a Consumer Testing Exercise' (2015), *CONSOB Quaderni di Finanza, No. 82.*

—— 'Financial Advice Seeking, Financial Knowledge and Overconfidence. Evidence from the Italian Market' (2016) *CONSOB Quaderni di Finanza, No. 83.*

Georgosouli A, 'The FSA's `Treating Customers Fairly' (TCF) Initiative: What is So Good About It and Why It May Not Work' (2011) *38 Journal of Law and Society* 424.

Giliker P, *The Europeanisation of English Tort Law* (Oxford, Hart Publishing, 2014).

Gilson RJ, Sabel CF and Scott RE, 'Contract and Innovation: The Limited Role of Generalist Courts in the Evolution of Novel Contractual Forms' (2013) 188 *New York University Law Review* 171.

Giudici P, 'Independent Financial Advice' in D Busch, G Ferrarini (eds). Regulation of the EU Financial Markets. MiFID II & MiFIR (Oxford, Oxford University Press, 2017) 162.

Glover J, 'The Structural Role of Private Enforcement Mechanisms in Public Law' (2012) *William and Mary Law Review* 1162.

Goodhart C, Hartman P, Llewellyn DT, Rojas-Suarez L and Weisbrod S, Financial Regulation: Why, How and Where Now? (London and New York, Routledge, 1998).

Gower LCB, '"Big Bang" and City Regulation' (1988) 51 *Modern Law Review* 11.

Greco F, 'Informazione pre-contrattuale e rimedi nella disciplina dell'intermediazione finanziaria' (Milano, Giuffrè, 2010).

Grundfest JA, 'Damages and Reliance Under Section 10(b) of the Exchange Act' (2013) *Stanford Law School andThe Rock Center for Corporate Governance.*

Grundmann S, 'The Bankinter Case on MiFID Regulation and Contract Law' (2013) 9 *European Review of Contract Law* 267.

—— 'The Banking Union Translated into (Private Law) Duties: Infrastructure and Rulebook' 16 European Business Organization Law Review (2015): 1.

Grundmann S and Hacker P, 'Conflicts of Interest' in D Busch and G Ferrarini (eds), *Regulation of the EU Financial Markets. MiFID II & MiFIR* (Oxford, Oxford University Press, 2017) 176.

Grundmann S and Kerber W, 'Information Intermediaries and Party Autonomy', in S Grundmann, W Kerber and S Weatherill (eds), *Party Autonomy and the Role of Information in the Internal Market* (Berlin, Walter de Gruyter, 2001) 290.

Guerrero C, Las acciones y participaciones preferentes: acciones judiciales y estrategias de defensa (2012) 6 *Revista Aranzadi Doctrinal.*

Haar B, 'Civil Liability of Credit Rating Agencies after CRA 3 – Regulatory All-or-Nothing Approaches Between Immunity and Over-Deterrence', University of Oslo Faculty of Law Legal Studies Research Paper Series No. 2013-02.

Hadjiemmanuil C, 'The Banking Union and Its Implications for Private Law: A Comment (2015) 16 *European Business Organization Law Review* 383.

Hesselink MW, 'Contract Theory and EU Contract Law' in C Twigg-Flesner (ed), *Research Handbook on EU Consumer and Contract Law* (Cheltenham, Edward Elgar, 2016) 531.

Hudson A, *The Law of Finance*, 1st edn (London, Sweet and Maxwell, 2013).

—— 'The Synthesis of Public and Private in Finance Law' in K Barker and D Jensen (eds), *Private Law: Key Encounters with Public Law* (Cambridge, Cambridge University Press, 2013) 233.

Imbruglia D, 'La creazione razionale dell'alea nei derivati OTC e la nullità dello swap per vizio di causa' in Persona e Mercato (2013): 332. Available at: www.personaemercato.it.

—— *La Regola di Adequatezza e il Contratto* (Milano, Giuffré, 2017).

Issacharoff S and Samuel IJ, 'The Institutional Dimension of Consumer Protection', in F Cafaggi, H-W Micklitz (eds), *New Frontiers of of Consumer Protection: Combining Private and Public Enforcement* (Antwerp: Intersentia, 2009) 4.

Jackson HE and Roe MJ, 'Public and Private Enforcement of Securities Laws: Resource-based Evidence' (2009) 93 *Journal of Financial Economics* 207.

James R and Morris PE, 'The Financial Ombudsman Service: A Brave New World in Ombudsmary' (2002) Public Law 640.
Jansen JD, 'Passion to Inform – BGH Expands Banks' Advisory Duties' (2011) 12 *German Law Journal* 1504.
Kelemen D, *Eurolegalism. The Transformation of Law and Regulation in the European Union* (Cambridge MA, Harvard University Press, 2012).
Kingsford Smith D and Dixon O, 'The Consumer Interest and the Financial Markets' in N Moloney, E Ferran, J Payne (eds), *The Oxford Handbook of Financial Regulation* (Oxford, Oxford University Press, 2015) 698.
Köndgen J, 'Rules of Conduct: Further Harmonisation?', in G Ferrarini (ed), *European Securities Markets: The Investment Services Directive and Beyond* (London / The Hague / Boston, Kluwer Law International, 1998) 117.
Kruithof M and Van Gerven W, 'A Differentiated Approach to Client Protection: The Example of MiFID', *Financial Law Institute, Working Paper 2010/07.*
Leczykiewicz D, 'Private Party Liability in EU Law: In Search of the General Regime' (2009–2010) 12 *Cambridge Yearbook of European Legal Studies* 257.
Lehmann M, 'Civil Liability of Rating Agencies – An Insipid Sprout from Brussels' (2016) 11 *Capital Markets Law Journal* 62.
Lieverse K, 'The Scope of MiFID II', in D Busch, G Ferrarini (eds), *Regulation of the EU Financial Markets. MiFID II & MiFIR* (Oxford, Oxford University Press, 2017) 41.
Lo Schiavo G, *The Role of Financial Stability in EU Law and Policy* (Alphen aan den Rijn: Wolters Kluwer, 2017).
Lomnika E, 'Private Damages Claims for Breaches of Securities Regulation Law' in R Plender (ed). *Legal History and Comparative Law. Essays in Honour of Albert Kiralfi* (London, Frank Cass., 1990) 133.
MacNeil I, 'Enforcement and Sanctioning' in E Ferran, N Moloney, N Payne (eds), *Oxford Handbook on Financial Regulation* (Oxford, Oxford University Press, 2015) 293.
Mager A, 'Oltre la violazione dei doveri informativi nei servizi di investimento. La cassazione e il nesso di causalità' (2018) 6 *Rivista di diritto bancario* 41.
Maggiolo M, *Servizi ed attività di investimento, Prestatori e prestazione*, in Tratt. Cicu-Messineo-Mengoni-Schlesinger (Milano, Giuffré, 2012) 396.
Mak C, 'Rights and Remedies: Article 47 EUCFR and Effective Judicial Protection in European Private Law Matters, in H-W Micklitz (ed), *Constitutionalization of European Private Law* (Oxford, Oxford University Press, 2014) 253.
Marcacci A, *Regulating Investor Protection under EU Law. The Unbridgeable Gaps with the U.S. and the Way Forward* (Palgrave, 2018).
Martinez Escribano C, 'Delimitacion del error en los contractos de swaps' (2013) *Revista de Derecho Bancario y Bursátil* 130.
Micklitz H-W, 'The Politics of Judicial Co-operation in the EU Sunday Trading, Equal Treatment and Good Faith' (Cambridge, Cambridge University Press, 2005).
—— 'Monistic Ideology versus Pluralistic Reality – Towards a Normative Design for European Private Law' in L Niglia (ed), Pluralism and European private law (Oxford, Hart Publishing, 2013) 47.
—— 'On the Intellectual History of Freedom of Contract and Regulation' (2015) 4 *Penn State Journal of Law & International Affairs* 11.
—— 'The ECJ between the Individual Citizen and the Member States: A Plea for a Judge-made European Law on Remedies', in H-W Micklitz and B De Witte (eds). The European Court of Justice and the Autonomy of Member States, Cambridge: Intersentia, 2012, p. 352.
—— 'The Visible Hand of European Regulatory Private Law: The Transformation of European Private Law from Autonomy to Functionalism in Competition and Regulation' (2009) 28 *Yearbook of European Law* 1.
—— 'Unfair Contract Terms – Public Interest Litigation', in Evellyn Terryn et al (eds), Landmark Cases of EU Consumer Law: In Honour of Jules Stuyck (Cambridge, Intersentia, 2013) 651.

—— 'The EU as a Federal Order of Competences and the Private Law" in L Azoulai "The Question of Competence in the European Union", Oxford: Oxford University Press, 2014, p 125.

—— 'The Transformation of Enforcement in European Private Law: Preliminary Considerations' (2015) 4 *European Review of Private Law* 491.

Micklitz H-W and Comparato G, 'Regulated Autonomy between Market Freedoms and Fundamental Rights', in U Bernitz, X Groussot, F Schulyok (eds), *General Principles of EU Law and European Private Law* (Alphen aan den Rijn, Kluwer, 2013).

Micklitz H-W and Reich N, 'The Court and Sleeping Beauty: The revival of the Unfair Contract Terms Directive (UCTD) (2014) 51 *Common Market Law Review* 804.

Micklitz H-W, Comparato G, Svetiev Y, 'The Regulatory Character of European Private Law', in C Twigg-Flesner (ed), *Research Handbook on EU Consumer and Contract Law* (Cheltenham, Edward Edgar, 2016) 41.

Micklitz H-W, Svetiev Y and Comparato G (eds), 'European Regulatory Private Law – The Paradigms Tested', LAW 2014/04 Department of Law European Regulatory Private Law Project (ERC-ERPL – 07).

Mitu Gulati G, 'Contract as Statute' (2006) 104 *Michigan Law Review* 1146.

Moloney N, 'Effective Policy Design for the Retail Investment Services Market: Challenges and Choices Post FSAP' in G Ferrarini and E Wymeersch (eds), *Investor Protection in Europe. Corporate Law Making, the MiFID and Beyond* (Oxford, Oxford University Press, 2007) 391.

—— *How to Protect Investors? Lessons from the EC and the UK* (Cambridge, Cambridge University Press, 2010).

—— 'The Investor Model Underlying the EU's Investor Protection Regime: Consumers or Investors?' (2012) 13 *European Business Organization Law Review* 169.

—— *EU Securities and Financial Markets Regulation*, 3rd edn (Oxford, Oxford University Press, 2014).

—— 'Institutional Governance and Capital Markets Union: Incrementalism or a "Big Bang"?' (2016) 2 *European Company and Financial Review* 418.

Möslein F, 'Third Parties in the European Banking Union: Regulatory and Supervisory Effects on Private Law Relationships Between Banks and their Clients or Creditors' (2015) 16 *European Business Law Review* 547.

Möslein F and Riesenhuber K, 'Contract Governance – A Draft Research Agenda' (2009) 3 *European Review of Contract Law* 248.

Mülbert PO, 'The Eclipse of Contract Law in the Investment Firm-Client-Relationship: The Impact of the MiFID on the Law of Contract from a German Perspective' in G Ferrarini and E Wymeersch (eds) *Investor Protection in Europe: Corporate Law Making, The MiFID and Beyond* (Oxford, Oxford University Press, 2006) 317.

Nebbia P, 'The Double Life of Effectiveness' (2007–2008) 10 *Cambridge Yearbook of European Legal Studies* 288.

Pascual JG, 'La protección de consumidores y usuarios en la contratación de permuta financiera o swap' (2013) *Revista Doctrinal Aranzadi Civil-Mercantil* 9.

Perrone A, 'Tanto rumore per nulla? Per un ripensamento della disciplina sugli inducements' (2016) 2 *Banca Borsa Titoli di Credito* 129.

Perrone A and Valente S, 'Against All Odds: Investor Protection in Italy and the Role of Courts' (2012) 13 *European Business Organization Law Review* 31.

Poser NS, *International securities regulation: London's 'Big Bang' and the European securities markets* (New York, Little, Brown & Co, 1990).

—— 'Why the SEC Failed: Regulators Against Regulation (2009) 2 *Brooklyn Journal of Corporate Finance and Commercial Law* 290.

Powell JL and Stewart R (eds), *Jackson & Powell on Professional Liability* (London, Sweet and Maxwell, 2016).

Prechal S 'Community Law in National Courts: The Lessons from Van Schijndel' (1998) 35 *Common Market Law Review* 681.

—— 'The Court of Justice and Effective Judicial Protection: What Has the Charter Changed? in Paulussen, Ch., Takacs, T., Lazic, V., van Rompuy, B. (eds), *Fundamental Rights in International and European Law* (The Hague, Springer, 2015) 154.
Prum A, 'Le dilemme de la jurisprudence: protege' (2015) *Droit & Patrimonie* 85.
Quaglia L, 'Financial Sector Committee Governance in the European Union' (2008) 30 *Journal of European Integration* 567.
Reich N, 'Horizontal Liability in EC Law: Hybridization of Remedies for Compensation in Case of Breaches of EC Rights' (2007) 44 *Common Market Law Review* 708.
—— 'The Interrelation between Rights and Duties in EU Law: Reflections on the State of Liability Law in the Multilevel Governance System of the Union: Is there a Need for a More Coherent Approach in European Private Law? (2010) 29 *Yearbook of European Law* 121.
—— '*General Principles of EU Civil Law*' (Cambridge, Intersentia, 2013).
—— The Principle of Effectiveness and EU Private Law, in U Bernitz, X Groussot and F Schulyok (eds), *General Principles of EU law and European Private Law* (Kluwer Law International, 2013) 308.
Reynolds P, 'Selling Financial Products: The Interface between Regulatory and Common Law Standards' (2014) 29 *Journal of International Banking Law and Regulation* 269.
Reynolds P and Collins A, 'Non-advised Sales of Financial Products: An End to caveat emptor?' (2018) 33 *Journal of International Banking Law and Regulation*, 148.
Roppo V, 'La tutela del risparmiatore fra nullità, risoluzione e risarcimento (ovvero, l'ambaradan dei rimedi contrattuali)' (2005) *Contratto e Impresa* 905.
Safjan M and Dusterhaus D, 'A Union of Effective Judicial Protection: Addressing a Multi-level Challenge through the Lens of Article 47 CFREU' (2014) *Yearbook of European Law* 1.
Sainz de Baranda YB, 'El caso Lehman Brothers en la jurisprudencia española. Alcance de la responsabilidad de las entidades bancarias y de las empresas de servicios de inversión' (2012) 128 *Revista de Derecho Bancario y Bursátil* 211.
Sangiorgio G, 'Problemi della pratica un esempio di giustizia 'domestica' alternativa a quella dell'a.g.o.: l'ombudsman - giurì bancario' (2009) 3 *Banca Borsa Titoli di Credito* 344.
Sartori F, *Le regole di condotta degli intermediari finanziari. Disciplina e forme di tutela* (Milano, Giuffré, 2004).
Schammo P, *EU Prospectus Law. New Perspectives on Regulatory Competition in Securities Markets* (Cambridge, Cambridge University Press, 2011).
—— 'EU Day-to-Day Supervision or Intervention-based Supervision: Which Way Forward for the European System of Financial Supervision?' (2012) 32 *Oxford Journal of Legal Studies* 771.
Segré C, 'The Development of a European Capital Market. Report of a Group of Experts appointed by the EEC Commission'. November 1966.
Shavell S, 'The Fundamental Divergence between the Private and the Social Motive to Use the Legal System' (1997) 16 *The Journal of Legal Studies* 599.
Silverentand L, Sprecher J and Simons L, 'Inducements', in D Busch and G Ferrarini (eds), *Regulation of the EU Financial Markets, MiFID II & MiFIR* (Oxford, Oxford University Press, 2017) 205.
Simoncini M, '*Administrative Regulation Beyond the Non-Delegation Doctrine. A study on EU Agencies*' (Oxford, Hart Publishing, 2018).
Smerdon R and Morse G, *Palmer's Company Law. The Protection of Investors and the Regulation of Financial Services*, vol 3 (London, Sweet and Maxwell, 2017).
Stephenson MC, 'Public Regulation of Private Enforcement: The Case for Expanding the Role of Administrative Agencies' (2005) 91 *Virginia Law Review* 103.
Storck M 'La responsabilité encourue pour le défaut d'exigence de couverture sur le marché à terme' (2001) *Revue Trimestrelle de Droit Commercial* 175.
—— 'Le particularisme de l'obligation d'information en matière de gestion d'instruments financiers' (2006) *Revue Trimestrielle de Droit Commercial* 157.
—— 'Disproportion du montant de la couverture avec le risque spéculatif' (2010) 4 *Revue de Droit bancaire et financier* 162.

Svetiev Y, and Ottow A, 'Financial Supervision in the Interstices Between Private and Public Law' (2014) 10 *European Review of Contract Law* 496.

Timmermans C,'Horizontal Direct/Indirect Effect or Direct/Indirect Horizontal Effect: What's in a Name?' (2016) 4 *European Review of Private Law* 677.

Tison M, 'The Civil Law Effects of MiFID in a Comparative Law Perspective' *Financial Law Institute Working Paper Series* (2010).

Tountopoulos V, 'Market Abuse and Private Enforcement' (2014) 3 *European Company and Financial Law Review* 312.

Tresnjack V and Beysen E, 'European Consumer Protection Law: Curia Semper Dabit Remedium?' (2011) 48 *Common Market Law Review* 105.

Tridimas T, Black, White, and Shades of Grey: Horizontality of Directives Revisited (2001) 21 *Yearbook of European law* 328.

—— 'EU Financial Regulation: Federalization, Crisis Management and Law Reform' in P Craig, G De Burca (eds) *The Evolution of EU Law*, 2nd ed (Oxford, Oxford University Press, 2011) 794.

—— 'Financial Supervision and Agency Power: Reflections on ESMA' in N Shuibhne and L W Gormley (eds). From Single Market to Economic Union (Oxford, Oxford University Press, 2012) 56.

—— 'The ECJ and National Courts: Dialogue, Cooperation and Instability' in D Chalmers, A Arnull (eds). *The Oxford Handbook of European Union Law* (Oxford, Oxford University Press, 2015) 409.

Tucci A, Il contratto inadeguato e il contratto immeritevole (2017) *Contratto e Impresa* 921.

Tuch A, 'Conduct of Business Regulation', in N Moloney, E Ferran, and J Payne (eds), *The Oxford Handbook of Financial Regulation* (Oxford, Oxford University Press, 2015) 557.

Tuori K, 'On legal Hybrids and Perspectivism' in M Maduro, K Tuori, S Sankari (eds), *Transnational Law: Rethinking European Law and Legal Thinking* (Cambridge, Cambridge University Press, 2014) 14.

Turner A, 'The Turner Review. A regulatory response to the global banking crisis' March 2009.

Van Gerven W 'Of Rights, Remedies and Procedures' (2001) 37 *Common Market Law Review* 501.

Vettori G, 'Contract Without Numbers and Without Adjectives. Beyond the Consumer and the Weak Enterprise' (2013) 9 *European Review of Contract law* 233.

Wagner G, 'Private Law Enforcement through ADR: Wonder Drug or Snake Oil?' (2014) 51 *Common Market Law Review* 176.

Walker G and Purves R (eds), *Financial Services Law* (Oxford, Oxford University Press, 2014).

Weatherill S, 'The Limits of Legislative Harmonization Ten Years after Tobacco Advertising: How the Court's Case Law has become a "Drafting Guide' (2011) 12 *German Law Journal* 843.

Weber F and Faure M, 'The Interplay between Public and Private Enforcement in European Private Law: Law and Economics Perspective' (2015) 4 *European Review of Private Law* 533.

Widdershoven R and Prechal S, Redefining the Relationship between 'Rewe-effectiveness' and Effective Judicial Protection (2011) 2 *Review of European Administrative Law* 44.

Wilman F, '*Private Enforcement of EU Law Before National Courts. The EU Legislative Framework*' (Cheltenham, Edward Elgar, 2015).

Wymeersch E, 'The Implementation of the ISD and CAD in National Legal Systems', in G Ferrarini (ed), *European Securities Markets – The Investment Services Directive and Beyond* (London – Den Haag – Boston, Kluwer Law International, 1998) 40.

Zoppini A, 'Diritto Privato vs Diritto Amministrativo (ovvero alla ricerca dei confini tra stato e mercato) (2013) 3 *Rivista di diritto civile* 527.

Zunzunegui F, 'Mis-selling of Preferred Shares to Spanish Retail Clients' (2014) 29 *Journal of International Banking Law and Regulation* 174.

Zunzunegui Pastor F, 'Aproximación a la responsabilidad contractual de los prestadores de servicios de inversión' (2016) 35 *Revista de derecho bancario y bursátil* 142.

INDEX

Note: Alphabetical arrangement is word-by-word, where a group of letters followed by a space is filed before the same group of letters followed by a letter, eg 'expert knowledge' will appear before 'expertise'. In determining alphabetical arrangement, initial articles and prepositions are ignored.

www.ingramcontent.com/pod-product-compliance
Lightning Source LLC
Chambersburg PA
CBHW071301180926
51613CB00001B/92
9781509925292